RÉGION ET DÉVELOPPEMENT

n° 43-2016

Varia

REVUE RÉGION ET DÉVELOPPEMENT

Revue fondée en 1995 par Gilbert Benhayoun et Maurice Catin

Revue semestrielle référencée dans ECONLIT et dans IDEAS (REPEC)

Site web : www.regionetdeveloppement.org
ISSN 2117-0843

5-7, rue de l'Ecole-Polytechnique, 75005 Paris

http://www.harmattan.fr
diffusion.harmattan@wanadoo.fr

ISBN : 978-2-343-09842-5
EAN : 9782343098425

Région et Développement

n° 43 - 2016

Varia

COMPLEXITY OF PRODUCTION PROCESSES AND THE NEED FOR PROXIMITY

Sandrine NOBLET[*], Antoine BELGODERE[**]

Abstract - *This paper studies the effect of globalization on the geography of trade. More specifically we present the deepening integration process (i.e. the fall in transport costs) and the need for proximity as two sides of the same phenomenon. We propose a theoretical model in which both international fragmentation and increasing need for proximity in input-output relationships are endogenous responses to an exogenous fall in transport costs. Indeed, in a Dixit-Stiglitz' framework, a fall in transport costs increases the varieties of tasks making production process more complex. This increasing complexity implies that input-output linkages require a higher level of coordination. Coordination is assumed to be achieved more easily between nearby than between distant countries.*

Key-words - INTERNATIONAL TRADE, COMPLEXITY, PROXIMITY, TRANSPORT COSTS, COORDINATION COSTS

Classification JEL - F12, F15

[*] Université de Corse, UMR CNRS LISA 6240 ; noblet@univ-corse.fr
[**] Université de Corse, UMR CNRS LISA 6240 ; belgodere@univ-corse.fr

1. INTRODUCTION

Current globalization seems to exhibit two somehow paradoxical trends. The first is the increasing fragmentation of production on an international basis. International trade flows are characterized by an important share of intermediate goods or, more broadly, goods in process as documented by Ng and Yeats (2001), Hummels et al. (2001), Jones and Kierzkowski (2005) and Kimura et al. (2007) among others. According to Miroudot et al. (2009) trade in intermediates represents 56,2% of total trade for OECD countries between 1995 and 2007. The increasing fragmentation has been triggered by what Richard Baldwin called the "two great unbundlings" (Baldwin, 2006). More precisely, the fall in transport costs has weakened the need for proximity between firms and consumers and the fall in communication costs has weakened the need for proximity between upstream and downstream firms.

The second trend, that may look paradoxical with the first, is that this increasing fragmentation seems, in turn, to foster some need for geographical proximity between trade partners.

Indeed, according to Johnson and Noguera (2012), trade in intermediates has grown faster between nearby countries than between long distance partners. This echoes Hillberry and Hummels (2002) who explain home bias effect through the localized nature of intermediates trade flows suggesting that trade in intermediates is a factor of industrial concentration[1]. More recently, Baldwin and Venables (2013) argue that the need for proximity between producers can offset comparative advantages.

Thus, distance seems to count less, because production is more internationally fragmented, but distance seems to count more because more fragmented production processes are organized essentially among nearby countries. We believe both trends can be regarded as consistent with each other, if one acknowledges that more fragmented production processes are more complex, and that complexity requires proximity for coordination purposes.

Fragmentation is often associated with productivity gains[2]. However, since Kremer (1993), increasing fragmentation is also associated to an increase in complexity of production process. The underlying assumption is that the higher is the number of tasks, the higher is the risk of failure (Kremer, 1993; Costinot, 2009; Minondo and Requena-Silvente, 2013). According to Hidalgo and Hausmann (2009) the level of complexity depends on the diversity of capabilities available in a country. Finally, the complexity of production process can be linked to the nature of tasks performed. For instance, Autor et al. (2003) and Spitz (2004) have shown respectively for the United-States and Europe that there has been a switch in the nature of tasks from routine to non-routine tasks (interactive or analytical), that can be considered as more complex.

In this paper, we propose a theoretical model in which both international fragmentation and increasing need for proximity in input-output relationship are

[1]This idea has been suggested by Wolf (2000).
[2]These productivity gains are a property of Dixit-Stiglitz' production function.

endogenous responses to an exogenous fall in transport costs. In our Dixit-Stiglitz model, based upon increasing returns to scale technology, a fall in transport costs may increase the international division of labour. The increasing international division of labour can be interpreted as increasing specialization of intermediate goods. As a consequence, we assume that production processes become more complex, which, in turn, implies that input-output linkages require a higher level of coordination. Coordination is assumed to be achieved more easily between nearby than between distant countries. As a result, trade increases with all partners, but more quickly for nearby than for distant countries.

Hence, our paper adds to the recent literature on complexity. Hidalgo and Haussmann (2009) use the concept of complexity in order to explain growth differential between high wage and low wage countries. Minondo and Requena-Silvente (2013) show that the level of complexity was able to predict the structure of trade flows. Finally this link between complexity and international trade has also been studied through the quality of institutions. Berkowitz et al. (2006) show that institutional quality matters more for trade in complex goods than in simple ones since the level of contract incompleteness is higher for complex goods. Some other papers have emphasized the importance of institutional quality for trade in differentiated goods (Levchenko, 2007; Nunn, 2007; Ranjan and Lee, 2007; Feenstra et al., 2013).

The remainder of the paper is organized as follows: section 2 presents a micro model of coordination costs, section 3 introduces this micro model in a general equilibrium model of international trade, section 4 shows the unambiguous effect of the fall in transport costs regarding to the geography of trade. Section 5 provides a discussion of our result and the last section concludes.

2. COMPLEXITY IN INPUT-OUTPUT LINKAGES

Here, we consider production processes that consist of assembling a continuum of intermediate goods of mass N. A specific intermediate good can be used only if its characteristics fit perfectly with the characteristics of all the other intermediate goods. The final good producer both assembles the intermediate goods, and coordinates the various intermediate producers in a bid to avoid any mismatch among them. This coordination activity requires proximity, so the probability that a given intermediate good fits with another one is a decreasing function of geographical distance (d) between the intermediate and the final good producers. We assume this probability is given by $1/(1+\phi d)$ (with $\phi > 0$), which is equal to 1 when $d = 0$, and tends toward 0 for infinite distance. Since an intermediate good must fit not only with one other good but also with all the others that are part of the production process, the probability it can be used is $1/(1+\phi d)^N$ (this modelling isinspired by Michael Kremer's O'ring theory (Kremer, 1993). It follows then, that a risk-neutral final good producer must buy a quantity $x(1+\phi d)^N$ of an intermediate good in order to use an expected value of x. A more realistic interpretation is that the final good producer can buy an insurance contract (or equivalently add a clause to its contract with the supplier) that guarantees free replacement of the intermediate good should it not incorporate the appropriate characteristics. If p is the price of this intermediate good, then the price of the insurance contract would be $p((1+\phi d)^N - 1)$. In what follows, we refer to this insurance price as the "coordination cost" (as in Noblet, 2011), although it is more accurately the cost of lack of coordination in input-output relations.

In addition to this coordination cost, downstream firms have to bear transport costs. We assume that the transport cost is an iceberg cost, which increases the cost by $p\theta d$, where $\theta > 0$ is a parameter that denotes the transport technology. This means that a fall in transport costs is modelled as a fall in θ.

Finally, the expected cost of using one unit of the intermediate good is given by the following expression:

$$p(1+\theta d)(1+\phi d)^N \quad (1)$$

This equation provides some insight for the point we want to make in this paper. Modern models of international trade based on a Dixit-Stiglitz framework exhibit an increasing variety of goods. Here, an increasing integration corresponds to a fall in θ, whereas an increasing variety of goods corresponds to an increase in N. Let us assume a final good producer has both short-distance and long-distance trading partners. If a fall in θ is accompanied by an increase in N, then the non-linearity of expression 1 implies that the global transfer costs for both types of partners does not evolve proportionally. In those conditions, the impact of integration on the shape of international trade depends crucially on two things: the parameter ϕ, and the importance of the increase in N in response to the fall in θ. In other words, globalization can strengthen the impact of distance on trade if this globalization increases the complexity of production processes, and if distance matters for the coordination of intermediate good suppliers.

We address these issues in the next two sections by plugging the model of coordination costs summarized by relation 1 into an international trade model.

3. INTERNATIONAL TRADE

In this section and section 4, we study an international trade model where firms support a coordination cost as previously defined. This section presents the structure of our model, while section 3 discusses the implications of our model in terms of distance of trade.

The model is a symmetric multi-country model. In order to simplify the notations, we do not use country-specific subscripts.

3.1. Consumers

In each country, a representative consumer has a utility function given by $U(x_A, X) = \left(x_A^{\frac{\sigma-1}{\sigma}} + X^{\frac{\sigma-1}{\sigma}}\right)^{\frac{\sigma}{\sigma-1}}$, where x_A and X are the quantities of agricultural good and (final) industrial good that are consumed, and $\sigma > 1$ is the elasticity of substitution between both goods. The agricultural good is chosen as the *numeraire*, and P is the price of the industrial good. The budget constraint is

$y = x_A + PX$ where y is the national income. Utility maximization results in the following demand functions:

$$x_A = \frac{y}{1 + P^{1-\sigma}} \tag{2}$$

$$X = \frac{y}{P + P^{\sigma}} \tag{3}$$

3.2. Agricultural sector

In each country, a representative firm produces the agricultural good out of labour, with constant returns to scale:

$$x_A = AL_A \tag{4}$$

where L_A is the quantity of labour employed in the sector, and $A > 0$ is a productivity parameter. The profit in the sector can be written as $AL_A - \omega L_A$, where ω is the wage rate. Since this sector is competitive, the equilibrium wage rate is simply:

$$\omega = A \tag{5}$$

and the profit is nil at equilibrium.

3.3. Industrial downstream sector

In each country, a representative firm builds a final industrial good out of intermediate goods, with a CES production function $X = \left[\int_0^N x_i^{(\sigma-1)/\sigma}\, di\right]^{\sigma/(\sigma-1)}$, where x_i is the quantity of intermediate good of variety i. Intermediate goods can be bought locally or from foreign countries. The production cost can be written as $\int_0^N \tau_i\, x_i p_i di$, where p_i is the price of variety i and τ_i is the transfer cost of variety i. Following the modeling presented in section 1, we define τ_i as:

$$\tau_i = (1 + \theta d_i)(1 + \phi d_i)^N \tag{6}$$

Minimizing this cost for a given production results in the following demand:

$$x_i = (\tau_i p_i)^{-\sigma} c^{\sigma} X \tag{7}$$

where $c \equiv \left[\int_0^N \left(\tau_j p_j\right)^{1-\sigma} dj\right]^{1/(1-\sigma)}$

Replacing the optimal value of x_i in the definition of production cost, gives the cost function $COST(X) = cX$. Since the final good sector is competitive, the equilibrium price equates to the marginal cost:

$$P = c \tag{8}$$

3.4. Industrial upstream sector

The industry upstream sector is characterized by monopolistic competition. Each firm supplies both local and foreign downstream firms. Let p be the price imposed by a typical firm in this sector. Downstream firms in different locations do not face the same transfer costs, but, according to equation 7, their individual demand for a typical variety is always: $constant \times p^{-\sigma}$. It follows that $-\sigma$ is the price-elasticity of aggregate demand.

Technology in this sector exhibits increasing returns to scale. A typical firm hires a quantity L_x of labour, and produces a quantity $x = L_x - f$ of output, where $f > 0$ is a fixed requirement. It follows that the marginal cost is simply ω. Thus, each firm applies the standard pricing:

$$p = \omega \frac{\sigma}{\sigma - 1} \tag{9}$$

At equilibrium, the classical no-profit condition applies:

$$x = f(\sigma - 1) \tag{10}$$

3.5. Physical geography

This model needs to include more than two countries, so that we can compare trade between neighbours with trade between distant partners. We also need to respect a perfect symmetry between countries, in order to keep the model as tractable as possible. The simplest way to fulfil these conditions is to assume the four-country world depicted in figure 1, where the lines represent the roads between the countries.

Figure 1. The 4-country world

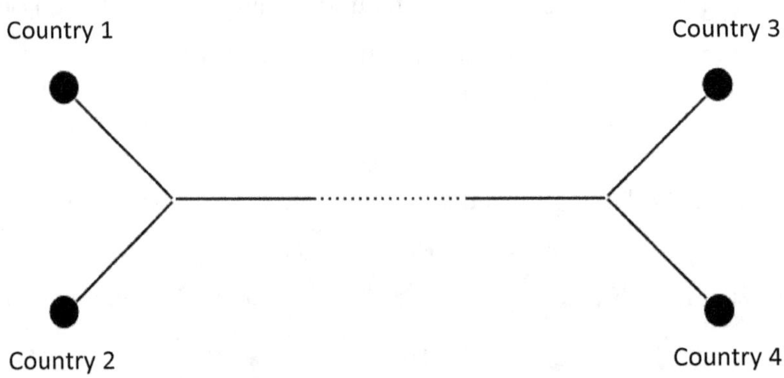

Let $\underline{d}(> 0)$ be the distance between neighbours, and $\bar{d}(> \underline{d})$ the distance between distant partners. Here, perfect symmetry prevails, because each country has one neighbour and two distant partners.

Under these assumptions, we can define three different levels of transfer costs:

$\tau_i = 1$ for local trade

$\tau_i = \underline{\tau} \equiv (1 + \theta \underline{d})(1 + \phi \underline{d})^N$ for trade between neighbours (11)

$\tau_i = \bar{\tau} \equiv (1 + \theta \bar{d})(1 + \phi \bar{d})^N$ for trade between distant partners

Perfect symmetry implies that $N/4$ varieties are produced in each country. Thus, the price of the final industrial good, given by equation 8, can be written as:

$$P = \left[\frac{N}{4}\left(\frac{\omega\sigma}{\sigma-1}\right)^{1-\sigma} + \frac{N}{4}\left(\frac{\omega\sigma}{\sigma-1}\right)^{1-\sigma}\underline{\tau}^{1-\sigma} + \frac{N}{2}\left(\frac{\omega\sigma}{\sigma-1}\right)^{1-\sigma}\bar{\tau}^{1-\sigma}\right]^{1/(1-\sigma)} \\ = \left(\frac{N}{4}\right)^{1/(1-\sigma)}\left(\frac{\omega\sigma}{\sigma-1}\right)\left(1+\underline{\tau}^{1-\sigma}+2\bar{\tau}^{1-\sigma}\right)^{1/(1-\sigma)} \quad (12)$$

Demand for intermediate goods defined in equation 7 also has three different values:

$$x_i = x^0 \equiv \left(\frac{\omega\sigma}{\sigma-1}\right)^{-\sigma} P^\sigma X \text{ for local trade}$$
$$x_i = \underline{x} \equiv x^0\underline{\tau}^{-\sigma} \text{ for trade between neighbours} \quad (13)$$
$$x_i = \bar{x} \equiv x^0\bar{\tau}^{-\sigma} \text{ for trade between distant partners}$$

3.6. Closing the model

There are three more equations required to solve the model. The first clearing condition concerns the labour market. Let L be the each country's total labour force. This labour force is used by the upstream industry sector and the agriculture sector:

$$\frac{N}{4}L_X + L_A = L \quad (14)$$

The second clearing condition relates to the intermediate good market. In this market, each firm supplies x and faces four demands: x^0 from the local market; $\underline{x}$ from the neighbouring country; and $\bar{x}$ from each of the two distant countries. However, when foreign downstream firms want to use $\underline{x}$ and $\bar{x}$, they must purchase $\underline{x\tau}$ and $\bar{x}\bar{\tau}$ to compensate for the transport and coordination losses. Thus, at equilibrium (using equation feq:x):

$$x = x^0\left(1+\underline{\tau}^{1-\sigma}+2\bar{\tau}^{1-\sigma}\right) \quad (15)$$

The third one is the definition of national income, which is simply the workers' income since the profit is nil in the three sectors:

$$y = wL \quad (16)$$

3.7. Summarizing, simplifying

The model presented in this section can be expressed in a quite tractable way, although it has no analytical solution.

Four variables have trivial solutions: $\omega = A$, $y = AL$, $p = \frac{A\sigma}{\sigma-1}$ and $x = f(\sigma-1)$. Using those values reduces the model to a 11-equation 11-variable system. Variables are: L_A, L_X, x_A, X, P, N, $\underline{\tau}$, $\bar{\tau}$, x^0, $\underline{x}$ and $\bar{x}$. Equations are:

$$L_A = x_A/A \quad (17)$$

$$\frac{N}{4}L_x + L_A = L \tag{18}$$

$$x_A = \frac{AL}{1 + P^{1-\sigma}} \tag{19}$$

$$X = \frac{AL}{P + P^{\sigma}} \tag{20}$$

$$x^0 = X\left(\frac{A\sigma}{\sigma - 1}\right)^{-\sigma} P^{\sigma} \tag{21}$$

$$\underline{x} = x^0 \underline{\tau}^{-\sigma} \tag{22}$$

$$\bar{x} = x^0 \bar{\tau}^{-\sigma} \tag{23}$$

$$P = \left(\frac{N}{4}\right)^{1/(1-\sigma)} \left(\frac{A\sigma}{\sigma - 1}\right)\left(1 + \underline{\tau}^{1-\sigma} + 2\bar{\tau}^{1-\sigma}\right)^{1/(1-\sigma)} \tag{24}$$

$$x^0 = \frac{f(\sigma - 1)}{1 + \underline{\tau}^{1-\sigma} + 2\bar{\tau}^{1-\sigma}} \tag{25}$$

$$\underline{\tau} = (1 + \theta\underline{d})(1 + \phi\underline{d})^N \tag{26}$$

$$\bar{\tau} = (1 + \theta\bar{d})(1 + \phi\bar{d})^N \tag{27}$$

Variables $\underline{\tau}$, $\bar{\tau}$, P, x_A, X, L_A and L_x can easily be expressed as a function of the parameters and N[3], whereas $\underline{x}$ and $\bar{x}$ can be expressed as a function of the parameters, N and x^0 [4]. This leaves a system of two variables, x^0 and N, and two equations, 21 and 25. By removing x^0 from these equations, we get:

$$\frac{[A\sigma/(\sigma - 1)]^{\sigma-1}}{1 + \left[(1 + \theta\underline{d})(1 + \phi\underline{d})^N\right]^{1-\sigma} + 2\left[(1 + \theta\bar{d})(1 + \phi\bar{d})^N\right]^{1-\sigma}} = \frac{L}{f\sigma} - \frac{N}{4} \tag{28}$$

Equation 28 is the cornerstone of the model, because solving this equation would allow us to solve the entire model. Although equation 28 is clearly not solvable, it provides an interesting insight into the ambiguous effect of a fall in transport costs on the geography of trade, which is discussed in the next section.

[3]By using equations 26, 27, 24, 19, 20, 17 and 18, in this order.
[4]By using equations 22 and 23.

4.THE GEOGRAPHY OF TRADE

We focus here on the impact of a fall in θ, the pure transport cost, on the ratio $\frac{\underline{x}}{\overline{x}}$, namely the ratio of neighbour to distant exchanges. This fall in transport costs strengthens the importance of distance if this ratio increases when θ decreases. Notice that, according to equations 22 and 23, $\frac{\underline{x}}{\overline{x}} = \left(\frac{\overline{\tau}}{\underline{\tau}}\right)^{\sigma}$, so we can focus alternatively on the ratio of both transfer costs:

$$\frac{\overline{\tau}}{\underline{\tau}} = \left(\frac{1+\theta\overline{d}}{1+\theta\underline{d}}\right)\left(\frac{1+\phi\overline{d}}{1+\phi\underline{d}}\right)^{N} \tag{29}$$

The right-hand side (RHS) of equation 29 highlights the two opposite forces in globalization: the fall in transport costs (θ) clearly increases $\left(\frac{1+\theta\overline{d}}{1+\theta\underline{d}}\right)$ (since $\underline{d} < \overline{d}$), which is the transport cost ratio, whereas increased complexity, measured by an increase in N, clearly decreases $\left(\frac{1+\phi\overline{d}}{1+\phi\underline{d}}\right)^{N}$, which is the coordination cost ratio. Two points matter in order to know whether distance will have more or less importance as a result of globalization: 1) the impact of changes in θ on N; 2) the size of ϕ. Obviously, if the fall in θ has only a small impact on N, then the transport cost effect is likely to outdo the coordination cost effect. The same applies if ϕ is very small, *ie.* if the probability of mismatch for distant produced intermediate goods is low[5].

Formally, the derivative of the log of expression 29 with respect to θ is written as:

$$\frac{\partial log(\overline{\tau}/\underline{\tau})}{\partial\theta} = \frac{\overline{d}-\underline{d}}{(1+\theta\underline{d})(1+\theta\underline{d})} + \frac{\partial N}{\partial\theta}\left[log(1+\phi\overline{d}) - log(1+\phi\underline{d})\right] \tag{30}$$

where $\frac{\partial N}{\partial\theta}$ is the reaction of the number of varieties to an increase in the transport costs in the model presented in section 2. The direct effect (the transport cost effect) is measured by $\frac{\overline{d}-\underline{d}}{(1+\theta\underline{d})(1+\theta\underline{d})}$, which is clearly positive. The indirect effect is measured by $\frac{\partial N}{\partial\theta}\left[log(1+\phi\overline{d}) - log(1+\phi\underline{d})\right]$, which clearly has the same sign as $\frac{\partial N}{\partial\theta}$, which, as we will see, is negative.

Distance becomes more important when transport costs fall if expression 30 is negative, which requires:

$$\frac{\partial N}{\partial\theta} < \frac{\overline{d}-\underline{d}}{(1+\theta\underline{d})(1+\theta\underline{d})\left[log(1+\phi\overline{d}) - log(1+\phi\underline{d})\right]} (< 0) \tag{31}$$

The impact of θ on N can be depicted using equation 28. In figure 2, where the decreasing line represents the RHS of equation 28, whereas the three increasing curves represent the left-hand-side (LHS), for three different values of θ. The grey area represents all the possible locations for the curve representing

[5] If $\phi = 0$, the coordination cost ratio reduces to 1^{N}.

the LHS, for values of θ ranging from 0 to ∞. Whatever the value of θ, this curve tends asymptotically toward $[A\sigma/(\sigma-1)]^{\sigma-1}$ when $N \to \infty$. When $\theta = 0$, the curve starts from $\frac{[A\sigma/(\sigma-1)]^{\sigma-1}}{4}$ (for $N = 0$) then converges toward $[A\sigma/(\sigma-1)]^{\sigma-1}$. When $\theta \to \infty$, the curve tends toward the dashed horizontal line.

Figure 2. Determination of N, for 3 different values of θ

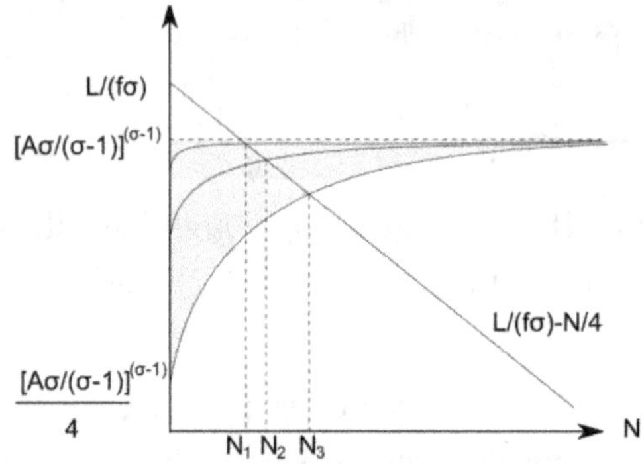

The mechanism behind this increase in N is quite simple: a fall in θ decreases the price P of the final industrial good (see equation 24). Since σ, the elasticity of substitution between both types of consumption goods is higherthan 1, the fall in P results in an increase in the expenditure in industrial goods. This expenditure is equal to the expenditure on intermediate goods, because they are the only input to final good production and the returns to scale are constant. This increase in demand results in an increase in N, because x and p are constant.

In order to know whether the impact of θ on N is large enough to fulfil condition 31, we need an analytical expression of this impact. Applying implicit functions theorem to equation 28 gives:

$$\frac{\partial N}{\partial \theta} = \frac{4p^{\sigma-1}(1-\sigma)\left(\underline{d}(1+\phi\underline{d})\underline{\tau}^{-\sigma} + 2\overline{d}(1+\phi\overline{d})\overline{\tau}^{-\sigma}\right)}{B^2 - 4p^{\sigma-1}(1-\sigma)\left(log(1+\phi\underline{d})\underline{\tau}^{1-\sigma} + 2log(1+\phi\overline{d})\overline{\tau}^{1-\sigma}\right)} \quad (32)$$

where p, $\underline{\tau}$ and $\overline{\tau}$ are defined as in equations 9, 26 and 27, and $B \equiv 1 + \underline{\tau}^{1-\sigma} + 2\overline{\tau}^{1-\sigma}$.

Proving that a fall in transport costs *can* strengthen the impact of distance on trade requires us to show that equation 32 can be compatible with condition 31. Although the complexity of equation 32 does not allow for an analytical proof, it can be used to show numerically that, for some sets of parameters, this outcome can occur.

For instance, with the parameters $\underline{d} = 1$, $\overline{d} = 10$, $\sigma = 4$, $\theta = 1$, $A = 5$, $f = 1$, $L = \sigma f(A\sigma/(\sigma-1))^{\sigma-1}$ and $\phi = 0.000001$, it can be computed that $N = 133.0403$ is the solution to equation 28. We use equation 32 to calculate $\frac{\partial N}{\partial \theta} = -178.8048$. The direct effect of a change in θ is $\frac{\overline{d}-\underline{d}}{(1+\theta\overline{d})(1+\theta\underline{d})} = 0.409$, while the indirect effect is $\frac{\partial N}{\partial \theta}\left[log(1+\phi\overline{d}) - log(1+\phi\underline{d})\right] = -0.0016$. Thus, here, the net effect is clearly positive: a fall in θ decreases the importance of distance in trade. The very small value of ϕ gives a very small weight to the coordination cost ratio. In contrast, for $\phi = 0.001$, the other parameters remaining unchanged, we get: $N = 100.4212$ and $\frac{\partial N}{\partial \theta} = -107.9839$. Here, the direct effect is still 0.409 (note that neither N nor ϕ has an impact on the direct effect), whereas the indirect effect is -0.9665 which makes the net effect negative $-0.409 - 0.9665 = 0.5575$.

Figure 3 depicts the ratio $\frac{\bar{\tau}}{\underline{\tau}}$ as a function of θ, for three values of ϕ: a small value ($\phi = 0.000001$); an intermediate value ($\phi = 0.005$) and a high value ($\phi = 0.001$). Here, the impact of ϕ is clear: when uncertainty is low in the input-output relationship (low ϕ), a fall in transport costs lowers the importance of distance. When uncertainty is important (high ϕ), a fall in transport costs has a non-monotonic impact on the importance of distance. At some stages, the increased complexity of the production processes *can* result in an increased need for proximity. In the most extreme case ($\phi = 0.001$), distance matters more for nil than for infinite transport costs.

Figure 3. The ratio $\frac{\bar{\tau}}{\underline{\tau}}$ as function of θ

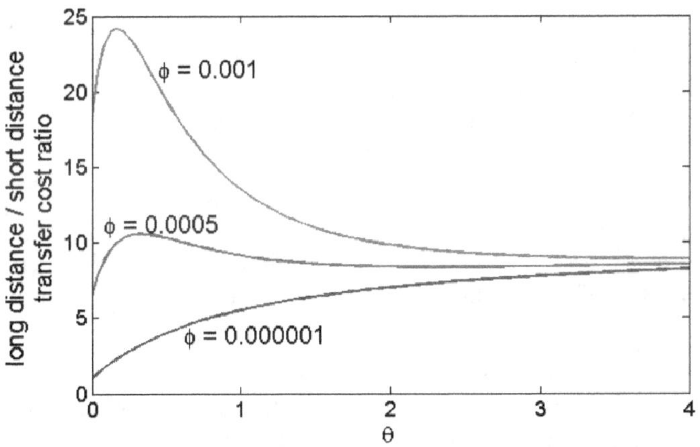

5. DISCUSSION

In this paper we argued that the increasing complexity of the production process, triggered by a fall in transport costs, strengthens the need for proximity between downstream firms and their suppliers. Consequently, a fall in transport costs leads to an overall increase in trade, but can make short distance trade increase more rapidly than long distance. Now, we want to discuss several empirical implications of our model.

Our model could be interpreted in light of Baldwin's two unbundlings[6] framework. This framework distinguishes the first unbundling triggered by a fall in transport costs, from the second unbundling triggered by a fall in com-

[6]Baldwin (2006).

munication and coordination costs. The first allows firms to be located at a distance from their customers, the second (currently happening), allows different tasks in the production process to be located apart from each other. Clearly, in our model the first unbundling corresponds to an exogenous fall in θ. However, regarding the second unbundling, things are more complicated. At first sight, it seems that the second unbundling could be modelled as an exogenous fall in ϕ, but in our model, the first unbundling endogenously increases coordination costs through an increase in N, which tends to limit the second undbundling (recall that the coordination costs coefficient is given by $(1+\phi d)^N$). This effect recalls the Kremer's O'ring theory since it underlines the importance of the number of tasks. An empirical implication is that the second unbundling would be delayed with respect to the improvement in communication technologies.

Another empirical implication of our model is production processes should be more complex today than a few decades ago. Let us present some evidences. Spitz (2004) shows that an important feature of the fragmentation of production processes is the decreasing share of routine tasks performed by workers, whatever their skill level. More precisely, among these non-routine tasks, he highlights a particular increase in interactive tasks. In our view, this switch from routine to non-routine and interactive tasks might reflect the increasing complexity of production processes. Also, Minondo and Requena-Silvente (2013) show that the division of labour between Northern and Southern countries is related more to the level of complexity than factor intensity. These previous works allow us to interpret the increasing complexity of the production process as a consequence of the increasing share of non-routine tasks in production, which require greater coordination and proximity.

If the complexity of the production process increases the need for proximity, then we should observe that the distances in trade of intermediate goods are shorter than the distances involved in trade in final goods. Indeed, this point is suggested by Wolf (2000) and emphasized by Hilleberry and Hummels (2002) as mentioned in introduction.

Finally, our results echoes the so called *distance puzzle* literature. This distance puzzle has been widely discussed in the literature since Leamer and Medburry (1993) first drew attention to it. The puzzle is that "the world is not getting smaller": distance still matters in trade, despite declining trade costs. Most studies based on gravity equations show increasing or constant distance coefficients (see among others Leamer and Medberry, 1993; Brun et al., 2005; Disdier and Head, 2008; Berthelon and Freund, 2008), and decreasing or constant trends for distance of trade (DOT) (Carrère and Schiff, 2005; Berthelon and Freund, 2008). Our model suggests that it should be tested for the most complex goods.

6. CONCLUDING REMARKS

Our goal in this paper was to bring together several features of the current globalization process generally considered important by the international trade literature: (i) the importance of trade in intermediate goods, which reflects a switch in specialization from a sectoral to a task basis (Grossman and Rossi-

Hansberg, 2006); (ii) the emergence of production processes coordinated on a regional scale, which leads to distinguish short-distance (regional trade) from long-distance trade (inter-continental trade) (Hilleberry and Hummels, 2002); (iii) the increasing complexity of production processes, which corresponds to a deepening of the division of labour (Krugman, 1995)[7]; (iv) the need to distinguish between improvements in transport technology and improvements in communication-coordination technology (Baldwin, 2006); and (v) the importance of coordinating complexifying production processes, which echoes Kremer's intuition that the number of task increases the probability of failure (Kremer, 1993).

In doing so, we presented a model that exhibits endogenous increase in coordination costs as a consequence of a fall in transport costs, via an increase in the number of tasks. Although the empirical implications of this model seem supported by several contributions, as discussed in section 5, a robust test of this model would require a relevant measure of complexity, in order to check if: (i) production processes are becoming more complex, (ii) complexity increases the need for geographical proximity between downstream firms and their suppliers. We would expect future work to perform those tests would prove fruitful.

REFERENCES

Asheim, B.T., Coenen, L., 2005, "Knowledge Bases and Regional Innovation Systems: Comparing Nordic Clusters", *Research Policy*, 34(8), 1173-1190.

Autant-Bernard, C., Massard, N., Charlot, S., 2008, « Les déterminants géographiques de l'innovation : Diffusion spatiale des connaissances et choix de localisation », in: Madiès, T., Prager, J.-C. (Eds.), *Innovation et compétitivité des régions*, La Documentation Française, Paris, 227-265.

Hamdouch, A., Depret, M.-H., 2009, "Surveying the Literature on Territorial Innovation Systems: A Suggested Interpretation Framework", *SSRN Working Papers Series*, December.

Autor, D. H., Levy, F., Murnane, R. J., 2003, The Skill Content Of Recent Technological Change: An Empirical Exploration. *The Quarterly Journal of Economics* 118 (4), 1279-1333.

Baldwin, R., Venables, A. J., 2013, Spiders and snakes: offshoring and agglomeration in the global economy. *Journal of International Economics* 90 (2), 245-254.

Baldwin, R. E., 2006, Globalisation: The great unbundling(s). Tech. rep., Paper prepared for Finnish Prime Minister's Office for EU Presidency.

Berkowitz, D., Moenius, J., Pistor, K., 2006, Trade, Law, and Product Complexity. *The Review of Economics and Statistics* 88 (2), 363-373.

[7]"Manufactured goods today are more complex than those of our great-grandfathers' days; not only are they more finely differentiated, their manufacture involves the use of a much greater variety of specialized intermediate goods"(p.7).

Berthelon, M., Freund, C., 2008, On the consevration of distance in international trade. *Journal of International Economics* 75, 310-320.

Brun, J.-F., Carrère, C., Guillaumont, P., de Melo, J., 2005, Has distance died? evidence from a panel gravity model. *World Bank Economic Review* 19 (56), 99-120.

Carrère, C., Schiff, M., 2005, On the geography of trade: distance is alive and well. *Revue Économique* 6 (56), 1249-1274.

Costinot, A., 2009, On the origins of comparative advantage. *Journal of International Economics* 77, 255-264.

Disdier, A.-C., Head, K., 2008, The puzzling persistence of the distance effect on bilateral trade. *The Review of Economics and Statistics* 90 (1), 37-48.

Feenstra, R. C., Hong, C., Ma, H., Spencer, B. J., 2013, Contractual versus non-contractual trade: The role of institutions in China. *Journal of Economic Behavior & Organization* 94 (C), 281-294.

Grossman, G. M., Rossi-Hansberg, E., 2006, Trading tasks: A simple theory of offshoring. *American Economic Review* 98 (5), 1978-97.

Hidalgo, C. A., Hausmann, R., 2009, The building blocks of economic complexity. *Proceedings of the National Academy of Sciences* 106 (26), 10570-10575.

Hillberry, R., Hummels, D., 2002, Explaining home bias in consumption: The role of intermediate input trade. *NBER Working Papers 9020, National Bureau of Economic Research, Inc.*

Hummels, D., Ishii, J., Yi, K.-M., 2001, The nature and growth of vertical specialization in world trade. *Journal of International Economics* 54 (1), 75-96.

Johnson, R. C., Noguera, G., 2012, Proximity and production fragmentation. The American Economic Review 102 (3), 407-411.

Jones, R., Kierzkowski, H., 2005, International fragmentation and the new economic geography. *North American Journal of Economics and Finance* 16 (1), 1-10.

Kimura, F., Takahashi, Y., Hayakawa, K., 2007, Fragmentation and parts and components trade: Comparison between east asia and europe. *The North American Journal of Economics and Finance* 18 (1), 23-40.

Kremer, M., 1993, The o-ring theory of economic development. *The Quarterly Journal of Economics* 108, 551-575.

Krugman, P., 1995, Growing world trade: Causes and consequences. *Brookings Papers on Economic Activity* 26, 327-377.

Leamer, E. E., Medberry, C. J., 1993, U.s. manufacturing and an emerging mexico. *NBER Working Papers 4331, National Bureau of Economic Research, Inc.*

Levchenko, A. A., 2007, Institutional Quality and International Trade. *Review of Economic Studies* 74 (3), 791-819.

Minondo, A., Requena-Silvente, F., 2013, Does complexity explain the structure of trade? *Canadian Journal of Economics* 46 (2), 928-955.

Miroudot, S., Lanz, R., Ragoussis, A., 2009, Trade in intermediate goods and services. *OECD Trade Policy Working Papers* 93, OECD Publishing.

Ng, F., Yeats, A., 2001, Production sharing in East Asia: who does what for whom, and why?, in: Cheng L.K., Kierzkowski H. (Eds.), *Global production and trade in East Asia*, Springer.

Noblet, S., 2011, Coordination costs and the redispersion of industrial activities. *Papers in Regional Science* 90 (4), 813-828.

Nunn, N., 2007, Relationship-Specificity, Incomplete Contracts, and the Pattern of Trade. *The Quarterly Journal of Economics* 122 (2), 569-600.

Ranjan, P., Lee, J. Y., 2007, Contract Enforcement And International Trade. *Economics and Politics* 19 (2), 191-218.

Spitz, A., 2004, Are skill requirements in the workplace rising? Stylized facts and evidence on skill-biased technological change. Tech. rep., *ZEW Discussion Paper* No. 04-33.

Wolf, H. C., November 2000, International home bias in trade. *The Review of Economics and Statistics* 82 (4), 555-563.

COMPLEXITÉ DES PROCESSUS DE PRODUCTION ET BESOIN DE PROXIMITÉ

Résumé - *Cet article étudie les effets de la globalisation sur la géographie des flux commerciaux. Plus précisément, nous présentons l'approfondissement du processus d'intégration (à savoir la baisse des coûts de transport) et le besoin de proximité comme les deux faces d'un même phénomène. Nous proposons un modèle théorique dans lequel la fragmentation et le besoin de proximité dans les liens input-output sont endogènes à la baisse des coûts de transport. En effet, dans un cadre à la Dixit-Stiglitz, la baisse des coûts de transport entraîne une augmentation du nombre de variétés de biens intermédiaires – ou tâches – rendant les processus de production plus complexes. Cette complexification implique une augmentation du besoin de coordination dans les relations input-output. La coordination est supposée être plus facile à réaliser entre pays voisins qu'entre pays lointains.*

Mots-clés - COMPLEXITÉ, PROXIMITÉ, COÛTS DE TRANSPORT, COÛTS DE COORDINATION ET COMMERCE INTERNATIONAL

REGIONAL ECONOMIC GROWTH AND STEADY STATES WITH FREE FACTOR MOVEMENT: A THEORETICAL MODEL WITH EVIDENCE FROM EUROPE

Sascha SARDADVAR*

Abstract - *This paper develops a spatial theoretical growth model in order to study the impact of physical and human capital relocations on the growth of open economies. Analytical and simulation results show how the respective neighbours determine an economy's development, why convergence and divergence may alternate in the medium run, and that interregional migration as a consequence of interregional wage inequalities causes disparities to prevail in the long run. The empirical part applies spatial econometric specifications for European regions on the NUTS2 level for the observation period 2000-2013. The estimations underline the importance of human capital endowments and its relation with spatial location.*

Key-words - NEOCLASSICAL GROWTH THEORY, HUMAN CAPITAL, INTERREGIONAL MIGRATION, CONVERGENCE, DIVERGENCE, EUROPEAN INTEGRATION

JEL Classification - F43, R11, C31

Acknowledgment - The author wishes to thank Lauren Landsmann and Assma Hajji for their helpful support.

* Institute for Economic Geography and GIScience, WU Vienna, Welthandelsplatz 1/D4, 1020 Vienna, Austria. Email: sascha.sardadvar@wu.ac.at

1. INTRODUCTION

Studies released in the 1990s and 2000s generally display a trend of interregional convergence in Europe (Sala-i-Martin 1996, Paci and Pigliaru 2002, Fischer and Stirböck 2006, Pfaffermayr 2009), although some point out that this process is not consistent but rather changing over time (Neven and Gouymte 1995, Tondl 2001). This issue is of particular importance for the European Union, where differences in levels of gross regional product (GRP) per capita reach up to 30fold, which is extreme by any standard. If the famous two per cent rule of β-convergence speed applies, then interregional disparities would halve in around 35 years. Although this may be considered as rather slow, β-convergence and σ-convergence were considered as robust empirical results (see Islam 2003) – at least until recently.

In addition to the well-known problems with growth equations,[1] some problems regarding the empirics of interregional development in Europe continue to exist. By considering only medium run observation periods, empirical results are often biased because of disequilibria and/or shocks which appear shortly before or during the observation period. In particular, recessions and subsequent recoveries, such as the transitions of formerly centrally planned economies or financial crises, may lead to interpretations which depend mostly on the observation period considered.

In the European context, the two decades before the current crises were characterised by high growth rates in the cohesion countries (Greece, Ireland, Portugal, Spain) as well as in the former centrally planned economies which accessed the EU during the 2000s. However, the cohesion countries simultaneously have enjoyed substantial financial support from the EU's structural funds since the late 1980s, which probably supported their high growth numbers during the 1990s. In addition, the introduction of the euro led to unprecedented low interest rates which in turn led to unsustainable private debt and, consequently, high growth during the 2000s until the start of the ongoing crises 2007/2008. At the same time, most empirical studies which include former members of the Council for Mutual Economic Assistance (Comecon) start only at 1995. During the early 1990s, these countries suffered severe recessions due to the transition process, and the high growth numbers afterwards at least partly reflect merely catching-up processes to their long run growth paths.

Taking on a long run perspective, the maps in Figures 1, 2 and 3 display gross domestic product (GDP) for European countries at purchasing power parities (PPP) in percentage to the European mean for 1900, 1960 and 2008, respectively. In particular, when comparing 1900 to 1960, a period during which countless economic transitions took place, it is remarkable how little has changed. Apart from an apparent catching-up process in Northern European countries, which matters visually due to the area size but not so much economically,

[1] Acemoğlu (2009) mentions three major problems, namely (i) endogeneity of explanatory variables and growth, (ii) ambiguity regarding an explanatory variable's magnitude of impact and (iii) ignoring the openness of considered economies and their interactions.

a core-periphery pattern is persistent over the decades: Central western European countries are the most advanced, while the southern, eastern and far western European countries lag behind. The picture hints at club-convergence, as discussed by Baumol (1986). According to his study, the western market economies as well as the eastern centrally planned economies would not converge towards each other but rather form two clubs, differing substantially from each other. Shortly after Baumol's study, the eastern European economies opened themselves to migration, investment and trade-flows from and to the west. In this context, it seems interesting to note that Alexiadis (2013) finds comparable geographical patterns of club-convergence within the EU now that economic systems are more similar than ever before. Indeed, the picture of 2008 differs insofar as the divide between the west and the east is even more pronounced from 1900 and 1960.

Figure 1. GDP at PPP per inhabitant relative to the European mean, 1900

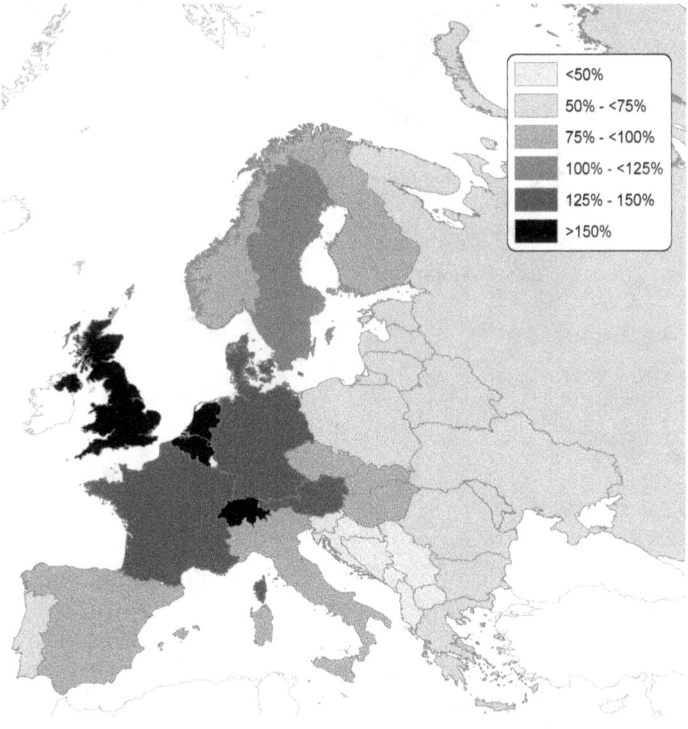

Notes: Total European GDP including Russia, excluding Cyprus and Turkey, European white areas indicate missing data. Data source: World Economics (www.worldeconomics.com)

As of today, more than two thirds of the European population live in member states of the European Union, where capital, people, goods and services are free to move. Figure 4 displays GRP per inhabitant at market prices relative to the EU's mean on the regional NUTS2 level. It can be seen that within Italy and Spain, those regions which lie geographically close to the core are also the most advanced. In contrast, the peripheral regions within these countries are lagging behind. Hence it may be stated that 200 years after the industrialisation of continental Europe commenced, almost 60 years after the foundation of the European Union, and 25 years after the transition of the former Comecon, the European core's economic advance appears to be as robust as ever.

Figure 2. GDP at PPP per inhabitant relative to the European mean, 1960

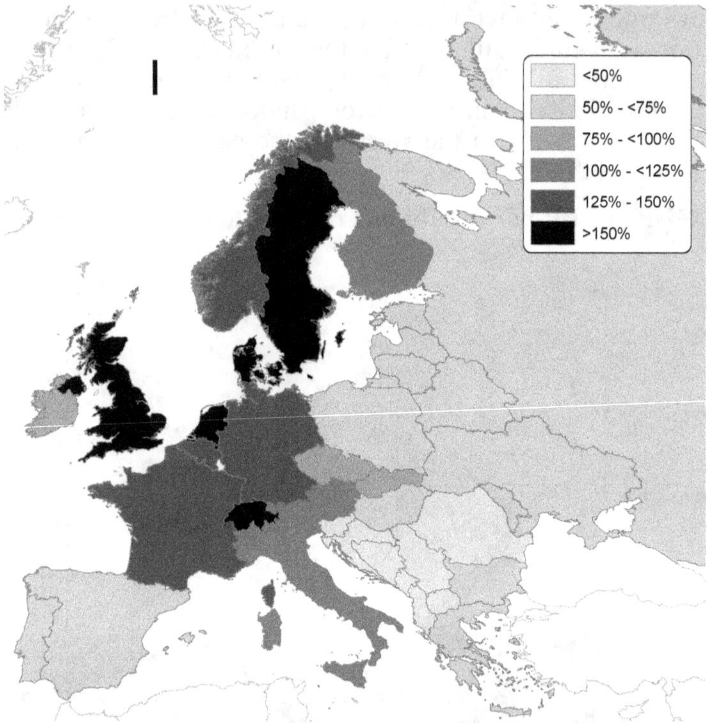

Notes: See Figure 1.

A recent report by the European Bank for Reconstruction and Development (2013) casts doubts on whether the countries and regions which lag behind economically will ever converge to their peers. The report notes that the transition economies of central and eastern Europe achieved impressive growth rates from the mid-1990s until the outbreak of the crises in 2007/2008. According to the report, the high growth rates were fuelled by a rapid catching-up with respect to productivity in the wake of opening their economies to western technology – a process which has now come to an end, with long run growth-problems on prospects of future convergence dynamics. In addition, brain drain has proven to be an obstacle for socio-economic development, and the EU's new member states' brain drain has even accelerated after their accessions in 2004 and 2007. The report (pp. 63) argues that for transition economies to converge towards their mature economy peers, human capital's returns within the former need to be comparable to or even greater than within the latter.

Figure 3. GDP at PPP per inhabitant relative to the European mean, 2008

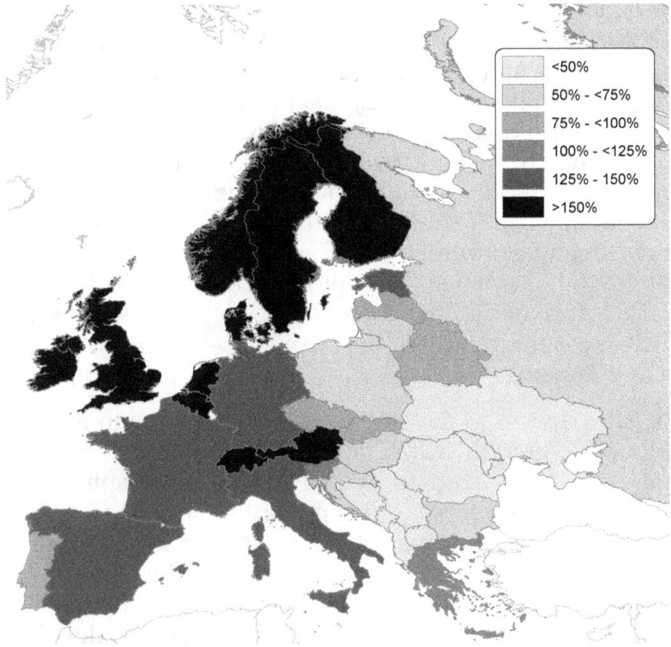

Notes: See Figure 1.

Figure 4. GRP per inhabitant relative to the EU's mean, 2010

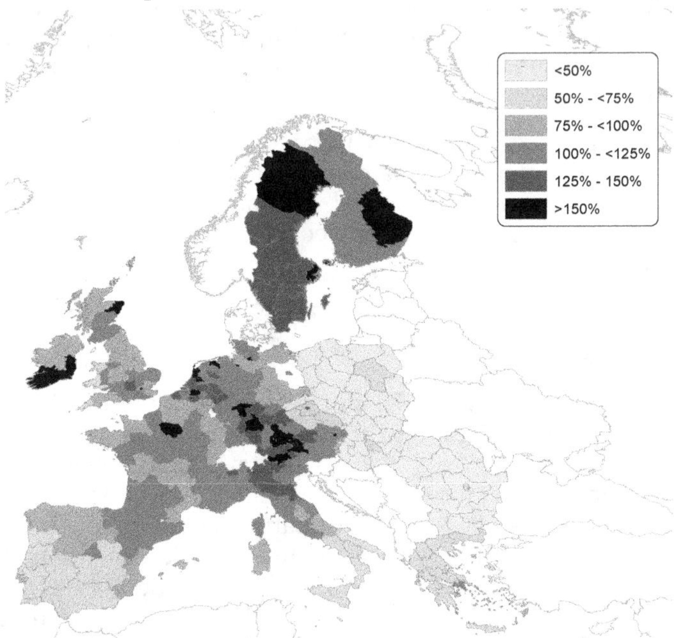

Notes: Data corresponds to GRP at current market prices; data source: Eurostat (epp.eurostat.ec.europa.eu).

As discussed by many authors (North 1990, Landes 1998, Acemoğlu and Robinson 2012), improving institutions is a means of improving economic performance. Whether the report's proposed solution of improving the institutional environment in these countries is enough to stop human capital outflows and to enforce convergence is, however, questionable. It seems too simple to regard an improvement of institutional settings as a cure-all, as it is implausible that if institutional environments within two given economies are identical, then the dynamics between these economies would come to a halt. Rather, dynamics between two economies with similar institutions may be to the advantage of one as it is to the disadvantage to the other if productivity levels differ. To illustrate the case, it is hard to believe that the population decrease of 15.5 per cent within the territory of the former German Democratic Republic since German unification – of which most migrated within Germany – is solely caused by inferior institutional environments.

The aim of this paper is to develop a neoclassical growth model for a system of regional economic growth which takes into account that physical as well as human capital relocations tend to decrease with geographical distance. The quality of institutions and access to technology are assumed to be identical for all regional economies that are part of the system. It is shown that under these conditions, steady state levels depend on geographical location as well as initial conditions. Furthermore, medium run developments can be quite turbulent and do not necessarily allow for conclusions regarding long run development, which may show a completely different pattern. Finally, by means of spatial econometrics, the model's predictions are confronted with interregional developments of the EU before and after the crises. It is argued that possibly the system of the EU's regional economies currently moves towards a new equilibrium which is not caused by the financial and euro crises but rather economic integration of the recent past.

The paper is set up as follows. The theoretical model is presented in the next section. After that, the model's dynamics are described by means of differential equations and simulations. The spatial econometric specifications, data and regions as well as the results are discussed in the fourth section. The final section concludes.

2. THE MODEL

2.1. Theoretical background

In the neoclassical growth model as developed by Solow (1956) and Swan (1956), different steady states result from variations in the determinants of growth within the economy, e.g. the saving rate. Since then, the notion that growth is also shaped by relations to other economies has been considered by a number of theoretical models, which is of particular relevance for issues related to globalisation as well as regional economies. Models in the tradition of the Solow model have incorporated the effects of labour migration (Borts and Stein 1964), trade (Thirlwall 1979), knowledge spillovers (Ertur and Koch 2007), investment flows (Sardadvar 2012), agglomeration effects (De Dominicis 2014) or public capital (Dall'erba and Llamosas-Rosas 2015).

In addition, human capital is acknowledged as a key driver of economic growth at least since the release of Mankiw, Romer and Weil's (1992) influential essay. However, because human capital is embodied in workers, the integration of human capital relocations and its interplay with other factors becomes more complex. Maybe for this reason, theoretical models which integrate human capital relocations show no clear results regarding economic disparities. For instance, in a model of national economies by Barro and Sala-i-Martin (1995, 2004), immigration of human capital suppliers to highly productive economies leads to physical capital dilution and hence accelerates the convergence processes. In contrast, Docquier and Rapoport (2012) consider the benefits of sending and receiving countries. Since it is usually the wealthy economies that attract human capital, the authors' main concern is the extent to which sending countries suffer from negative effects due to brain drain. In a model of regional development by Gennaioli et al. (2013), human capital suppliers migrate from unproductive to productive regions, where the latter may become even more productive as a matter of human capital externalities. In equilibrium, regional economies fall either into the productive or unproductive category, where the former benefits from migration from the latter. As a result, disparities persist also in equilibrium.

Ertur and Koch (2007) develop a spatial growth model where national economies benefit from the knowledge in neighbouring economies, which is embodied in physical capital. The model results in individual steady states, but the economies are not open in the strict sense of the word as factor relocations are not allowed for. In contrast, Sardadvar (2012) considers regional economies and allows for physical capital relocations which depend on human capital stocks relative to neighbouring regions, with possible divergence in the medium run but convergence to identical steady states in the long run. Sardadvar (2013) shows at the example of two economies that the introduction of human capital relocations may further strengthen economies which are already richly endowed with human capital.

Against this background, the aim of the present paper is to provide a theoretical model that is able to explain the persistence of economic and geographic disparities in an integrating economic system such as the European Union. Special attention is paid to (i) the double role of human capital, which is considered as a type of capital but embodied in workers, and (ii) the role of distance, which is assumed to have an impact on factor's mobility. The research question of the paper may be expressed as follows: If an economic system with free but spatially bounded factor movement is integrated to an extent where institutional environments among its regional economies are comparable, which long run pattern of economic development will emerge?

2.2. The Production Function

Consider a neoclassical growth model in the spirit of Mankiw, Romer and Weil (1992) for a finite set of regional economies $i = 1, 2, ..., N$, over continuous time t. Output per unit of effective labour $q_{i,t}$ is assumed to be produced via a Harrod-neutral production function with constant returns to scale

$$q_{i,t} = f(k_{i,t}, h_{i,t}) \tag{1}$$

where the inputs are physical capital per unit of effective labour $k_{i,t}$, and human capital per unit of effective labour $h_{i,t}$. It is assumed that the current level of technology is available everywhere within the superordinate economy, so that $A_{i,t} = A_{j,t}\ \forall i, j, t$, where A symbolises technology.

In addition, in order to facilitate calculations it is assumed that population sizes are identical, that is $L_{i,t} = L_{j,t}\ \forall i, j, t$.

Hence at any t, total regional stocks of factors equal $K_{i,t} = k_{i,t}A_{i,t}L_{i,t}$, $H_{i,t} = h_{i,t}A_{i,t}L_{i,t}$ and thus $Q_{i,t} = f(K_{i,t}, H_{i,t}, A_{i,t}L_{i,t})$.

Since constant returns are assumed, it follows that $Q_{i,t} = q_{i,t}A_{i,t}L_{i,t}$.

In addition, the basic assumptions of the Solow model (continuity, differentiability, positive and diminishing marginal products) apply.

The regions are part of a superordinate economy, whose output is simply the sum of the N regional economies, $\sum_{i=1}^{N} Q_{i,t}$. Since population sizes are assumed to be identical in each region, the superordinate economy's output per unit of effective labour equals the arithmetic mean of the individual regional economies' output values, or simply:

$$\bar{q}_{i,t} = \frac{\sum_{i=1}^{N} Q_{i,t}}{NA_{i,t}L_{i,t}} = \frac{\sum_{i=1}^{N} q_{i,t}}{N} \tag{2}$$

2.3. Evolutions of Stocks of Factors

Factor mobility takes place between directly connected regions and depends on individual choices based on future expectations. Connectivity between any two regions i and j is captured by the term w_{ij}. If $w_{ij} > 0$ for any two regions $i \neq j$ then they are directly connected and considered as neighbours. If they are not considered as neighbours then $w_{ij} = 0$. Note that according to this definition neighbours neither have to share a common physical border, nor do the values $w_{ij} > 0$ have to be identical among pairs of regions.

Expected future profits from investments in physical capital equal their marginal productivity and depend on geographical proximity. The assumption of identical population sizes allows to express the evolution of the physical capital stock as

$$\dot{k}_{i,t} = s_k \mu_{k,t} q_{i,t} \prod_{i \neq j}^{N} \left(\frac{\partial q_{i,t} / \partial k_{i,t}}{\partial q_{j,t} / \partial k_{j,t}} \right)^{\lambda w_{ij}} - (n + g + d) k_{i,t} \tag{3}$$

where the dot over k denotes its derivation with respect to time. s_k is the saving rate, n is the population growth rate, g is the technology growth rate, and d is the rate of depreciation, all of which are exogenously given and assumed to be identical for each region. It can be seen how differences in marginal productivity determine investment flows between the two regions i and j. The size of net investment flows is influenced by λ, a measure of the degree of integration, and the respective value of w_{ij}. $\mu_{k,t}$ is a variable that ensures that the sum of investment outflows equals inflows within the superordinate economy at any t.

In contrast to physical capital investments, expected income of human capital suppliers does not solely depend on human capital's current marginal product but rather on the wage a worker with human capital receives. Therefore, the evolution of the human capital stock per unit of effective labour takes the form

$$\dot{h}_{i,t} = s_h \mu_{h,t} f(k_{i,t}, h_{i,t}) \prod_{i \neq j}^{N} \left(\frac{v_{h,i,t}}{v_{h,j,t}} \right)^{\lambda w_{ij}} - (n+g+d) h_{i,t} \tag{4}$$

where $v_{h,i,t}$ is the wage of human capital suppliers in i at t. s_h is the education expenditure rate (or, equivalently, the saving rate for human capital), which is assumed to be determined by the superordinate economy and hence identical for all regions, while $\mu_{h,t}$ ensures that the sum of regional outflows of human capital within the superordinate economy equals the sum of inflows at any t. From the assumptions of identical technology and population sizes it follows that $\dot{K}_{i,t} = \dot{k}_{i,t} A_{i,t} L_{i,t}$ and $\dot{H}_{i,t} = \dot{h}_{i,t} A_{i,t} L_{i,t}$.

For simplicity, the superordinate economy is assumed an open economy which constantly runs a balanced current account, or, alternatively, simply a closed economy. In that case, the actual superordinate economy's net investment at t including the intraregional flows must equal the sum of all net investments of all regions at t:

$$\sum_{i=1}^{N} \left(s_k Q_{i,t} - dK_{i,t} \right) = \mu_{k,t} \sum_{i=1}^{N} \dot{K}_{i,t} \tag{5}$$

where dividing both sides by $A_{i,t} L_{i,t} = A_{j,t} L_{j,t} \forall i, j, t$ and expressing by $\mu_{k,t}$ yields

$$\mu_{k,t} = \frac{\sum_{i=1}^{N} q_{i,t}}{\sum_{i=1}^{N} \left(q_{i,t} \prod_{i \neq j}^{N} \left(\frac{\partial q_{i,t} / \partial k_{i,t}}{\partial q_{j,t} / \partial k_{j,t}} \right)^{\lambda w_{ij}} \right)} > 0 \tag{6}$$

Likewise, for simplicity it is assumed that net human capital migration beyond the superordinate economy's borders equals zero, so that

$$\sum_{i=1}^{N}\left(s_h Q_{i,t} - dH_{i,t}\right) = \mu_{h,t}\sum_{i=1}^{N}\dot{H}_{i,t} \tag{7}$$

and consequently

$$\mu_{h,t} = \frac{\sum_{i=1}^{N} q_{i,t}}{\sum_{i=1}^{N}\left(q_{i,t}\prod_{i\neq j}^{N}\left(\frac{v_{h,i,t}}{v_{h,j,t}}\right)^{\lambda w_{ij}}\right)} > 0 \tag{8}$$

From eqs. (6) and (8) it can be seen that $\mu_{k,t}$ and $\mu_{h,t}$ will always be greater than zero, since all terms and hence both the nominator and the denominator must be positive.

2.4. The Cobb-Douglas Case

Output per unit of effective labour with a Cobb-Douglas production function equals

$$q_{i,t} = k_{i,t}^{a} h_{i,t}^{b} \tag{9}$$

from which it follows that

$$\dot{k}_{i,t} = s_k \mu_{k,t} k_{i,t}^{a} h_{i,t}^{b} \prod_{i\neq j}^{N}\left(\frac{k_{i,t}^{a-1} h_{i,t}^{b}}{k_{j,t}^{a-1} h_{j,t}^{b}}\right)^{\lambda w_{ij}} - \eta k_{i,t} \tag{10}$$

where $\eta = n + g + d$ to save space.

Human capital is usually defined as 'the total contribution of workers of different skill levels to production' (Romer 2005, pp. 134). Therefore, H is to be distinguished from raw labour L as it represents acquired skills. Accordingly, two types of workers exist: Those who supply only raw labour, and those who additionally supply the skills which are considered to be human capital as defined above. The latter are supposed to earn a higher wage which consists of a compensation for raw labour plus a premium for their human capital supply. Thus the difference between workers who supply human capital and workers who don't equals the profits of foregone human capital investments, i.e. its marginal product. Put differently, although human capital represents a form of capital, its revenues are part of wages.

In terms of national accounts, the share of income earned by the owners of physical capital in equilibrium takes the following form:

$$V_{K,i,t} = K_{i,t}\frac{\partial Q_{i,t}}{\partial K_{i,t}} \tag{11}$$

where V symbolises a factor's total compensation, with the first subscript referring to the respective factor. In the Cobb-Douglas case, eq. (11) simply equals $aQ_{i,t}$. It follows that the share of income that is found on the payrolls is the sum of compensations for raw labour plus human capital

$$V_{L,i,t}+V_{H,i,t}=L_{i,t}\frac{\partial Q_{i,t}}{\partial L_{i,t}}+H_{i,t}\frac{\partial Q_{i,t}}{\partial H_{i,t}} \tag{12}$$

which in the Cobb-Douglas case consequently equals $(1-a)Q_{i,t}$.

Assume that $x_{i,t}$ measures the share of workers who represent one unit of human capital in i at t. Under this scenario, those workers who qualify as human capital receive a premium in addition to marginal product of labour which equals the marginal product of the human capital they supply. In contrast, those workers who do not qualify as human capital just receive compensation for raw labour. In the Cobb-Douglas case we thus have

$$V_{L,i,t}=Q_{i,t}\left(1-x_{i,t}\right)\left(1-a-b\right) \tag{13}$$

$$V_{H,i,t}=Q_{i,t}\left(x_{i,t}\left(1-a-b\right)+b\right) \tag{14}$$

To save space, let $c=1-a-b$ and, for simplicity, consider $x_{i,t}=h_{i,t}$. Then the total compensation for one unit of human capital equals $v_{h,i,t}=q_{i,t}(h_{i,t}c+b)$, and hence

$$\dot{h}_{i,t}=s_h\mu_{h,t}k_{i,t}^a h_{i,t}^b\prod_{i\neq j}^{N}\left(\frac{q_{i,t}(b+ch_{i,t})}{q_{j,t}(b+ch_{j,t})}\right)^{\lambda w_{ij}}-\eta h_{i,t} \tag{15}$$

3. DYNAMICS

3.1. Economic Growth

The total differential of the production function with respect to time equals

$$\frac{dq_{i,t}}{dt}=\frac{\partial q_{i,t}}{\partial k_{i,t}}\frac{dk_{i,t}}{dt}+\frac{\partial q_{i,t}}{\partial h_{i,t}}\frac{dh_{i,t}}{dt} \tag{16}$$

By setting $\mu_{k,t}=\mu_{h,t}=1$ for simplicity, output growth at t may be expressed as

$$\frac{\dot{q}_{i,t}}{q_{i,t}}=as_k\left(\frac{q_{i,t}}{k_{i,t}}\right)^{1+\phi_i}\prod_{i\neq j}^{N}\left(\frac{k_{j,t}}{q_{j,t}}\right)^{\lambda w_{ij}}+bs_h\frac{q_{i,t}v_{h,i,t}^{\phi_i}}{h_{i,t}}\prod_{i\neq j}^{N}\left(\frac{1}{v_{h,j,t}}\right)^{\lambda w_{ij}}-\eta(a+b) \tag{17}$$

where $\phi_i=\lambda\sum_{i=1}^{N}w_{ij}$. Note that this variable becomes higher, the more the neighbours i has and the closer it lies to them. Hence the more centrally located a region, the greater the effects of other regions' attributes will be. To avoid extreme fluctuations or the explosion of the model, the integration of i within the system is constrained so that $\phi_i < 1 \forall i$.

It follows that for any $j \neq j'$

$$\frac{\partial(\dot{q}_{i,t}/q_{i,t})}{\partial h_{j,t}} = -b\lambda w_{ij}\frac{q_{i,t}}{h_{j,t}} \times$$
$$\left(\begin{array}{l} as_k \dfrac{q_{i,t}^{\phi_i} k_{j,t}^{\lambda w_{ij}} h_{j,t}^b}{k_{i,t}^{1+\phi_i}\left(k_{j,t}^a + h_{j,t}^b\right)^{1+\lambda w_{ij}}} \prod_{j' \neq i}^{N} \left(\dfrac{k_{j',t}}{q_{j',t}} \right)^{\lambda w_{ij'}} + \\ s_h \dfrac{b^2 + c(1+b)h_{j,t}}{h_{i,t}\left(b + ch_{j,t}\right) v_{h,j,t}^{\lambda w_{ij}}} \prod_{j' \neq i}^{N} \left(\dfrac{1}{v_{h,j',t}} \right)^{\lambda w_{ij'}} \end{array} \right) \tag{18}$$

which is unambiguously negative since all variables must be positive. Therefore, an increase in human capital endowment in neighbouring regions has a decreasing effect on output growth of region i. This is because the latter becomes less attractive for both types of capital. Equation (18) also shows that this effect is stronger, the stronger the connectivity between the two regions is, i.e. the higher w_{ij}.

The effect of a change in the human capital stock within i has a contrasting effect:

$$\frac{\partial(\dot{q}_{i,t}/q_{i,t})}{\partial h_{i,t}} = b\frac{q_{i,t}}{h_{i,t}^2} \times$$
$$\left(\begin{array}{l} as_k\left(1+\phi_i\right) \dfrac{q_{i,t}^{\phi_i}}{k_{i,t}^{1+\phi_i} h_{i,t}} \prod_{i \neq j}^{N} \left(\dfrac{k_{j,t}}{q_{j,t}} \right)^{\lambda w_{ij}} + \\ s_h \dfrac{v_{h,i,t}^{\phi_i}\left(\left(1+b\right)\left(c\phi_i h_{i,t} - 1\right) + b^2\left(1+\phi_i\right) + ch_{i,t}\right)}{b + ch_{i,t}} \prod_{i \neq j}^{N} \left(\dfrac{1}{v_{h,j,t}} \right)^{\lambda w_{ij}} \end{array} \right) \tag{19}$$

The first term in brackets is unambiguously positive, the second term is positive if $h_{i,t} > \left(1+b-b^2(1-\phi_i)\right) / \left(c\left(1+\phi_i\left(1+b\right)\right)\right)$, which, with plausible values for the parameters, takes on values around one. Considering the positive value of the first term, it is very unlikely yet principally possible for regions with very low human capital endowments that eq. (19) becomes negative. Therefore, the equation shows how under normal circumstances an increase in a region's own human capital stock benefits its further development: A large stock of human capital will attract further human as well as physical capital, and an increase in i's human capital stock will also increase i's output growth. However, the actual magnitude of this effect depends on the interplay of the stocks of factors in the various regions plus the connectivities of i.

Considering i's current output level, an increase may have a positive or negative effect on growth:

$$\frac{\partial(\dot{q}_{i,t}/q_{i,t})}{\partial q_{i,t}}=(1+\phi_i)\times$$

$$\left(-s_k(1-a)\left(\frac{h_{i,t}^{b(1+\phi_i)}}{q_{i,t}^{1+(1-a)\phi_i}}\right)^{\frac{1}{a}}\prod_{j'\neq i}^{N}\left(\frac{k_{j,t}}{q_{j,t}}\right)^{\lambda w_{ij}}+bs_h\frac{v_{h,i,t}^{\phi_i}}{h_{i,t}}\prod_{j'\neq i}^{N}\left(\frac{1}{v_{h,j,t}}\right)^{\lambda w_{ij}}\right) \tag{20}$$

On the one hand, i benefits from its increased attractiveness on foreign factors. On the other hand, an increase above steady state must decrease i's output as a matter of depreciation. However, plausible parameters imply that $1-a>b$, thus a tendency for negative levels of eq. (20) exists.[2]

An output-increase in a particular region j affects i's growth depending on the relative sizes of factors in both regions, with the total effect remaining ambiguous:

$$\frac{\partial(\dot{q}_{i,t}/q_{i,t})}{\partial q_{j,t}}=\frac{\lambda w_{ij}}{b}\frac{q_{i,t}}{q_{j,t}}\times$$

$$\left(\begin{array}{l}a(1-b)s_k\left(\dfrac{h_{i,t}^{a(1+\phi_i)}}{q_{i,t}^{1+(1-b)\phi_i}}\left(\dfrac{q_{j,t}^{1-b}}{h_{j,t}^{a}}\right)^{\lambda w_{ij}}\right)^{\frac{1}{b}}\displaystyle\prod_{\substack{j'\neq i\\ j'\neq j}}^{N}\left(\dfrac{q_{j',t}^{1-b}}{h_{j',t}^{a}}\right)^{\frac{\lambda w_{ij'}}{b}}-\\ b^2 s_h\dfrac{v_{h,i,t}^{\phi_i}}{h_{i,t}v_{h,j,t}^{\lambda w_{ij}}}\displaystyle\prod_{\substack{j'\neq i\\ j'\neq j}}^{N}\left(\dfrac{1}{v_{h,j',t}}\right)^{\lambda w_{ij'}}\end{array}\right) \tag{21}$$

The interpretation is analogous to eq. (20), but this time the tendency for positive levels exists, as $1-b>b^2$.

To summarise, an increase of human capital endowments in neighbouring regions will reduce economic growth of region i, while an increase within its own borders will increase growth. The effect of output in region i or its neighbours depends on the interplay of human capital, physical capital and neighbourship. Therefore, it is possible that regions with low initial output levels will not converge to the mean if its connectivities are unfavourable and if its human capital endowment is low compared to its neighbours. Furthermore, the impacts of neighbouring regions are stronger, the more centrally located a region is, i.e. the more neighbours it has.

[2] Note that a negative impact of initial output would resemble β-convergence, although the interpretation in this paper is different.

3.2. Steady states

Equilibrium is defined a state of the system in which there are no further changes with respect to the capital stocks per unit of effective labour, i.e. it must be that $\dot{k}_i^* = \dot{h}_i^* = 0 \; \forall i$, with the stars indicating equilibrium levels. Because physical capital relocations depend on relative marginal productivity, the condition $\dot{k}_i^* = 0 \; \forall i$ implies that in equilibrium $\partial q_i^* / \partial k_i^* = \partial q_j^* / \partial k_j^* \; \forall i, j$. It follows that in equilibrium, the nominator and denominator of eq. (6) are identical, and therefore $\mu_k^* = 1$.

In contrast, for human capital the equilibrium condition $\dot{h}_i^* = 0 \; \forall i$ allows for $v_{h,i}^* \neq v_{h,j}^*$ which is due to the incentive to migrate based on wages. This means that a particular level of human capital can be upheld even under permanent emigration, as human capital is simultaneously reproduced while depreciating. In other words, in order to keep a relatively high level of human capital a region must permanently attract human capital from neighbouring regions if both terms on the right hand side of eq. (15) are to have identical values. Simultaneously, a region with a relatively low human capital level permanently produces and loses human capital to its neighbours, but needs less gross investments to uphold its relatively low equilibrium level.

By solving both eqs. (10) and (15) for η, it follows that in equilibrium

$$s_h \mu_h^* \frac{q_i^{*1+\phi_i} (h_i^* c + b)^{\phi_i}}{h_i^*} \prod_{i \neq j}^{N} \left(\frac{1}{k_j^{*a} h_j^{*b} (h_j c + b)} \right)^{\lambda w_{ij}} = s_k \left(\frac{h_i^{*b}}{q_i^{*1-a}} \right)^{\frac{1}{a}} \tag{22}$$

Solving this equation for q_i yields steady state output as

$$q_i^* = \left(\left(\frac{s_k}{s_h \mu_h^*} \right)^a \frac{h_i^{*a+b}}{(b + c h_i^*)^{a\phi_i}} \prod_{i \neq j}^{N} \left(q_j^* (b + c h_j^*) \right)^{a \lambda w_{ij}} \right)^{\frac{1}{1+a\phi_i}} \tag{23}$$

A special case arises if each connectivity $w_{ij} = w_{ij'} \forall w_{ij} > 0$ and simultaneously $\phi_i = \phi_j \forall i, j$ or, expressed verbally, if each of a particular region's connectivities is considered as equally important and if, in addition, each region is as centrally located as any other region.[3] In this case, cancelling and restructuring of eq. (23) leads to:

$$\frac{k_i^*}{h_i^*} = \frac{s_k}{s_h \mu_h^*} \prod_{i \neq j}^{N} \frac{v_j^{*\frac{\phi}{\omega(i)}}}{v_i^{*\phi}} \forall w_{i,j} > 0 \tag{24}$$

[3] Note that this case corresponds to a row-standardised spatial weight matrix based on binary connectivities.

where $\phi = \lambda \sum_{i=1}^{N} w_{ij} \forall i$ and $\omega(i)$ equals i's number of non-zero connectivities (i.e. the number of regions which are considered as neighbours to i). Note that $\prod_{i \neq j}^{N} v_j^{*\phi/\omega(i)} / v_i^{*\phi} \approx 1$, from which it follows that the neighbours' impact on long run levels almost disappears, hence they will be almost identical. Furthermore, from almost identical output levels across all regions it follows from eq. (8) that $\mu_h^* \approx 1$. But if this is the case, then eq. (24) collapses to $k_i^* / h_i^* \approx s_k / s_h$ and each region converges to the same steady state levels which are identical to the ones in Sardadvar (2012).

Therefore, from eq. (23) a number of the model's key conclusions can be drawn.

- Firstly, each region's eventual levels of factors depend on their neighbours' values. The higher the individual neighbours' steady state levels are, the higher is i's steady state output level. From this it follows that all regions approach individual levels of factor endowments and output in the long run.
- Secondly, equilibrium is dependent on the parameter of integration λ, the connectivities w_{ij}, and the values of s_k, s_h, a and b. Therefore, the system evolves towards an equilibrium that is determined by these factors. Considering that λ, s_k and s_h result from political decision-making, equilibrium can be influenced and changed.
- Thirdly, equilibrium also depends on starting levels as displayed by the inclusion of h_i^* on the right hand side of eq. (23).
- Fourthly, from eqs. (18) to (21) it follows that development in the medium run may be quite turbulent, depending on connectivities, the degree of integration and initial factor endowments. Until equilibrium is eventually reached, regions may surpass each other with respect to output, possibly displaying trends of β- and σ-convergence and -divergence subsequently or even simultaneously.
- Fifthly, if all connectivities are equally important and each region is as central as any other region, then all regions converge to the same steady state level.

In addition, steady state output of i is an increasing function of h_i^*:

$$\frac{\partial q_i^*}{\partial h_i^*} = \frac{h_i^*\left(ac\left(1-\phi_i\right)+b\right)+b\left(a+b\right)}{1+a\phi_i} \times \left(\left(\frac{s_k}{s_h \mu_h^*}\right)^a \frac{1}{h_i^{*1-a(1-\phi_i)-b}\left(b+ch_i^*\right)^{1+2a\phi_i}} \prod_{i \neq j}^{N}\left(q_j^*(b+ch_j^*)\right)^{a\lambda w_{ij}}\right)^{\frac{1}{1+a\phi_i}} \quad (25)$$

which is unambiguously positive. In contrast to the effect on medium run growth, the steady state of i is positively influenced by h_j^*:

$$\frac{\partial q_i^*}{\partial h_j^*}=\frac{a\lambda w_{ij}}{1+a\phi_i}\left(q_j^*\left(c\left(1+b\right)+\frac{b}{h_j^*}\right)\right)\times$$

$$\left(\left(\frac{s_k}{s_h\mu_h^*}\right)^a\frac{h_i^{a+b}}{\left(b+ch_i^*\right)^{a\phi_i}}\frac{1}{\left(q_j\left(b+ch_j^*\right)\right)^{1+a\left(\phi_i-\lambda w_{ij}\right)}}\prod_{i\neq j'}^{N}\left(q_{j'}^*\left(b+ch_{j'}^*\right)\right)^{a\lambda w_{ij'}}\right)^{\frac{1}{1+a\phi_i}} \qquad (26)$$

Finally, q_i^* is positively influenced by q_j^*

$$\frac{\partial q_i^*}{\partial q_j^*}=\frac{a\lambda w_{ij}}{1+a\phi_i}\times$$

$$\left(\left(\frac{s_k}{s_h\mu_h^*}\right)^a\frac{h_i^{*a+b}}{\left(b+ch_i^*\right)^{a\phi_i}}\frac{\left(b+ch_j^*\right)^{a\lambda w_{ij}}}{q_j^{*1+a\left(\phi_i-\lambda w_{ij}\right)}}\prod_{i\neq j'}^{N}\left(q_{j'}^*\left(b+ch_{j'}^*\right)\right)^{a\lambda w_{ij'}}\right)^{\frac{1}{1+a\phi_i}} \qquad (27)$$

From eqs. (25), (26) and (27) it follows that steady state levels are expected to be *similar* across neighbouring regions. This positive influence of the neighbours' steady state output despite its negative effect on economic growth is due to feedback effects which emerge in the long run. In the medium run, high human capital endowments attract investments and hence a region may grow at its neighbours' expense. At some point, however, marginal productivity becomes so low that the region's neighbours start to benefit. Therefore, in the long run all regions converge to their individual steady state output levels, which are more similar among neighbouring regions.

3.3. Simulation Results

In order to illustrate the model, in this section three simulations are run. The first scenario shows how the model behaves if the initial factor endowments are arbitrarily given. The second scenario considers identical initial endowments among regions, but at some point an exogenous shock leads to a small increase of human capital endowment in one particular region, leading to a collapse of the old equilibrium. In the third scenario, one region starts out with much more human capital than the others, where due to its initial advantage the respective region remains the most productive region in the long run despite the occurrence of σ-convergence in the medium run.

Consider those variables which are identical across regions to equal $a=0.3$, $b=0.2$, $\eta=0.08$, $s_k=0.25$, $s_h=0.15$, and $\lambda=0.1$. The superordinate economy consists of 12 regions A, B, ..., L, whose borders are displayed by the accompanying spatial weights matrix:

$$\mathbf{W} = \begin{pmatrix} 0 & 1 & 0 & 1 & 0 & 0 & 1 & 0 & 0 & 1 & 0 & 0 \\ 1 & 0 & 1 & 1 & 1 & 0 & 1 & 0 & 0 & 0 & 0 & 0 \\ 0 & 1 & 0 & 0 & 1 & 1 & 1 & 0 & 0 & 0 & 0 & 0 \\ 1 & 1 & 0 & 0 & 1 & 0 & 0 & 0 & 1 & 1 & 0 & 0 \\ 0 & 1 & 1 & 1 & 0 & 1 & 0 & 0 & 0 & 1 & 0 & 0 \\ 0 & 0 & 1 & 0 & 1 & 0 & 1 & 0 & 0 & 0 & 0 & 0 \\ 1 & 1 & 1 & 0 & 0 & 1 & 0 & 1 & 0 & 0 & 0 & 0 \\ 0 & 0 & 0 & 0 & 0 & 0 & 1 & 0 & 1 & 0 & 0 & 0 \\ 1 & 0 & 0 & 1 & 0 & 0 & 0 & 1 & 0 & 1 & 1 & 0 \\ 0 & 0 & 0 & 1 & 1 & 0 & 0 & 0 & 1 & 0 & 1 & 0 \\ 0 & 0 & 0 & 0 & 0 & 0 & 0 & 0 & 1 & 1 & 0 & 1 \\ 0 & 0 & 0 & 0 & 0 & 0 & 0 & 0 & 0 & 0 & 1 & 0 \end{pmatrix} \qquad (28)$$

For the first simulation, the initial factor endowments are arbitrarily given, with the corresponding vectors of the values of $k_{i,0}$ and $h_{i,0}$ equalling:

$$\mathbf{k}_0^{'} = \begin{pmatrix} 10 & 9 & 5 & 8 & 9 & 7.5 & 8.5 & 7 & 8 & 7.5 & 5 & 4 \end{pmatrix}$$

$$\mathbf{h}_0^{'} = \begin{pmatrix} 7 & 6 & 5 & 4.5 & 5.5 & 4 & 5 & 3.5 & 5 & 4 & 3 & 1.5 \end{pmatrix}$$

As can be seen from Figure 5, disparities regarding output reduce during the first 60 periods. Although overall σ-convergence applies during these first 60 periods, a closer look also reveals that some regions do not converge to the mean but rather diverge: E and I move upwards, while D moves downwards. From $t = 61$ onwards, variance increases. Put differently, the observation of σ-convergence during the first 60 periods is deceptive for two reasons: Firstly, some regions diverge during this period despite global convergence. Secondly, others are caught in a downward spiral, i.e. their continuous shrinking (in efficiency units) leads to a decreasing variance in the first 60 periods, while others rise, which leads to σ-divergence in the medium run.

Figure 5. First simulation of the model, 200 periods

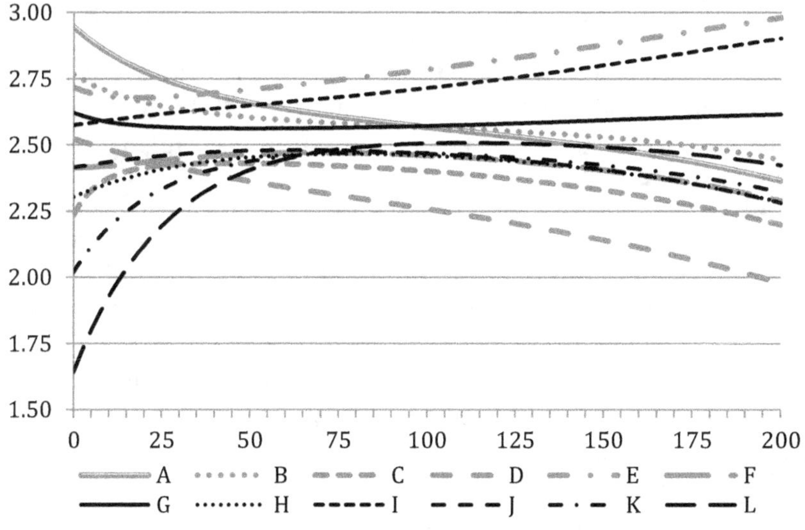

Figure 6 displays the development for the same scenario over 2,000 periods. It can be seen that after many position changes and periods of σ-convergence as well as σ-divergence, all regions eventually converge to their individual balanced growth paths. Three regions are found clearly above the mean, while the others are below, some of which display similar output levels. Therefore, in the long run, growth rates converge, but output levels differ substantially. In addition, during certain periods some groups of regions may converge, while others diverge. This issue of simultaneous convergence and divergence may, as in Figures 5 and 6, depend on the current output level, an issue which has recently been taken up by Monastiriotis (2014). However, occurrences of convergence of some regions do not lead to convergence clubs of the same regions, as they may overpass each other in the long run.

Figure 6. First simulation of the model, 2,000 periods

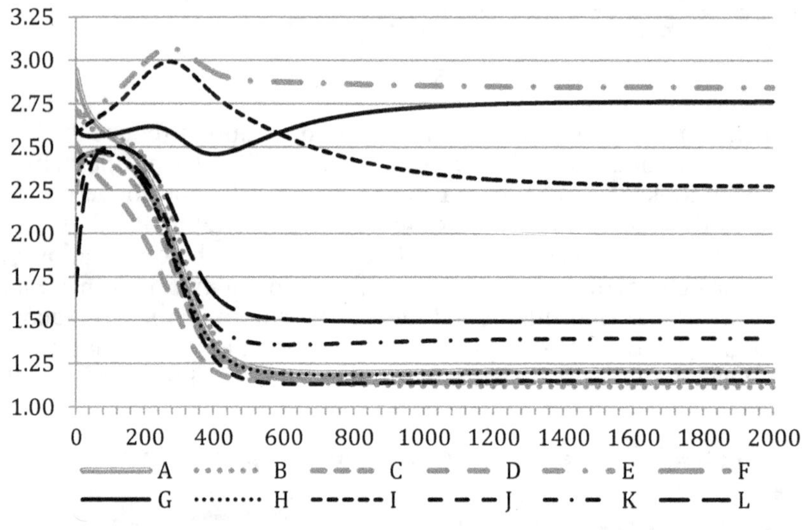

In the second simulation, displayed in Figure 7, all regions start out with identical initial factor endowments of $k_0 = 5$ and $h_{i,0} = 3$. With factor endowments and hence output and wages being identical in each region, there is no incentive for factor relocations, and each region converges to the levels that would prevail in the case of closed economies.[4] However, this is an unstable equilibrium: At $t = 200$, region B exogenously receives 0.1 extra units of h, which has a devastating effect to the system. This small deviation initiates large factor relocations, from which region B benefits the most. At $t = 876$, region B has accumulated a human capital stock of $h_{B,876} = 11.29$, which is four times higher than the mean $\bar{h}_{876} = 2.82$. Five periods later, B's output level has reached its maximum $q_{B,881} = 3.27$. After that, B's level shrinks slightly but remains way above the other regions.

[4] The corresponding steady states are identical to the ones in the model by Mankiw et al. (1992).

Figure 7. Second simulation of the model, 2,000 periods

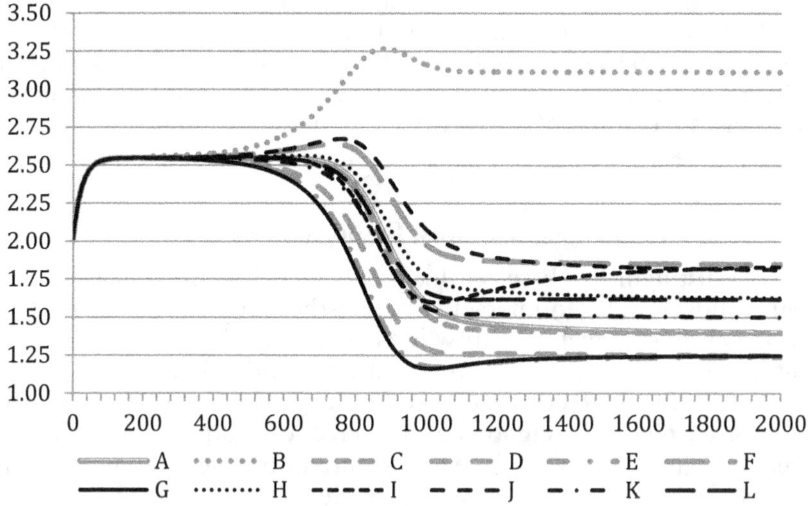

Figure 8. Third simulation of the model, 2,000 periods

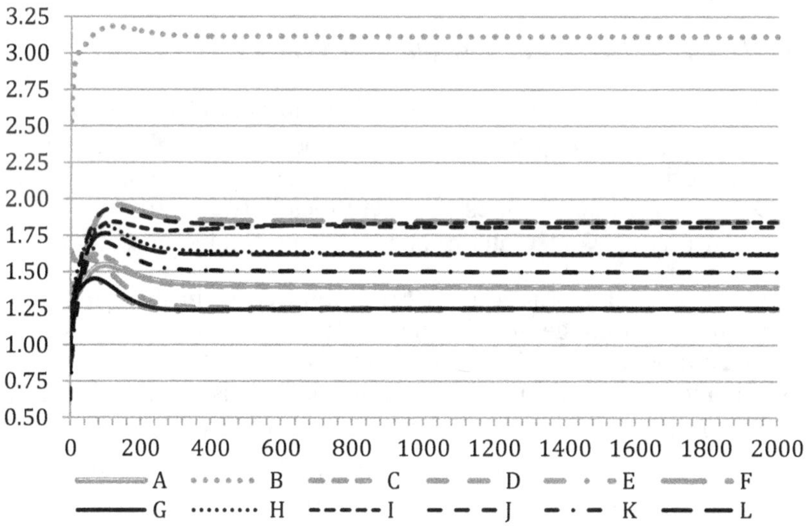

Figure 8 illustrates a third simulation, representing a scenario in which region B starts out with more human capital than the sum of all other regions, while other values are relatively small and similar across the regions:

$$\mathbf{k}_0' = \begin{pmatrix} 2 & 3 & 4 & 1.5 & 0.5 & 3 & 2 & 1 & 1 & 0.75 & 0.25 & 0.5 \end{pmatrix}$$
$$\mathbf{h}_0' = \begin{pmatrix} 1 & 20 & 1.5 & 2 & 1.5 & 0.5 & 1 & 1.5 & 1 & 1 & 0.75 & 1 \end{pmatrix}$$

In this case, B's human capital level immediately starts to fall due to depreciation. However, the high human capital level attracts physical capital investments, and its output increases until B has reached its highest level with $q_{B,124}$ = 3.18. 15 periods later, B's physical capital endowment has reached its peak with $q_{B,139}$ = 9.97. Although both decline slightly afterwards, B remains the most productive region by far and in that sense the system's core. In Figure 8, it is also interesting to note that during the first 50 periods of high growth rates, variance decreases, i.e. times of prosperity coincide with σ-convergence.

4. EMPIRICS

4.1. Spatial Econometric Specifications, Regions and Data

LeSage (2014) distinguishes between local and global spillover specifications, where local spillovers refer to interaction effects between pairs of spatial units. From this perspective, effects on growth as in eqs. (18) to (21) capture *local* effects. Furthermore, from eqs. (18) to (21) it follows that human capital within region i has a positive effect on i's economic growth, while human capital levels in regions which are neighbours to i have a negative effect. Regarding output levels, it follows that the effect of the current output level in region i on its neighbours depends on how far away these levels are from steady states, in addition to the interplay with other factors. In order to test these medium run predictions, a specification is needed which includes spatial effects of the explanatory variables:

$$(\mathbf{q}_\mathrm{T}-\mathbf{q}_0)/T=\alpha\boldsymbol{\iota}+\beta_1\mathbf{q}_0+\gamma_1\mathbf{h}_0+\beta_2\mathbf{W}\mathbf{q}_0+\gamma_2\mathbf{W}\mathbf{h}_0+\mathbf{u} \tag{29}$$

where $\mathbf{q}$ and $\mathbf{h}$ are $N\times 1$ vectors which contain the natural logarithms of output and human capital levels per labour unit, respectively, with 0 symbolising the observation period's initial year and T representing the number of years. $\mathbf{W}$ is an $N\times N$ matrix that captures connectivities between all regions via its elements w_{ij}, and $\boldsymbol{\iota}$ is an $N\times 1$ vector of ones. $\mathbf{u}$ is an $N\times 1$ vector of residuals.

A regression specification as in eq. (29) is referred to in the spatial econometrics literature (e.g. LeSage and Fischer 2008, LeSage and Pace 2009) as a spatial lag of X model (SLXM). It contains a home region's as well as its neighbours' characteristics. From eqs. (18) and (19) it is expected that $\gamma_1>0$ and $\gamma_2<0$, while eqs. (20) and (21) display how β_1 depends on the state of the system while it is expected that $\beta_2>0$ as discussed above. Furthermore, if the system experiences no recession then α should be positive as it captures global economic growth. A restricted regression of eq. (29) which tests for $\beta_1=-\beta_2$ and $\gamma_1=-\gamma_2$ takes the form

$$(\mathbf{q}_\mathrm{T}-\mathbf{q}_0)/T=\alpha\boldsymbol{\iota}+\beta(\mathbf{q}_0-\mathbf{W}\mathbf{q}_0)+\gamma(\mathbf{h}_0-\mathbf{W}\mathbf{h}_0)+\mathbf{u} \tag{30}$$

where the coefficients β and γ reveal whether within-region effects and neighbouring effects outweigh each other.

With the theoretical model assuming the same quality of institutions and equal access to technology within the European Union, respective differences may diminish over time but are probably still present. Furthermore, relative similarities regarding these and other differences may be spatially lagged and be captured by spatial autocorrelation of the residuals as measured by Moran's I (see Goodchild 1986), which takes on values between -1 and 1:

$$I = \frac{\sum_{i=1}^{N}\sum_{j=1}^{N} w_{ij}\left(u_i - \bar{u}\right)\left(u_j - \bar{u}\right)}{\sum_{i=1}^{N}\left(u_i - \bar{u}\right)^2} \tag{31}$$

Concerning the model's long run predictions, from eq. (23) it follows that region i 's steady state output level is dependent on the respective levels in neighbouring regions as well as human capital levels in i and its neighbouring regions. In the sense of LeSage (2014) in this case *global* spillovers apply, as they refer to a scenario where changes in one spatial unit set in motion a sequence of adjustments in (potentially) all spatial units such that a new long run steady state equilibrium arises. From eqs. (25), (26) and (27) it is expected that all of these effects are positive. Therefore, the econometric specification where the dependent variable is output *level* has the form

$$\mathbf{q}_t = \rho \mathbf{W}\mathbf{q}_t + \alpha \boldsymbol{\iota} + \mu_1 \mathbf{h}_t + \mu_2 \mathbf{W}\mathbf{h}_t + \mathbf{u} \tag{32}$$

An econometric specification as in eq. (32) is referred to in the literature as a spatial Durbin model (SDM) (e.g. LeSage and Fischer 2008, LeSage and Pace 2009). In contrast to the SLXM, the SDM's coefficients are not identical to the partial derivatives of the dependent variable. Rather, a change in the explanatory variable for a single region can potentially affect the dependent variable in all other regions. This can be seen by expressing eq. (32) as:

$$\mathbf{q}_t = \left(\mathbf{I}_N - \rho\mathbf{W}\right)^{-1}\left(\mu_1\mathbf{I}_N + \mu_2\mathbf{W}\right)\mathbf{h}_t + \left(\mathbf{I}_N - \rho\mathbf{W}\right)^{-1}\alpha\boldsymbol{\iota} + \left(\mathbf{I}_N - \rho\mathbf{W}\right)^{-1}\mathbf{u}$$

where $\mathbf{I}_N$ represents an $N \times N$ identity matrix. As shown by LeSage and Pace (2009), the derivative of $q_{i,t}$ with respect to $h_{j,t}$ is potentially non-zero and determined by the element in row i, column j of the matrix $\left(\mu_1\mathbf{I}_N + \mu_2\mathbf{W}\right)$. From this it follows that a change in the explanatory variable for a single region can potentially affect the dependent variable in all other regions (LeSage and Pace 2009, pp. 35).

The interpretation of the parameters therefore differs from linear regressions and becomes more complicated. The present paper follows LeSage and Pace (2009) in estimating direct, indirect and total impacts in order to draw inference from the regression results. Firstly, the average direct impacts capture the effect of a change in $h_{i,t}$ on $q_{i,t}$ and includes feedback influences that arise from the fact that $\left(\mathbf{I}_N - \rho\mathbf{W}\right)^{-1} = \mathbf{I}_N + \rho\mathbf{W} + \rho^2\mathbf{W}^2 + \rho^3\mathbf{W}^3 + \ldots$, i.e. impacts passing through neighbouring regions and back to region i. This effect corresponds to eq. (25), where a positive value implies a positive impact of an increase in i 's human capital stock on i's equilibrium output level. Secondly, the average indirect impacts capture the effect of a change in $h_{j,t}$ by the same amount across all regions on $q_{i,t}$ and thus capture the impact of an increase in human capital within the neighbours of region i on the latter. This effect corresponds to the sum for all regions $j \neq i$ in eq. (26), i.e. $\sum_{i \neq j}^{N} \partial q_i^* / \partial h_j^*$, where a positive value implies a positive effect of an increase in the human capital stocks of i's neighbours on i's equilibrium output. Thirdly, the average total impacts capture the effect of a change of h_t in the jth region over all $q_{i,t}$, i.e. direct plus indirect effects. A positive value implies that an increase of human capital stocks in the whole systems increases total equilibrium output.

The model is tested for 250 European Union's regions on the NUTS2[5] level for the years 2000-2013, based on ESA10.[6] Although actual population sizes are not identical, they are comparable as most NUTS2 regions' population sizes lie between the official population thresholds of 800,000 and 3,000,000 (European Parliament and Council of the European Union 2003, Article 3) Output per labour unit is measured by GRP at current market prices in euros per inhabitant.[7] Human capital is estimated by the percentage of inhabitants with tertiary education to the number of gainfully active persons. The source of all data is Eurostat.

Distances between regions are taken by car travel times between NUTS2 regions as calculated by Schürmann and Talaat (2000). Results in this paper are based on the concept of two regions as being considered as neighbours if the distance between them lies below a *critical cut-off* value, with

$$\begin{cases} w_{ij}^* = 0 \text{ if } i = j \\ w_{ij}^* = 1 \text{ if } \delta_{ij} \leq \delta^* \\ w_{ij}^* = 0 \text{ if } \delta_{ij} > \delta^* \end{cases}$$

where δ_{ij} equals the distance between two regions i and j in time units and δ^* is a pre-defined critical cut-off distance. If a region happens to have no neighbour for whom $\delta_{ij} \leq \delta^*$ applies, then the closest region is considered to be

[5] The study covers the European territory of the EU on the NUTS2 level. Due to lack of data, the classification used in this study deviates from the official classification as of December 2011 in the following cases: Croatia, Cyprus, Estonia, Latvia, Lithuania, Luxemburg, and Malta are not included; the NUTS2 regions Brandenburg-Nordost and Brandenburg-Südwest as well as the NUTS2 regions of Denmark and Slovenia have been merged to one region, respectively. By focussing on Europe, the study excludes the French regions Guadeloupe, Martinique, Guyana and Réunion, the Portuguese regions Região Autónoma dos Açores and Região Autónoma da Madeira, and the Spanish regions Ciudad Autónoma de Ceuta, Ciudad Autónoma de Melilla and Canarias.

[6] In cases of missing data on the NUTS2 level, growth rates for the respective periods of the superordinate NUTS1 regions are assumed for their corresponding NUTS2 regions.

[7] It does no harm to rely on nominal values as relative growth rates are studied (see Sardadvar (2011, Chapter 9) for a discussion).

the sole neighbour. The i th row and j th column of **W** consists of the element $w_{ij} = \sum_{i=1}^{N}\sum_{j=1}^{N} w_{ij}^{*}$, i.e. the spatial weights matrix is standardised so that both the average row and the average column sums equal one.

Note that the spatial weights matrix as specified here is neither row- nor column-standardised. Rather, regions which happen to lie more centrally located display higher row sums as compared to peripheral regions. This way, one of the basic characteristics of the capital accumulation functions – centrally located regions being more exposed to influences of other regions – is reflected by the empirical specification.

For instance, if $\delta^{*} = 3$ h, then the applied travel time distances correspond to 1,738 neighbourhoods within all 250 regions. Standardisation in this case leads to each non-zero element of **W** equalling 0.1438, which is also necessarily equal to the row sums of those regions which have only one neighbour assigned to. Regions with exactly two neighbours have row sums of 0.2877, regions with three neighbours have row sums of 0.4315 and so on.[8] In the case of $\delta^{*} = 4$ h, **W** has 2,973 non-zero elements, equalling 0.0841 each.[9] From this it also follows that a greater cut-off distance reduces the impact of individual regions classified as neighbours. In contrast, the average total impact a region is exposed to remains unchanged, as the average row-sum across all regions equals one as discussed above.

4.2. Results

Before estimating the regressions, it may be helpful calculating the variances of the natural logarithms of GRP per capita, i.e. testing for what is referred to in the literature as σ-convergence (see Sala-i-Martin 1996). Figure 9 displays the observation area's corresponding values for each year. It is striking to see that until the outbreak of the recession in 2008, the variance shows a clear downward trend. Since then, it stagnates.

The regression estimations which correspond to eq. (29) are displayed in Tables 1 and 2 for $\delta^{*} = 3$ h and $\delta^{*} = 4$ h, respectively. The results are given for the whole observation period 2000-2013, for the period before the outbreak of the recession 2000-2008, and for the period afterwards 2008-2013. Additional results for $\delta^{*} = 2$ h and $\delta^{*} = 5$ h can be found in Tables 5 and 6 in the Appendix.

It can be seen that the results for 2000-2013 clearly support the model's predictions: Within one region, initial output, β_1, is negative, while human capital, γ_1, is positive, with the respective values for neighbouring regions, β_2 and γ_2,

---

[8] The regions with most neighbours in the case of $\delta^{*} = 3$ h is Düsseldorf (NUTS code: DEA1) with 26 neighbours and a row sum of 3.7399, closely followed by North Brabant (NL41) and Limburg (NL42) with 25 neighbours each and corresponding row sums of 3.5961.

[9] With $\delta^{*} = 4$ h Düsseldorf remains the most central region with 40 neighbours and a row sum of 3.3636, this time closely followed by Cologne (DEA2) and Münster (DEA5) with 39 neighbours each and corresponding row sums of 3.2795.

displaying contrasting signs. Spatial autocorrelation of the residuals is positive and significant in both cases, but the values are remarkably low, especially for 2000-2013 with $\delta^* = 4$ h. The restricted regression corresponds to eq. (30) and displays a total negative impact of initial output, β, and a total positive impact of initial human capital, γ. However, the likelihood ratio test rejects the restricted regression.

Figure 9. Variance of the natural logarithms of GRP per inhabitant, 2000-2013

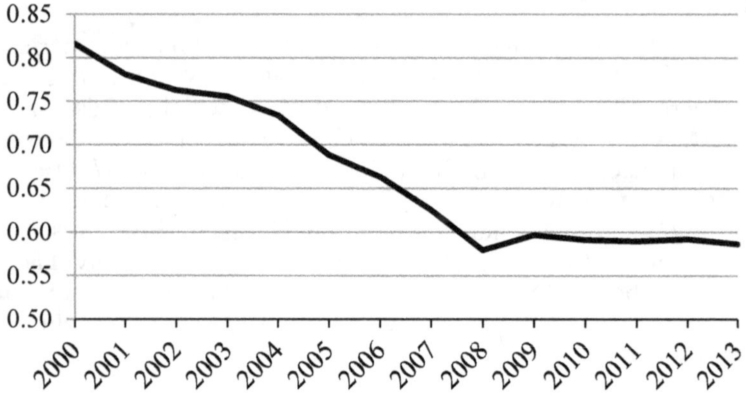

When looking at the results for 2000-2008 and 2008-2013, it can be seen that the value of β_1 is about three times as large before as after the crises. This might be interpreted as a decrease in the speed of convergence, as a negative value of β_1 is usually interpreted as evidence for β-convergence as defined by Sala-i-Martin (1996). However, as displayed in Fig. 9, σ-convergence during the same period does not apply. It is also interesting to note that for 2008-2013 statistical explanation power is lowest, the spatial autocorrelation of the residuals is highest and the likelihood ratio test does not reject the restricted version.

Therefore, although a negative value of β_1 implies a corresponding effect of high initial output on growth, it does not necessarily imply convergence of GRP levels. As shown by the model, a region rich in physical capital is able to remain attractive to new investments as well as human capital suppliers by simultaneously displaying high human capital levels. This interpretation is supported by the unambiguously positive effects of human capital endowments within one region, as displayed by γ_1, and output in neighbouring regions, as displayed by β_2. The strong negative impact of human capital in neighbouring regions, γ_2, confirms eq. (18) and has also been found in a number of empirical studies (among them Olejnik 2008, Ramos et al. 2010, Fischer et al. 2010, Resende et al. 2013). Taken together, the estimations underline that a negative impact of initial output on growth is not necessarily an evidence for convergence, as it is more than outweighed by human capital endowments within one region as well as in neighbouring regions.

Table 1: SLXM estimations with 3 hours travel time as threshold distance

	without dummy			including NMS dummy		
	2000-2013	2000-2008	2008-2013	2000-2013	2000-2008	2008-2013
α	0.275 (0.000)	0.431 (0.000)	-0.014 (0.609)	0.188 (0.000)	0.367 (0.000)	-0.122 (0.015)
β_1	-0.031 (0.000)	-0.045 (0.000)	-0.015 (0.000)	-0.022 (0.000)	-0.038 (0.000)	-0.003 (0.489)
γ_1	0.019 (0.000)	0.018 (0.001)	0.021 (0.000)	0.016 (0.000)	0.016 (0.002)	0.020 (0.000)
β_2	0.012 (0.000)	0.015 (0.000)	0.020 (0.000)	0.010 (0.000)	0.014 (0.000)	0.019 (0.000)
γ_2	-0.039 (0.000)	-0.049 (0.000)	-0.025 (0.000)	-0.033 (0.000)	-0.044 (0.000)	-0.024 (0.000)
NMS	—	—	—	0.019 (0.011)	0.014 (0.256)	0.019 (0.003)
σ^2	0.012	0.018	0.019	0.012	0.018	0.019
R^2	0.750	0.772	0.110	0.771	0.777	0.153
LIK	752.31	652.35	633.89	764.09	655.19	640.58
AIC	-1,492.61	-1,292.69	-1,255.78	-1,514.18	-1,296.37	-1,267.17
F-stat	187.3 (0.000)	212.2 (0.000)	8.714 (0.000)	168.8 (0.000)	174.0 (0.000)	10.01 (0.000)
M's I	0.141 (0.000)	0.187 (0.000)	0.290 (0.000)	0.155 (0.000)	0.194 (0.000)	0.313 (0.000)
			restricted regression			
α	0.031 (0.000)	0.048 (0.000)	0.002 (0.161)	0.021 (0.000)	0.033 (0.000)	0.001 (0.674)
β	-0.005 (0.002)	-0.004 (0.114)	-0.015 (0.000)	-0.003 (0.000)	-0.002 (0.200)	-0.012 (0.002)
γ	0.0189 (0.001)	0.018 (0.040)	0.019 (0.000)	0.012 (0.000)	0.007 (0.097)	0.015 (0.003)
NMS	—	—	—	0.048 (0.000)	0.072 (0.000)	0.007 (0.042)
LR-t	319.71 (0.000)	339.23 (0.000)	1.46 (0.482)	69.67 (0.000)	103.92 (0.000)	11.48 (0.003)

Notes: The estimations have been carried out with *R* using the *spdep* and *sandwich* packages. *p*-values of the heteroscedasticity-consistent standard errors are given in parentheses for the regression coefficients. σ^2 is the residual variance, R^2 refers to adjusted values. *LIK* and *AIC* are the maximised log-likelihood and the Akaike information criterion, respectively. *F-stats* refers to the *F*-statistic with the *p*-values given in parentheses. *M's I* is the Moran's *I* of the residuals, where the *p*-values are based on 10,000 sampled raw parameter estimates. *LR-t* is the χ^2 value of the likelihood ratio test, with the *p*-value for rejecting the restricted regression given in parentheses.

Table 2: SLXM estimations with 4 hours travel time as threshold distance

	without dummy			including NMS dummy		
	2000-2013	2000-2008	2008-2013	2000-2013	2000-2008	2008-2013
α	0.275 (0.000)	0.428 (0.000)	-0.006 (0.817)	0.195 (0.000)	0.370 (0.000)	-0.116 (0.018)
β_1	-0.032 (0.000)	-0.046 (0.000)	-0.015 (0.000)	-0.024 (0.000)	-0.040 (0.000)	-0.004 (0.420)
γ_1	0.022 (0.000)	0.022 (0.000)	0.020 (0.000)	0.019 (0.000)	0.020 (0.001)	0.020 (0.000)
β_2	0.015 (0.000)	0.018 (0.000)	0.020 (0.000)	0.013 (0.000)	0.017 (0.000)	0.018 (0.000)
γ_2	-0.047 (0.000)	-0.059 (0.000)	-0.025 (0.000)	-0.041 (0.000)	-0.055 (0.000)	-0.023 (0.001)
NMS	—	—	—	0.018 (0.015)	0.013 (0.306)	0.019 (0.002)
σ^2	0.012	0.017	0.019	0.011	0.017	0.019
R^2	0.768	0.785	0.131	0.786	0.788	0.175
LIK	761.77	659.36	636.82	772.70	661.82	643.90
AIC	-1,511.54	-1,306.71	-1,261.63	-1,531.39	-1,309.65	-1,273.81
F-stat	206.8 (0.000)	227.9 (0.000)	10.37 (0.000)	184.3 (0.000)	186.2 (0.000)	11.59 (0.000)
M's I	0.073 (0.005)	0.113 (0.001)	0.233 (0.000)	0.077 (0.004)	0.120 (0.001)	0.236 (0.000)
			restricted regression			
α	0.031 (0.000)	0.048 (0.000)	0.002 (0.234)	0.021 (0.000)	0.033 (0.000)	0.000 (0.891)
β	-0.006 (0.001)	-0.004 (0.084)	-0.015 (0.000)	-0.004 (0.000)	-0.002 (0.154)	-0.011 (0.003)
γ	0.020 (0.000)	0.020 (0.023)	0.019 (0.000)	0.013 (0.000)	0.009 (0.068)	0.014 (0.005)
NMS	—	—	—	0.048 (0.000)	0.071 (0.000)	0.008 (0.016)
LR-t	336.49 (0.000)	348.14 (0.000)	0.77 (0.679)	84.69 (0.000)	114.13 (0.000)	10.01 (0.007)

Notes: See Table 1.

Table 3: SDM estimations with 3 hours travel time as threshold distance

	2000	2001	2002	2003	2004	2005	2006	2007	2008	2009	2010	2011	2012	2013
α	0.767	-0.050	0.085	0.026	-0.059	0.108	0.114	0.385	0.641	0.623	0.605	0.583	0.510	0.582
	(0.000)	(0.872)	(0.788)	(0.935)	(0.858)	(0.747)	(0.748)	(0.286)	(0.095)	(0.104)	(0.116)	(0.127)	(0.199)	(0.146)
μ_1	0.647	0.629	0.656	0.676	0.706	0.762	0.729	0.752	0.794	0.807	0.847	0.889	0.901	0.909
	(0.000)	(0.000)	(0.000)	(0.000)	(0.000)	(0.000)	(0.000)	(0.000)	(0.000)	(0.000)	(0.000)	(0.000)	(0.000)	(0.000)
μ_1	-0.458	-0.462	-0.502	-0.527	-0.543	-0.611	-0.560	-0.600	-0.655	-0.686	-0.722	-0.773	-0.762	-0.783
	(0.000)	(0.000)	(0.000)	(0.000)	(0.000)	(0.000)	(0.000)	(0.000)	(0.000)	(0.000)	(0.000)	(0.000)	(0.000)	(0.000)
Direct	0.713	0.691	0.701	0.726	0.763	0.802	0.771	0.775	0.797	0.804	0.842	0.878	0.896	0.900
	(0.000)	(0.000)	(0.000)	(0.000)	(0.000)	(0.000)	(0.000)	(0.000)	(0.000)	(0.000)	(0.000)	(0.000)	(0.000)	(0.000)
Indirect	0.663	0.643	0.477	0.510	0.588	0.374	0.418	0.209	0.013	-0.021	-0.056	-0.101	-0.031	-0.092
	(0.019)	(0.030)	(0.118)	(0.127)	(0.063)	(0.211)	(0.167)	(0.435)	(0.960)	(0.941)	(0.834)	(0.727)	(0.913)	(0.752)
Total	1.376	1.335	1.178	1.235	1.351	1.176	1.189	0.983	0.810	0.783	0.785	0.777	0.865	0.808
	(0.000)	(0.000)	(0.001)	(0.001)	(0.000)	(0.001)	(0.001)	(0.001)	(0.005)	(0.016)	(0.011)	(0.019)	(0.008)	(0.016)
ρ	0.862	0.874	0.871	0.880	0.878	0.870	0.856	0.843	0.827	0.842	0.841	0.850	0.839	0.842
	(0.003)	(0.000)	(0.000)	(0.000)	(0.000)	(0.000)	(0.000)	(0.000)	(0.000)	(0.000)	(0.000)	(0.000)	(0.000)	(0.000)
σ^2	0.077	0.066	0.064	0.056	0.054	0.052	0.053	0.053	0.055	0.054	0.052	0.049	0.050	0.048
LIK	-71.97	-54.99	-50.25	-35.33	-28.85	-22.86	-23.27	-22.77	-23.40	-24.35	-20.03	-13.11	-14.72	-10.43
BP	11.914	8.947	7.291	4.501	3.471	1.769	1.648	1.789	3.544	4.616	3.636	2.414	2.718	0.362
	(0.003)	(0.011)	(0.026)	(0.105)	(0.176)	(0.413)	(0.439)	(0.409)	(0.170)	(0.162)	(0.162)	(0.299)	(0.257)	(0.835)
Wald	1887.6	2286.8	2164.9	2536.0	2446.1	2145.7	1741.5	1434.4	1165.2	1407.5	1403.1	1580.6	1358.6	1413.3
	(0.000)	(0.000)	(0.000)	(0.000)	(0.000)	(0.000)	(0.000)	(0.000)	(0.000)	(0.000)	(0.000)	(0.000)	(0.000)	(0.000)

Notes: The estimations have been carried out with *R* using the *spdep* package. *p*-values of the regression coefficients are given in parentheses. σ^2 is the residual variance, *LIK* refers to the value of the maximised log-likelihood value. 'Direct', 'indirect' and 'total' refer to the impacts of an increase of the spatially lagged variable as discussed by LeSage and Pace (2009), with the corresponding *p*-values in parentheses being based on 1,000 sampled raw parameter estimates. *BP* refers to the spatially adjusted version of the Breusch-Pagan test for heteroskedasticity, using studentised values (see Anselin 1988), *Wald* is the square of the asymptotic standard error.

Table 4: SDM estimations with 4 hours travel time as threshold distance

	2000	2001	2002	2003	2004	2005	2006	2007	2008	2009	2010	2011	2012	2013
α	0.534	-0.304	-0.185	-0.200	-0.269	-0.041	-0.103	0.126	0.387	0.420	0.335	0.356	0.312	0.417
	(0.002)	(0.352)	(0.576)	(0.549)	(0.443)	(0.908)	(0.785)	(0.743)	(0.343)	(0.298)	(0.407)	(0.378)	(0.461)	(0.333)
μ_1	0.601	0.579	0.599	0.628	0.662	0.718	0.676	0.688	0.737	0.759	0.789	0.840	0.848	0.860
	(0.000)	(0.000)	(0.000)	(0.000)	(0.000)	(0.000)	(0.000)	(0.000)	(0.000)	(0.000)	(0.000)	(0.000)	(0.000)	(0.000)
μ_1	-0.416	-0.411	-0.445	-0.479	-0.501	-0.579	-0.516	-0.535	-0.600	-0.652	-0.670	-0.731	-0.719	-0.747
	(0.000)	(0.000)	(0.000)	(0.000)	(0.000)	(0.000)	(0.000)	(0.000)	(0.000)	(0.000)	(0.000)	(0.000)	(0.000)	(0.000)
Direct	0.667	0.646	0.656	0.682	0.723	0.755	0.720	0.723	0.751	0.765	0.796	0.842	0.857	0.860
	(0.000)	(0.000)	(0.000)	(0.000)	(0.000)	(0.000)	(0.000)	(0.000)	(0.000)	(0.000)	(0.000)	(0.000)	(0.000)	(0.000)
Indirect	0.983	1.020	0.858	0.837	0.888	0.572	0.668	0.467	0.198	0.089	0.117	0.047	0.103	0.031
	(0.010)	(0.012)	(0.047)	(0.061)	(0.045)	(0.186)	(0.096)	(0.208)	(0.564)	(0.815)	(0.768)	(0.907)	(0.788)	(0.939)
Total	1.650	1.666	1.514	1.519	1.611	1.327	1.389	1.190	0.950	0.854	0.912	0.889	0.960	0.891
	(0.000)	(0.000)	(0.001)	(0.002)	(0.001)	(0.005)	(0.002)	(0.003)	(0.012)	(0.035)	(0.035)	(0.043)	(0.023)	(0.042)
ρ	0.887	0.899	0.898	0.904	0.901	0.895	0.885	0.868	0.854	0.874	0.872	0.878	0.867	0.868
	(0.008)	(0.000)	(0.000)	(0.000)	(0.000)	(0.000)	(0.000)	(0.000)	(0.000)	(0.000)	(0.000)	(0.000)	(0.000)	(0.000)
σ^2	0.078	0.067	0.064	0.058	0.055	0.053	0.053	0.055	0.056	0.054	0.053	0.051	0.052	0.051
LIK	-67.06	-48.22	-42.38	-31.49	-24.67	-18.65	-17.95	-21.01	-21.02	-19.23	-16.64	-11.25	-13.77	-10.85
BP	9.783	5.807	4.182	2.622	2.074	1.008	0.617	0.633	1.002	2.450	2.317	2.083	2.990	1.291
	(0.008)	(0.055)	(0.124)	(0.270)	(0.355)	(0.604)	(0.734)	(0.729)	(0.606)	(0.294)	(0.314)	(0.353)	(0.224)	(0.525)
Wald	2010.8	2520.0	2493.5	2782.2	2645.2	2323.2	1936.7	1455.4	1178.8	1578.2	1546.3	1698.6	1418.5	1437.2
	(0.000)	(0.000)	(0.000)	(0.000)	(0.000)	(0.000)	(0.000)	(0.000)	(0.000)	(0.000)	(0.000)	(0.000)	(0.000)	(0.000)

Notes: See Table 3.

In order to control for a catching-up of the formerly centrally planned economies – which may be due to technology and/or a convergence to their own steady states as discussed in the Introduction – the estimations are run again by inclusion of a dummy control variable for those regions that accessed the EU in 2004 or 2007 ('new member states', NMS). The results can be found in the corresponding columns in Tables 1 and 2. It can be seen that while the NMS coefficients as such have positive signs, the values of β_1 decrease. Furthermore and perhaps most strikingly, β_1 becomes statistically non-significant for 2008-2013. In contrast, γ_2 remains negative and highly significant in each case. It should also be mentioned that the NMS coefficients are statistically not significant at the ten per cent level for 2000-2008 in the unrestricted specification, while the inclusion of the NMS dummy leads to a rejection of the restricted specification in each case.

The SDM specification estimations which correspond to eq. (32) are displayed in Tables 3 and 4 for $\delta^* = 3\text{ h}$ and $\delta^* = 4\text{ h}$, respectively. As with the SLXM estimations, additional results for $\delta^* = 2\text{ h}$ and $\delta^* = 5\text{ h}$ can be found in Tables 7 and 8 in the Appendix. Results are given for each year of the observation period. α, μ_1, μ_2 and ρ are the coefficients for the intercept, human capital in i, human capital in i's neighbours as well as output in i's neighbours, respectively. 'Direct', 'indirect' and 'total' are the respective impacts of human capital as discussed in the previous section.

The direct impacts are positive for each year in each case, i.e. an increase in the human capital stock within one region has a positive effect on output levels. Total impacts are – as expected – also positive, but they decrease over time. Indirect impacts are initially positive, but around 2007/2008 they start to decrease in values with their *p*-values increasing at the same time. This development continues until the end of the observation period.

An intercept is included in the regressions for control reasons but is non-significant for each year starting with 2001. Output in neighbouring regions, ρ, has a positive effect on i's output. Therefore, all of these results confirm the predictions of eqs. (25), (26) and (27) except for the vanishing indirect impacts of human capital. In general, the results in Tables 3 and 4 are very similar although explanatory power is slightly higher for $\delta^* = 4\text{ h}$.

One particular aspect of the theoretical model relates to vertical integration (as captured by λ) as well as horizontal integration (as captured by the w_{ij} terms). As illustrated by simulation results, if variables change, then the system inevitably moves towards a new steady state. What is hence of particular interest when examining the SDM estimations is their development over time. Although steady states are a theoretical concept and cannot be measured in the real world, changes in the variables' impacts hint at equilibrium level changes. In this respect, the SDM estimations display that the influence of human capital in neighbouring regions on output level loses its statistical significance somewhere around 2006. Furthermore, the total impact of human capital on output levels starts to decrease in 2005. What is remarkable about these developments is that they begin clearly before the outbreak of the crises.

On the one hand, it is difficult to distinguish medium run effects as caused by the acts of vertical integration such as the introduction of the euro in 1999, horizontal integration such as the accession of the new member states in 2004 and 2007, the consequences of the crises that broke out in 2007/2008, and the recovery of transition-induced recession in the NMS that started around 1995. On the other hand, the present paper's regression estimations hint at decisive changes occurring before the current crises, hence the immediate halt of the convergence process as displayed in Figure 9 should be interpreted in this context. Taking everything together, the results indicate that the system of the European Union's regions moves towards a new equilibrium as a consequence of its recent integration processes.

5. CONCLUSIONS AND OUTLOOK

Only a handful of neoclassical growth models have so far studied interdependencies of regional economies by simultaneously considering the effects of space and time. In addition, neoclassical growth models have usually little to tell about the roles of historical coincidence, alternation of convergence and divergence trends, persisting core-periphery patterns, and human capital migration. Models of economic geography have been successful in explaining these phenomena in an environment with increasing returns to scale, of which the most influential model is Krugman's (1991a, 1991b) core-periphery model. However, this as well as its succeeding models are most often restricted to two regions, and growth is not modelled as such. The main objective of this paper was to incorporate the effects of factor relocations into a neoclassical growth model which is able to explain alternating convergence and divergence trends as well as persisting core-periphery patterns in a scenario with free factor movement, where the regional economies under consideration have access to the same technology and are big enough to display constant returns to scale.

The theoretical model assumes that human capital migration decisions depend on expected wages for human capital suppliers, while physical capital relocations depend on expected profits. Both types of movement are spatially bounded, and more centrally located regions are subject to greater dependence on circumstances in other regions. The model explains why regions with high initial levels of human capital are attractive for both human capital suppliers as well as investment flows. Furthermore, in the long run, the levels of wages for human capital suppliers are region-specific and consequently, the physical capital levels approach differing levels, too. Each region's steady state level is positively dependent on its neighbours' levels as well as on its own initial levels.

Simulation results illustrate that in the medium run, convergence and divergence may alternate until each region has reached its own steady state growth path. In the long run, therefore, disparities prevail, with similar levels across regions which are spatially close. It should also be stressed that during transition periods some groups of regions may converge, while others diverge.

A further aspect of the model relates to the indeterminateness of the eventual equilibrium, as exogenous events and shocks inevitably alter the relationships between the economies. For instance, if a region – for whatever reason – is confronted with a sudden change in the endowments in one or more factors, its relative position to other regions will change. Since all regions are connected to each other, this will have an effect on future factor movements and steady state equilibrium. The latter aspect is of particular importance when studying the developments within the European Union, which is characterised by continuously changing framework conditions while expanding its territory. For this reason, the empirical part of the paper tests for economic growth as well as output levels for the observation period 2000-2013, a time which is characterised by the EU's eastern enlargements on the one hand, and the outbreak of the financial and euro crises on the other hand.

Spatial lag of X as well as spatial Durbin error model specifications for 250 regions are applied to confront the model with European data. The study area comprises the regions of the European Union on the NUTS2 level, the observation periods is split into 2000-2008, 2000-2008 and 2008-2013. The results confirm both the model's predictions regarding human capital, with positive effects within one region's borders, and negative effects in neighbouring regions. In contrast, initial output in neighbouring regions has a positive effect. Perhaps most importantly, the effect of initial output levels within regions is negative until 2008, but becomes statistically non-significant for the period 2008-2013. An accompanying display of the evolution of variance of output levels confirms this trend reversal.

Spatial Durbin model specifications are applied for each year during the observation period 2000-2013. As predicted by the model, the results show that neighbouring regions are expected to have similar levels. Furthermore, human capital endowments both within a region and in neighbouring regions have positive impacts, although the latter disappear somewhere around 2006. These results indicate the system of the European Union's regions may move towards a new equilibrium in the wake of its own integration processes.

The empirical record of interregional disparities within Europe over the past 120 years is one of persistent disparities, with strong spatial autocorrelation. The same economies which were highly developed back then are the most advanced today, and most of them are neighbours to each other. Within these economies, those which lie geographically closer to the economic core-regions are also more advanced. There is little evidence that the interlude during which some European economies were centrally planned had any effect on long run growth. Rather, it seems as if the years of high growth rates that followed the transition-induced recession are just a temporary phenomenon.

Only very few national economies have managed to catch up to the highest developed economies so far. It is remarkable that Asian economies such as Japan or the Republic of Korea were considerably regulated and closed during their catching-up processes, and with respect to investment and migration flows to a large extent still are. Within the European Union, the crises have hit the cohesion countries hardest, and the gap has widened again. For instance, Germany attracts immigrants from other member states, who are relatively highly qualified (Gathmann et al. 2014). Hence, peripheral countries and regions are losing human capital to the core, which may alleviate the burden of unemployment in the short-run, but hinder development in the long run.

Taking on a long run perspective, European economic history since industrialisation provides little evidence of long run convergence. Rather, historical coincidence and neighbourhood relations shape the spatial distribution of productivity and wealth down to the present day. This paper's theoretical model has incorporated these issues by showing how investment flows and the migration of skilled workers have the potential to stabilise or deepen existing disparities. Temporary convergence of some regions or the whole system may occur as the system moves towards a new equilibrium in the wake of parameter changes or external shocks.

The empirical section underlines the importance of human capital endowments and spatial locations. Furthermore, it is shown that the convergence process has come to a halt at around 2008. In this context, the present paper hypothesises that this trend reversal is only partly due to the current crises. Rather, more attention should be paid to changing interregional relations and dynamics in the wake of the European Union's own integration processes, as these are expected to have severe impacts on interregional growth rates and the persistence of disparities in the long run.

APPENDIX

Table 5: SLXM estimations with 2 hours travel time as threshold distance

	without dummy			including NMS dummy		
	2000-2013	2000-2008	2008-2013	2000-2013	2000-2008	2008-2013
α	0.270 (0.000)	0.432 (0.000)	-0.027 (0.340)	0.169 (0.000)	0.355 (0.000)	-0.139 (0.007)
β_1	-0.029 (0.000)	-0.044 (0.000)	-0.011 (0.003)	-0.018 (0.000)	-0.035 (0.000)	0.001 (0.839)
γ_1	0.013 (0.000)	0.011 (0.016)	0.018 (0.002)	0.011 (0.000)	0.010 (0.028)	0.016 (0.004)
β_2	0.008 (0.000)	0.012 (0.000)	0.013 (0.020)	0.006 (0.000)	0.011 (0.000)	0.010 (0.071)
γ_2	-0.024 (0.000)	-0.036 (0.000)	-0.016 (0.022)	-0.020 (0.000)	-0.033 (0.000)	-0.013 (0.075)
NMS	—	—	—	0.023 (0.002)	0.018 (0.147)	0.020 (0.003)
σ^2	0.013	0.018	0.020	0.012	0.018	0.019
R^2	0.717	0.761	0.052	0.749	0.768	0.098
LIK	736.88	646.12	625.99	752.76	650.38	632.75
AIC	-1,461.76	-1,280.23	-1,239.98	-1,491.53	-1,286.76	-1,251.51
F-stat	158.4 (0.000)	198.9 (0.000)	4.429 (0.002)	149.9 (0.000)	165.6 (0.000)	6.438 (0.000)
M's I	0.346 (0.000)	0.344 (0.000)	0.389 (0.000)	0.364 (0.000)	0.347 (0.000)	0.418 (0.000)
			restricted regression			
α	0.032 (0.000)	0.049 (0.000)	0.003 (0.044)	0.021 (0.000)	0.033 (0.000)	0.001 (0.414)
β	-0.004 (0.006)	-0.004 (0.139)	-0.012 (0.001)	-0.003 (0.001)	-0.002 (0.210)	-0.009 (0.029)
γ	0.015 (0.003)	0.015 (0.064)	0.015 (0.001)	0.009 (0.001)	0.006 (0.139)	0.011 (0.035)
NMS	—	—	—	0.048 (0.000)	0.073 (0.000)	0.006 (0.047)
LR-t	295.71 (0.000)	337.13 (0.000)	0.99 (0.609)	52.02 (0.000)	101.33 (0.000)	11.47 (0.003)

Notes: See Table 1.

Table 6: SLXM estimations with 5 hours travel time as threshold distance

	without dummy			including NMS dummy		
	2000-2013	2000-2008	2008-2013	2000-2013	2000-2008	2008-2013
α	0.275 (0.000)	0.425 (0.000)	-0.001 (0.974)	0.199 (0.000)	0.367 (0.000)	-0.108 (0.031)
β_1	-0.033 (0.000)	-0.046 (0.000)	-0.016 (0.000)	-0.024 (0.000)	-0.040 (0.000)	-0.005 (0.310)
γ_1	0.022 (0.000)	0.022 (0.000)	0.020 (0.000)	0.020 (0.000)	0.020 (0.001)	0.019 (0.000)
β_2	0.015 (0.000)	0.020 (0.000)	0.020 (0.000)	0.015 (0.000)	0.018 (0.000)	0.019 (0.000)
γ_2	-0.052 (0.000)	-0.065 (0.000)	-0.025 (0.000)	-0.047 (0.000)	-0.060 (0.000)	-0.024 (0.001)
NMS	—	—	—	0.017 (0.017)	0.013 (0.305)	0.019 (0.003)
σ^2	0.011	0.017	0.019	0.011	0.017	0.018
R^2	0.781	0.788	0.159	0.798	0.791	0.201
LIK	768.99	661.18	640.87	779.47	663.66	647.83
AIC	-1,525.99	-1,310.36	-1,269.74	-1,544.93	-1,313.32	-1,281.65
F-stat	222.8 (0.000)	232.2 (0.000)	12.73 (0.000)	197.2 (0.000)	189.7 (0.000)	13.52 (0.000)
M's I	0.053 (0.011)	0.097 (0.000)	0.179 (0.000)	0.054 (0.006)	0.106 (0.000)	0.166 (0.000)
			restricted regression			
α	0.032 (0.000)	0.0481 (0.000)	0.001 (0.289)	0.021 (0.000)	0.033 (0.000)	0.000 (0.995)
β	-0.006 (0.001)	-0.004 (0.089)	-0.015 (0.000)	-0.004 (0.000)	-0.002 (0.181)	-0.012 (0.001)
γ	0.021 (0.000)	0.020 (0.023)	0.019 (0.000)	0.013 (0.000)	0.009 (0.080)	0.014 (0.003)
NMS	—	—	—	0.048 (0.000)	0.071 (0.000)	0.008 (0.012)
LR-t	352.65 (0.000)	352.66 (0.000)	0.66 (0.719)	97.77 (0.000)	117.44 (0.000)	8.97 (0.011)

Notes: See Table 1.

Table 7: SDM estimations with 2 hours travel time as threshold distance

	2000	2001	2002	2003	2004	2005	2006	2007	2008	2009	2010	2011	2012	2013
α	1.179	-0.056	0.002	-0.064	-0.208	-0.066	0.014	0.300	0.590	0.563	0.546	0.486	0.350	0.459
	(0.000)	(0.863)	(0.995)	(0.839)	(0.529)	(0.844)	(0.969)	(0.400)	(0.117)	(0.138)	(0.153)	(0.196)	(0.371)	(0.251)
μ_1	0.656	0.655	0.689	0.714	0.751	0.799	0.781	0.798	0.827	0.839	0.871	0.898	0.916	0.917
	(0.000)	(0.000)	(0.000)	(0.000)	(0.000)	(0.000)	(0.000)	(0.000)	(0.000)	(0.000)	(0.000)	(0.000)	(0.000)	(0.000)
μ_1	-0.383	-0.416	-0.452	-0.482	-0.495	-0.549	-0.524	-0.552	-0.593	-0.621	-0.652	-0.687	-0.672	-0.693
	(0.000)	(0.000)	(0.000)	(0.000)	(0.000)	(0.000)	(0.000)	(0.000)	(0.000)	(0.000)	(0.000)	(0.000)	(0.000)	(0.000)
Direct	0.751	0.747	0.772	0.801	0.847	0.875	0.855	0.844	0.849	0.855	0.883	0.910	0.940	0.930
	(0.000)	(0.000)	(0.000)	(0.000)	(0.000)	(0.000)	(0.000)	(0.000)	(0.000)	(0.000)	(0.000)	(0.000)	(0.000)	(0.000)
Indirect	0.575	0.556	0.507	0.520	0.575	0.438	0.433	0.268	0.126	0.098	0.080	0.073	0.144	0.074
	(0.002)	(0.004)	(0.006)	(0.010)	(0.003)	(0.019)	(0.023)	(0.128)	(0.431)	(0.569)	(0.644)	(0.684)	(0.408)	(0.680)
Total	1.327	1.303	1.279	1.320	1.421	1.313	1.288	1.112	0.976	0.952	0.962	0.983	1.084	1.004
	(0.000)	(0.000)	(0.000)	(0.000)	(0.000)	(0.000)	(0.000)	(0.000)	(0.000)	(0.000)	(0.000)	(0.000)	(0.000)	(0.000)
ρ	0.793	0.818	0.813	0.824	0.819	0.811	0.798	0.778	0.759	0.771	0.773	0.785	0.773	0.776
	(0.001)	(0.000)	(0.000)	(0.000)	(0.000)	(0.000)	(0.000)	(0.000)	(0.000)	(0.000)	(0.000)	(0.000)	(0.000)	(0.000)
σ^2	0.090	0.073	0.070	0.061	0.058	0.055	0.056	0.057	0.058	0.059	0.057	0.053	0.054	0.053
LIK	-94.30	-73.47	-67.33	-52.44	-44.17	-37.28	-35.54	-34.50	-34.17	-38.53	-33.73	-26.85	-27.95	-25.65
BP	14.510	11.347	10.721	7.595	6.846	4.526	5.258	5.032	6.190	8.101	7.572	4.955	6.252	1.941
	(0.001)	(0.003)	(0.005)	(0.022)	(0.033)	(0.104)	(0.072)	(0.081)	(0.045)	(0.017)	(0.023)	(0.084)	(0.044)	(0.379)
Wald	1449.7	1948.2	1844.1	2114.8	1998.0	1790.4	1518.7	1217.1	989.4	1121.0	1147.1	1308.4	1141.2	1185.0
	(0.000)	(0.000)	(0.000)	(0.000)	(0.000)	(0.000)	(0.000)	(0.000)	(0.000)	(0.000)	(0.000)	(0.000)	(0.000)	(0.000)

Notes: See Table 3.

Table 8: SDM estimations with 5 hours travel time as threshold distance

	2000	2001	2002	2003	2004	2005	2006	2007	2008	2009	2010	2011	2012	2013
α	0.417	-0.481	-0.385	-0.383	-0.489	-0.287	-0.393	-0.182	0.049	0.216	0.197	0.189	0.121	0.239
	(0.020)	(0.173)	(0.275)	(0.290)	(0.197)	(0.456)	(0.327)	(0.651)	(0.907)	(0.609)	(0.641)	(0.653)	(0.784)	(0.602)
μ_1	0.553	0.539	0.559	0.588	0.618	0.651	0.605	0.603	0.642	0.699	0.735	0.781	0.786	0.789
	(0.000)	(0.000)	(0.000)	(0.000)	(0.000)	(0.000)	(0.000)	(0.000)	(0.000)	(0.000)	(0.000)	(0.000)	(0.000)	(0.000)
μ_1	-0.359	-0.357	-0.389	-0.427	-0.441	-0.494	-0.421	-0.427	-0.484	-0.589	-0.621	-0.673	-0.654	-0.670
	(0.000)	(0.000)	(0.000)	(0.000)	(0.000)	(0.000)	(0.000)	(0.000)	(0.000)	(0.000)	(0.000)	(0.000)	(0.000)	(0.000)
Direct	0.621	0.608	0.618	0.650	0.684	0.701	0.662	0.646	0.671	0.717	0.750	0.793	0.803	0.799
	(0.000)	(0.000)	(0.000)	(0.000)	(0.000)	(0.000)	(0.000)	(0.000)	(0.000)	(0.000)	(0.000)	(0.000)	(0.000)	(0.000)
Indirect	1.260	1.354	1.209	1.210	1.303	0.967	1.126	0.816	0.560	0.301	0.258	0.227	0.341	0.230
	(0.013)	(0.014)	(0.023)	(0.034)	(0.022)	(0.075)	(0.026)	(0.074)	(0.196)	(0.555)	(0.582)	(0.653)	(0.467)	(0.642)
Total	1.881	1.962	1.827	1.860	1.986	1.669	1.788	1.462	1.232	1.018	1.008	1.020	1.144	1.029
	(0.000)	(0.001)	(0.001)	(0.002)	(0.001)	(0.004)	(0.001)	(0.003)	(0.007)	(0.058)	(0.042)	(0.057)	(0.022)	(0.049)
ρ	0.896	0.907	0.906	0.912	0.911	0.905	0.895	0.881	0.872	0.891	0.890	0.895	0.883	0.880
	(0.000)	(0.000)	(0.000)	(0.000)	(0.000)	(0.000)	(0.000)	(0.000)	(0.000)	(0.000)	(0.000)	(0.000)	(0.000)	(0.000)
σ^2	0.084	0.071	0.067	0.062	0.059	0.056	0.056	0.058	0.058	0.056	0.055	0.053	0.055	0.056
	(0.000)													
LIK	-69.68	-50.14	-42.25	-34.20	-26.59	-20.86	-18.92	-21.18	-19.78	-19.02	-16.04	-11.39	-16.37	-18.19
BP	15.394	9.832	8.308	5.667	4.640	7.582	7.221	8.178	7.280	8.637	8.124	10.156	8.320	7.205
	(0.000)	(0.007)	(0.016)	(0.059)	(0.098)	(0.023)	(0.027)	(0.017)	(0.026)	(0.013)	(0.017)	(0.006)	(0.016)	(0.027)
Wald	1918.2	2378.7	2362.3	2684.0	2600.9	2293.0	1877.7	1440.7	1218.2	1694.0	1677.6	1839.7	1459.3	1397.3
	(0.000)	(0.000)	(0.000)	(0.000)	(0.000)	(0.000)	(0.000)	(0.000)	(0.000)	(0.000)	(0.000)	(0.000)	(0.000)	(0.000)

Notes: See Table 3.

REFERENCES

Acemoğlu, D., 2009, *Introduction to Modern Economic Growth*, Princeton and Oxford, Princeton University Press

Acemoğlu, D., Robinson, J.A., 2012, *Why Nations Fail - The Origins of Power, Prosperity, and Poverty*, Crown Business, New York.

Alexiadis, S., 2013, *Convergence Clubs and Spatial Externalities: Models and Applications of Regional Convergence in Europe*, Berlin and Heidelberg, Springer.

Barro, R., Mankiw, G., Sala-i-Martin, X.X., 1995, "Capital Mobility in Neoclassical Models of Growth", *American Economic Review*, 85, 103-115.

Barro, R.J., Sala-i-Martin, X.X., 2004, *Economic Growth* [2nd ed.], New York, McGraw-Hill.

Baumol, W.J., 1986, "Productivity Growth, Convergence, and Welfare: What the Long Run Data Show", *American Economic Review*, 76, 1072-1085.

Blonigen, B.A., Davies, R.B., Waddell, G.R., Naughton H.T., 2007, "FDI in Space: Spatial Autoregressive Relationships in Foreign Direct Investment", *European Economic Review*, 51, 1303-1325.

Borts, G.H., Stein, J.L., 1964, *Economic Growth in a Free Market* [Reprint 1966], New York, Columbia University Press.

Dall'erba, S., Llamosas-Rosas, I., 2015, "The Impact of Private, Public and Human Capital on the US states' economies: theory, extensions and evidence", in Karlsson, C., Andersson, M., Norman, T. (eds.), *Handbook of Research Methods and Applications in Economic Geography*, Cheltenham and Northampton [MA], Edward Elgar, 436-467.

De Dominicis, L., 2014, "Inequality and Growth in European Regions: Towards a Place-based Approach", *Spatial Economic Analysis*, 9, 120-141.

Docquier, F., Rapoport, H., 2012, "Globalization, Brain Drain, and Development", *Journal of Economic Literature*, 50, 681-730.

Ertur, C., Koch, W., 2007, "Growth, Technological Interdependence and Spatial Externalities: Theory and Evidence", *Journal of Applied Econometrics*, 22, 1033-1062.

European Bank for Reconstruction and Development, 2013, "Transition Report 2013: Stuck in Transition?". http://www.ebrd.com/pages/research/publications/flagships/transition.shtml

European Parliament and Council of the European Union, 2003, "Regulation (EC) No 1059/2003 O". http://eur-lex.europa.eu/legal-content/EN/TXT/?uri=CELEX:32003R1059&qid=1435677832364

Fischer, M.M., Bartkowska, M., Riedl, A., Sardadvar, S., Kunnert, A., 2009, "The Impact of Human Capital on Regional Labour Productivity in Europe", in Fischer, M.M., Getis, A. (eds.), *Handbook of Applied Spatial Analysis*, Berlin, Heidelberg and New York, Springer, 583-597.

Fischer, M.M., Stirböck, C., 2006, "Pan-European Regional Income Growth and Club-Convergence – Insights from a Spatial Econometric Perspective", *Annals of Regional Science* 40, 1-29.

Gathmann, C., Keller, N., Monscheuer, O., Straubhaar, T., Schäfer, H., Zimmermann, K.F., Brücker, H., 2014, "Zuwanderung nach Deutschland – Problem und Chance für den Arbeitsmarkt", *Wirtschaftsdienst*, 94, 59-179.

Gennaioli, N., La Porta, R., Lopez-de-Silanes, F., Shleifer, A., 2013, "Human Capital and Regional Development", *The Quarterly Journal of Economics*, 128, 105-164.

Islam, N., 2003, "What Have We Learnt from the Convergence Debate?", *Journal of Economic Surveys*, 17, 309-362.

Krugman, P., 1991a, "Increasing Returns and Economic Geography", *Journal of Political Economy*, 99, 483-499.

Krugman, P., 1991b, *Geography and Trade* [Reprint 1992], Leuven and Cambridge [MA], Leuven University Press and MIT Press.

Landes, D. S., 1998, *The Wealth and Poverty of Nations: Why Some Are so Rich and Some so Poor*, New York, W. W. Norton.

Le Gallo, J., Ertur, C., Baumont, C., 2003, "A Spatial Econometric Analysis of Convergence across European Regions, 1980-1995", in Fingleton, B. (ed.), *European Regional Growth*, Berlin, Heidelberg and New York, Springer.

LeSage, J., 2014, "What Regional Scientists Need to Know about Spatial Econometrics".
https://www.gate.cnrs.fr/IMG/pdf/Lesage2014.pdf

LeSage, J., Fischer, M.M., 2008, "Spatial Growth Regressions: Model Specification, Estimation and Interpretation", *Spatial Economic Analysis*, 3, 275-304.

LeSage, J., Pace, R.K., 2009, *Introduction to Spatial Econometrics*, CRC Press, Boca Raton, London and New York.

Mankiw, N.G., Romer, D., Weil, D.N., 1992, "A Contribution to the Empirics of Economic Growth", *Quarterly Journal of Economics*, 107, 407-437.

Maya, A. M., 2012, "International Migration: A Panel Data Analysis of the Determinants of Bilateral Flows", *Journal of Population Economics*, 23, 1249-1274.

Monastiriotis, V., 2014, "Regional Growth and National Development: Transition in Central and Eastern Europe and the Regional Kuznets Curve in the East and the West", *Spatial Economic Analysis*, 9, 142-161.

Neven, D., Gouymte, C., 1995, "Regional Convergence in the European Community", *Journal of Common Market Studies* 33, 47-65.

North, D.C., 1990, *Institutions, Institutional Change, and Economic Performance*, Cambridge University Press, New York.

Olejnik, A., 2008, "Using the Spatial Autoregressively Distributed Lag Model in Assessing the Regional Convergence of per-Capita Income in the EU25", *Papers in Regional Science*, 87, 371-385.

Paci, R., Pigliaru, F., 2002, "Technological Diffusion, Spatial Spillovers and Regional Convergence in Europe", in Cuadrado-Roura, J. R., Parellada, M., (eds.), *Regional Convergence in the European Union*, Berlin and Heidelberg, Springer.

Pfaffermayr, M., 2009, "Conditional β- and σ-Convergence in Space: A Maximum Likelihood Approach", *Regional Science and Urban Economics* 39, 63-78.

Ramos, R., Suriñach, J., Artís, M., 2010, "Human Capital Spillovers, Productivity and Regional Convergence in Spain", *Papers in Regional Science*, 89, 435-447.

Resende, G.M., de Carvalho, A.X.Y., Sakowski, P.A.M., 2013, "Evaluating Multiple Spatial Dimensions of Economic Growth in Brazil Using Spatial Panel Data Models (1970 - 2000)", Instituto de Pesquisa Econômica Aplicada Discussion Paper, 1830a

Romer, D., 2005, *Advanced Macroeconomics* [3rd ed.], New York, McGraw-Hill/Irwin.

Sala-i-Martin, X.X., 1996, "Regional cohesion: Evidence and Theories of Regional Growth and Convergence", *European Economic Review*, 40, 1325-1352.

Sardadvar, S., 2011, *Economic Growth in the Regions of Europe: Theory and Empirical Evidence from a Spatial Growth Model*, Berlin and Heidelberg, Physica.

Sardadvar, S., 2012, "Growth and Disparities in Europe: Insights from a Spatial Growth Model", *Papers in Regional Science*, 91, 257-274.

Sardadvar, S., 2013, "Does the Neoclassical Growth Model Predict Interregional Convergence? On the Impact of Free Factor Movement and the Implications for the European Union", *Economics and Business Letters*, 2, 161-168.

Schürmann, C., Talaat, A., 2000, "Towards a European Peripherality Index: Final Report", Berichte aus dem Institut für Raumplanung, 53.

Solow, R.M., 1956, "A Contribution to the Theory of Economic Growth", *Quarterly Journal of Economics*, 70, 65-94.

Swan, T.W., 1956, "Economic Growth and Capital Accumulation", *Economic Record*, 32, 334-361.

Thirlwall, A.P., 1979, The Balance of Payments Constraint as an Explanation of International Growth Rate Differences", *Banca Nazionale del Lavoro Quarterly Review*, 32, 45-53.

Tondl, G., 2001, *Convergence After Divergence? Regional Growth in Europe*, Vienna, Heidelberg and New York, Springer.

CROISSANCE ÉCONOMIQUE RÉGIONALE ET ÉTATS STATIONNAIRES AVEC DES FACTEURS DE PRODUCTION MOBILES : MODÈLE THÉORIQUE ET APPLICATION À L'EUROPE

Résumé - *L'article présente un modèle théorique spatial de croissance permettant d'étudier l'effet de la mobilité du capital physique et humain sur la croissance des économies ouvertes. Les résultats analytiques et les simulations montrent la manière dont le développement d'une économie est influencé par ses voisins, comment à moyen terme des processus de convergence et de divergence peuvent s'enchaîner et comment la migration interrégionale due aux différences de salaires entraîne un maintien des disparités à long terme. Sur le plan empirique, un modèle économétrique spatial est appliqué aux régions européennes (niveau NUTS2) sur la période 2000-2013. Les estimations soulignent le rôle de la localisation du capital humain et de son évolution.*

Mots-clés - THÉORIE DE LA CROISSANCE NÉOCLASSIQUE, CAPITAL HUMAIN, MIGRATION INTERRÉGIONALE, INTÉGRATION EUROPÉENNE, CONVERGENCE, DIVERGENCE

LES INVESTISSEMENTS DE SÉCURISATION DES SITES INDUSTRIELS À RISQUE ET LA CONCERTATION ENTRE FIRMES ET RIVERAINS : UNE APPROCHE THÉORIQUE

Nicolas PILUSO [*], Clément RAU [**]

Résumé - *Cet article propose une modélisation de la concertation entre industries à risque et riverains sur les investissements de sécurité à mettre en œuvre. Le modèle permet de déterminer à quels niveaux tendent à se fixer le taux de profit espéré et le taux d'investissement de sécurisation. L'intérêt des riverains, favorables à plus de sécurité, n'est pas forcément incompatible avec l'intérêt de la firme : une exigence plus grande des riverains en matière de sécurité peut s'accompagner d'une hausse simultanée de l'investissement de sécurisation et du taux de profit espéré. Dans cette situation, nous suggérons la nécessité de rendre la concertation plus équilibrée en permettant aux riverains de commander des contre-expertises en matière d'études de danger.*

Mots-clés - CONCERTATION, INVESTISSEMENTS DE SECURISATION, INDUSTRIES À RISQUE

Classification JEL - L10, L20, L69

Nous tenons à remercier les rapporteurs de la revue pour leurs commentaires qui ont largement aidé à l'amélioration de cet article.

* Certop, UMR 5044, Université de Toulouse, CNRS, UPS, UT2J; nicolas.piluso@iut-tlse3.fr
** Institut Mathématiques de Toulouse, Université de Toulouse 3 Paul Sabatier; clement.rau@iut-tlse3.fr

INTRODUCTION

L'histoire récente montre que les États européens ont progressivement renforcé leur politique de prévention des risques industriels, à la suite de la survenue d'accidents et la montée de la contestation.

Le risque industriel majeur est généralement défini comme la possibilité de réalisation d'un événement accidentel se produisant sur un site industriel et entraînant des conséquences immédiates graves pour le personnel, les populations avoisinantes, les biens ou l'environnement (ministère de l'Écologie, du Développement et de l'Aménagement durables, 2007). Il est souvent lié à l'utilisation, au stockage ou à la fabrication de substances dangereuses. Les générateurs de ce risque sont classés en deux familles : les industries chimiques (production de substances chimiques de base, de produits destinés à l'agroalimentaire, de produits pharmaceutiques ou de consommation courante) et les industries pétrochimiques (production de tout type de dérivé du pétrole).

Suite à la catastrophe industrielle survenue à Seveso en 1976, la directive dite Seveso réclame aux États et aux entreprises d'identifier les risques associés à certaines activités industrielles et de prendre des mesures pour y faire face. Cette directive a été plusieurs fois modifiée, ce qui a permis d'élargir son champ. La directive Seveso 2 impose aux établissements considérés comme dangereux de mettre en place un système de gestion de la sécurité proportionné à la menace liée aux installations[2].

La réglementation publique française s'est construite autour de l'idée d'obliger les entreprises dites Seveso à produire et diffuser les données d'information concernant les risques auxquels peuvent être exposées les populations résidant à proximité des établissements dangereux. La catastrophe de l'usine toulousaine AZF en 2001 a cependant poussé l'État à restructurer sa politique de prévention des risques majeurs. C'est ainsi que les CLIC (comités locaux d'information et de concertation) et les PPRT (plans de prévention des risques technologiques) ont vu le jour avec la loi Bachelot[3]. Les PPRT visent à la réorientation de l'urbanisation par la prise en compte de zones de danger ; les CLIC, quant à eux, institutionnalisent la concertation publique sur le sujet des risques technologiques majeurs. Cette concertation vise à réduire l'asymétrie (informationnelle et décisionnelle) caractéristique des relations entre industriels et riverains (Spangler, 1982 ; Luhmann, 1993 ; Chaskiel, 2008 ; Piluso, 2013).

Une étude récente sur la perception qu'ont les riverains dunkerquois de la menace liée aux établissements à risque montre qu'ils se considèrent comme exposés de façon importante à la possibilité d'un accident industriel (Zwarte-

---

[2] En France, après la loi sur les installations classées du 19 juillet 1976 concernant toute activité potentiellement nuisible pour l'environnement, les directives européennes Seveso ont été transposées en droit français, en particulier avec l'arrêté du 10 mai 2000. La loi du 30 juillet 2003 concerne les établissements industriels à haut risque relevant de la directive Seveso 2. Ces derniers doivent réaliser et mettre à jour une étude de danger qui quantifie le risques et justifie les mesures de réduction de ces risques prises par le chef d'établissement exploitant les installations dangereuses.

[3] Loi du 31 juillet 2003 relative aux risques technologiques et naturels majeurs.

rook, 2010), tant d'un point de vue spatial que d'un point de vue social, même si les habitants « en première ligne » jugent qu'ils sont relativement plus exposés que les habitants « en seconde ligne ». Les riverains estiment majoritairement par ailleurs que les investissements dans la sécurité réalisés par les industriels sont insuffisants. La concertation des riverains sur la question de la prévention à mettre en œuvre peut, de là, contribuer à atténuer la perception de la menace liée aux établissements dangereux (*ibid.*, 2010).

Selon Ruegg (1997), la gestion de l'environnement à l'échelle locale doit répondre à quatre critères : l'efficacité territoriale (capacité d'un territoire à créer des richesses, des emplois, des avantages de proximité), l'équité territoriale (réduction des inégalités d'accès aux ressources stratégiques, possibilité de participation et d'adhésion des usagers et riverains aux décisions les concernant), la durabilité des territoires (solidarité intergénérationnelle) et la créativité territoriale (création de projets partagés par tous).

En tant qu'espaces de concertation de la population sur les conditions de maintien d'un établissement dangereux dans un espace urbanisé, les CLIC s'inscrivent dans cette recherche d'une gestion des problèmes environnementaux dans un territoire. Environ cinq cents CLIC ont été créés, chaque comité correspondant à l'existence d'un établissement dit Seveso en espace urbain. Les secrétariats permanents pour la prévention des pollutions industrielles créés trente ans plus tôt ont permis d'expérimenter le principe de la concertation. Mais l'une des nouveautés induites par la création des CLIC, comme le souligne Suraud (2013), est « la possibilité pour les membres du CLIC d'avoir accès aux dossiers industriels et, plus spécifiquement, aux études de danger produites par l'entreprise ». Les études de danger, réalisées par les industriels et validées par l'administration publique, présentent les sources de danger, les zones potentiellement touchées et les mesures de prévention adoptées.

L'un des aspects les plus importants de la concertation concerne les investissements qui visent à la sécurisation des installations (Suraud, 2013). L'objectif de la concertation est clair : il s'agit à la fois d'informer le citoyen, mais aussi de prendre en compte son point de vue dans le but de diminuer les risques. Le rôle des riverains au sein des CLIC est à la fois de récolter l'information pour la relayer, mais aussi d'infléchir les décisions des industriels (Suraud, 2013). Ces derniers ne disposent pas à proprement parler de droit de vote, mais influencent par l'échange de points de vue les décisions des industriels en matière de sécurisation (Zwarterook, 2013).

L'objet de l'article est de formaliser un des aspects de la concertation, celui de la mise en œuvre d'investissements pour la sécurité. Nous définissons les termes de concertation/négociation par la prise en compte de la part des industriels de l'intérêt des riverains dans la décision d'investir pour la sécurité.

Les travaux existant en sciences sociales montrent que la mise en œuvre de débats citoyens permet l'intégration des exigences de la société civile dans les décisions des entreprises et de la sphère étatique. Pour certains sociologues, les CLIC tels qu'organisés aujourd'hui seraient donc une avancée significative permettant à la population riveraine de peser sur les politiques de prévention des risques (Revel *et alii,* 2007 ; Bourg *et alii*, 2005 ; Reber, 2011).

Cette expression citoyenne pousse ainsi l'industrie à sécuriser davantage les installations. Or, la mise en place d'investissements de sécurisation peut se traduire par des effets positifs à plusieurs niveaux (Blanchet, Paquiet, Zampa, 1996) :

- la conception de nouveaux procédés de fabrication peut conduire à accroître les rendements de la production ;

- la modification de l'organisation du travail peut rendre le personnel plus productif et plus réactif à la survenue d'événements imprévus ;

- la conception de produits plus respectueux de l'environnement est susceptible d'élargir le marché des firmes ;

- surtout, l'accroissement des besoins de sécurité intensifie les relations entre centres de formation, laboratoires de recherche et universités au sein d'un territoire donné (création de formations spécifiques, financement de recherches par un système de bourses, créations de partenariats CNRS-industries…).

Le développement de la pratique de la concertation entre riverains et industriels qui mène à sécuriser davantage le site de production peut favoriser le développement du territoire : pour Gay et Picard (2001), le « territoire vécu, organisé, où peuvent s'exprimer pouvoir, stratégie et confiance, offre une configuration idéale pour l'émergence des activités d'innovation en servant de catalyseur aux interactions qui les engendrent. […] *Last but not least*, la capacité innovante attachée au territoire en fait un instrument privilégié de développement endogène qui justifie sa mobilisation dans l'action publique ». D'après Blanchet et Paquiet (1999), les acteurs d'un territoire permettent de mieux maîtriser les conséquences environnementales de l'activité économique des industries à risque lorsque ces derniers sont dotés d'une véritable capacité d'influence. Ils peuvent même devenir la composante clé d'un vrai projet de développement. Enfin, pour Blanchet, Paquiet, Zampa (1996), « la présence des industries chimiques est un atout qu'une agglomération doit pouvoir valoriser. Il faut pour cela se concerter plus pour résoudre les points conflictuels en matière d'environnement et de risque ». C'est ainsi que le développement de la logique de concertation, couplé au développement de la logique d'une sécurisation plus grande, constituent potentiellement des catalyseurs de la révélation d'un territoire au sens où l'entendent Colletis et Pecqueur (2005). Pour résumer et sans entrer dans le détail de cette analyse, un territoire n'existe pas *ex ante*, mais est révélé dans le cadre d'un processus dynamique de « spécification » de ses ressources. Les ressources d'un territoire sont spécifiées lorsque leur valeur devient dépendante de leur usage, et que leur transfert d'une activité à l'autre entraîne un coût de conversion irrécouvrable. Ces ressources fondent non pas un « avantage comparatif », mais un « avantage différenciatif » pour le territoire. Le développement de la concertation et des investissements de sécurisation peuvent de ce point de vue créer des ressources spécifiques, à savoir des compétences, des savoir-faire, ou expériences spécifiques à l'activité et au territoire dans laquelle cette concertation s'insère[4].

[4] Pour une présentation détaillée de la théorie de l'avantage concurrentiel différencié d'un territoire, voir Colletis et Pecqueur (2005) et Colletis (2010).

Pour poursuivre et développer cet argumentaire, nous tentons de montrer formellement que le développement des investissements de sécurité va dans certains cas dans le sens des intérêts des riverains et de l'industrie.

Le but de notre recherche est double. Il s'agit d'une part d'analyser les grands déterminants des investissements de sécurité qui font l'objet de la concertation ; il s'agit d'autre part de montrer qu'une augmentation des investissements de sécurité (dans le sens de l'intérêt du riverain) n'est pas toujours contraire à l'intérêt propre à la firme.

Notre analyse utilise le modèle de négociation de Nash (Binmore, Rubinstein et Wolinsky, 1986) qui fait appel à la théorie des jeux coopératifs. La grandeur à maximiser correspond au produit des gains que chaque partie parvient à obtenir en cas d'accord, pondérés par le poids de chaque agent dans la négociation. Ce modèle a connu diverses applications, notamment dans le champ de l'économie du travail (Layard, Nickell, et Jackman, 1991). Le présent article tente de déterminer le taux d'investissement de sécurisation optimal issu de la concertation.

Dans une première section, nous exposons la structure du modèle de négociation adopté. Dans une seconde section, les principaux résultats de l'analyse sont mis en exergue.

1. UN MODÈLE DE NÉGOCIATION SUR LES INVESTISSEMENTS DE SÉCURISATION

Deux types d'intervenants sont analysés dans le modèle : l'entrepreneur ou manager de la firme (1.1), une association de riverains (1.2). Les riverains sont consultés en vue de décider du niveau de l'investissement de sécurisation mis en œuvre par la firme (1.3).

1.1. Modélisation du comportement de la firme

Nous retenons plusieurs hypothèses simplificatrices concernant le comportement de la firme et celui des riverains.

H1. Le taux d'endettement de la firme est nul. On suppose qu'elle autofinance ses investissements.

H2. Dans la pratique, les firmes réduisent le caractère aléatoire de leurs résultats économiques par le biais de dépenses d'autoprotection (au sens d'Ehrlich et Becker, 1972), de dépenses d'autoassurance et enfin d'assurance. Les dépenses de prévention se composent de l'ensemble des moyens mis en œuvre pour faire diminuer la probabilité d'accident (autoprotection), mais aussi de ceux mis en œuvre pour limiter les dommages en cas de réalisation d'un risque (autoassurance). Les investissements de sécurisation recouvrent toutes les dimensions de la prévention (autoprotection et autoassurance). Ils peuvent par exemple viser à rendre la technologie de production moins dangereuse, mais aussi à protéger salariés et riverains en cas de réalisation d'un risque. Cependant, pour simplifier le modèle, nous supposerons que la firme ne noue pas de contrat avec une compagnie d'assurance et que l'investissement de sécurisation n'affecte que la probabilité d'accident.

H3. La littérature en sciences sociales montre que les riverains perçoivent un *danger*, tandis que les firmes et les actionnaires perçoivent un *risque*. Il existe, d'après les sociologues, une asymétrie de perception entre industriels et riverains, autrement dit entre ceux qui produisent le risque et ceux qui y sont exposés involontairement : les premiers réalisent un calcul coût-bénéfice des installations sur la base de probabilités d'occurrence tandis que les riverains ne perçoivent que le danger représenté par l'existence de ces équipements indépendamment de toute probabilité d'occurrence (Chaskiel, 2008). Pour éclairer cette analyse, on peut rappeler qu'une firme a fréquemment la possibilité de mutualiser les risques de plusieurs d'établissements (ce qui permet de réduire, dans certains cas, le risque global). À cet égard, on peut la considérer comme neutre au risque. À l'inverse, les riverains ne peuvent, le plus souvent, avoir recours à ce type de mutualisation et portent un jugement critique sur la menace (ou la perte potentielle) liée à l'installation. Ils manifestent, notamment à l'égard de la menace « à développement long », une crainte vis-à-vis de sa nature diffuse, de sa capacité à avoir des conséquences sur les générations futures. À plus court terme, d'un point de vue matériel, les riverains craignent la menace à laquelle est exposée leur habitation, acquise le plus souvent sur le long terme. On supposera ainsi que les riverains veulent conjurer cette menace en pesant sur la mise en œuvre par les industriels de la politique de prévention.

Les hypothèses étant présentées, il est possible de formaliser le comportement de la firme.

Le profit net π de la firme qui investit dans la sécurité est défini comptablement par :

$$\pi = P - \delta K - S$$

avec P le profit brut de la firme, S le montant de l'investissement de sécurisation au cours de la période considérée, K le capital productif total accumulé considéré comme exogène et δ son taux de déclassement. Cette épargne nette de la firme est supposée être entièrement distribuée sous forme de dividendes.

En divisant le profit net π par le stock total de capital, on obtient la relation suivante :

$$\pi / K = g - s$$

où s correspond au montant de l'investissement de sécurisation par unité de capital. Le taux de rendement économique g dépend d'un paramètre α de répartition incluant le taux de marge, le partage salaire-profit et les impôts indirects. Il dépend aussi de la productivité moyenne de capital *(Y/K)* :

$$g = [\alpha(Y / K)] - \partial$$

On suppose que g est un paramètre du modèle. Cette fonction de taux de profit net dépend donc du partage salaire-profit au sein de la firme et de l'importance de l'investissement de sécurisation à mettre en place. Plus le taux d'investissement dans la sécurité est important, plus le taux de profit se réduit, toutes choses étant égales par ailleurs.

La firme exerce une activité productive porteuse de risque : cette dernière est susceptible d'engendrer un accident. D'un point de vue strictement économique, cet accident altère la rentabilité de l'entreprise (Barro, 2006).

Il est particulièrement délicat de spécifier une fonction de probabilité d'accident. Cette dernière résulte en effet le plus souvent d'études empiriques sur les fréquences d'occurrences qui sont exogènes[5] (Levêque, 2013 ; Gollier, 2007 ; Godard, 1993). Par ailleurs, elle peut être modifiée en fonction des experts qui sont mandatés (ICSI, 2009). Autrement dit, il n'existe pas, par définition, de fondement microéconomique à l'établissement d'une telle fonction.

On choisit donc une fonction de probabilité d'accident simple $\phi(s)$ qui décroît avec le taux d'investissement de sécurisation[6] :

$$\phi(s) = 1/as$$

Le paramètre a représente le degré d'efficacité de l'investissement de sécurisation ou, de façon équivalente, le degré de dangerosité de l'installation une fois l'investissement réalisé. Lorsque a augmente, un même taux d'investissement de sécurisation engendre une probabilité d'accident plus faible. Plus le paramètre est élevé, plus l'investissement est efficace ou, dit autrement, moins l'installation sera considérée comme dangereuse. Ce paramètre est estimé par des services d'expertise internes à la firme (ICSI, 2009) et est rendu public par le rapport exposant l'étude de danger.

La grandeur que le manager cherche à maximiser est donc le taux de profit net espéré par unité de capital :

$$w = (g - s)(1 - 1/as)$$

L'effet d'un investissement de sécurisation sur le taux de profit espéré est ambigu : il contribue certes à augmenter mécaniquement les coûts pour la firme, mais il est susceptible de diminuer la probabilité d'accident. C'est précisément ce dont nous discutons dans la suite de l'article.

1.2. Modélisation du comportement des riverains

L'objectif des riverains est de minimiser les risques d'accident liés à l'activité productive de la firme. Elle tire son bien-être de l'importance des investissements de sécurité mis en œuvre. On considère un agent représentatif des riverains doté d'une fonction d'utilité U[7] :

$$U = (a(s - \bar{s}))$$

Ses arguments sont :

---

[5] On peut considérer que ces dernières sont généralement calculées à partir d'un ensemble de firmes appartenant au même secteur d'activité.

[6] En utilisant d'autres types de fonction de probabilité d'accident (fonction exponentielle, etc.), les résultats obtenus ne sont pas modifiés.

[7] On suppose implicitement que les riverains ont tous la même perception de la menace technologique, ce qui nous permet de raisonner à partir d'un agent représentatif.

- la différence entre le montant de l'investissement de sécurisation par unité de capital investi s et le montant de l'investissement de sécurisation unitaire de réservation $\overline{s}$ (celui en dessous duquel le riverain est amené à quitter la négociation et à déménager de la zone). Cet investissement de sécurisation unitaire de réservation dépend bien sûr du danger perçu par le riverain représentatif ;

- le paramètre a d'efficacité de l'investissement mis en œuvre, mesuré par les experts mandatés par la firme.

Cette fonction d'utilité possède donc deux paramètres : le coefficient d'efficacité de l'investissement a et l'option extérieure $\overline{s}$. La grandeur U est maximisée par rapport à la variable s (le taux d'investissement dans la sécurité) qui est l'objet même de la négociation. La fonction est croissante en s et a et décroissante en $\overline{s}$.

1.3. Modélisation de la négociation

Le critère de Nash consiste à maximiser les gains obtenus par chaque partie en cas d'accord, pondérés par leur poids respectif dans la négociation. On supposera pour simplifier les calculs que la négociation se fait entre parties de poids égal. Lorsque tel n'est pas le cas, on obtient de façon relativement évidente que le taux d'investissement de sécurisation issu de la négociation est d'autant plus important que le poids des riverains est élevé.

Le cadre institutionnel du marchandage oriente le choix de modélisation à partir de la théorie des jeux coopératifs. En effet, dans le cadre des CLIC, les parties prenantes sont invitées à communiquer entre elles pour passer un « contrat » sur la meilleure solution à adopter pour la collectivité dans son ensemble. Ce cadre institutionnel correspond au cadre théorique des jeux coopératifs : ces derniers supposent, d'une part, la rationalité des agents et, d'autre part, la communication entre les acteurs pour définir une solution collective (Cahuc, Zylberberg, 1996). Dans ce type de jeu, les joueurs gagnent ou perdent ensemble. Ainsi, si la négociation échoue, les riverains sont susceptibles de quitter la région ou d'engager un conflit (avec les coûts que cela implique pour les riverains comme pour la firme). Si la négociation réussit, le niveau de sécurisation décidé profite aux deux parties prenantes : la firme peut poursuivre son activité en bénéficiant des externalités positives du territoire dans lequel elle est implantée, et les craintes des riverains sont apaisées. Conformément aux principes de cette approche, nous supposons que le contrat signé entre les joueurs est « stable » au sens où l'une des deux parties prenantes n'est pas incitée à modifier le contrat en formant une coalition différente[8].

L'objectif commun à poursuivre à travers la concertation est la réduction des risques technologiques. Après discussion préliminaire entre les deux parties prenantes (diffusion d'informations et partage des points de vue [ICSI, 2009 et Suraud, 2013]), le jeu de marchandage à proprement parler commence. Dans

[8] Il existe néanmoins un lien entre l'approche stratégique de Nash propre aux jeux non coopératifs et l'approche institutionnelle propre aux jeux coopératifs : lorsque le délai entre les énoncés des propositions tend vers zéro dans le jeu de Rubinstein, la solution de ce dernier jeu converge vers la solution de Nash (Binmore et al., 1986).

notre modèle, il s'agit d'un jeu simultané (les parties prenantes énoncent en même temps une valeur de la variable négociée), à somme non nulle (les intérêts des participants ne sont pas toujours opposés), et non fini (la stratégie adoptée prend ses valeurs potentielles sur l'ensemble des réels positifs). Le jeu est répété jusqu'à ce qu'une solution correspondant au critère de Nash soit trouvée.

Le gain de la firme est représenté par le produit de son taux de profit net et de la probabilité d'absence d'accident $(g-s)(1-1/as)$. Le gain de l'association de riverains est représenté par l'utilité qu'elle retire de l'investissement de sécurisation $(a(s-\overline{s}))$. La négociation autour du taux de l'investissement de sécurisation à mettre en œuvre peut donc consister à résoudre le problème :

$$Max\,\theta = (g-s)(1-1/as)(a(s-\overline{s}))$$
$$s \geq 0$$

Nous pouvons réécrire le programme de la façon suivante :

$$Max\,\theta = \ln(g-s) + \ln(1-1/as) + \ln(a(s-\overline{s}))$$
$$s \geq 0$$

Le produit des gains nets de chaque partie prenante de la négociation est maximisé si la condition de premier ordre est vérifiée, à savoir si :

$$\frac{1}{s(as-1)} - \frac{1}{g-s} + \frac{1}{s-\overline{s}} = 0$$

On obtient alors l'investissement de sécurisation s* correspondant au point d'équilibre de la négociation. Cet investissement de sécurisation optimal dépend bien sûr de l'ensemble des paramètres du modèle :

$$s^* = f(g, a, \overline{s})$$

Il est possible de spécifier la valeur de s* grâce aux formules de Cardan permettant de résoudre les équations du troisième degré. Néanmoins, ces dernières sont peu aisées à manipuler. C'est pourquoi nous étudierons les déterminants de l'investissement optimal à l'aide de la condition du premier ordre.

L'investissement de sécurisation optimal étant connu, il est possible de déterminer le taux de profit espéré de la firme, donné par l'expression :

$$w = (g-s^*)(1-1/as^*)$$

2. LES ENSEIGNEMENTS DU MODÈLE

Le modèle permet de mettre en exergue deux catégories de résultats. La première catégorie concerne les conséquences d'une variation des paramètres du modèle sur le niveau d'investissement de sécurisation. La seconde catégorie de résultats permet d'analyser l'effet d'une variation de l'investissement de sécurisation sur le profit espéré de la firme.

2.1. Les déterminants de l'investissement de sécurisation optimal

L'investissement de sécurisation optimal, c'est-à-dire celui satisfaisant simultanément les deux parties prenantes, dépend des trois paramètres du modèle que sont le taux de rendement économique de la firme g, l'efficacité des investissements à mettre œuvre a, et le taux d'investissement de sécurisation minimum acceptable $\bar{s}$ pour les riverains.

Une augmentation du taux de rendement économique entraîne une augmentation de l'investissement de sécurisation mis en œuvre. De la même façon, une hausse du taux d'investissement minimum acceptable pour le riverain (l'option extérieure) accroît l'investissement de sécurisation. L'accroissement du taux de rendement permet à la firme d'accroître le financement interne pour ces investissements (voir preuve dans l'annexe 1). Une plus grande capacité d'autofinancement lui permet donc d'investir plus dans la prévention. Par ailleurs, une plus forte perception par les riverains de la menace technologique se traduit par une augmentation de leur option extérieure. Cela incite la firme à investir davantage, dans la mesure où le dépeuplement et la désertification de sa zone d'implantation n'est guère dans son intérêt. Ce résultat est proche de celui obtenu par Maxwell, Lyon et Hackett (2000). Ces auteurs montrent en effet que lorsque la contestation citoyenne d'une activité économique est forte, la firme peut avoir intérêt à répondre à l'attente des riverains, car la survenue d'un « conflit » peut se solder par des coûts plus élevés et une réglementation plus drastique. De même, Hommel (2004) met en évidence que l'amplification d'une contestation des consommateurs ou des riverains incite la firme à adopter un comportement « vertueux » dès lors que les coûts de redéploiement de son activité sont élevés.

Une révision à la baisse de l'efficacité des investissements à mettre en œuvre (baisse du paramètre a) accroît le niveau de sécurisation, d'une part pour compenser la perte d'utilité des riverains, et d'autre part pour compenser le risque accru d'accident, quand bien même les coûts fixes de production augmentent. Or, ce paramètre clé de la concertation est entre les mains exclusives de la firme : les experts qui évaluent le risque font partie des services internes à la firme (ICSI, 2009). L'association de riverains est dépossédée d'un des principaux paramètres influant le résultat de la négociation : il est évident que plus l'efficacité estimée de chaque unité d'investissement sera grande, moins la firme aura à investir en sécurité.

La concertation gagnerait ainsi en équité, au-delà de toute considération sur le poids de chaque partie prenante, si l'association de riverains avait la possibilité de mandater son propre expert pour l'évaluation de l'efficacité de la prévention. Elle pourrait ainsi confronter son propre paramètre a à celui annoncé par la firme.

Certes, les études de danger sont obligatoires pour toute installation classée pour la protection de l'environnement (ICPE) et sont prises en compte par les pouvoirs publics. Ces derniers ont la possibilité de commander une contre-expertise, mais celle-ci n'est pas systématique (ICSI, 2009). Le point de vue défendu ici est que l'ouverture au public de l'information sur la sécurité industrielle est insuffisante en l'état : la transparence simple (accès aux documents techniques) ou la transparence accompagnée (accès à des documents rendus accessibles au grand public) ne suffisent pas à faire disparaître l'asymétrie de la concertation. Il n'est pas question ici de rétention de l'information, mais de controverses scientifiques : les études de danger s'appuient sur des données fragiles et sont susceptibles d'être remises en question. La confrontation de points de vue pluriels, sur le modèle des forums hybrides (Callon *et al.*, 2001), est susceptible d'accroître l'efficacité sociale et environnementale de la concertation. On parle de forum hybride lorsqu'est organisé un espace de concertation ouvert à une pluralité de groupes sociaux hétérogènes (Callon *et al.*, p. 36). Dans ce cadre, il n'y a pas de conflit opposant profanes et spécialistes. Pour reprendre les termes des auteurs, c'est une « démocratie dialogique » qui réalise expérimentations et apprentissages en vue de débattre des controverses scientifiques. Le but est ainsi *d'apprendre du collectif*[9] dans un cadre plus général où l'information probabiliste sur le risque technologique est à tout le moins imprécise.

Reste à savoir si l'augmentation des investissements de sécurité est à l'avantage ou non de la firme.

2.2. Paramètres du modèle, investissement de sécurisation et profit espéré de la firme

Il s'agit à présent d'analyser les effets d'une modification des paramètres du modèle sur le taux de profit espéré par la firme (2.2.1). Le cas d'une baisse du paramètre a sera étudié séparément, car ses effets sur le taux de profit espéré sont ambigus (2.2.2).

2.2.1. Effets sur le taux de profit espéré d'une augmentation de l'option extérieure des riverains et du taux de rendement économique de la firme

Supposons que les riverains révisent à la hausse leur utilité collective de réservation suite à une plus forte prise de conscience du danger qui les menace. Supposons alternativement que le taux de rendement économique de la firme augmente. Dans les deux cas, il s'ensuit une augmentation de l'investissement de sécurisation mis en œuvre. Cette augmentation est-elle contre-productive pour la firme ?

[9] Pour rendre notre propos plus précis, il est possible de citer Gaudilliere (2002) qui s'est livré à un commentaire des travaux de Callon : « Hybrides, ces arènes le sont parce qu'elles rassemblent des acteurs que l'on a peu l'habitude de voir dialoguer : des ingénieurs, des représentants d'association, des fonctionnaires, des chercheurs et des industriels ; autrement dit toute la palette des groupes intéressés à tel ou tel objet technique. Plus fondamentalement, ces forums sont hybrides parce qu'ils remettent en cause la démocratie « délégative ». Pour nos auteurs, celle-ci repose sur une séparation rigide entre représentants politiques et mandataires, doublée d'une séparation tout aussi radicale entre savants et profanes. Cette « double délégation » est fondamentale et problématique, car elle est à l'origine de l'incapacité de la grande majorité à peser sur la plupart des décisions qui engagent notre avenir. Ce qui importe dans les forums hybrides c'est donc qu'ils offrent un terrain pour repolitiser les questions de science et de technique, un terrain permettant aux gens ordinaires, aux non-professionnels de venir troubler la mécanique classique de l'expertise » (*Ibid.*, p. 191).

Pour répondre à la question, il est nécessaire d'étudier la fonction du taux de profit espéré.

La fonction du taux de profit espéré est une courbe en cloche (voir la preuve dans l'annexe 2). Cette fonction w est croissante sur $]0;\sqrt{g/a}]$ et décroissante sur $]\sqrt{g/a},+\infty[$. Lorsque le taux d'investissement de sécurisation prend des valeurs faibles, c'est-à-dire inférieures à $\sqrt{g/a}$, son augmentation induit une baisse de la probabilité d'accident plus rapide que l'augmentation des coûts supportés par la firme. Ainsi, sur cet intervalle, l'augmentation du taux d'investissement de sécurisation entraîne une hausse du taux de profit espéré. Le taux de profit espéré est maximum lorsque le taux d'investissement de sécurisation prend la valeur $\sqrt{g/a}$. Lorsque le taux d'investissement de sécurisation prend des valeurs élevées, c'est-à-dire supérieures à $\sqrt{g/a}$, l'augmentation des coûts est plus rapide que la diminution de la probabilité d'accident. Le taux de profit espéré diminue donc avec le taux d'investissement dans la sécurité.

On peut mettre en évidence trois résultats.

R1. Il existe sur l'intervalle $V=]0;+\infty[$ deux valeurs s_1 et s_2 du taux d'investissement de sécurisation (avec $s_2>s_1$) qui assurent le même niveau de profit espéré (voir la preuve dans l'annexe 2). Si l'option extérieure des riverains augmente, toute augmentation du taux d'investissement de sécurisation s à partir de s_1 et contenue entre s_1 et s_2 conduit au mieux à l'accroissement du profit espéré, au pire à un taux de profit espéré identique (voir Graphique 1).

Graphique 1. Impact d'une modification de l'option extérieure des riverains sur le taux d'investissement de sécurisation et le taux de profit espéré

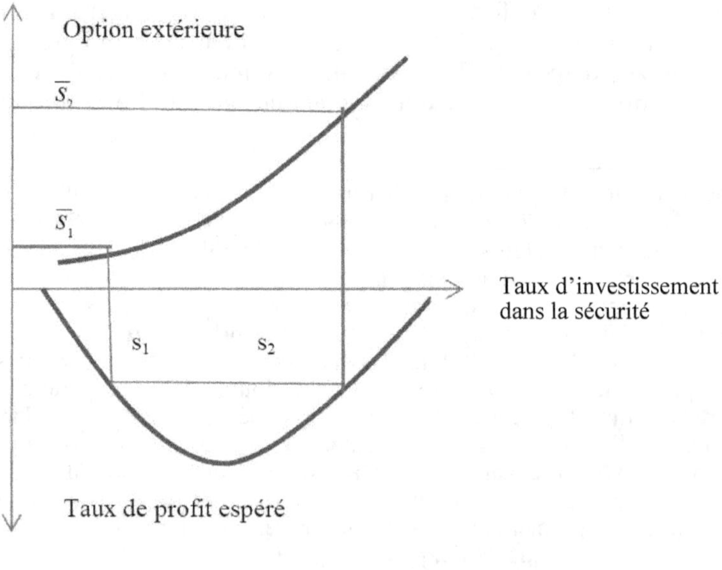

R2. En partant d'un taux d'investissement de sécurisation initial nul, toute augmentation de l'option extérieure des riverains entraîne une augmentation du taux d'investissement qui accroît le profit espéré dès lors que s est compris dans l'intervalle $V' = [0; \sqrt{g/a}]$ des valeurs faibles du taux d'investissement dans la sécurité. Si s n'est pas compris dans cet intervalle, alors l'intérêt de la firme et celui des riverains sont contradictoires, car l'augmentation de l'option extérieure des riverains fait diminuer le taux de profit espéré de la firme.

R3. En partant de n'importe quelle valeur initiale du taux d'investissement de sécurisation, toute augmentation du taux de rendement économique entraîne une augmentation du taux de profit espéré, quelle que soit la nouvelle valeur du taux d'investissement de sécurisation (la courbe de profit est translatée vers le nord avec l'augmentation du taux de rentabilité).

Les deux premiers résultats mettent en évidence que les intérêts des riverains et de la firme ne sont pas toujours rivaux. Dans la mesure où un même profit espéré peut être obtenu à partir d'un taux d'investissement faible (s_1) ou fort (s_2), il n'y a aucune raison a priori de ne pas entendre la voix des riverains et de ne pas faire en sorte d'assurer la sécurisation la plus grande.

Le dernier résultat peut justifier une politique de subvention publique à l'investissement de sécurisation : elle permet à la firme d'augmenter simultanément ses efforts en matière de sécurité et son profit espéré sur l'intervalle entier des valeurs possibles du taux d'investissement.

Lorsque les intérêts de la firme et des riverains s'opposent, cette politique publique de subvention à l'investissement dans la prévention apparaît également souhaitable.

Quelles sont donc les configurations microéconomiques favorables ou défavorables à la convergence des intérêts des deux parties ? Lorsque le taux d'investissement de sécurisation se situe dans un intervalle de valeurs faibles, les intérêts des riverains et de la firme sont parfaitement convergents puisque toute augmentation du taux d'investissement de sécurisation génère une hausse du profit espéré. Il est possible d'élargir ce résultat en soulignant, comme nous l'avons fait plus haut, qu'un même taux de profit espéré peut être obtenu avec une valeur faible (qu'on note s_1) ou forte (qu'on note s_2) du taux d'investissement dans la sécurité. Supposons que la firme ait décidé, avant concertation, de fixer provisoirement son taux à s_1. Si la concertation aboutit à la fixation finale et définitive d'un taux inférieur ou égal à s_2, alors la concertation n'entre pas en contradiction avec l'intérêt de la firme puisque son taux de profit espéré est au pire égal au taux de profit initialement espéré avec s_1.

La convergence des intérêts de la firme et des riverains suppose donc que la concertation ne débouche pas sur un taux d'investissement de sécurisation trop élevé. Cela implique que le paramètre a d'efficacité de l'investissement de sécurisation soit suffisamment élevé et/ou que l'option extérieure des riverains ne soit pas trop importante. En effet, nous avons établi que plus l'efficacité de l'investissement de sécurisation est forte, plus le taux d'investissement négocié est faible. De même, plus l'option extérieure des riverains est grande, plus le taux d'investissement négocié est élevé[10] (voir preuve dans l'annexe 1). Lorsque ces conditions ne sont pas remplies, une subvention publique à l'investissement est nécessaire pour que ne soit pas dégradée la situation économique de la firme. Lorsqu'une telle politique est mise en œuvre, la convergence des intérêts est à nouveau assurée puisqu'elle aboutit à augmenter le taux de rendement économique de la firme, le taux de profit espéré et le taux d'investissement dans la sécurité (conformément à R3).

2.2.2. Conséquences d'une révision à la baisse du paramètre a sur le taux de profit espéré

Nous avons vu précédemment qu'une révision à la baisse du paramètre *a*, mesurant l'efficacité de l'installation de sécurisation, entraîne une augmentation du taux d'investissement négocié. Néanmoins, l'effet sur le profit espéré est ambigu. La baisse de *a* diminue mécaniquement le sommet de la courbe du taux de profit espéré (elle diminue le taux de profit espéré maximum réalisable), mais peut augmenter le taux de profit espéré enregistré par la firme si à la fois :

- l'augmentation du taux d'investissement se positionne sur la partie croissante de la courbe du taux de profit espéré ;
- l'augmentation du taux d'investissement permet de compenser la baisse mécanique du profit espéré liée à la hausse de la probabilité d'accident.

Graphique 2. Impact d'une hausse de la probabilité d'accident sur le taux d'investissement de sécurisation et le taux de profit espéré (cas d'une hausse du taux de profit consécutive à une révision de la probabilité d'accident)

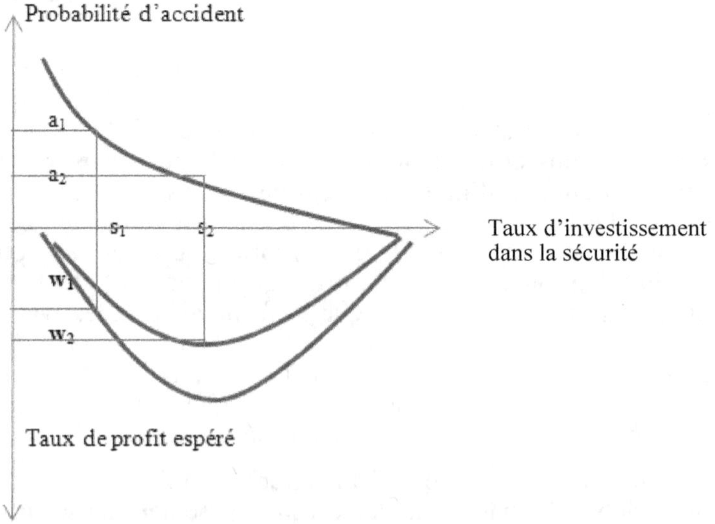

[10] Il est possible d'obtenir précisément l'intervalle théorique dans lequel doivent être compris ces deux paramètres en spécifiant la valeur de s*. Nous avons exclu cette analyse dans le cadre du présent article pour éviter un excès de formalisme n'apportant pas de valeur ajoutée significative à la discussion.

Une ouverture de l'expertise au public est donc souhaitable sur le plan démocratique et sécuritaire, mais l'effet sur le taux de profit espéré de la firme est incertain (voir Graphique 2).

CONCLUSION

Le modèle exposé dans cet article permet de décrire le processus de décision des industries à risque en matière d'investissement de sécurisation. Il montre qu'avec la mise en place d'instances de concertation, les firmes prennent en compte le point de vue de la population riveraine pour la détermination de leur investissement. Nous avons pu mettre en évidence les principaux paramètres qui influent sur le résultat de la négociation. Par ailleurs, nous avons montré que dans certains cas, les intérêts de la firme et des riverains peuvent être convergents. L'intérêt de la négociation est qu'elle permet, sous certaines conditions portant sur l'efficacité des investissements de sécurité et l'option extérieure des riverains, d'augmenter à la fois le niveau de sécurité et le taux de profit espéré de la firme. Ainsi, l'efficacité des investissements de sécurité doit être suffisamment élevée pour que le taux d'investissement de sécurisation ne se situe pas à l'intérieur d'un intervalle de valeurs trop grandes. Lorsque les conditions de convergence des intérêts des parties prenantes ne sont pas vérifiées, il est possible d'envisager une politique de subvention publique à l'investissement pour rendre compatibles les exigences de rentabilité de la firme et de sécurité des riverains.

Nous suggérons, à l'instar des sociologues spécialistes du risque technologique, d'encourager l'approfondissement de la négociation. Celle-ci peut être dans l'intérêt des firmes sur le strict plan de la rentabilité à court terme, mais aussi de la rentabilité à plus long terme par le biais de l'acquisition d'avantages différenciatifs et le développement d'externalités positives sur le territoire mis en évidence dans la littérature en économie spatiale. La concertation peut en effet contribuer à modifier la perception qu'ont les riverains de la menace que représentent ces établissements. Si le danger perçu par les riverains est atténué, la menace de contestations sociales devient moins importante. Les firmes qui doivent assurer la pérennité de leurs sites ainsi que leur capacité d'évolution peuvent alors conforter leur développement et susciter de nouveaux investissements. Le respect d'une double exigence de rentabilité et d'efficacité environnementale – garanti ou non par les pouvoirs publics, selon les cas – ouvre la voie à l'apparition d'économies d'agglomération dont sont bénéficiaires à la fois les firmes et les riverains. Le développement régional peut ainsi être à la fois durable et inclusif.

ANNEXE 1 : Démonstration des résultats de la section 2.1.

On réécrit la condition de premier ordre de la façon suivante :

$$(1)\frac{1}{s(as-1)}=\frac{1}{g-s}+\frac{1}{\overline{s}-s}$$

Les paramètres a, g et $\overline{s}$ sont fixés et on cherche s dans $I=]1/a;\min(g,\overline{s})[$ la solution de (1).

Posons $\psi(s)=\frac{1}{s(as-1)}$ et $\phi(s)=\frac{1}{g-s}+\frac{1}{\overline{s}-s}$.

La fonction $\psi(s)$ est strictement décroissante et continue sur I ; elle tend vers $+\infty$ à droite de 1/a. La fonction $\phi(s)$ est strictement croissante et continue sur I et tend vers à $+\infty$ gauche de $\min(g,\overline{s})$.

Ainsi, par le théorème des valeurs intermédiaires appliqué par exemple à la fonction $\phi(s)$ - $\psi(s)$, qui est strictement croissante, continue et positive au voisinage de $\min(g,\overline{s})$, et négative au voisinage de 1/a, on déduit qu'il existe un unique point noté $s^*=f(g,a,\overline{s})$ dans I tel que (1) soit satisfaite.

Proposition

(i) La fonction $a\to s^*(a)$ est strictement décroissante

(ii) La fonction $g\to s^*(g)$ est strictement croissante

(iii) La fonction $\overline{s}\to s^*(\overline{s})$ est strictement croissante

Preuve

Pour (i), soit $a_1<a_2$, montrons que $s^*(a_2)<s^*(a_1)$. On a :

$\psi_{a_2}[s^*(a_2)]=\phi[s^*(a_2)]$ et $\psi_{a_1}[s^*(a_1)]=\phi[s^*(a_1)]$.

On a rajouté l'indice *a* dans la fonction ψ pour mettre en évidence sa dépendance en *a*. Notons également que pour tout s, $a\to\frac{1}{s(as-1)}$ est décroissante.

Supposons $s^*(a_2)>s^*(a_1)$, avec les variations des fonctions déjà mentionnées, on aurait alors :

$$\psi_{a_2}[s^*(a_2)]<\psi_{a_1}[s^*(a_2)]<\psi_{a_2}[s^*(a_1)]=\phi[s^*(a_1)]<\phi[s^*(a_2)]$$

Cela contredit la définition de $s^*(a_2)$.

On raisonne par des arguments similaires pour les points (ii) et (iii).

ANNEXE 2 : Démonstration des résultats de la section 2.2.

Soit la fonction de taux de profit espéré $w(x)=(g-x)(1/ax)$ avec $x=s$, à savoir le taux d'investissement de sécurisation. On a sur l'intervalle $]0;+\infty[$ la dérivée première $w'(x)=\frac{g-ax^2}{ax^2}$, positive sur l'intervalle $]0;\sqrt{g/a}]$ et négative sur l'intervalle $]\sqrt{g/a},+\infty[$. Par conséquent, la fonction w est croissante sur $]0;\sqrt{g/a}]$ et décroissante sur $]\sqrt{g/a},+\infty[$.

Par le théorème des valeurs intermédiaires appliqué sur les intervalles $]0;\sqrt{g/a}]$ et $]\sqrt{g/a},+\infty[$ pour tout $z\in[0;\sqrt{g}-1/\sqrt{a})^2[$, on déduit l'existence de 2 points x et x' tels que $z=w(x)=w(x')$.

REFERENCES

Barro, R. J, 2006, "Rare disasters and asset markets in the twentieth century", *The Quarterly Journal of Economics*, 121(3), 823-866.

Binmore, K, Rubinstein, A., Wolinsky, A., 1986, "The nash bargaining solution in economic modeling", *The Rand Journal of Economics*, 176-188.

Bourg, D., Boy, D., 2005, *Conférences de citoyens, mode d'emploi*, Ed. Charles Léopold Mayer.

Blanchet, P., Paquiet, P., 1999, "Qualité des territoires et performance des entreprises. Démarches territoriales pour un management environnemental", *Revue de géographie de Lyon*, 74 (3), 199-207.

Blanchet, P., Paquiet, P., Zampa, C., 1996, "Industries chimiques et territoires : contraintes et opportunités de développement", *Revue géographique de Lyon*, 71(1), 23-30.

Cahuc, P., Zylberberg, A., 1996, *Économie du travail*, De Boeck Université, Série ouvertures économiques, Paris.

Callon, M., Lascoumes, P., Barthe, Y., 2001, *Agir dans un monde incertain. Essai sur la démocratie technique*, Le Seuil, Paris.

Chaskiel, P., 2008, "Luhmann et le mystère du risque technologique - Un retour de l'opinion publique ? ", *Réseaux*, 151, 63-90.

Chevassus-au-Louis, B., 2007, *L'analyse des risques. L'expert, le décideur et le citoyen*, Ed. Quae, Paris.

Colletis, G., 2010, "Co-évolution des territoires et de la technologie : une perspective institutionnaliste", *Revue d'économie régionale et urbaine*, 2, 235-249.

Colletis, G., Pecqueur, B., 2005, "Révélation des ressources spécifiques et coordination située", *Économie et institutions*, 6, 51-74.

Ehrlich, I., Becker, G., 1972, "Market Insurance, Self-Insurance, and Self-Protection", *Journal of Political Economy*, University of Chicago Press, 80(4), 623-648.

Gaudillière, J.P, 2002, "À propos de « démocratie technique »", *Mouvements*, 21-22, 191-193.

Gay, C., Picard, F., 2001, "Innovation, agglomération et espace : une mise en perspective de la littérature", *Économie et Société*, série W - Dynamique technologique et organisation, 6, 679-716.

Godard, O., 1993, "Stratégies industrielles et conventions d'environnement : de l'univers stabilisé aux univers controversés", *INSEE Méthode*, 39-40, 145-174.

Gollier, C., 2007, "Comment intégrer le risque dans le calcul économique ? ", *Revue d'économie politique*, 117 (2), 209-223.

Hommel, T., 2004, *Stratégie industrielle et contestation sociale*, coédition Cemagref-Cirad-Inra, Paris.

ICSI, 2009, "Etudes de danger et ouvertures au publics", *Cahiers de la sécurité industrielle*, février.

Layard, R., Nickell, S., Jackman, R., 1991, *Unempoyment, macroeconomic performance and the labour market*, Oxford University Press.

Levêque, F., 2013, "Le risque d'accident nucléaire majeur : calcul et perception des probabités", *working paper 13-ME-02*, CERNA, Mines, Paris.

Luhmann, N., 1993, *Risk: A Sociological Theory*, Ed. Walter de Gruyter, New York.

Maxwell, J.W, Lyon, T. P, Hackett, S. C, 2000, "Self-regulation and social welfare: the political economy of environmentalism", *Journal of Law and Economics*, 43, 583-617.

Ministère de l'Écologie, du Développement et de l'Aménagement durables, 2007, *Le risque industriel*, Dossier informatif.

Piluso, N., 2013, "Choix technologiques des firmes et équilibres de consommation contestée", *Revue d'économie industrielle,* 143, 109-131.

Reber, B., 2011, *La démocratie génétiquement modifiée,* Presses de l'université Laval, Québec.

Revel, M., Blatrix, C., Blondiaux, L., Fourniau, J.M., Dubreuil, B., Lefebvre, R., 2007, *Le débat public : une expérience française de démocratie participative,* La Découverte, Paris.

Ruegg, J., 1997, "Dans quelle mesure le management territorial peut-il contribuer à la gestion de l'environnement ? ", *Revue de géographie alpine*, 85 (2), 145-156.

Spangler, M.B., 1982, "The Role of Interdisciplinary Analysis in Bridging the Gap Between the Technical and Human Sides of Risk Assessment", *Risk Analysis*, 2 (2), 101-114.

Suraud, M.G, 2013, "L'espace public des risques : communication et concertation", *Document de travail du CERTOP*, décembre.

Zwarterook, I., 2013, "La concertation sur les risques industriels : 10 pistes d'amélioration", *les Cahiers de la sécurité industrielle*, septembre.

Zwarterook, I., 2010, "Les risques et pollutions industriels sur le territoire dunkerquois : des perceptions à la concertation", *les Cahiers de la sécurité industrielle*, septembre.

RISK-REDUCTION INVESTING FOR HAZARDOUS INDUSTRIES AND COOPERATING WITH LOCAL CITIZENS: A THEORETICAL APPROACH

Abstract - *This article presents a model for cooperation between hazardous industries and local citizens over safety investments. This model determines the expected rate of profit and the level of risk-reduction investments to be done. In so doing, it brings to light the determinants of these investments and shows that the interests of local citizens, who favor more safety, are not necessarily incompatible with those of the company: citizens' demands for greater safety and a simultaneous increase in risk-reduction investments can result in an increase in the expected profit rate. We therefore recommend greater cooperation and making that cooperation more balanced by allowing residents to commission their own hazard studies.*

Key-words - COOPERATION, HAZARDOUS INDUSTRIES, INVESTING IN RISK REDUCTION

ANALYSE SPATIALE DE L'ESPACE URBAIN : LE CAS DE L'AGGLOMÉRATION LYONNAISE

Emilie ARNOULT[*], Florent SARI[**]

Résumé - *L'objectif de ce travail est d'analyser la répartition de la population et de l'emploi au sein de la Communauté Urbaine de Lyon, appelée « le Grand Lyon », sur la période 1999-2009, en mettant en perspective sa configuration spatiale et son évolution. Nous mobilisons dans un premier temps les outils de l'Analyse Exploratoire des Données Spatiales (ESDA) afin de déterminer s'il existe un ou plusieurs centroïdes autour desquels se répartissent l'emploi et la population. Nous effectuons ensuite différentes analyses économétriques à partir des résultats de l'ESDA afin de déterminer si tout ou partie des centres mis en avant ont un impact significatif sur la répartition de l'emploi et de la population au sein de la Communauté Urbaine de Lyon, et de déterminer quel type de modèle décrit le mieux cet espace urbain. Nos résultats montrent que la localisation des emplois est fortement dépendante de la proximité au centre de Lyon, ainsi qu'une rupture de la densité d'emploi à partir de 8 kilomètres. L'analyse de la répartition de la population confirme l'effet significatif de la distance au centre-ville mais nous montrons également que les modélisations classiques de l'économie urbaine ne nous permettent pas de traiter du rôle significatif des centres d'emplois secondaires sur les stratégies de localisation des ménages. Nous observons cependant un recul de l'effet de la distance au centre-ville, confirmant ainsi le phénomène d'étalement urbain que connaissent grand nombre d'agglomérations françaises.*

Mots-clés - SCHÉMA URBAIN, ÉTALEMENT URBAIN, FONCTIONS DE DENSITÉ, ÉCONOMÉTRIE SPATIALE

Classification JEL - C21, J11, R23

[*] Université Paris-Est Marne-la-Vallée, ERUDITE, TEPP ; emilie.arnoult@u-pem.fr
[**] Université de Nantes, LEMNA, TEPP ; florent.sari@univ-nantes.fr

1. INTRODUCTION

Au cours des dernières années, une grande partie des agglomérations françaises ont dû faire face au processus d'étalement urbain. Concrètement, la périurbanisation autour des grandes villes a pris le pas sur les anciennes terres agricoles induisant de nouvelles problématiques en termes d'aménagement des territoires. Ce phénomène s'est accompagné d'un accroissement des mobilités quotidiennes, rendu possible par le développement de réseaux de transport routier. Ces infrastructures ont permis de rapprocher les banlieues des emplois en réduisant les temps de transport pour rejoindre les centres villes. L'étalement urbain engendre des problématiques socioéconomiques et environnementales ; Les villes ont dû mettre en place une planification de l'aménagement des territoires qui tienne compte de ces enjeux contrôlant ainsi des risques locaux. D'autres facteurs micro et macroéconomiques interviennent également. C'est par exemple le marché foncier, les stratégies résidentielles des ménages relevant de préférences individuelles de localisation, la mise en place de politiques publiques sur l'occupation des sols à différentes échelles, etc.

Les travaux de l'économie urbaine montrent que, de ces interactions, résultent différents schémas urbains. Traditionnellement, on oppose la forme monocentrique, où la répartition de la population se fait uniquement en fonction de la distance à un centre dynamique regroupant l'ensemble des activités, à la forme multicentrique où la localisation des individus ne relève pas uniquement de la distance au centre-ville mais également de pôles d'emploi secondaires qui apparaissent en-dehors du centre d'activité historique.

L'objectif de ce travail est d'étudier la forme spatiale de la Communauté Urbaine de Lyon, et de révéler si celle-ci relève plus du schéma monocentrique ou multicentrique. Parallèlement, cette analyse réalisée à partir des données de 1999 et 2009 doit nous permettre de confirmer ou infirmer les résultats obtenus par Buisson et al. (2001) et, lorsque les données sont disponibles, de voir s'il y a eu une évolution au cours de la dernière décennie. Sachant que la population a augmenté de plus de cent mille habitants sur cette période[1], il nous semble judicieux de regarder quel a été l'impact de cette croissance démographique sur l'organisation spatiale du Grand Lyon.

Dans ce travail, nous analysons la répartition des emplois et de la population au sein de la Communauté Urbaine de Lyon. Après avoir regardé le poids de celle-ci dans la région Rhône-Alpes, nous déterminons s'il existe un ou plusieurs centroïdes autour desquels se répartissent emplois et populations. Nous réalisons nos analyses en 1999 et en 2009 afin de voir si la structure urbaine a évolué. Nous testons ensuite différents modèles économétriques afin de vérifier la robustesse des configurations obtenues par l'analyse exploratoire des données spatiales (ESDA) puis déterminer quelle forme urbaine correspond le mieux aux réalités de la Communauté Urbaine de Lyon. Cette analyse nous permet d'étudier les stratégies résidentielles des ménages en fonction de leur distance aux emplois.

[1] La population de la Communauté Urbaine de Lyon a augmenté de 116 670 habitants entre 1999 et 2009 (Source INSEE).

Dans une première partie, nous revenons sur les éléments de littérature existant mettant en évidence les différentes formes urbaines, à travers les modèles théoriques de choix de localisation des individus et les études empiriques menées pour analyser la distribution des populations. Dans une seconde partie, nous choisissons quels sont les outils appropriés à notre analyse en nous basant sur les résultats de l'ESDA. Dans une troisième partie, nous présentons les résultats de notre travail, en identifiant la forme monocentrique ou multicentrique de la Communauté Urbaine de Lyon. Finalement, nous concluons en mettons en perspective nos résultats et les pistes de recherche qu'ils ouvrent.

2. L'ÉTUDE DES FORMES URBAINES DANS LA LITTÉRATURE

Dans cette partie, nous regardons dans un premier temps quels sont les mécanismes qui influencent les choix de localisation. Nous présentons ensuite les résultats de différentes études empiriques qui s'intéressent à la répartition des emplois et de la population.

2.1. Etalement urbain et stratégies de localisation des ménages : du schéma monocentrique au multicentrisme

Dans la littérature, deux courants de pensées se distinguent sur l'analyse de l'étalement urbain. Le premier est porté par l'école de la Nouvelle Economie Urbaine et s'appuie sur des modèles théoriques mis en place pour traiter de la répartition des populations en fonction de la localisation des emplois (Alonso, 1964; Mills, 1967; Muth, 1969; Fujita, 1997). Ces travaux montrent que la répartition de la population peut s'expliquer par la seule distance aux emplois. La seconde approche, au contraire, rejette l'hypothèse d'homogénéité des espaces résidentielles et avancent l'idée d'une discontinuité entre les espaces, urbains, périphériques et ruraux (Bussiere, 1972). En effet, ce courant met en évidence la diversité des formes urbaines, portées par la présence de réseaux de transport plus ou moins développés (Peguy, 2000). L'isolement des certaines zones ne relève alors pas de leur distance au centre-ville, puisque deux espaces voisins peuvent se distinguer par leur accessibilité par les transports en commun ou routiers.

Le modèle standard de l'Economie Urbaine, développé par Alonso (1964) et Muth (1969), met en avant la forme monocentrique des espaces métropolitains. Ces derniers possèdent un quartier des affaires *(CBD : central business district)* et les choix de localisation résidentielle vont entièrement dépendre de celui-ci. Il existe alors un unique centre d'activité qui regroupe l'ensemble des emplois et des activités et la densité d'emploi des autres quartiers dépend uniquement de la distance qui les sépare de celui-ci. Les ménages n'ont, a priori, pas de préférence révélée quant à leur lieu de résidence. Seule la distance à leur lieu de travail impacte leur choix de localisation. Du fait de la concurrence pour l'occupation des sols dans le centre-ville, le prix du foncier y est élevé et décroit avec la distance au CBD (Fujita, 1989). Les ménages vont alors chercher la localisation optimale qui leur permet de maximiser l'accès à une quantité de terre, de biens et de services sous contraintes des coûts associés au logement et aux transports. Deux paramètres entrent en compte dans le choix de localisation des ménages : les coûts induits par la mobilité quotidienne et le profil socioéconomique des ménages.

Ce type de modèle nous montre que plus les infrastructures de transport sont développées, moins les coûts liés à la mobilité quotidienne sont élevés et plus l'étalement urbain est important. En effet, le développement de réseaux de transport permet de rapprocher des territoires éloignés les rendant ainsi plus attractifs pour les ménages. La densité de population est donc décroissante de la distance au centre-ville et convexe, celle-ci déclinant plus rapidement avec l'éloignement au centre (Hamilton, 1982). Des études récentes appréhendent les espaces urbains comme le résultat des mobilités quotidiennes (Bertaud, 2001). Les politiques mises en place dans le secteur des transports au cours des dernières décennies ont conduit à un accroissement des infrastructures de transports, routiers et ferrés, permettant ainsi de connecter les banlieues éloignées aux centres d'emplois. L'efficacité des transports en commun a également été optimisée permettant ainsi d'étendre les aires métropolitaines (Wiel, 2010). Les ménages s'installent alors en-dehors des villes-centres et peuvent profiter des aménités engendrées par la propriété, tout en conservant les mêmes durées de transport pour se rendre sur le lieu de travail. Ceci conduit donc à une accélération de l'étalement urbain, au désengorgement des villes-centres et à la densification des espaces périphériques (Crozet, 2007).

Une forme « naturelle » de stratification apparait pour l'occupation des sols en fonction de la catégorie socio-professionnelle des ménages ; lorsque l'élasticité-revenu du logement est inférieure à l'élasticité-revenu des transports, les ménages les plus aisés se localisent à proximité des centres d'emploi (Brueckner, 1999). Donc lorsque le prix des logements diminue avec l'éloignement au CBD, les ménages les plus riches vivent à proximité des emplois et les plus pauvres se retrouvent éloignés du marché du travail. Cependant, lorsque le niveau de vie attendu est accru avec la distance au centre, et que l'accès aux emplois est rendu possible par les infrastructures de transports, les ménages aisés choisissent de vivre en dehors du centre-ville.

Les choix de localisation, contraints par les revenus, dépendent donc du profil socioéconomique des ménages et de l'accessibilité des territoires. Les tensions sur le marché de l'immobilier expliquent que les prix y soient plus élevés et qu'ils diminuent avec la distance. Le développement des réseaux de transport permet donc l'accès à des logements de meilleure qualité en termes de taille, de nombre de pièces, de type de logement. L'accès à la propriété en maison individuelle est alors rendu possible ; il est plus aisé de devenir propriétaire en zone périurbaine où les prix du marché sont moins élevés. La distance à l'emploi reste cependant un critère central dans les choix de localisation des ménages, quels qu'ils soient (Aguilera, 2006).

Dans le modèle monocentrique le choix de localisation des ménage résulte d'un arbitrage entre les prix des logements et les coûts de transports (Alonso, 1964; Anas, 1998), ce qui influence la répartition des ménages en fonction de leurs niveaux de revenus. Fujita (1997) prolonge la réflexion et, en s'appuyant sur les mêmes arguments, démontre l'apparition de centres d'emploi secondaires dans les espaces métropolitains. McMillen (2004) explique qu' « un centre secondaire d'emploi se définit par une concentration d'entreprise assez importante pour avoir un impact significatif sur la distribution de la population, des emplois et sur les prix fonciers ».

La concurrence économique et pour l'occupation des sols s'intensifiant dans le quartier des affaires, une partie des entreprises prennent la décision de se délocaliser en périphérie afin de réduire leurs frais d'infrastructures. L'accès au centre-ville ayant été rendu possible par le développement des infrastructures de transport, les coûts d'accès au centre sont également réduits pour ces entreprises qui choisissent de se localiser le long des grands axes d'accès. Ces entreprises vont former des centres d'emploi secondaires et pourront se permettre de proposer des salaires moins élevés qu'en centre-ville. La vie étant moins couteuse en périphérie que dans la ville-centre, les individus accepterons des salaires moins élevés si la baisse des coûts de logement et de transport engendrée par la mobilité en zone périurbaine est supérieure ou égale à la perte de salaire engendrée par le changement de poste. La périurbanisation donne accès aux entreprises à une main d'œuvre prête à travailler à des niveaux de salaires inférieurs si les bénéfices attendus de cette mobilité professionnelle sont supérieurs aux coûts induits par la baisse de revenu. D'autre part, cela permet de rapprocher des emplois les individus qui ne pouvaient pas s'offrir la vie en centre-ville. Avec le temps, les centres secondaires se forment et modifient la répartition de la population et donc le schéma urbain de l'aire métropolitaine.

2.2. Les formes urbaines : les enseignements des études empiriques

Depuis la création des modèles d'économie urbaine, de nombreux travaux se sont intéressés à leur validation empirique.

2.2.1. La répartition de l'emploi et de la population dans les travaux empiriques

Une grande partie des études empiriques menées sur données étrangères montrent la pertinence du modèle monocentrique, en trouvant un gradient de la distance au CBD négatif et significatif. Cela confirme l'idée selon laquelle la densité de population diminue au fur et à mesure que l'on s'éloigne du centre-ville. Ces résultats sont confirmés non seulement dans des villes de pays développés, mais aussi pour des pays en développement. Clark (1968) a réalisé les travaux empiriques pionniers sur l'estimation de fonctions de densité. Il montre, pour les années 1960, que onze grandes villes de pays développés correspondaient au schéma urbain monocentrique ; Celles-ci avaient connu différentes vagues de croissance de leur population, en particulier lié au recul de l'agriculture et au développement des emplois du secondaire et surtout du tertiaire. Ceci s'est traduit par un exode rural vers les grandes villes, et a entrainé l'étalement des aires urbaines. Ce fut par exemple le cas de Paris, New-York, Sidney et Frankfurt. Lambert (1998) confirme également la forme monocentrique de plusieurs villes des Pays-Bas, Peguy (2000) et Pouyanne (2004) également pour les grandes villes françaises. Des études menées sur données de pays en voie de développement révèlent aussi la prépondérance d'un centre d'emploi expliquant à lui seule la structure urbaine des grandes villes ; c'est par exemple le cas à Haïti (Myrtho, 2010) mais aussi dans de nombreuses autres villes (Mills, 1980).

Cependant, la significativité du gradient ainsi que la magnitude varie en fonction des espaces étudiés, toutes les villes étant différentes. Le modèle monocentrique a même été rejeté dans plusieurs travaux (Baumont, 1999; McMillen, 1998ab; Fujita, 1997) mettant en avant l'apparition de centres secondaires ; le schéma multicentrique serait donc plus approprié. Dans l'analyse des schémas multicentriques, on ne prend pas uniquement en compte la distance au centre d'emploi principal mais aussi à des centres d'emplois secondaires. La distance aux centres d'emploi secondaires peut être introduite de différentes façons dans les analyses, méthodes que nous expliquerons et testerons dans la suite de cette étude. Le principal avantage de cette approche est qu'elle ne réfute pas l'hypothèse d'un centre d'activité principale ; et si la distance aux centres secondaires ne joue pas de rôle significatif sur la répartition des populations, c'est que l'aire métropolitaine est de forme monocentrique.

Depuis les années 1990, de nombreuses études ont testé et validé ce modèle, dans des pays développés[2] et en développement[3]. Des études ont également été menées sur données françaises : Baumont *et al.* (2004) ont étudié la distribution urbaine de l'emploi et de la population de l'aire urbaine de Dijon, Gaschet (2000) et Pouyanne (2004) ont travaillé sur données bordelaises, Boiteux (2003), Baccaini (2009) et Guillain (2007) se sont intéressés à la région parisienne, tandis que Blanc (2007) a étudié les bassins de vie français[4].

2.2.2. La répartition de l'emploi et de la population au sein de l'Aire Urbaine Lyonnaise

A notre connaissance, seulement deux études empiriques se sont intéressées à la répartition des emplois et de la population au sein de l'agglomération lyonnaise : Buisson *et al.* (2001) et Mignot (2013). Notre travail prolonge ces études tout en étant complémentaire. Dans le premier article, les auteurs proposent une analyse spatiale de la répartition des établissements par secteur d'activité entre les communes qui composent l'aire métropolitaine. Ils montrent l'émergence de centres d'emploi périphériques, supposant une modification de l'aire urbaine vers une organisation multicentrique. Dans le second travail cité, l'auteur effectue une analyse comparative de trois grandes métropoles françaises : Lyon, Marseille et Lille. Il montre que la mobilité résidentielle et les choix de localisation ne dépendent pas seulement des caractéristiques sociodémographiques des ménages mais aussi du schéma urbain des aires métropolitaines. En effet, la forme urbaine a un impact sur les mobilités quotidiennes et peut entrainer des phénomènes de ségrégation au sein des grandes villes. A partir des données des

[2] McMillen (1998ab) à Chicago, Waddell (1993) à Dallas, Small (1994), Heikkila (1989) et Gordon (1986) à Los Angeles, Cervero (1997) à San Francisco, Coffey (1996) à Montreal.

[3] Alperovich (1996) à Jérusalem, Chen (1997) à Taipei, Wu (1998) à Guanghzou, Amara (2010) and Ben Said (2011) à Tunis.

[4] Les bassins de vie correspondent au plus petit territoire sur lequel les habitants ont accès aux équipements et services les plus courants (INSEE).

recensements de la population de 1975 à 1999 (INSEE), il conclut que Lille et Marseille sont des villes multicentriques, avec respectivement quatre et deux centres d'emploi secondaires. Alors que Lyon conserve une forme monocentrique avec un centre d'emploi unique, les centres secondaires n'ayant pas un impact significatif sur la répartition de la population dans son aire.

En utilisant des données plus récentes, nous souhaitons voir si cette tendance est restée la même ou bien si des modifications dans l'organisation de l'aire urbaine ont été opérées entre 1999 et 2009.

3. MÉTHODE : IDENTIFICATION DES CENTRES D'EMPLOI ET CHOIX DES MODÈLES ÉCONOMÉTRIQUES

Pour analyser l'impact de la localisation des activités sur la répartition de la population, on estime des fonctions de densité de la population qui prennent en compte la distance au marché du travail local. La méthode utilisée consiste à observer dans un premier temps la répartition de l'emploi dans l'aire métropolitaine afin de déterminer s'ils se concentrent en un seul et unique centre ou bien si les activités se regroupent également dans des centres secondaires. Si le gradient de la distance au centre-ville est significatif et de signe négatif, l'aire urbaine étudiée correspond au schéma monocentrique. Si au moins un des centres d'emploi secondaires a également un impact significatif, l'aire urbaine est dite multicentrique.

Après avoir révélé le poids de la Communauté Urbaine de Lyon dans la région Rhône-Alpes, l'objectif de notre travail est d'en analyser la forme urbaine. Dans un premier temps, il nous faut observer la localisation de la population et des emplois à l'échelle du quartier[5]. En se basant sur les travaux de Anselin (1995, 1996) nous effectuons une Analyse Exploratoire des Données Spatiales (ESDA) ; en s'appuyant sur la répartition des emplois et de la population, nous déterminons quels sont les centres de concentration d'emplois.

3.1. La localisation des activités : une analyse exploratoire des données spatiales

Nous mobilisons deux concepts centraux de l'analyse spatiale : l'autocorrélation spatiale globale, et l'autocorrélation spatiale locale. Le premier est obtenu par le calcul de la statistique *I* de Moran, le second grâce aux indicateurs locaux d'autocorrélation spatiale (LISA)[6]. L'objectif de L'ESDA est de visualiser les densités d'emploi et de population afin de tester l'autocorrélation aux deux échelles retenues, et de déterminer quels sont les centres d'emploi. Afin de définir la connexion spatiale entre les zones géographiques, nous testerons deux formes de matrices de pondération spatiales et retiendrons la plus adaptée pour décrire nos données[7]. À partir du calcul des LISA[8], le central business district

[5] Les IRIS sont le plus petit découpage propose par l'INSEE et correspondent à des quartiers.
[6] Voir Anselin (1995) pour plus de détails relatifs à ces méthodes.
[7] Une matrice de contiguïté à l'ordre 2, où sont considérées comme voisines les zones partageant une frontière commune ou une zone voisine en commun; et une matrice de distance ou les unités sont voisines lorsque leurs centres sont éloignés au maximum de 2 kilomètres.

est identifié comme un quartier où la densité d'emploi est élevée et celle des zones voisines également. Les centres d'emploi secondaires se définissent par une densité d'emploi élevée et des valeurs faibles pour dans les zones voisines (Baumont *et al.*, 2004). L'analyse économétrique permet par la suite de définir si un ou plusieurs centres d'emploi influencent de façon significative la répartition spatiale des emplois et de la population.

3.2. Présentation des modèles empiriques

La majeure partie des premiers travaux réalisés pour estimer les fonctions de densité de population et d'emploi ont utilisé la méthode des moindres carrés ordinaires (MCO), mais des méthodes économétriques plus appropriées ont été développées pour traiter des données spatialisées (Lesage, 1999 ; Anselin, 2001). Dans la littérature, différentes modélisations ont été établies pour analyser les formes urbaines. Dans le cadre de notre étude, nous estimons les fonctions de densité d'emploi et de population en comparant deux types de schémas urbains : le modèle monocentrique et le modèle multicentrique. Nos données nous ont conduits à penser qu'il était pertinent d'estimer deux types de modèles monocentriques, le premier considérant une continuité de la baisse de densité avec la distance au centre-ville et la seconde spécification supposant une rupture de la densité à une distance donnée, distance à partir de laquelle les densités d'emploi et de populations diminueraient plus rapidement.

3.2.1. Le modèle monocentrique

L'objectif du modèle monocentrique est de montrer que les densités d'emplois et de population se réduisent avec la distance au centre d'activité, précédemment identifié à partir de l'analyse exploratoire des données spatiales. Au fur et à mesure que l'on s'éloigne du centre-ville, les concentrations des emplois et résidentielle sont décroissantes, et dans ce type de modèle, on suppose que la distance au centre peut expliquer à elle seule la répartition des emplois et de la population. Cette modélisation est le résultat de travaux menés par Clark (1951), McDonald et McMillen (1998a) qui ont montré que les densités d'emploi et de population ne sont pas linéaires mais suivent une loi négative exponentielle :

$$D(x) = D_0 e^{-\beta x} \quad \rightarrow \quad \ln D(x) = \ln D_0 - \beta x$$

avec $D(x)$ la densité d'emploi d'un quartier localisé à une distance x du CBD, D_0 la densité au centre-ville et β le paramètre de densité qui mesure l'intensité de la baisse de la densité avec la distance. D'où le modèle économétrique :

$$y_i = \alpha + \beta\, DCBD_i + u_i$$

avec $y_i = \ln D(x)$ la densité de population ou d'emploi estimée par le modèle, $\alpha = \ln D_0$ la constant (qui correspond à la densité à l'origine) et $DCBD_i = x$ la distance entre le quartier i et le CBD.

[8] Les LISA sont une décomposition de la statistique I de Moran et obtenus de la façon suivante: $I_i = \frac{(x_i - \bar{x})}{m_0} \sum_j w_{ij}(x_j - \bar{x})$ et $m_0 = \frac{\sum_i (x_i - \bar{x})^2}{N}$.

3.2.2. La fonction spline-exponentielle

Ce type de spécification arrive en prolongement de la fonction négative-exponentielle. Son utilisation est adaptée lorsque la densité d'emploi et/ou de population ne décroit pas de façon monotone avec la distance au centre-ville (Baumont *et al.*, 2004). On définit des intervalles de distances au sein desquels la baisse de la densité est homogène mais on fait l'hypothèse que le gradient de la densité varie d'un intervalle à l'autre. Dans le cadre de notre étude, nous retenons une unique borne à huit kilomètres du centre[9]. Après cette distance, nous faisons l'hypothèse que la densité d'emploi et de population sont inférieures, le découpage des zones géographiques étant plus large (les communes étant moins peuplées, elles ne sont pour la plupart plus découpées en IRIS). Nous supposons alors que les densités d'emploi et de population sont plus élevées dans le premier cercle, et se réduisent fortement une fois dépassés les huit kilomètres au centre. La fonction spline exponentielle s'écrit de la façon suivante :

$$y_i = \alpha + \beta DCBD_i + \gamma x_{ri} + u_i$$

où y_i, *a*, β and $DCBD_i$ sont identiques au modèle précédent, et *k* est défini de la façon suivante :

$$\begin{cases} 0 & si \;\; x \leq r \\ x - r & si \;\; x > r \end{cases} \qquad \text{avec r = 8 kilomètres.}$$

Dans ce modèle, γ est le paramètre qui décrit le changement du gradient de la fonction de densité une fois la borne des huit kilomètres dépassée. Si ce paramètre est positif et significatif, le modèle confirme une rupture de la densité d'emploi ou de population à cette borne.

3.2.3. Le modèle multicentrique

La spécification de ce modèle est également une extension du modèle *spline-exponentiel*. Il suppose que les densités d'emploi et de population ne dépendent pas uniquement de la distance au centre dans sa forme négative exponentielle mais également de la distance aux centres d'emploi secondaires définis dans l'analyse exploratoire des données spatialisées. Ce modèle suppose que les centres d'emplois secondaires peuvent impacter à un niveau local la répartition des emplois et de la population. La distance au centre-ville reste la principale source d'explication, la distance aux centres secondaires étant introduite dans le modèle dans leur forme inverse. Cette spécification prend en compte le fait que la distance aux centres d'emploi secondaires a un impact beaucoup plus local et que leur influence décroit plus rapidement que celle du CBD (McMillen, 2004). Le modèle empirique s'écrit sous la forme suivante :

$$y_i = \alpha + \beta DCBD_i + \sum_{k=1}^{n} \delta DSUB_i^{-1} + u_i$$

avec y_i, α, β et $DCBD_i$ identiques aux modèles précédents. $DSUB_i$ est la distance qui qui sépare la zone *i* de chaque centre secondaire, et δ le vecteur des paramètres qui y sont associés.

9 Les centres d'emplois secondaires estimés dans la section 3.2 sont situés dans ce rayon.

Nous effectuons également une estimation alternative à celle présentée précédemment. Au lieu de considérer l'effet de l'ensemble des centres secondaires sur les densités d'emploi et de population, nous prenons uniquement en compte la distance au centre d'emploi secondaire le plus proche. Cette méthode peut en effet paraitre plus réaliste ; le choix de localisation des ménages va dépendre de la distance au centre d'emploi principal et au centre secondaire le plus proche. Il est difficile de croire que sur un territoire l'ensemble des pôles d'emplois isolés impactent la densité d'emploi et de population de chacune des zones qui le composent. Ce modèle alternatif prend donc la forme suivante :

$$y_i = \alpha + \beta DCBD_i + \delta DSUB_i^{-1} + u_i$$

avec $DSUB^{-1}$ la distance qui sépare la zone géographique considérée du centre d'emploi secondaire le plus proche et δ le paramètre associé à cette distance.

3.2.4. Stratégie d'estimation

Les différents modèles empiriques sont dans un premier temps estimés par la méthode des moindres carrés ordinaires. Cette première étape nous permet d'identifier quelle méthode d'estimation est la plus pertinente pour expliquer la configuration urbaine de la Communauté Urbaine de Lyon. Cependant, pour faire face aux problématiques induites par la dépendance spatiale de nos observations, la méthode des MCO est biaisée, la covariance entre les observations n'étant pas égale à zéro (Anselin, 1988).

Une première forme de dépendance survient lorsque la densité observée dans une zone géographique influence celle des zones voisines. Afin de la prendre en compte, une variable spatialement décalée est introduite parmi les variables explicatives. Dans ce cas, nous utilisons la méthode SAR (Spatial Autoregressive Model), estimée par la méthode du maximum de vraisemblance. Une autre forme de dépendance spatiale apparait lorsque les termes d'erreur sont spatialement corrélés entre les observations. Dans ce cas, l'autocorrélation spatiale est considérée comme une nuisance statistique, qui peut s'expliquer par une mauvaise spécification du modèle (omission de variables explicatives, mauvaise échelle géographique, etc.). Même si les équations sont spécifiées correctement, les paramètres estimés sont erronés et potentiellement biaisés. Ce biais peut être corrigé en utilisant un modèle de type SEM (Spatial Error Model), que nous estimons par la méthode du maximum de vraisemblance et par la méthode des moments généralisés (GMM). Le fait de décliner ces deux méthodes d'estimation nous permet de vérifier la robustesse de nos résultats.

Dans le cas de notre étude, nous pensons que c'est la deuxième forme de dépendance spatiale qui domine. Les modèles empiriques que nous testons ne prennent en compte que très peu de variables explicatives, et même si celles-ci ont un impact statistiquement significatif, la distance aux emplois pourrait ne pas être la seule source explicative de la répartition de la population et des emplois. Pour chaque modèle, nous réalisons deux types de tests de l'autocorrélation spatiale (LM-lag, LM-error et leurs versions robustes) afin de confirmer ou infirmer cette intuition. Par conséquent, les modèles précédemment présentés doivent être modifiés pour intégrer explicitement l'autocorrélation spatiale, afin d'obtenir des estimateurs non biaisés. Dans le cas de la première forme d'autocorrélation spatiale, la variable spatialement décalée est introduite de la façon suivante :

$$y = \alpha + \rho Wy + \beta\, DCBD + u\,.$$

où Wy est la variable endogène spatialement décalée et ρ le paramètre indiquant l'intensité des interactions spatiales entre les observations.

La seconde forme d'autocorrélation spatiale suppose la décomposition du terme d'erreur suivante :

$$y = \alpha + \beta\, DCBD + u$$

$$u = \lambda Wu + \varepsilon \quad and \quad u \sim N(0, \sigma^2 I)$$

avec W la matrice de pondération de taille $n \times n$ mentionnée précédemment.

Les différents modèles sont estimés en utilisant les deux méthodes (SEM et SAR) et nous retenons les résultats appropriés en fonction des résultats des tests de l'autocorrélation spatiale.

Nous testons également un modèle d'économétrie spatiale plus général développé par Anselin (1988). Le modèle de Durbin suppose qu'il peut simultanément exister une autocorrélation spatiale entre les observations qui soit liée à la distribution des observations (variable dépendante spatialement décalée) et à la distribution des variables explicatives (variable explicative spatialement décalée). Le modèle prend alors la forme suivante :

$$y = \alpha + \rho Wy + \beta\, DCBD + WX\theta + u$$

où WX correspond aux variables explicatives spatialement décalées et θ un vecteur mesurant l'intensité des interactions spatiales qui y sont liées. Il existe des modèles mixes spatiales prenant simultanément en compte l'ensemble des formes d'autocorrélation spatiale, mais le modèle de Durbin est ici préféré puisqu'il permet d'obtenir des coefficients non biaisés même si la distribution des observations correspond à un modèle SAR ou SEM. Ces deux modélisations spatiales sont en fait des formes particulières du modèle de Durbin. Nous choisirons les résultats qui sont les plus appropriés à nos données en s'appuyant sur les tests du ratio de vraisemblance dont la méthode est détaillée en Annexe 3.

4. RÉSULTATS

Nous réalisons notre étude à partir des données des recensements de la population de 1999 et de 2009 à l'échelle des IRIS afin d'analyser la forme urbaine la Communauté Urbaine de Lyon. Dans un premier temps, nous nous intéressons à l'influence de celle-ci au sein de la région Rhône-Alpes. Par la suite nous identifions les centres d'emploi, principal et secondaires, à partir de l'ESDA. Finalement, nous testons différentes spécifications économétriques afin d'estimer les fonctions de densité d'emploi et de population au sein du territoire étudié, en mobilisant les outils de l'économétrie spatiale.

4.1. La Communauté Urbaine de Lyon au sein de la région Rhône-Alpes

La région Rhône-Alpes occupe une place centrale en France, et plus largement dans l'Union européenne. Parmi les vingt-deux régions métropolitaines françaises, elle occupe la seconde position en termes de surface (derrière la région Midi-Pyrénées) et de population, la région la plus peuplée étant l'Ile-de-France. Au sein de l'Union européenne, elle est la sixième région en termes de performance économique, avec un PIB de 193 milliards d'euros en 2012[10].

Tableau 1. Population et emploi en région Rhône-Alpes

	Rhône-Alpes	Rhône	C.U. de Lyon
Surface totale	43 746,10	6 018,62	527,02
Population 1999	6 091 121	1 947 120	1 195 519
Population 2009	6 653 843	2 142 732	1 281 002
Variation de la population	9,2%	10,0%	7,2%
Emploi 1999	2 515 638	822 985	567 078
Emploi 2009	2 883 742	965 231	664 457
Variation de l'emploi	14,6%	17,3%	17,2%
Observations	2 879	514	58

Légende : Population et emploi à l'échelle de la région, du département, et de la Communauté Urbaine de Lyon.
Source : Recensement National de la Population – INSEE.

Dans la région, la communauté urbaine de Lyon concentre une part importante des emplois et de la population. Avec plus de 1,2 millions d'habitants en 2009, elle regroupe près de 20% de la population de la région. Cependant, le taux de croissance démographique est inférieur à la moyenne de la région, avec +7.2% entre 1999 et 2009. Elle regroupe également 22,5% des emplois en 1999, et 23,0% en 1999. Donc, une part importante de la population et des emplois se concentrent dans la Communauté Urbaine de Lyon, qui représente moins de 1% de la surface de la région dans son ensemble. C'est pourquoi, il nous semble pertinent de se focaliser sur ce territoire, afin de souligner la structure urbaine d'une zone qui concentre une part importante des emplois et de la population.

4.2. L'identification des centres d'emploi principal et secondaires

Nous mobilisons les outils de l'Analyse Exploratoire des Données Spatiales afin d'observer les densités d'emploi et de population au sein de la Communauté Urbaine de Lyon, et de déterminer quels sont les centres d'emploi. Nous utilisons les données des Recensements de la Population de 1999 et 2009 à l'échelle de l'IRIS en ce qui concerne la répartition de la population, et les données de 2009 concernant la localisation des emplois, ces derniers n'étant pas disponibles pour des dates d'enquête plus anciennes.

4.2.1. L'autocorrélation spatiale globale

L'autocorrélation spatiale sur l'ensemble du territoire nous est donnée par la mesure de la statistique de Moran. Les résultats présentés dans le tableau 2

[10] Source : INSEE.

montrent la présence d'autocorrélation spatiale globale en 1999 et 2009, pour les densités d'emploi et de population. Les *I* de Moran calculés à partir de la matrice de contiguïté (à l'ordre 2) et de la matrice de distance (à 3 kilomètres) révèlent tous les deux une autocorrélation spatiale positive et significative. Au sein de la Communauté Urbaine de Lyon, la population et l'emploi ne se répartissent donc pas de manière aléatoire, mais on observe un phénomène de concentration des zones géographiques ayant des densités d'emploi et de population élevées. Finalement, la comparaison de la statistique de Moran de la densité de population en 1999 et en 2009 montre un accroissement de la dépendance spatiale entre les observations.

Tableau 2. La statistique I de Moran

	Matrice de contiguïté (ordre 2)		Matrice de distance (3 km)	
	I de Moran	P-value	I de Moran	P-value
Population 1999	0,076	0,001	0,043	0,001
Densité de pop. 1999	0,416	0,001	0,360	0,001
Population 2009	0,079	0,001	0,048	0,002
Densité de population 2009	0,440	0,001	0,379	0,001
Emploi 2009	0,022	0,084	0,014	0,055
Densité d'emploi 2009	0,230	0,001	0,138	0,001

Lecture : la statistique I de Moran de la distribution de la population en 1999 montre une autocorrélation spatiale positive et significative au seuil de 1% (0,076>E(I)= -0,002).
Source : Recensement National de la Population – INSEE.

Dans la suite de notre étude, nous retenons la matrice de contiguïté à l'ordre 2, celle-ci nous permettant d'obtenir des statistiques plus élevées pour l'emploi, la population et leurs densités respectives en 1999 et en 2009.

4.2.2. L'autocorrélation spatiale locale

Les résultats de la section précédente nous permettent d'affirmer la présence d'autocorrélation spatiale globale au sein de la communauté urbaine de Lyon, nous menant à mesurer les indicateurs d'association spatiale locale au sein du territoire. Nos résultats sont représentés dans la Carte 1 en ce qui concerne la densité d'emploi, et dans les Cartes 2 et 3 en ce qui concerne la distribution de la population.

La densité d'emploi de chaque zone est comparée à celle de ses voisins afin de décrire la distribution de l'emploi en termes d'associations spatiales locales. Le tableau 3 montre les associations spatiales locales entre chaque zone et ses voisines. Concernant la distribution de l'emploi au sein de la Communauté Urbaine de Lyon, 42% des observations sont caractérisées par une autocorrélation spatiale positive (31,1% de *HH,* 10,4% de *BB*) et 58% par une autocorrélation spatiale négative.

Tableau 3. Les associations spatiales locales

Associations locales	Densité de population (1999)		Densité de population (2009)		Densité d'emploi (2009)	
Haut-Haut	90	31,14%	92	31,19%	52	19,85%
Bas-Bas	30	10,38%	29	9,83%	6	2,29%
Haut-Bas	154	53,29%	158	53,56%	200	76,34%
Bas-Haut	15	5,19%	16	5,42%	4	1,53%
Non significatif	217	-	211	-	244	-

Lecture : Dans la Communauté Urbaine de Lyon, 31,14% des quartiers ont une configuration Haut-Haut, avec une densité élevée en 1999 entourés de quartiers aux densités de population également élevées.
Source : Recensement National de la Population – INSEE.

La Carte 1, représentant les associations spatiale au niveau local, révèle la présence d'un centre d'emploi principal dans le centre-ville Lyonnais, où les quartiers ont une densité d'emploi élevée et sont entourés de quartiers aux densités d'emploi également élevées (configurations *Haut-Haut* dans le graphique de Moran). On identifie également cinq centres d'emploi secondaires potentiels, caractérisés par des densités d'emploi supérieures à celles des quartiers voisins (configurations *Haut-Bas*). Ceux-ci seront utilisés dans l'analyse économétrique du modèle multicentrique, afin de tester leur significativité sur la configuration spatiale de la Communauté Urbaine Lyonnaise.

Carte 1. Carte de significativité de Moran concernant la densité d'emploi en 2009 (matrice de contiguïté à l'ordre 2)

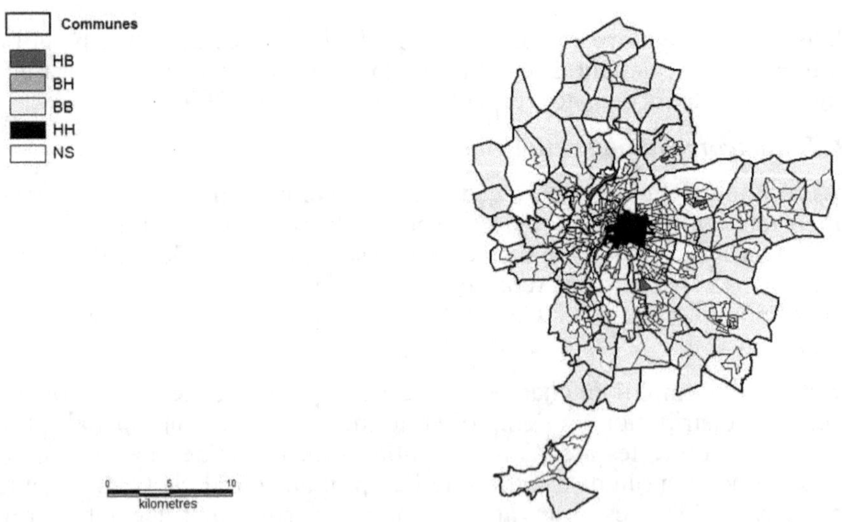

Source : Recensement National de la Population (2009) – INSEE.

Carte 2. Carte de significativité de Moran concernant la densité de population en 1999 (matrice de contiguïté à l'ordre 2)

Source : Recensement National de la Population (1999) – INSEE.

Carte 3. Carte de significativité de Moran concernant la densité de population en 2009 (matrice de contiguïté à l'ordre 2)

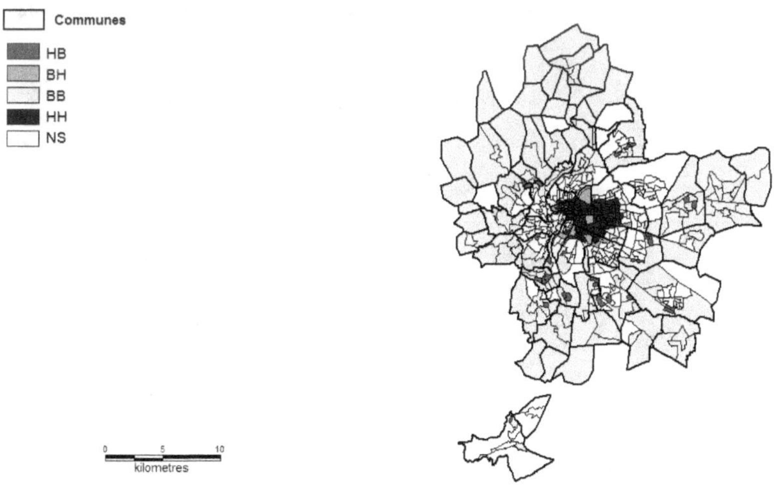

Source : Recensement National de la Population (2009) – INSEE.

Les mêmes outils sont utilisés pour décrire la répartition de la population en 1999 et en 2009. Les résultats présentés dans les cartes 2 et 3 révèlent une distribution similaire au schéma de distribution de l'emploi, avec une forte concentration de densités élevées au centre-ville (associations locales *Haut-Haut*) et plusieurs zones secondaires de concentration de la population (configurations

Haut-Bas et *Bas-Haut* dans le graphique de Moran). En comparant les résultats de 1999 et de 2009, on constate que la configuration spatiale de la répartition de la population est restée similaire au cours de la dernière décennie, la proportion de chaque type d'associations locales étant restée identique. Cette hypothèse est testée dans la section suivante, en comparant les gradients de la densité de population obtenus dans l'analyse économétrique du modèle multicentrique.

4.3. Estimation des fonctions de densité de population et d'emploi

Nous estimons les fonctions de densité de la population et de l'emploi selon trois types de formes urbaines : monocentrique suivant une loi négative exponentielle, monocentrique suivant une loi spline-exponentielle et multicentrique. La comparaison des résultats de nos régressions économétriques nous permet de déterminer quelle forme urbaine correspond le mieux à la distribution de la population et de l'emploi au sein de la Communauté Urbaine de Lyon. Les spécifications retenues sont estimées pour deux périodes (1999 et 2009) pour la population, et pour une période (2009) concernant l'emploi[11]. Une telle démarche nous permet d'analyser l'évolution de la configuration spatiale au cours de la période, et de confirmer ou infirmer les résultats des études sur données lyonnaises citées précédemment.

Tableau 4. Modèle monocentrique, fonction négative exponentielle – Population 1999

Variables	MCO-White	SEM-ML	SEM-GMM	DURBIN-ML
Ln D0	9,662***	9,757***	9,782***	6,678***
	(0,119)	(0,168)	(0,218)	(0,841)
DCBD	-0,220***	-0,219***	-0,219***	-0,442***
	(0,017)	(0,023)	(0,030)	(0,079)
w.DCBD				0,329***
				(0,091)
λ		0,314***	0,514***	
		(0,087)	(0,059)	
ρ				0,293***
				(0,088)
R^2	0,243	0,243	0,243	
Test de Moran	4,787			
p-valeur	*0,000*			
Test LM-Lag	11,869			
p-valeur	*0,001*			
Test Robuste LM-Lag	10,094			
p-valeur	*0,001*			
Test LM-Error	19,824			
p-valeur	*0,000*			
Test Robuste LM-Error	18,049			
p-valeur	*0,000*			
Observations			497	

*Légende : ***, ** et * pour une significativité au seuil de 1%, 5% et 10% respectivement. Les écarts-types sont présentés entre parenthèses, les p-values des tests d'autocorrélation spatiale sont en italique. Les résultats de la première colonne sont obtenus par la méthode des MCO en utilisant les outils de White (1980) pour corriger l'hétéroscédasticité.*
Source : Recensement National de la Population de 1999 – INSEE.

[11] Nous ne disposons pas des données sur l'emploi à l'échelle de l'IRIS en 1999.

4.3.1. Les densités de population

Les tableaux 4 et 5 présentent les résultats des estimations du modèle monocentrique suivant une loi négative exponentielle, en 1999 et en 2009. Les résultats de l'estimation par la méthode des MCO sont donnés dans la première colonne, et révèlent un gradient de la densité négatif et significatif au seuil de 1%, en 1999 et en 2009. Ce résultat confirme le déclin de la densité de population avec la distance au centre. La valeur du gradient montre un recul de l'effet de la distance au centre avec une baisse de 2,7% entre 1999 (-0,220) et 2009 (-0,214). Cette baisse du gradient peut traduire un recul de l'attractivité du centre-ville pour les ménages. Les tests de Lagrange, LM-error et LM-lag ainsi que leurs versions robustes révèlent la présence d'autocorrélation spatiale entre les termes d'erreurs plutôt qu'entre les observations[12]. Les colonnes 2 et 3 nous donnent les résultats du même modèle, mais en utilisant les outils de l'économétrie spatiale afin de corriger de ce biais, par la méthode du maximum de vraisemblance (SEMM-ML) et par la méthode des moments généralisés (SEM-GMM). Les résultats de l'estimation restent significatifs, quelle que soit la méthode d'estimation.

Tableau 5. Modèle monocentrique, fonction négative exponentielle – Population 2009

Variables	MCO-White	SEM-ML	SEM-GMM	DURBIN-ML
Ln D0	9,614***	9,664***	9,683***	7,516***
	(0,137)	(0,171)	(0,198)	(0,911)
DCBD	-0,214***	-0,213***	-0,212***	-0,432***
	(0,02)	(0,024)	(0,028)	(0,093)
w.DCBD				0,301***
				(0,106)
λ		0,215**	0,348***	
		(0,095)	(0067)	
ρ				0,201**
				(0,095)
R^2	0,186	0,186	0,186	
Test de Moran	2,967			
p-valeur	*0,003*			
Test LM-Lag	4,088			
p-valeur	*0,043*			
Test Robuste LM-Lag	6,606			
p-valeur	*0,010*			
Test LM-Error	7,165			
p-valeur	*0,007*			
Test Robuste LM-Error	9,683			
p-valeur	*0,002*			
Observations		497		

*Légende : ***, ** et * pour une significativité au seuil de 1%, 5% et 10% respectivement. Les écarts-types sont présentés entre parenthèses, les p-values des tests d'autocorrélation spatiale sont en italique. Les résultats de la première colonne sont obtenus par la méthode des MCO en utilisant les outils de White (1980) pour corriger l'hétéroscédasticité.*
Source : Recensement National de la Population de 2009 – INSEE.

[12] La valeur du gradient et le niveau de significativité est supérieur pour le test LM-error à celui du test LM-lag.

On observe une baisse de la densité de population de 21.9% en 1999 pour chaque kilomètre depuis le centre. La régression par la méthode des MCO et sans correction de l'autocorrélation spatiale donnait des résultats biaisés et surestimés. Le déclin de la densité est moins important en 2009, avec une baisse de 21.3% de la densité par kilomètre. La quatrième colonne nous donne les résultats du modèle de Durbin spatial. L'effet de la distance au centre-ville est ici confirmé et plus élevé, avec une baisse de 44.2% par kilomètre de la densité de population en 1999. On confirme également la baisse de l'effet de la distance au centre avec un effet diminué de 1% entre les deux périodes.

Tableau 6. Modèle monocentrique, fonction spline-exponentielle – Population 1999

Variables	MCO-White	SEM-ML	SEM-GMM	Durbin-ML
Ln D0	9,789***	9,887***	9,913***	6,741***
	(0,149)	(0,206)	(0,258)	(0,877)
DCBD	-0,253***	-0,253***	-0,254***	-0,792***
	(0,030)	(0,038)	(0,048)	(0,136)
x	0,091	0,088	0,089	0,479***
	(0,065)	(0,079)	(0,090)	(0,156)
w.DCBD				0,686***
				(0,155)
w.x				-0,479**
				(0,211)
λ		0,308***	0,495***	
		(0,088)	(0,060)	
ρ				0,280***
				(0,089)
R^2	0,243	0,246	0,246	
Test de Moran	4,718			
p-valeur	*0,000*			
Test LM-Lag	9,987			
p-valeur	*0,002*			
Test Robuste LM-Lag	18,348			
p-valeur	*0,000*			
Test LM-Error	18,318			
p-valeur	*0,000*			
Test Robuste LM-Error	26,679			
p-valeur	*0,000*			
Observations			497	

*Légende : ***, ** et * pour une significativité au seuil de 1%, 5% et 10% respectivement. Les écarts-types sont présentés entre parenthèses, les p-values des tests d'autocorrélation spatiale sont en italique. Les résultats de la première colonne sont obtenus par la méthode des MCO en utilisant les outils de White (1980) pour corriger l'hétéroscédasticité.*
Source : Recensement National de la Population de 1999 – INSEE.

Nous retenons les résultats du modèle SEM comme étant les plus proches de la réalité. En nous appuyant sur les tests du ratio de vraisemblance, dont la méthode est détaillée dans l'Annexe 3, et les résultats en Annexes 4 et 5, il apparait comme plus approprié que ne l'est le modèle de Durbin.

La forme négative-exponentielle présentée précédemment suppose l'homogénéité de la fonction de densité à travers l'ensemble du territoire étudié. Nous supposons à présent une forme d'hétérogénéité de la densité de population avec la distance au centre, avec une rupture à un rayon de 8 kilomètres du centre d'activité ; au-delà de cette distance, on ne distingue plus de zones de fortes concentration de population ou d'emploi. Les tableaux 6 et 7 présentent les résultats du modèle monocentrique *spline-exponentiel*. Dans la première colonne, on voit que le gradient de la distance est également négatif et significatif, même si sa valeur est modifiée. A l'inverse, le coefficient associé à *x*, la borne de 8 kilomètres, n'est pas significatif. Cela pourrait indiquer l'absence de rupture dans la densité d'emploi à travers l'ensemble du territoire. Ce résultat n'est pas lié à une mauvaise spécification du modèle ; la prise en compte de la présence d'autocorrélation spatiale sur le terme d'erreur ne modifie pas la significativité de nos résultats.

Tableau 7. Modèle monocentrique, fonction spline-exponentielle – Population 2009

Variables	MCO-White	SEM-ML	SEM-GMM	Durbin-ML
Ln D0	9,761***	9,805***	9,822***	7,647***
	(0,171)	(0,209)	(0,237)	(0,966)
DCBD	-0,253***	-0,250***	-0,250***	-0,773***
	(0,034)	(0,040)	(0,045)	(0,158)
x	0,106	0,099	0,098	0,463**
	(0,075)	(0,085)	(0,092)	(0,182)
w.DCBD				0,637***
				(0,182)
w.x				-0,428*
				(0,247)
λ		0,203**	0,323***	
		(0,096)	(0,069)	
ρ				0,185*
				(0,097)
R^2	0,186	0,190	0,190	
Test de Moran	2,834			
p-valeur	*0,005*			
Test LM-Lag	2,885			
p-valeur	*0,084*			
Test Robuste LM-Lag	12,876			
p-valeur	*0,000*			
Test LM-Error	6,028			
p-valeur	*0,014*			
Test Robuste LM-Error	16,019			
p-valeur	*0,000*			
Observations			497	

*Légende : ***, ** et * pour une significativité au seuil de 1%, 5% et 10% respectivement. Les écarts-types sont présentés entre parenthèses, les p-values des tests d'autocorrélation spatiale sont en italique. Les résultats de la première colonne sont obtenus par la méthode des MCO en utilisant les outils de White (1980) pour corriger l'hétéroscédasticité.*
Source : Recensement National de la Population de 2009 – INSEE.

Cependant, dans le modèle Durbin spatial, le gradient associé à cette borne de 8 kilomètre est significatif et de signe attendu, que ce soit en 1999 (+0.479) ou en 2009 (+0.463). Ces résultats s'interprètent comme une discontinuité dans la répartition de la population, celle-ci déclinant d'autant plus vite avec la distance au centre au-delà de la borne de 8 kilomètres.

Les tests du ratio de vraisemblance (Annexe 4) nous mènent à retenir les résultats de la régression par la méthode SEM : nous rejetons donc l'hypothèse de discontinuité dans la distribution de la population en fonction de la distance au centre.

Tableau 8. Fonctions de densité multicentriques - Population

	1999	2009
Variables	MCO-White	MCO-White
Ln D0	9,252***	9,220***
	(0,153)	*(0,179)*
DCBD	-0,252***	-0,245***
	(0,018)	*(0,021)*
1/(dist. à Rillieux la Pape)	0,485*	0,513
	(0,268)	*(0,313)*
1/(dist. à Vaulx en Velin)	0,810***	0,829***
	(0,274)	*(0,319)*
1/(dist. à Venicieux)	0,796***	0,738**
	(0,253)	*(0,295)*
1/(dist. à Saint-Priest)	1,271***	1,251***
	(0,234)	*(0,273)*
1/(dist. à Oullins)	0,234	0,159
	(0,275)	*(0,320)*
R^2	0,303	0,231
Test de Moran	2,473	1,259
p-valeur	*0,013*	*0,208*
Test LM-Lag	2,700	0,420
p-valeur	*0,100*	*0,517*
Test Robuste LM-Lag	0,014	0,000
p-valeur	*0,907*	*0,986*
Test LM-Error	3,323	0,461
p-valeur	*0,068*	*0,497*
Test Robuste LM-Error	0,636	0,041
p-valeur	*0,425*	*0,839*
Observations	497	497

*Légende : ***, ** et * pour une significativité au seuil de 1%, 5% et 10% respectivement. Les écarts-types sont présentés entre parenthèses, les p-values des tests d'autocorrélation spatiale sont en italique. Les résultats de la première colonne sont obtenus par la méthode des MCO en utilisant les outils de White (1980) pour corriger l'hétéroscédasticité.*
Source : Recensement National de la Population (1999 et 2009), INSEE.

Les résultats de l'ESDA ont révélé l'existence de potentiels centres d'emploi secondaires. De ce fait, nous testons l'éventualité d'une forme multicentrique de la Communauté Urbaine de Lyon. Nous considérons le centre de Lyon comme étant le centre d'emploi principal (CBD) et nous testons l'effet des cinq centres secondaires identifiés : Rillieux-la-Pape, Vaulx-en-Velin, Venissieux, Saint-Priest et Oullins. Les résultats de l'estimation sont présentés dans le tableau 8.

De nouveau, le paramètre associé à la distance au centre d'emploi principal est négatif et significatif, même si d'amplitude inférieure relativement au modèle monocentrique (colonne 1). Donc, malgré la prise en compte des centres d'emploi secondaires, la distance au centre-ville lyonnais a une importance significative dans la répartition de la population. De plus, sur les cinq centres secondaires, quatre ont une influence significative au seuil de 1 et 10%. C'est le cas de Rillieux-la-Pape et Vaulx-en-Velin situés au Nord-Est de Lyon, ainsi que de Saint-Priest et Venissieux au Sud-Est. On constate également que les coefficients sont de signe attendu ; la relation positive entre la densité de population et l'inverse de la distance aux centres secondaires s'interprète comme une baisse de la densité lorsque la distance augmente. Par exemple, chaque kilomètre supplémentaire depuis Saint-Priest se traduit par une baisse de la densité de population de 127.1%. De ce fait, la baisse du gradient entre 1999 et 2009 se traduit par une hausse de l'attractivité des centres secondaires, la densité de population diminuant moins rapidement qu'auparavant avec la distance. C'est le cas pour Venissieux et Saint-Priest qui ont vu leur attractivité croitre au cours de la dernière décennie. Si l'on s'intéresse de nouveau au cas de Saint-Priest, en 2009, la densité de population diminue de 125.1% pour chaque kilomètre, soit une réduction de 2% en dix ans.

Les tests d'autocorrélation spatiale confirme la présence d'autocorrélation spatiale globale sur le territoire (la valeur du I de Moran est positive et significative au seuil de 5%). Cependant, les tests LM-Lag et LM-Erreur ainsi que leurs versions robustes ne sont pas significatifs. Cette situation laisse à penser que la spécification du modèle étant simpliste, et ne prenant en compte que la distance aux centres d'emploi, ne permet pas de traiter de l'autocorrélation spatiale sur le territoire. Cela indique qu'il y a des erreurs dans la spécification du modèle qui biaisent les résultats sur lesquels se basent les tests robustes du multiplicateur de Lagrange (Anselin, 2005).

Les travaux de Lesage et Pace (2009) synthétisé par Elhorst (2010) mènent à penser que l'estimation des modèles SAR et SEM doivent malgré tout être réalisés. Les résultats complets sont présentés dans l'Annexe 1. Si les coefficients ρ et/ou λ, mesurant l'autocorrélation spatiale dans chacun de ces modèles, sont significatifs, nous retenons les résultats de la régression SAR, SEM ou Durbin. Dans notre cas, et pour les deux années d'étude, les deux coefficients ne sont pas significatifs[13]. Nous retenons donc les résultats estimés par la méthode des Moindres Carrés Ordinaires. Cependant, ces résultats sont à interpréter avec précaution; le fait de ne pas prendre en compte l'autocorrélation spatiale dans la régression laisse à penser que les résultats présentés et la significativité des centres d'emploi secondaires dans la répartition de la population peuvent être biaisés. Nous interprétons l'absence de significativité des tests de Lagrange comme l'inadaptation du modèle multicentrique dans sa forme classique aux données de la Communauté Urbaine de Lyon.

Les résultats des différentes estimations confirment le rôle central de la distance au centre-ville Lyonnais sur la répartition de la population, en 1999 et en 2009. La baisse de la densité de population avec la distance est continue et ne connait pas d'effet de seuil à 8 kilomètre du centre. Finalement, l'hypothèse d'une forme urbaine multicentrique est rejetée, confirmant ainsi les résultats des études empiriques sur données lyonnaises.

[13] Le coefficient ρ n'est pas significatif, ce qui confirme le rejet de l'hypothèse d'autocorrélation spatiale entre les observations. Le coefficient λ n'est significatif que pour l'estimation par la méthode des GMM. ; ce résultat n'étant pas robuste (non significatif lors de l'estimation par maximum de vraisemblance), nous rejetons également l'hypothèse d'autocorrélation spatiale entre les termes d'erreur.

4.3.2. La densité d'emploi

Dans cette dernière section, nous réalisons les mêmes analyses afin d'estimer la fonction de densité de l'emploi. Notre objectif est de pouvoir comparer la répartition de l'emploi à la répartition de la population afin de savoir s'ils répondent aux mêmes logiques en termes d'organisation spatiale. Les tableaux 9 et 10 présentent les résultats des fonctions de densité du modèle monocentrique, dans sa forme négative exponentielle et *spline-exponentiel*. Dans les deux cas, le test de Moran confirme la présence d'autocorrélation spatiale et les tests de Lagrange montrent que celle-ci est liée aux termes d'erreur spatialement corrélés. Quelle que soit la méthode d'estimation retenue, par maximum de vraisemblance ou par la méthode des moments généralisés, le gradient de la densité au centre d'emploi principal est négatif et significatif au seuil de 1%. Dans le premier modèle, cela signifie que la densité d'emploi décroît de 42% pour chaque kilomètre parcouru, et de 58% dans le second modèle.

Tableau 9 : Le modèle monocentrique – Fonction négative exponentielle – Emploi

Variables	MCO-White	SEM-ML	SEM-GMM	Durbin Model
Ln D0	8,830***	8,847***	8,846***	5,265***
	(0,202)	(0,308)	(0,321)	(0,767)
DCBD	-0,414***	-0,419***	-0,418***	-0,519***
	(0,030)	(0,044)	(0,045)	(0,135)
Wx_DCBD				0,286*
				0,154
λ		0,401***	0,430***	
		(0,084)	(0,057)	
rho				0,393***
				(0,084)
R²	0,281	0,282	0,282	
Test de Moran	6,299			
p-valeur	*0,000*			
Test LM-Lag	27,909			
p-valeur	*0,000*			
Test Robuste LM-Lag	1,728			
p-valeur	*0,189*			
Test LM-Error	35,127			
p-valeur	*0,000*			
Test Robuste LM-Error	8,946			
p-valeur	*0,003*			
Observations		497		

*Légende : ***, ** et * pour une significativité au seuil de 1%, 5% et 10% respectivement. Les écarts-types sont présentés entre parenthèses, les p-values des tests d'autocorrélation spatiale sont en italique. Les résultats de la première colonne sont obtenus par la méthode des MCO en utilisant les outils de White (1980) pour corriger l'hétéroscédasticité.*
Source : Recensement National de la Population 2009 – INSEE.

Tableau 10. Le modèle monocentrique – Fonction spline-exponentielle – Emploi

Variables	MCO-White	SEM-ML	SEM-GMM	Durbin Model
Ln D0	9,434***	9,473***	9,470***	6,429***
	(0,250)	(0,351)	(0,367)	(0,896)
DCBD	-0,573***	-0,580***	-0,579***	-0,952***
	(0,050)	(0,067)	(0,069)	(0,230)
Wx_DCBD				0,569**
				(0,263)
x	0,436***	0,411***	0,412***	0,526**
	(0,109)	(0,135)	(0,138)	(0,263)
Wx_x				-0,122
				(0,359)
λ		0,345***	0,382***	
		(0,089)	(0,061)	
rho				0,304***
				(0,090)
R^2	0,302	0,304	0,304	
Test de Moran	5,124			
p-valeur	*0,000*			
Test LM-Lag	15,069			
p-valeur	*0,000*			
Test Robuste LM-Lag	6,141			
p-valeur	*0,013*			
Test LM-Error	21,836			
p-valeur	*0,000*			
Test Robuste LM-Error	12,908			
p-valeur	*0,000*			
Observations			497	

*Légende : ***, ** et * pour une significativité au seuil de 1%, 5% et 10% respectivement. Les écarts-types sont présentés entre parenthèses, les p-values des tests d'autocorrélation spatiale sont en italique. Les résultats de la première colonne sont obtenus par la méthode des MCO en utilisant les outils de White (1980) pour corriger l'hétéroscédasticité.*
Source : Recensement National de la Population 2009 – INSEE.

De plus, et contrairement à l'analyse de la répartition de la population, on constate que le coefficient associé à la distance *x* est positif et significatif, révélant un changement du gradient de la densité après 8 kilomètres. Toutes choses étant égales par ailleurs, la densité d'emploi diminue de 57,9% par kilomètre pour les quartiers situés à moins de 8 kilomètres du centre, alors qu'elle ne diminue plus que de 16,7% pour les quartiers situés à plus de 8 kilomètres.

D'autre part, en comparant densité d'emploi et de population, il est également important de souligner que l'effet de la distance au centre a un impact plus important sur la répartition des emplois que sur la répartition de la population, les coefficients associés étant plus élevés quelle que soit la méthode d'estimation retenue. Nous avons également testé le modèle de Durbin qui donne les mêmes résultats pour les deux spécifications. Finalement, quelle que soit la méthode économétrique utilisée, le modèle monocentrique est validé.

Bien que les résultats du modèle monocentrique soient statistiquement significatifs, nous souhaitons vérifier si la distribution de l'emploi correspond au modèle multicentrique (résultats présentés dans le tableau 11). Nous retenons comme centres secondaires potentiels les zones de concentration d'emploi identifiées par l'ESDA et utilisées pour l'estimation des fonctions de densité de population.

Les résultats de la première colonne confirment le rôle du centre d'emploi principal, pour lequel le gradient est négatif et significatif. Le test de Moran révèle la présence d'autocorrélation spatiale entre les observations, et les tests de Lagrange montrent que celle-ci est plutôt liée à un effet de dispersion entre zones géographiques voisines. Il nous faut donc utiliser un modèle de type SAR (colonne 2).

Tableau 11. Fonction de densité multicentrique - Emploi

Variables	MCO-White		SAR		Durbin Model	
Ln D0	8,504***	(0,268)	5,948***	(0,821)	7,032***	(0,932)
DCBD	-0,448***	(0,031)	-0,333***	(0,046)	-0,395***	(0,137)
1/(dist. à Rill. la P.)	0,335	(0,469)	0,365	(0,459)	0,348	(0,701)
1/(dist. à V. en V.)	1,047**	(0,479)	0,841*	(0,473)	-0,182	(0,963)
1/(dist. à Ven.)	0,924**	(0,442)	0,831*	(0,434)	0,558	(0,821)
1/(dist. à Saint-P.)	1,220***	(0,409)	0,856**	(0,415)	-0,218	(0,536)
1/(dist. à Oul.)	-0,341	(0,480)	-0,072	(0,477)	1,777**	(0,788)
Wx_DCBD					-0,016	(0,165)
Wx_1/(dist. à RLP)					-0,151	(1,339)
Wx_1/(dist. à VV)					1,696	(1,520)
Wx_1/(dist. à Ven.)					0,502	(1,312)
Wx_1/(dist. à SP)					2,819***	(0,965)
Wx_1/(dist. à Oul.)					-3,401***	(1,256)
Rho			0,299***	(0,091)	0,186*	(0,099)
R^2	0,300					
test de Moran	3,928	*0,000*				
Test LM-Lag	13,820	*0,000*				
Test Robuste LM-Lag	4,603	*0,032*				
Test LM-error	10,196	*0,001*				
Test Robuste LM-error	0,980	*0,322*				
Observations			497			

*Légende : ***, ** et * pour une significativité au seuil de 1%, 5% et 10% respectivement. Les écarts-types sont présentés entre parenthèses, les p-values des tests d'autocorrélation spatiale sont en italique. Les résultats de la première colonne sont obtenus par la méthode des MCO en utilisant les outils de White (1980) pour corriger l'hétéroscédasticité.*

Source : Recensement National de la Population 2009 – INSEE.

Dans le cas du modèle SAR, les effets des variables explicatives ne correspondent pas aux coefficients qui leurs sont associés du fait de l'introduction de la variable spatialement décalée[14]. Nous ne commentons ici que leur signe et leur significativité. Les résultats par la méthode de Durbin présentés en colonne 3 montrent que trois centres d'emploi secondaires semblent avoir un impact

[14] Le coefficient estimé par le modèle ne correspond pas aux effets marginaux d'une variation de la variable explicative sur la variable à expliquer. Cela signifie que les coefficients ne peuvent pas s'interpréter de la même façon que dans le cas de régression linéaire simple du fait de l'introduction de la variable spatialement décalée.

significatif sur la distribution des emplois, aux seuils de 10% et 5%. C'est le cas de Vaulx-en-Velin, Vénissieux et Saint-Priest. Le coefficient ρ étant positif et significatif, le modèle ainsi estimé corrige de l'autocorrélation spatiale et donne des résultats non biaisés.

L'analyse de la fonction de densité de l'emploi montre que la distance au centre principal a un impact fort et significatif sur la répartition de l'emploi dans l'ensemble de la Communauté Urbaine Lyonnaise. Cet effet est d'autant plus vrai pour les zones géographiques situées à moins de 8 kilomètres du centre. Il apparait également que certains centres d'emploi secondaires ont un impact significatif sur la distribution des activités au sein du territoire, confirmant ainsi la forme multicentrique de l'emploi trouvé dans la littérature.

En travaillant sur des données différentes, à une échelle plus fine et plus récentes, nous confirmons les résultats de la littérature qui traitaient de la répartition des emplois et de la population autour de l'agglomération Lyonnaise (Buisson et al. 2001 ; Mignot, 2013). L'apparition de centres d'emploi secondaires a modifié la répartition des activités au sein de la Communauté Urbaine de Lyon, même si celle-ci reste principalement déterminée par la distance au centre-ville. Malgré le fait que l'emploi suive un schéma multicentrique, la répartition de la population ne suit pas les schémas classiques de l'économie urbaine réfutant l'hypothèse du modèle multicentrique.

5. CONCLUSION

L'objectif de cet article était d'analyser la répartition de l'emploi et de la population au sein de la Communauté Urbaine de Lyon. Nous avons fait appel à différentes spécifications (monocentrique suivant une distribution négative exponentielle, ou suivant une distribution *spline exponentiel*, multicentrique) afin de tester la robustesse des résultats obtenus par l'analyse exploratoire des données spatialisées, et déterminer quel type de modèle correspond le mieux à la réalité de l'organisation spatiale du Grand Lyon.

Nos résultats montrent que la localisation des activités, bien que principalement déterminée par la distance au centre-ville Lyonnais, suit un schéma multicentrique avec une influence significative de trois centres d'emploi secondaires (Saint-Priest, Venissieux et Vaulx-en-Velin). L'analyse de la répartition de la population ne nous permet pas d'arriver aux mêmes conclusions ; bien que l'analyse exploratoire des données spatiales révélait la présence de zones de fortes concentrations de la population en dehors du centre Lyonnais, l'analyse économétrique ne nous a pas permis de confirmer ces résultats. Le modèle multicentrique, tel qu'il est établi dans sa forme simplifiée, ne permet pas de contrôler de l'autocorrélation spatiale par le biais des outils classiques de l'économétrie spatiale.

Pourtant, dans les faits, il apparait que les politiques d'aménagement du territoire mises en place vont dans le sens du passage d'un espace monocentré sur la ville de Lyon vers un schéma multicentrique, avec l'émergence de centre secondaires d'emploi qui impactent la répartition de la population. En effet, le plan d'aménagement du territoire « Lyon 2010 » présenté en 1988 avait pour objectif de maitriser l'étalement urbain. Il visait au développement de la multipolarité de la métropole et du réseau de transports collectifs. Les investissements réalisés au cours des deux dernières décennies ont permis de connecter le centre lyonnais à des pôles périphériques qui ont parallèlement développé leurs activités économiques. En 2010, le projet d'aménagement et de développement durable « SCOT 2030 » visait, entre autres, à renforcer la multipolarité de la Communauté Urbaine de Lyon. Dans ce sens, les centres d'emploi secondaires identifiés dans cette étude, Vaulx-en-Velin, Venissieux, Rillieux-la-Pape, Saint-Priest et Oullins font partie des «bassins de vie à structurer ».

Au cours des prochaines décennies, la multipolarité pourrait être accrue, par le biais du renforcement et de la restructuration des réseaux de transports, en vue de permettre un meilleur maillage du territoire et de réduire les mobilités quotidiennes.

REFERENCES

Aguilera, A., Massot, M.H., Proulhac, L., 2006, "L'intégration du périurbain francilien à la métropole parisienne. Une mesure par les flux quotidiens de personnes", in A. Larceneux, C. Boiteux-Orain, *Paris et ses franges: étalement urbain et polycentrisme*, Université de Dijon, pp. 73–97.

Aguilera, A., Mignot, D., Bloy, D., Caubel, D., Madre, J.L., 2013, "Urban forms, mobility and segregation. A Lille-Lyon-Marseille comparison", *Dialogues in Urban Planning.*

Alonso, W., 1964, *Location and land use - Towards a general theory of land rent*, Cambridge, Harvard University Press.

Alperovich, G., 1996, "The effectiveness of spline urban density functions: an empirical investigation", *Urban Studies*, 32, pp.1537–1548.

Amara, M., Kriaa, M., Montacer, M., 2010, "Centralité des activités dans la région urbaine de tunis (1994-2004)", *Revue d'Économie Régionale et Urbaine*, pp. 473–509.

Anas, A., Arnott, R., Small, K., 1998, "Urban spatial structure", *Journal of Economic Perspectives*, 36.9.

Anselin, L, 1988, *Spatial Econometrics: Methods and Models*, MA: Kluwer Academic Publishers, Boston.

Anselin, L., 1995, "Local indicators of spatial association - LISA", *Geographical Analysis*, 27, pp. 93–115.

Anselin, L., 1996, *The Moran scatterplot as an ESDA tool to assess local instability in spatial association*, London: Taylor and Francis.

Anselin, L., 2001, "Spatial Econometrics", in B.H. Baltagi (Ed.), *A Companion to Theorical Econometrics,* Blackwell Publishing, on line 2007.

Baccaïni, B., Sémécurbe, F., 2009, "La croissance périurbaine depuis 45 ans", *Insee Première*, n°1240.

Baumont, C., Ertur, C., Le Gallo, J., 2004, "Spatial Analysis Of Employment And Population Density: The Case Of The Agglomeration Of Dijon 1999", *Geographical Analysis*, vol. 36(2), pp. 146-176.

Baumont, C., Le Gallo, J., 1999, "Empirical foundations of multicentric urban models", Technical Report, Laboratoire d'Economie et de Gestion (LEG), 46th North American Congress of the Regional Science Association International – Montreal (Canada).

Ben Said, F., Ayadi, M., 2011, "Analyse de l'étalement urbain selon le profil de la densité résidentielle dans le district de Tunis: application de la technique des "spline regression" spatiales" , JMA 2014.

Bertaud, A., 2001, "Metropolis: A measure of the spatial organization of 7 large cities", Technical report, NYU Stern Urbanization Project.

Blanc, M., Schmitt, B., Ambiaud, E., 2007, "Orientation économique et croissance locale de l'emploi dans les bassins de vie des bourgs et petites villes", *Economie et Statistique*, 402, pp. 57–74.

Boiteux-Orain, C., Guillain, R., 2003, "Changes in the intra-metropolitan location of producer services in Ile-de-France (1978-1997): do information technologies promote a more dispersed spatial pattern", LEG, Document de travail, Université de Bourgogne.

Brueckner, J. K., Thisse, J.-F., Zenou, Y., 1999, "Why is central Paris rich and downtown Detroit poor?: An amenity-based theory", *European Economic Review*, 43(1), pp. 91–107.

Buisson, M.-A., Mignot, D., Aguilera, A., 2001, "Métropolisation et polarités intra-urbaines. Le cas de Lyon", *Revue d'Economie Régionale et Urbaine*, 2, pp. 271–296.

Bumsoo, L., 2007, "'Edge' or 'edgeless' cities? Urban spatial structure in U.S. metropolitan areas, 1980 to 2000", *Journal of Regional Science*, 47(3), pp. 479–515.

Bussiere, R., 1972, "Modèle de localisation résidentielle", *Anales du centre de Recherche d'Urbanisme.*

Cadoret, I., 2009, *Econométrie Appliquée : Méthodes, Applications, Corrigés*, De Boeck.

Cervero, R., Wu, K., 1997, "Polycentrism, commuting, and residential location in San Francisco Bay area", *Environment and Planning A*, 29, pp.865–86.

Chen, H., 1997, "Models of urban population and employment density: the spatial structure of monocentric and polycentric functions in Greater Taipei and a comparison to Los Angeles", *Geographical and Environmental Modelling*, 1, pp.135–51.

Clark, C., 1968, *Population growth and land use*, New York, Saint Martin Press.

Cliff, A. D., Ord, J., 1973, *Spatial Autocorrelation*, Pion, London.

Coffey, W., Polèse, M., Drolet, R., 1996, "Examing the thesis of Central Business District decline: evidence from the Montreal metropolitan area", *Environment and Planning A*, 28, pp.1795–1814.

Crozet, Y., Joly, I., 2007, "La loi de Zahavi : quelle pertinence pour comprendre la construction et la dilatation des espaces-temps de la ville? ", 163, Recherche, PUCA edition.

Elhorst, J.P., 2010, "Applied Spatial Econometrics: Raising the Bar", *Spatial Economic Analysis*, 5,1, pp. 9-28.

Fujita, M., Ogawa, H., 1997, "Multiple equilibria and structural transition of non-monocentric urban configurations", *Regional Science and Urban Economics*, 12(2), pp. 161–196.

Fujita, M., Thisse, J.-F., 1997, "Economie géographique, problèmes anciens et nouvelles perspectives", *Annales d'Economie et Statistique*, (45), pp. 37–87.

Gaschet, F., 2000, "La structure d'un espace urbain polycentrique: la métropole bordelaise", dans P.H. Derycke (Dir.), *Structure des villes, entreprises et marchés urbains,* L'Harmattan, Coll. Emploi industrie et territoire, Paris, pp. 95–126.

Gordon, P., Richardson, H., Wong, H., 1986, "The distribution of population and employment in a polycentric city: the case of Los Angeles", *Environment and Planning A*, 18, pp.161–173.

Guillain, R., Le Gallo, J., 2007, "Agglomeration and dispersion of economic activities in Paris and its surroundings : An exploratory spatial data analysis", LEG - Document de travail - Economie 2007-01, Université de Bourgogne.

Hamilton, B.W., Röell, A., 1982, "Wasteful commuting", *Journal of Political Economy*, 90(5), pp. 1035–1053.

Heikkila, E., Gordon, P., Kim, J.I., Peiser, R.B., Richardson, H.W., Dale-Johnson D., 1989, "What happened to the CBD-distance gradient?: land values in a policentric city", *Environment and Planning A*, 21(2), pp. 221–232.

Horton, F. E., Reynolds, D. R., 1971, "Action space differentials in cities", *Perspectives in geography: Models of spatial interaction*, pp. 83–102.

Jayet, H., 1993, *Analyse spatiale quantitative: une introduction* , *Economica*, Paris.

Le Gallo, J., 2002, "Économétrie spatiale : l'autocorrélation spatiale dans les modèles de régression linéaire », *Economie et prévision*, n°155, pp. 139-157.

LeSage, J., 1999, *Spatial Econometrics*: *The Web Book of Regional Science*, Regional Research Institute, West Virginia University, Morgantown, WV.

LeSage, J., Pace, R.K., 2009, *Introduction to Spatial Econometrics*, Boca Raton, Taylor & Francis.

McMillen, D., McDonald, J., 1998a, "Population density in Chicago: a bird rent approach", *Urban Studies*, 7, pp.119–30.

McMillen, D., McDonald, J., 1998b, "Suburban subcenters and employment density in metropolitan Chicago", *Journal of Urban Economics*, 43, pp.157–80.

McMillen, D., 2004, "Employment densities, spatial autocorrelation, and subcenters in large metropolitan areas", *Journal of Regional Science*, 44(2), pp. 225–244.

Medam, A., 1998, *Villes pour un Sociologue*, L'Harmattan.

Mills, E.S., 1967, "An aggregative model of resource allocation in a metropolitan area", *The American Economic Review*, 57(2), pp.197–210.

Mills, E. S., Tan, J., 1980, "A comparison of urban population density functions in developed and developing countries", *Urban Studies*, 17.

Muth, R., 1969, *Cities and Housing: The Spatial Pattern of Urban Residential Land-Use*, Chicago and London, The University of Chicago Press.

Myrtho, J., Wang, F., 2010, "Population density patterns in Port-au-Prince, Haiti: A model of Latin American city?", *Cities*, 27(3), pp. 127 – 136.

Peguy, P.-Y., 2000, "Analyse économique des configurations urbaines et de leur étalement", Thèse de doctorat, Université Lumière Lyon 2.

Pouyanne, G., 2004, "The influence of urban form on travel patterns. An application to the metropolitan area of Bordeaux", ERSA conference papers ersa04p244, European Regional Science Association.

Sari F., 2011, "Expliquer les déplacements domicile-travail en Ile-de-France: le rôle de la structure urbaine et des caractéristiques socio-économiques", *Les Cahiers Scientifiques du Transport*, n°60.

Small, K. A., Song, S., 1994, "Population and employment densities: Structure and change", *Journal of Urban Economics*, 36, pp. 292–313.

Waddell, P., Shukla, V., 1993, "Employment dynamics, spatial restructuring, and the business cycle" *Geographical Analysis*, 25(1), pp. 35–52.

Wiel, M., 2010, *Etalement urbain et mobilité*, La documentation française.

Wu, F., 1998, "Polycentric urban development and land-use change in Transitional Economy: the case of Guangzhou", *Environment and Planning A*, 30, pp. 1077–1100.

ANNEXE 1

Le modèle multicentrique – Fonction de la densité de population en 1999

Variables	MCO-White		SEM-ML		SEM-GMM		DURBIN-ML	
Ln D0	9,252***	(0,153)	9,250***	(0,172)	9,253***	(0,218)	8,273***	(0,943)
DCBD	-0,252***	(0,018)	-0,248***	(0,020)	-0,245***	(0,026)	-0,366***	(0,080)
1/(dist. à RLP)	0,485*	(0,268)	0,577**	(0,290)	0,630**	(0,312)	1,036**	(0,408)
1/(dist. à VV)	0,810***	(0,274)	0,847***	(0,298)	0,870**	(0,346)	0,885	(0,558)
1/(dist. à Ven)	0,796***	(0,253)	0,787***	(0,273)	0,781**	(0,314)	0,531	(0,478)
1/(dist. à SP)	1,271***	(0,234)	1,197***	(0,251)	1,154***	(0,269)	0,805***	(0,312)
1/(dist. à Oul)	0,234	(0,275)	0,286	(0,297)	0,316	(0,337)	0,666	(0,459)
W.DCBD							0,158*	(0,096)
W.1/(dist. à RLP)							-1,355*	(0,779)
W.1/(dist. à VV)							-0,187	(0,871)
W.1/(dist. à Ven)							0,077	(0,764)
W.1/(dist. à SP)							0,679	(0,565)
W.1/(dist. à Oul)							-0,937	(0,727)
λ			0,159	(0,099)	0,398***	(0,065)		
ρ							0,119	(0,098)
R^2	0,303		0,310		0,310			
test de Moran	2,473	*0,013*						
Test LM-Lag	2,700	*0,100*						
Test Robuste LM-Lag	0,014	*0,907*						
Test LM-error	3,323	*0,068*						
Test Robuste LM-error	0,636	*0,425*						
Observations				497				

*Légende : ***, ** et * pour une significativité au seuil de 1%, 5% et 10% respectivement. Les écarts-types sont présentés entre parenthèses, les p-values des tests d'autocorrélation spatiale sont en italique. Les résultats de la première colonne sont obtenus par la méthode des MCO en utilisant les outils de White (1980) pour corriger l'hétéroscédasticité.*
Source : Recensement National de la Population 1999 – INSEE.

ANNEXE 2

Le modèle multicentrique – Fonction de la densité de population en 2009

Variables	MCO-White		SEM-ML		SEM-GMM		DURBIN-ML	
Ln D0	9,220***	*(0,179)*	9,215***	*(0,187)*	9,210***	*(0,211)*	9,106***	*(1,019)*
DCBD	-0,245***	*(0,021)*	-0,244***	*(0,022)*	-0,241***	*(0,025)*	-0,346***	*(0,094)*
1/(dist. à RLP)	0,513	*(0,313)*	0,547*	*(0,323)*	0,591*	*(0,338)*	0,976**	*(0,478)*
1/(dist. à VV)	0,829***	*(0,319)*	0,841**	*(0,330)*	0,856**	*(0,359)*	0,742	*(0,655)*
1/(dist. à Ven)	0,738**	*(0,295)*	0,740**	*(0,303)*	0,742**	*(0,329)*	0,598	*(0,561)*
1/(dist. à SP)	1,251***	*(0,273)*	1,221***	*(0,282)*	1,181***	*(0,294)*	0,798**	*(0,366)*
1/(dist. à Oul)	0,159	*(0,320)*	0,190	*(0,333)*	0,232	*(0,356)*	0,808	*(0,538)*
W.DCBD							0,117	*(0,112)*
W.1/(dist. à RLP)							-1,250	*(0,912)*
W.1/(dist. à VV)							0,085	*(1,021)*
W.1/(dist. à Ven)							-0,033	*(0,893)*
W.1/(dist. à SP)							0,821	*(0,660)*
W.1/(dist. à Oul)							-1,313	*(0,859)*
λ			0,066	*(0,106)*	0,212***	*(0,075)*		
ρ							0,030	*(0,105)*
R^2	0,231		0,240		0,240			
test de Moran	1,259	*0,208*						
Test LM-Lag	0,420	*0,517*						
Test Robuste LM-Lag	0,000	*0,986*						
Test LM-error	0,461	*0,497*						
Test Robuste LM-error	0,041	*0,839*						
Observations	497							

*Légende : ***, ** et * pour une significativité au seuil de 1%, 5% et 10% respectivement. Les écarts-types sont présentés entre parenthèses, les p-values des tests d'autocorrélation spatiale sont en italique. Les résultats de la première colonne sont obtenus par la méthode des MCO en utilisant les outils de White (1980) pour corriger l'hétéroscédasticité.*
Source : Recensement National de la Population 2009 – INSEE.

ANNEXE 3

La comparaison des modèles spatiaux

Elhorst (2010) se base sur les travaux de Lesage et Pace (2009) et montre que différents tests peuvent être réalisés afin de déterminer quel modèle économétrique est le plus approprié aux données étudiées. Lorsque les tests LM-Lag et LM-Error sont tous les deux significatifs, il est préférable de réaliser l'estimation par la méthode de Durbin, les modèle SAR et SEM étant des formes particulières du modèle de Durbin.
En effet, le modèle de Durbin prend simultanément en compte la présence de la variable endogène spatialement décalée et de variables explicatives spatialement décalées. Le modèle SAR correspond au cas spécifique où l'autocorrélation spatiale entre les observations est uniquement liée à l'influence des observations sur leurs voisines, $\theta = 0$. Quant au modèle SEM, il suppose la présence d'autocorrélation spatiale liée au terme d'erreur (ici, $\theta = \rho\beta$).
Lorsque les tests du Multiplicateur de Lagrange et leurs versions robustes sont significatifs, il est conseillé de réaliser des tests de vraisemblance afin de savoir quelle méthode d'estimation est la plus appropriée.
Nous faisons les tests d'hypothèses suivants :
$H_0 : \theta = 0$ contre $H_1 : \theta \neq 0$ pour le modèle SAR,
$H_0 : \theta - \rho\beta = 0$ contre $H_1 : \theta - \rho\beta \neq 0$ pour le modèle SEM.
La statistique du test du ratio de vraisemblance est formalisée de la façon suivante (Cadoret, 2009).
Soit $\hat{\beta}^*$ l'estimateur du modèle contraint – estimé par la méthode SEM ou SAR – et $e^{*\prime}e^*$ la somme des carrés des résidus correspondante, $\hat{\beta}$ l'estimateur du modèle non contraint – estimé par la méthode de Durbin – et $e'e$ la somme des carrés des résidus correspondante, la statistique du ratio de vraisemblance (LR) s'écrit :

$$LR = -2\left(LogL(\hat{\beta}^*) - LogL(\hat{\beta})\right) \text{ ou } LR = N\left(Log(e^{*\prime}e^*) - Log(e'e)\right).$$

Elle suit une loi du χ^2 à N degrés de liberté, avec N le nombre d'observations. Si $LR > \chi^2_\alpha(N)$, alors nous rejetons l'hypothèse nulle ; le modèle non contraint est accepté.
En d'autres termes, si l'hypothèse H_0 est rejetée dans les deux cas, le modèle Durbin décrit le mieux les données. Si l'hypothèse H_0 est acceptée, c'est le modèle SEM ou SAR qui convient. Ces résultats doivent venir conforter les résultats des tests du Multiplicateur de Lagrange, sinon nous retenons l'estimation du modèle de Durbin (Elhorst, 2010).

ANNEXE 4

Somme des carrés des résidus des régressions

Densité de population – 1999			
	(1)	(2)	(3)
SEM	1006,37	1002,26	909,76
SAR	1011,62	1007,34	909,46
Durbin	938,52	958,69	888,80
Densité de population - 2009			
SEM	1360,11	1353,49	1250,91
SAR	1358,10	1350,39	1251,29
Durbin	1337,71	1312,95	1229,49
Densité d'emploi - 2009			
SEM	3874,30	3733,65	3783,91
SAR	3874,30	3735,34	3727,67
Durbin	3870,53	3689,04	3596,62

Légende : (1) Modèle monocentrique, fonction négative-exponentielle,(2) modèle monocentrique, fonction spline-exponentielle, (3) Modèle multicentrique.

Source : Recensement National de la Population (1999 et 2009) – INSEE.

ANNEXE 5

Les ratios de vraisemblance

Densité de population – 1999			
	(1)	(2)	(3)
SEM/Durbin	34,69	22,09	11,58
SAR/Durbin	37,28	24,60	11,42
Densité de population - 2009			
SEM/Durbin	8,25	15,11	8,58
SAR/Durbin	7,52	13,97	8,74
Densité d'emploi - 2009			
SEM/Durbin	0,48	5,97	25,23
SAR/Durbin	0,36	6,20	17,79

Légende : (1) Modèle monocentrique, fonction négative-exponentielle,(2) modèle monocentrique, fonction spline-exponentielle, (3) Modèle multicentrique.

$\chi^2_{0.05}(500)=553,13$ donc pour l'ensemble des tests on accepte H_0 ; le modèle de Durbin n'est pas le plus approprié aux analyses réalisées.

Source : Recensement National de la Population (1999 et 2009) – INSEE.

SPATIAL ANALYSIS OF URBAN PATTERNS: THE CASE OF LYON

Abstract – *The main objective of this work is to analyze the spatial structure of the Urban Community of Lyon, also called "Grand Lyon". We aim to highlight not only the urban pattern of the area but also its changes over time. We first look at the location of both employment and population and realize an Exploratory Spatial Data Analysis to determine if it exists one or several potential centroids. Our work is based on data from the French National Population census of 1999 and 2009 to reveal its evolution during the last decade. The different econometrics analysis aim to determine if there is one or several employment centers influencing significantly the distribution of employment and population in the area. Finally, by testing different specification, we can conclude which one describes the best our data. Our results show that the location of employment is mainly determined by the distance to the city-center of Lyon, and a change in employment densities at 8 kilometers. Looking at the distribution of population enhance the attractiveness of city-center. We can also notice a fall in the effect of distance to CBD, highlighting an urban sprawl phenomenon. However, the original models of urban economics do not allowed handling subcenters influence in location strategies.*

Key-words - SPATIAL ECONOMETRICS, URBAN PATTERNS, URBAN SPRAWL, DENSITY FUNCTIONS

THE EFFECT OF FOREIGN DIRECT INVESTMENT ON ECONOMIC GROWTH: THE INSTITUTIONAL THRESHOLD

Ines TROJETTE[*]

Abstract - *This paper examines whether the effect of foreign direct investment on economic growth is dependent upon the institutional level for five regions (SSA, MENA, Europe, Asia and America). Using GMM system covering the period from 1984-2013, our results highlight the role of institutional development in moderating the ambiguous impacts of FDI on GDP growth. Under the threshold regression, technique developed by Caner and Hansen (2004) we find that the index of institutions matter for all groups except for the America group. The fact of taking the components of institutions reveal that above the threshold of government stability and the respect of law and order FDI enhances GDP growth.*

Key-words - FOREIGN DIRECT INVESTMENT; GROWTH; INSTITUTIONAL DEVELOPMENT; THRESHOLD EFFECT

Classification JEL - F21, C34, F43, O16

[*] LEAD, University of Toulon ; inestrojette@hotmail.fr

1. INTRODUCTION

A voluminous literature exists that explores the impacts of FDI on the host's socio-economic well-being (Borensztein et al., 1998; Carkovic and Levine, 2002). Yet, the findings are diverse, and sometimes far from conclusive (Meyer, Bevan, and Estrin, 2004). The aim of this paper is to assess the role of institutions on the effectiveness of FDI' effects on growth. One particularity of this study is the introduction of threshold analysis. This part relies on the idea that the impact of FDI on growth depends on a critical level of institutions developed by several authors (Meyer and Sinani, 2009; Jude and Levieuge, 2013). It leads us to consider 5 subsamples of countries according to the World Bank regional decomposition (MENA, Europe, America, Asia and SSA) and 3 income levels (high, middle and low income countries).

According to the economic literature, FDI may affects growth mainly through three channels. This works through first the linkages between FDI and foreign trade flows. Second, the spillovers and other externalities vis-à-vis the host country; and third the direct impact on structural factors in the host economy (OCDE, 2002). Theoretical models show different ways in which FDI affect growth. FDI can be a source of human capital augmentation and technological change in developing countries since it promotes the use of more advanced technology by domestic firms (De Mello Jr, 1997). Through capital accumulation in the host country, FDI is expected to boost growth by encouraging the incorporation of new inputs and technologies in production function of the recipient economy. Likewise, FDI stimulates a host economy's growth through the technological know-how transfer and human capital (Carkovic and Levine, 2002) creating the ''first-order'' effects. Subsequently, second-order effects, including the mobility of advanced technology, management system, and skilled labor for local firms will inflow to the host country (De Mello and Sinclair, 1995; Hale and Long 2006). This, in turn, enhances the host environment's ability to absorb other FDI, creating clusters of FDI and pools of talented managers and a skilled labor force in the host economy (Borensztein et al., 1998). FDI also offers demonstration effects, that is, their superior operational efficiency encourages local firms to place more emphases on technology investments for productivity gains that contribute to the economic growth of the host country (Meyer and Sinani, 2009). According to De Moello (1997), this impact should be lower in technological leaders than in technological laggards.

However, despite the arguments and evidence in support of the positive impacts of FDI on growth, some empirical findings suggest the contrary. Sen (1998) indicates that multinationals may have an adverse reaction in the host country R&D in order to continue to hold a technological advantage compared to local firms. He points out the increase in payments of royalties that will lead to a negative impact on the balance of payments. Vissak and Roolaht (2005) explain that the host country can become dependent on technologies introduced by multinationals. These authors argue that workers with high education may leave the country, since there are no R&D activities that they can engage in the host country. Furthermore, Ford et al. (2008) state that local authorities, verifying that multinationals are a source of training and improving the levels of education in the country, reduce public spending in this area which mitigate the effect of training of the labor force provided by FDI. Mencinger (2003) reports that FDI has a higher impact on imports than on exports, which influences negatively on the balance of payments. This can be explained by the fact that multinationals use goods and raw materials, which are most of the time not available in the host country (OECD, 2002). Vissak and Roolaht (2005) note that the purpose of improving the balance of payments through the initial financial flows received is not always achieved in the long run. This can be explained by the repatriation of multinationals subsidiaries profits to their countries of origin (OECD, 2002; Hansen and Rand, 2006; Ozturk, 2007). Finally, another negative effect of FDI on growth is caused by the competition created in access to credit. Lim (2001), Carkovic and Levine (2002) and Sylwester, (2005) explain that multinationals are partly financed by the host countries financial markets. This increase the costs of credit and the access to credit changes. Chakraborty and Basu (2002) show that the problems in access to credit are mainly experienced by local firms which have a smaller structure, and then find it difficult to support the increased costs of credit, plus their weak bargaining power with financial institutions (compared to multinationals).

It seems that FDI plays an ambiguous role in economic growth (Greenaway and Kneller, 2007; Alguacil, 2011) with little support for the positive effect (Meyer, 2004). A recent literature survey by Bruno and Campos (2013) shows that 50% of empirical studies report a significantly positive effect of FDI on growth, 11% find a negative effect while 39% find growth to be independent of FDI.

The explanations for these conflicting results have pointed to methodological issues (Moran et al., 2005) and to the different absorptive capacity of host countries (Blomström, Kokko, and Mucchielli, 2003; Lipsey and Sjöholm, 2005). Empirical research seems to converge to the conclusion that the effect of FDI on economic growth is conditional on several local circumstances. The literature has identified the level of development (Blomstrom et al., 1994), trade openness (Balasubramanyam, 1996), human capital (Borensztein et al., 1998), financial development (Alfaro et al., 2004), the business environment (Busse et al., 2008) and the sector allocation (Aykut and Sayek, 2007) to influence the effect of FDI on growth.

Since the late 1990s there has been a growing consensus among researchers that recognize the role of institutions the "rules of the game" in shaping multinational corporations (MNCs) activities and the spillover effects they produce (North, 2005; Acemoglu et al., 2005; Dunning and Lundan, 2008)). Institutions, broadly defined, consist of informal constraints such as norms, culture, and customs, or the more purposive formal ones embodied in particular political rules and organizational structures.

Institutions could be seen as one channel through which FDI promotes economic growth. Acemoglu et al. (2002) and Cantwell et al. (2010) argue that institutional environment significantly varies the degree and even the direction of FDI impacts in the host economy. This institutions-based view on FDI is particularly relevant to developing countries where institutions differ significantly from those in developed countries and forcefully shape the way multinationals behave and interact with local sectors. Hoskisson et al. (2000) and Peng et al. (2008) argue that local institutions in terms of private property protection, legal and regulatory enforcement, product and intermediary market development, can moderate the various impacts of FDI on growth. More specifically, a more developed institutional setting motivates and facilitates both foreign and local firms to compete for output rationalization and curtails the negative impacts of FDI on growth (Wang et al. 2013). However, poor institutions can bring additional costs to FDI. This can be the case of corruption for instance (Wei, 2000). Likewise, due to high sunk costs, FDI is especially vulnerable to any form of uncertainty, including uncertainty stemming from poor government efficiency, policy reversals, graft or weak enforcement of property rights and of the legal system in general. Stein and Daude (2001) use five out of six governance indicators provided by Kaufmann et al. (1999) and show that inward FDI is significantly influenced by the quality of institutions like political instability and violence, regulatory burden, rule of law and graft. Using the same database Globerman and Shapiro (2002) find good governance to impact positively both on FDI inflows and outflows, although the latter effect is only significant for relatively big and developed countries. Furthermore, Azman-Saini et al. (2010) find that the effect of FDI on growth is contingent on the level of economic freedom in the host countries. They point out that countries which promote greater freedom of economic activities will gain significantly from the presence of multinational corporations (MNCs).

Along this strand of research, some studies have also been aimed to analyze the existence of an institutional threshold beyond which FDI impacts positively growth. Jude and Levieuge (2013) use a Panel Smooth Transition Regression (PSTR) for 94 developing countries over the period 1984-2009. They find that, democratic accountability and bureaucracy have an immediate effect on fostering FDI-led growth as opposite to internal and external conflict. They find that any effort above the threshold of 2.09 for law and order increase the elasticity of FDI on growth by 0.126. Using the same method of the PSTR, Brahim and Rachdi (2014) point for a sample of 19 MENA countries over the period 1984-2011, that any improvement made by the MENA region just below the threshold value of 0.006 for Investment profile and 0.206 for government stability is likely to result in a sharp increase of the elasticity of growth with respect to FDI. Meyer and Sinani (2009) estimate an institutional threshold (economic freedom and corruption) for the advanced and less advanced economies employing the mathematical derivative method. Their results show that FDI impacts positively growth if the level of economic freedom and corruption are above respectively the threshold of 56.6 and 5.69.

There are a number of studies investigating the role of institutions in conditioning the positive impact of FDI flows on growth (Ali et al., 2010; Buchanan et al., 2012). However there is very limited research dealing with the threshold effect of institutions in explaining the positive effect of FDI on growth by region and by level of income (high, middle and low income). Seeking to refine the growth effect of FDI, we investigate its conditionality on the institutional quality. In this paper we argue that a well-developed institutions enhance the overall benefits of FDI on economic growth. As, we consider institutional heterogeneity to be a plausible explanation for the different results of empirical studies.

Our research has several original features compared to the existing literature. The empirical analysis shows that institutional quality conditions the effect of FDI on economic growth more in the middle-income countries than in high income ones. Furthermore, we highlight the importance of heterogeneity in analyzing the FDI-growth relationship, as we divide the 5 groups of SSA, MENA, Europe, Asia and America by level of income to determine the institutional threshold level. The existence of such a threshold level allows us in the one hand to analyze the indirect effect of FDI on growth through institutions for countries that are below and above the institutional threshold. In the other hand to compare the effect of FDI on growth between high, middle and low income countries that are above the institutional threshold. We take into account twelve components of the institutional quality (from ICRG database) to analyze the most important institutional variables that condition the positive impact of FDI on growth

The paper is organized as follows. Section 2 presents the model and methodology being used. Section 3 presents the results of the threshold estimation of institutions and section 4 discusses the threshold of its components. Section 5 highlights the main conclusions.

2. MODEL AND METHODOLOGY

2.1. Model

To test the hypothesis of the threshold effect of institutions on the impact of FDI in economic growth, the following Eq.(1) is particularly well suited to capture the presence of contingency effects. It also offers a rich way of modelling the influence of the institutional development on the impact of FDI in economic growth. We use the dynamic panel threshold regression approach suggested by Kremer, Bick and Nautz (2013) to explore the nonlinear behavior of FDI in relation to the economic growth[1]. The model such as (1) is based on lessons drawn from the literature review. It has been used in the analysis of trade and growth (El Khoury and Savvides, 2006), knowledge spillovers (Falvey, Foster, and Greenaway, 2007), foreign direct investment and growth (Azman-Saini et al., 2010), and FDI and income inequality (Wu and Hsu, 2012), among other topics. This study adopts a macroeconomic approach. It does not take into account the financial variables as they are highly correlated with the institutional factors (Minea and Villieu, 2010; Ayadi et al., 2015).

The model based on the threshold regression takes the following form:

[1] Kremer, Bick and Nautz (2013) extend the Hansen (1999) original static panel threshold estimation and the Caner and Hansen (2004) cross-sectional instrumental variable (IV) threshold model, where generalized methods of moments (GMM) type estimators are used to deal with endogeneity.

$$Y_{it} = \mu_i + \alpha_1 Y_{it-1} + \alpha_2 G_{it} + \alpha_3 GFCF_{it} + \alpha_4 INFRA_{it} + \alpha_5 CREATION_{it} + \alpha_6 KH_{it} + \alpha_7 TRADE_{it} + \alpha_8 FDI_{it} + \boldsymbol{\beta_1 FDI_{it}} * \mathbf{I}(\boldsymbol{INST_{it}} \leq \boldsymbol{\gamma}) + \boldsymbol{\delta_1} * \mathbf{I}(\boldsymbol{INST_{it}} \leq \boldsymbol{\gamma}) + \boldsymbol{\beta_2 FDI_{it}} * \mathbf{I}(\boldsymbol{INST_{it}} > \boldsymbol{\gamma}) + \varepsilon_{it} \quad (1)$$

where i is country index and t is time index.

Y is the log of GDP (constant 2005 US$), FDI is the stock of foreign direct investment, net inflows in percentage of GDP. Using the share of GDP allows us to take into account the relative country size.

Table 1. Macroeconomic variables

LABEL	DESCRIPTION	SOURCES
Y_{it}	Gross Domestic Product at market prices (constant 2005 US$).	WDI, 2014
Institutions (INST)	The resulting index ranges between zero and 100 and a larger value means lower political risk. It is computed through an average of twelve different indicators from the ICRG database.	International Country Risk Guide (ICRG), 2014
FDI	Foreign Direct Investment: inward stock, in percentage of GDP. It is the value of the share of their capital and reserves (including retained profits) attributable to the parent enterprise, plus the net indebtedness of affiliates to the parent enterprises.	UNCTAD, 2014
GFCF	Gross Fixed Capital Formation (% of GDP). It includes land improvements (fences, ditches, drains, and so on); plant, machinery, equipment purchases; the construction of roads, railways, including schools, offices, hospitals, private residential dwellings, and commercial and industrial buildings. According to the 1993 SNA, net acquisitions of valuables are also considered capital formation.	WDI, 2014
Technology creation (CREATION)	-Number of patent grants per 1 million people -Number of publications in scientific and technical journals per 1 million people	WIPO, World Bank (WDI), 2014
TRADE	Trade is measured by trade in goods and services as a percentage of GDP at constant price	WDI, 2014
Government consumption (G)	General government final consumption expenditure includes all government current expenditures for purchases of goods and services. It also includes most expenditure on national defense and security, but excludes government military expenditures.	WDI, 2014
Human capital (HK)	-Literacy rate, adult total (% of people ages 15 and below) -Enrolment in tertiary education per 100,000 inhabitants -Mean years of schooling of adults	World Bank (WDI) UNESCO, UNDP, 2014
Technology Infrastructure (INFRA)	-Fixed broadband Internet subscribers per 100 people -Telephone fixed-lines per 100 people -Mobile cellular subscriptions per 100 people -Electric power consumption (kWh per capita)	WDI, 2014

INST is institutional quality measured by ICRG. This database, compiled by the Political Risk Services (PRS) Group, provides information on several risk indicators grouped in three categories: political, economic and financial risks. For the purpose of our study we use the economy index risk. In every case the lower the value, the higher the risk, and the higher the value the lower the risk. (See Table 4 for the description of the institutional variables). This database covers a long period of study beginning from 1984 as opposite to the Kaufmann database which begins from 1996. Although, the ICRG database includes a large number of variables (12), however Kaufmann database provides only 6 variables. INST is the threshold variable used to split the sample into regimes or groups and γ is the unknown threshold parameter. INST is the threshold variable used to split the sample into regimes or groups and γ is the unknown threshold parameter.

I(.) is the indicator function, which takes the value 1 if the argument in the indicator function is valid, and 0 otherwise. This type of modeling strategy allows the role of FDI to differ depending on whether institutions are below or above some unknown level of γ. In this equation, institutions act as sample-splitting (or threshold) variables. The impacts of FDI on growth will be β_1 and β_2 for countries with a low and high regime, respectively. Following Bick (2010), we allow for differences in the regime intercepts (δ1). The variable institution is considered as an endogenous variable.

X_{it} denotes the vector of explanatory regressors, which include lagged values of the dependent variable Y_{it}. These control variables are hypothesized to affect economic growth. These determinants are: human capital, technology creation, gross fixed capital formation, trade openness, government consumption (used as an indicator of fiscal policy). Their definitions are presented in Table 1. The entire variables are in logarithm. μ_i is unobserved country-specific effect term, and ε_{it} is a white noise error term.

The matrix of correlation (Table 1A, Appendix 1) indicates the correlation between the explanatory variables. Most of the correlation's coefficients are low: they are between 0.02 and 0.47. As the sign of the Pearson correlation coefficient is positive, we can conclude that there is a positive correlation between Government consumption, GFCF, infrastructure, creation, HK, institutions and FDI with growth. That is, growth increases with these variables. The variable CREATION is correlated with HK (0.50) and with INST (0.63). For this reason, we run the Variance Inflation Factor to test the muticolinearity of this variable (CREATION). Results point that the VIF of the variable CREATION is 2.15 (Table 1B, Appendix 1). It is less than 10, we conclude that there is no evidence of multicollinearity.

We use five groups of countries: SSA, MENA, Europe, America and Asia. Each group is divided into high, middle and low income countries according to the World Bank classification[2]. The list of countries is given in Appendix 1, Table 1C.

2.2. Methodology

2.2.1. Estimation of a threshold effect

According to Kremer et al. (2013), the standard within transformation and first differencing methods to eliminate the country-specific fixed effects in the

[2] According to the World Bank, low-income economies are defined as those with a GNI per capita, calculated using the World Bank Atlas method, of $1,045 or less in 2014; middle-income economies are those with a GNI per capita of more than $1,045 but less than $12,736; high-income economies are those with a GNI per capita of $12,736 or more.

dynamic panel are not applicable because both violate the distribution assumptions underlying Hansen (1999) and Caner and Hansen (2004). Thus, the forward orthogonal deviations transformation suggested by (Arellano and Bover, 1995) is used to eliminate the fixed effects. The unique feature of this transformation is that serial correlation of the transformed error terms is avoided and it maintains the uncorrelatedness of the error terms. This ensures that the estimation procedure derived by Caner and Hansen (2004) for a cross-sectional model can be applied to the dynamic panel specification such as Eq.(1).

Following Caner and Hansen (2004), there are three steps to estimate the specification coefficients. First, a reduced form regression is estimated for the endogenous variables INST, as a function of the instruments, Z_{it} by the ordinary least squares (OLS) approach and obtain the fitted values of $\hat{b}$ $INST_{it}$. Second, by substituting the predicted values of $\hat{b}$ $INST_{it}$ into Eq.(1) we estimate the threshold parameter k with the OLS method. Denote the resulting sum of squared residuals by S (k). This step is repeated for a strict subset of the support of the threshold variable INST. Finally the estimator of the threshold value k is selected as the one associated with the smallest sum of squared residuals, i.e

$\gamma\hat{} = \text{argmin } \gamma \ Sn(\gamma)$.

In accordance with Hansen (2000) and Caner and Hansen (2004), the critical values for determining the 95% confidence interval of the threshold value are given by

$\Gamma = \{\gamma : LR(\gamma) \leq C(\alpha)\}$,

where $C(\alpha)$ is the 95% percentile of the asymptotic distribution of the likelihood ratio statistic $LR(\gamma)$. The underlying likelihood ratio has been adjusted to account for the number of time periods used for each cross section (see Hansen, 2000). Once $\gamma\hat{}$ is determined, the slope coefficients can be estimated by the generalized method of moments (GMM) for the previously used instruments and the previous estimated threshold $\gamma\hat{}$.

2.2.2. Econometric methodology

This study employs a system generalized-method-of moment (GMM) panel estimator, which was finalized by Blundell and Bond (1998). This estimator is better over others because (i) it is able to control for the presence of unobserved country-specific effects and (ii) it is also able to control for a simultaneity bias caused by the potential endogeneity of the explanatory variables. To eliminate the country specific effect Arellano and Bond (1991) imply first-difference transformation of Equation (1) as follows:

$$\Delta y_{it} = \alpha(\Delta y_{it-1}) + \beta_1(\Delta FDI_{it}) + \beta_2(\Delta INST_{it}) + \beta_3[\Delta(FDI * INST)_{it}] + \beta_4(\Delta X_{it}) + \Delta\varepsilon_{it} \quad (2)$$

In order to address the issue of endogeneity and the correlation between $\Delta y_{it\text{-}1}$and $\Delta\varepsilon_{i,t}$, this problem can be solved by using higher-order lag of the regressors as instrument (Arellano and Bond, 1991). However, the validity of the moment conditions must be fulfilled to yield unbiased and consistent estimators. In fact, this econometric method has one serious limitation where instrumental variables are weak if the explanatory variables are persistent

(Alonso-Borrego and Arellano, 1999; Blundell and Bond, 1998). To overcome this limitation, system GMM estimator has been introduced by Arellano and Bover (1995). Two specification tests are employed to test the validity of the model. Firstly, the consistency of the system GMM estimator requires no second order serial correlation in difference error term εit. Next, would be Hansen test of over identifying restrictions. The Non-rejection of the null of both tests indicates that the model is correctly specified and the instruments are valid.

System GMM estimator uses lagged differences of y_{it} as instruments for equations in levels and lagged levels of y_{it} as instruments for equations in first differences. In our case, we use these instruments with other instruments built by the method of Lewbel (2012). In the first stage, each endogenous variable is regressed on the Z vector (Z is a subset of the exogenous X vector included in the regression and excluding the endogenous variables). Then the vector of residuals (Re) is retrieved. Finally Y is regressed on the explanatory variables. The instruments are computed as follow: Instrument_X= (X- E(X)) * residual, with E(X) the mean of X.

3. THE EFFECT OF FDI ON GDP GROWTH: ESTIMATION OF THE INSTITUTIONAL THRESHOLD

The threshold values for institutions and the effect of FDI on GDP growth is displayed in Table 2. Given the p-value of AR(2) and Sargan tests, we accept all specifications. The p-values suggest that, for all the five groups, low debt regime slope coefficient ($\beta 1$) is significantly different from high debt regime slope coefficient ($\beta 2$) and therefore the threshold estimates are significant.

Table 2. The effect of FDI nexus institutions on growth by region

VARIABLES	MENA (1)	MENA (2)	AMER (3)	AMER (4)	ASIA (5)	ASIA (6)	EUROPE (7)	EUROPE (8)	SSA (9)	SSA (10)
Y_{it-1}	0.679***	0.620***	0.806***	0.817***	0.927***	0.921***	0.820***	0.858***	0.869***	0.881***
	(0.0297)	(0.0695)	(0.0241)	(0.0222)	(0.0118)	(0.0113)	(0.0153)	(0.0201)	(0.0144)	(0.0126)
G	0.234**	0.491*	-0.144*	-0.141	-0.171***	-0.183***	-0.0650	0.122	-0.133**	-0.129***
	(0.111)	(0.275)	(0.0781)	(0.0883)	(0.0491)	(0.0518)	(0.0707)	(0.151)	(0.0561)	(0.0459)
GFCF	-0.276	-0.0450	0.227*	0.225*	0.0874	0.0753	0.0799	0.00694	0.0395	0.0416
	(0.221)	(0.162)	(0.135)	(0.124)	(0.0775)	(0.0738)	(0.0725)	(0.0847)	(0.0518)	(0.0426)
INFRA	0.915	1.526***	0.190	0.160	0.111	0.106	-0.00584	-0.00919	-0.00440	0.0175
	(0.711)	(0.418)	(0.252)	(0.241)	(0.0924)	(0.0978)	(0.180)	(0.245)	(0.0143)	(0.0170)
CREATION	-0.0384	0.039	-0.0119	-0.0311	0.110***	0.072***	0.0327**	0.0639***	0.051	-0.0266
	(0.0252)	(0.0310)	(0.0274)	(0.0270)	(0.0406)	(0.0234)	(0.0260)	(0.0242)	(0.0176)	(0.0146)
HK	0.486	0.961**	-0.0204	0.251	0.378***	0.239**	0.0215*	0.143*	0.0809	0.0341
	(0.411)	(0.394)	(0.302)	(0.349)	(0.131)	(0.190)	(0.235)	(0.368)	(0.0655)	(0.0582)
TRADE	0.294***	0.520**	0.515***	0.450***	0.096***	0.125***	0.426***	0.442***	0.180***	0.165***
	(0.108)	(0.232)	(0.0717)	(0.0720)	(0.0296)	(0.0332)	(0.0518)	(0.0571)	(0.0516)	(0.0461)
FDI	0.310	0.438	0.399	0.0975	0.256*	0.635*	0.421***	0.530*	-0.196***	-0.116**
	(0.464)	(0.708)	(0.253)	(0.373)	(0.188)	(0.151)	(0.130)	(0.656)	(0.0609)	(0.0558)
FDI*INST	0.575*		0.654		0.426*		0.601***		0.385***	
	(0.726)		(0.390)		(0.269)		(0.183)		(0.131)	
FDI*(INST<= γ)		-0.377		0.0847		-0.325*		0.811		-1.063*
		(0.189)		(0.0651)		(0.467)		(0.257)		(0.658)
FDI*(INST> γ)		0.051**		0.0787*		0.133*		0.117***		0.325***
		(0.0421)		(0.0432)		(0.174)		(0.737)		(0.0990)
δ1		-0.555*		0.0552		-0.460*		-0.455		4.996**
		(0.464)		(0.160)		(1.010)		(0.457)		(2.012)
Threshold γ		**0.54**		**0.63**		**0.60**		**0.70**		**0.51**
Constant	0.559***	0.243**	1.746***	1.755***	0.699***	0.537***	0.480***	1.272***	0.487***	0.244***
	(1.157)	(0.337)	(0.943)	(0.431)	(0.474)	(1.274)	(1.085)	(0.449)	(0.475)	(0.411)
Observations	608	608	992	992	1,065	1,065	1,312	1,312	1,024	1,024
Number of id	19	19	31	31	34	34	41	41	32	32
AR(2) P-value	0.206	0.359	0.171	0.630	0.186	0.475	0.398	0.172	0.453	0.516
Sargan P-value	0.130	0.146	0.584	0.498	0.498	0.390	0.260	0.179	0.175	0.146

*Standard errors in parentheses, *** p<0.01, ** p<0.05, * p<0.1.*

Table 2 summarizes the results for the MENA, America, Asia, Europe and SSA groups using the threshold regressions of equation 1. The results show that institutions mitigate the negative effect of FDI on growth for the SSA group (column 9). The coefficient of FDI is negative; it turns to be positive for this group when we introduce INST (institutions). For the MENA (column 1), Asia (column 5) and Europe (column 7), the improvement of the level of institutions makes the impact of FDI on growth higher. It can be seen through the coefficient of the interaction (FDI*INST) as it becomes significant in the MENA region. For the Asia and the Europe group the additional effect of institutions on FDI has increased the impact of FDI on growth from 0.256 to 0.541 in the Asia group, and from 0.385 to 0.601 in the Europe group. The positive sign of the interaction (FDI*INST) means that the benefit of FDI is higher with a better institutional environment. Host countries should decrease the political risk in their countries to benefit more from FDI. Such a policy in a host country would generate a favorable environment for the spillover effects stemming from multinational companies to domestic companies. Also, the contribution of multinational companies would be easier and higher in a favorable business environment.

Table 3. The effect of threshold of institutions by income on FDI and growth by region

VARIABLES	MENA (1)	America (2)	Asia (3)	Europe (4)	SSA (5)
FDI	0.112	0.490	0.488**	0.228*	-0.0325*
	(0.129)	(0.285)	(0.606)	(0.0453)	(0.0229)
FDI*(INST ≤ ɣ)_high income			-		
FDI*(INST > ɣ)_high income			0.979**		
			(0.790)		
FDI*(INST ≤ ɣ)_middle income	0.070	-0.725	-0.809**	0.0107	1.646
	(0.482)	(0.934)	(0.552)	(0.146)	(1.110)
FDI*(INST > ɣ)_middle income	0.241*	0.564**	0.327*	0.572**	0.266***
	(0.377)	(0.753)	(1.779)	(0.267)	(0.0840)
Number of id	19	31	34	41	32

MENA region

According to the regression of the MENA region, FDI impacts positively growth only for countries with an institutional level (INST) above the threshold of 0.54 (column 2). Therefore 14 of the 19 countries in the regression pass the threshold (Figure 1). Conversely, FDI has a negative but a non significant effect on growth for 5 of the 19 countries in the sample (Algeria, Iraq, Lebanon, Libya and West Bank and Gaza). For these countries, the low level of institutions[3] (below 0.54) impedes them from the benefit of FDI on growth. This means that the existence of high political instability leads for example to corruption and restrain countries to benefit from FDI. For example, during the period 1984-2013, Iraq and Lebanon had the lowest level of institutions (0.39 and 0.43 respectively). More precisely, it is due to high level of corruption and others forms of cronyism.

[3] Lower level of institutions means higher level of political instability.

This means that institutions are important factors in influencing the effect of foreign direct investment on growth. A minimum level of institutions (0.54) is required in the MENA region to get a positive and significant effect of FDI on growth.

Table 3 presents a summary of the effect of FDI nexus institutions by income on growth for countries above and below the threshold of institutions. Details of the results including all explanatory variables are presented in Table 2A in Appendix 2. In Table 3 we compare between high, middle and low income countries that are above and beyond the threshold level of institutions. Results for the MENA region (column 1) confirm that the effect of FDI on growth is higher in the middle income countries than in the high income countries (0.241**) when the level of institutions is above 0.54.

Figure 1: Threshold level of institution in the MENA region

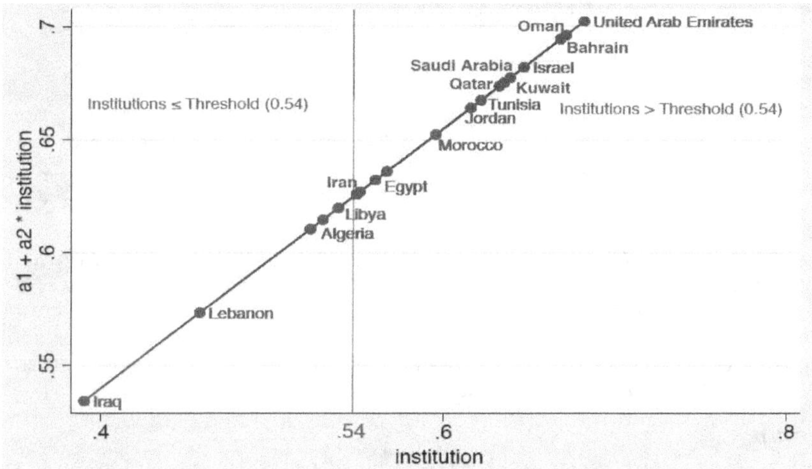

Countries below 0.54* (5 countries): High income: none, Middle income: Algeria, Iraq, Lebanon, Libya, West Bank and Gaza. **Countries above 0.54 (14 countries): High income: Bahrain, Israel, Kuwait, Oman, Qatar, Saudi Arabia, United Arab Emirates. Middle income: Egypt, Iran, Jordan, Morocco, Syria, Tunisia, Yemen.*

We conclude that for the MENA region institutions raise the effect of FDI on growth as the additional effect of institutions makes the effect of FDI on growth higher. The estimation of the threshold of institutions shows that the effect is positive only for countries, which are above the institutional threshold of 0.54. Furthermore, taking into account the level of income indicates that institutions are more important for FDI in the middle income countries than in the high income countries.

America group

For the America group, institutions add a positive and significant effect to the impact of FDI on growth (0.0787) only for countries above the institutional threshold of 0.63 (Table 2, column 4). Only 15 of 31 countries pass the threshold (Figure 2). We point that, the interaction (FDI*INST) is not significant (Table 2, column 3), but the fact that we divide the sample into countries that are below and above the threshold highlight that the effect is only positive for countries above the institutional threshold of 0.63. Furthermore, in Table 3 column (2), the effect of FDI on growth is bigger in the middle income countries than in the high income countries when the level of institutions is higher than 0.63.

Figure 2: Threshold level of institutions in the America group

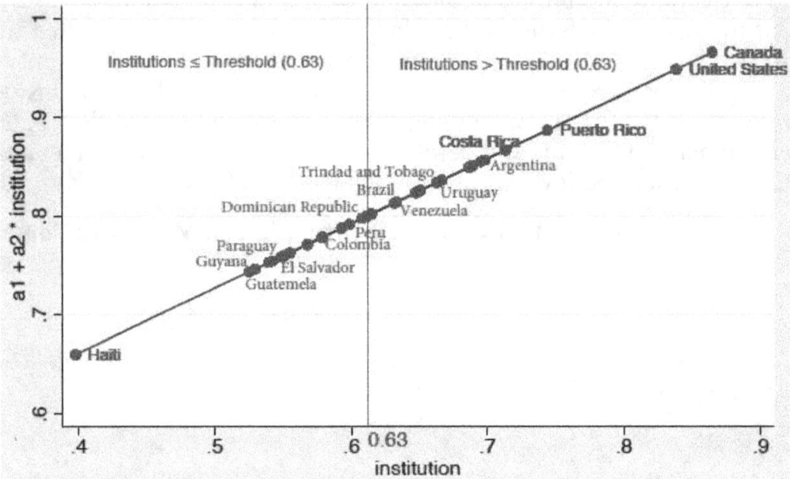

Countries below 0.63 (16 countries): High income: none, Middle income: Bolivia, Colombia, Cuba, Dominican Republic, Ecuador, El Salvador, Guatemala, Guyana, Honduras, Nicaragua, Panama, Paraguay, Peru, St. Vincent and the Grenadines, Suriname. **Countries above 0.63 (15 countries): High income: Canada, Chile, Puerto Rico, St. Kitts and Nevis, Trinidad and Tobago, United States, Uruguay. Middle income: Argentina, Brazil, Costa Rica, Dominica, Jamaica, Mexico, St. Lucia, Venezuela.*

Asia group

In the Asia group, institutions almost double the positive effect of FDI on growth (Table 2, column 5). More precisely the positive effect of FDI on growth appears on countries that are above the threshold institutions of 0.60 (column 6). Only 14 of 34 countries are above the threshold (Figure 3). When institutions are higher than 0.60, the effect of FDI on growth is higher in the high income countries than in the low income countries (Table 3). Furthermore, when institutions are below 0.60, the negative effect of FDI on growth is higher in the low income countries than in the middle income countries.

SSA group

In the SSA group (Table 2, column 9), institutions (INST) mitigate the negative effect of FDI on growth. One percent increase in FDI increases the GDP growth by 0.32 percent if the level of institutions is above 0.50 which represents the mean value of institutions (column 10). Ajide et al., (2014) find the same results for 27 countries of SSA. They show that FDI impacts positively growth if the level of governance is higher than its mean value. Now, if we consider countries that are below the level of institutions 0.5, the effect of FDI on growth is negative. It is the case for 13 of 32 countries (Figure 4).

Figure 3: Threshold level of institution in the Asia group

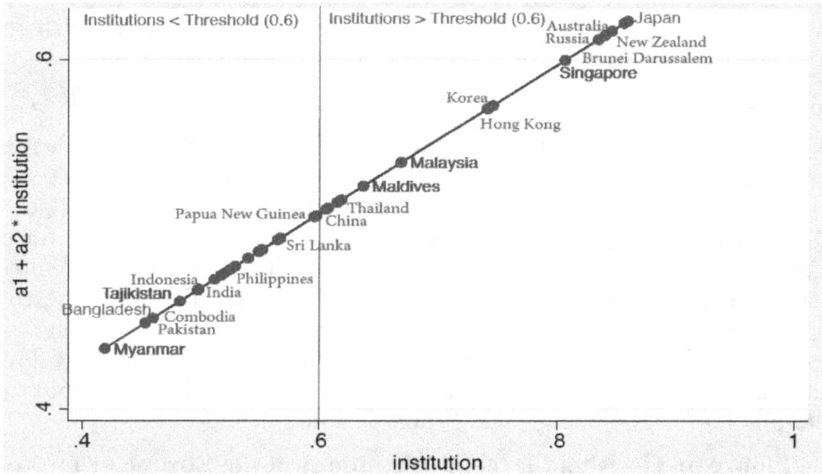

Countries below 0.6 (20 countries): High income: none, Middle income: India, Indonesia, Kazakhstan, Kyrgyz Republic, Mongolia, Pakistan, Papua New Guinea, Philippines, Solomon Islands, Sri Lanka, Timor-Leste, Turkmenistan, Uzbekistan, Vanuatu, Vietnam. Low Income: Bangladesh, Cambodia, Myanmar, Nepal, Tajikistan.* ***Countries above 0.6* *(14 countries): High income: Australia, Brunei Darussalam, Hong Kong, Ireland, Japan, Korea, New Zealand, Russia, Singapore. Middle income: China, Malaysia, Maldives, Thailand, Tonga.*

Figure 4: Threshold level of institution in the SSA group

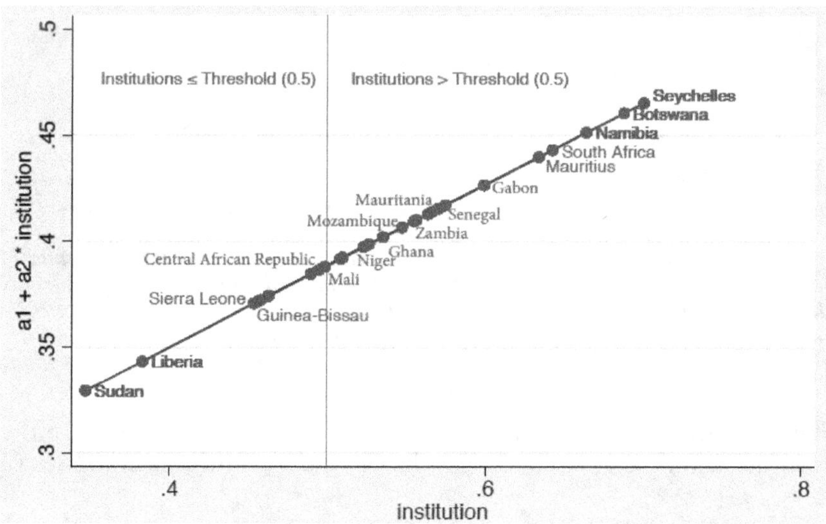

Countries below 0.5: Middle income: Nigeria, Sudan. Low Income: Central African Republic, Ethiopia, Guinea, Guinea-Bissau, Liberia, Mali, Niger, Rwanda, Sierra Leone, Togo, Uganda.* ***Countries above 0.5**: Middle Income: Botswana, Cameroon, Gabon, Ghana, Mauritania, Mauritius, Namibia, Senegal, Seychelles, South Africa, Swaziland, Zambia. Low income: Burkina Faso, Kenya, Madagascar, Malawi, Mozambique, Tanzania, Zimbabwe.*

The effect of FDI on growth becomes positive, once the level of institution is above 0.5. This positive effect is higher in the middle income than in the low countries (Table 3). Results explain that institutions are important in the effect of FDI on growth in the middle income countries that are above 0.50.

Europe group

For the Europe group, FDI has a positive effect. The additional effect of institutions, increase the impact of FDI on growth (Table 2, column 7). Like in the other groups, the threshold level of institutions condition the positive effect of FDI on growth. In this case, FDI contributes positively to growth for countries that are above the institutional threshold of 0.70. There are 27 countries of 41 that are above the threshold (see Figure 5). We highlight that the Europe group has the highest level of institutions, so the latter increase the effect of FDI on growth. In fact, the Europe group has achieved a high and stable level of institutions. Other factors like technology (creation) and human capital (HK) are determinant for FDI and growth (Table 2, column 7 and 8).

Figure 5: Threshold level of institutions in the Europe group

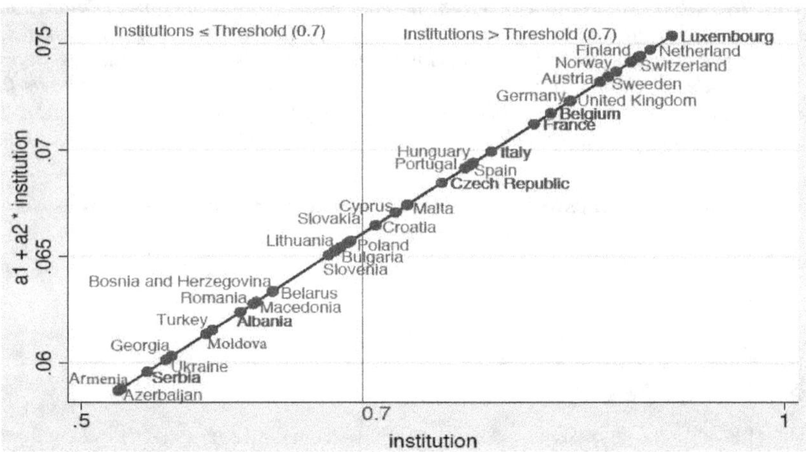

****Countries below 0.7**: High income: Estonia, Latvia, Lithuania, Poland, Slovenia. Middle Income: Albania, Armenia, Azerbaijan, Belarus, Bosnia and Herzegovina, Bulgaria, Georgia, Macedonia, Moldova, Romania, Serbia, Turkey, Ukraine. **Countries above 0.7**: High Income: Austria, Belgium, Croatia, Cyprus, Czech Republic, Denmark, Finland, France, Germany, Greece, Iceland, Italy, Luxembourg, Malta, Netherlands, Norway, Portugal, Slovakia, Spain, Sweden, Switzerland, United Kingdom. Middle income: Hungary.*

When the level of institutions is above 0.7 the effect of FDI on growth is higher in the middle income countries than in the high income countries (Table 3).

We conclude that FDI is not affected by the same level of institutions in the different groups. In fact, the effect of institutions is different across the groups and by level of income. Results show that the effect of institutions is more important in the middle income countries. Institutional quality is an important precondition for the positive effect of FDI on growth. This finding is consistent with (Azman-Saini et al., 2010), (Alfaro et al., 2004), (Durham, 2004),

(Borensztein et al., 1998) , among many others, who also find that the impact of FDI on growth depends on other conditions available in the host countries. FDI targeting strategies should therefore take into account the differentiated aspects that matter for FDI.

After studying the overall effect of the institutional threshold on FDI, we focus now on the components of this variable institutions in order to measure the threshold of each component that allows FDI to affect positively growth.

4. THE EFFECT OF THE SUBCOMPONENTS OF INSTITUTIONS NEXUS FDI ON GROWTH

The institutional variable "INST" is composed of 12 variables. These variables are: Government Stability, Socioeconomic Conditions, Investment Profile, Internal Conflict, External Conflict, Corruption, Military in Politics, Religious Tensions, Law and Order, Ethnic Tensions, Democratic Accountability and Bureaucracy Quality. Table 4 presents the definitions of the 12 components of the variable institutions (INST).

Table 4. The 12 components of the variable institutions (INST)

Label	Description	Sources
Government Stability	Measures the government's ability to carry out its policies and to stay in office.	PRS-ICRG (2014)
Socio-economic Conditions	Captures socio–economic pressures at work in society that might restrain government action or elevate social dissatisfaction and thus destabilize the political regime.	PRS-ICRG (2014)
Investment Profile	Assess the investment profile, that is, factors related to the risk of investment that are not covered by other (financial and economic) risk components, such as contract viability (expropriation), profits repatriation or payment delays.	PRS-ICRG (2014)
Internal Conflict	Stands for internal conflict, measuring political violence within the country and its actual or potential impact on governance by focusing on, for instance, civil war, terrorism, political violence or civil disorder.	PRS-ICRG (2014)
External Conflict	Weight external conflict, namely the risk to the incumbent government from foreign action, ranging from non-violent external pressure, such as diplomatic pressure, with holding aid or trade sanctions, to violent external pressures, ranging from cross-border conflicts to all-out war	PRS-ICRG (2014)
Corruption	It evaluates the degree of corruption within the political system	PRS-ICRG (2014)
Military in Politics	Represents the influence of the military in politics, which could signal that the government is unable to function effectively, therefore, the country might have unfavorable environment for business	PRS-ICRG (2014)
Religious Tensions	Measures religious tensions, stemming from the domination of society and/or governance by a single religious group seeking, for instance, to replace civil by religious law or to exclude other religious from the political and social press	PRS-ICRG (2014)
Law and Order	Quantifies Law and Order, that is, the strength and impartiality of the legal system.	PRS-ICRG (2014)
Ethnic Tensions	Assesses the degree of tensions among ethnic groups attributable to racial, nationality or languages divisions.	PRS-ICRG (2014)
Democratic Accoun-tability	Relates the democratic accountability of the government, that is, the responsiveness of the government to its citizens, but also to fundamental civil liberties and political rights.	PRS-ICRG (2014)
Bureaucracy Quality	Stands for the institutional strength and quality of the bureaucracy, which might act as a shock absorber tending to reduce policy revisions if governments change.	PRS-ICRG (2014)

Table 5 summarizes the threshold effect of institutions nexus FDI for the five regions using the twelve institutional variables. The details of the other explanatory variables are presented in Table 2B, 2C, 2D, 2E and 2F in Appendix 2. As an attempt to evaluate the individual effect of institutions on GDP growth and to avoid problems caused by multi-collinearity, we estimate equation (1) adding each institutional variable in succession. This approach was used in the literature by Walsh and Yu (2010).

Results indicate that FDI has a positive effect on growth for the MENA, America and the SSA groups when they are above the threshold level of government stability (column 1). The stability of government allows investors to have a warranty on the viability of their business project at least in the short term. This promotes the goals set by the investor and reduces political risks. Conversely, government instability exhibits the investors to very high risk (changes in laws, conventions or agreements), which can increase costs. We notice that, the coefficient is higher in the MENA region, which means that in case of government stability, the effect of FDI on growth is higher in the MENA region than in the SSA group or the America group. Improving government stability by one point will have an additional effect on growth by 0.24 percent in the MENA region if the level of government stability is higher than 0.42, and by 0.011 percent in the America group if the level of government stability is higher than 0.38. Our results are confirmed in the work of Brahim and Rachdi (2014). They found a threshold level for government stability of 0.5 for the MENA region, which is lower than our threshold (0.54). This difference can be explained by the sample that includes Sudan and Turkey, also by the method of PSTR used to estimate the threshold. Furthermore, in our estimation we take into account the effect for countries that are below and above the institutional threshold to get a clear idea about the effect of FDI on growth.

Table 5. Summary of the effect of FDI nexus institutions

		Government Stability (1)	Socieco. Conditions (2)	Investment Profile (3)	External Conflict (4)	Internal Conflict (5)	Corruption (6)	Military in Politics (7)	Religious Tensions (8)	Law and Order (9)	Ethnic Tensions (10)	Democratic Account. (11)	Bureaucracy Quality (12)
MENA	FDI	**-0.026**	**-0.027**	-0.054*	-0.055**	-0.018	**-0.017**	-0.013	-0.002	**-0.0514***	-0.017	-0.038	**-0.049***
	FDI*(INST≤ γ)	**-0.911***	**0.603**	0.380	-0.359	1.605	**0.060**	0.486	-0.132	**-0.271***	0.160	-0.472	**-0.233***
	FDI*(INST> γ)	**0.243***	**0.015***	0.027	0.0147	-0.015	**0.026***	0.018	0.001	**0.034***	-0.004	0.014	**0.021***
AMERICA	FDI	**0.022**	0.016	0.004	-0.005	0.010	-0.015	-0.010	0.020*	**0.021**	0.017	0.020*	0.010
	FDI*(INST≤ γ)	**0.006**	-0.025	-0.061	-0.006	-0.23***	0.056	0.041	0.241***	**-0.95*****	0.034	-0.033	0.272
	FDI*(INST> γ)	**0.0111***	0.001	-0.0061	0.001	-0.006	-0.001	0.005	-0.010	**0.029***	0.083*	-0.005	0.005
ASIA	FDI	0.0152	0.184	-0.017	**-0.018**	0.272***	0.075	**-0.200***	0.102	0.094	0.051	**-0.038**	0.288
	FDI*(INST≤ γ)	0.129	0.748	-0.271	**1.328**	-0.128	0.057	**-0.080***	0.799	0.534	0.071	**-0.089**	-0.386
	FDI*(INST> γ)	0.007	0.124	0.0537	**0.110***	0.030	0.022	**0.044***	0.0314	0.009	0.027	**0.070***	-0.017
SSA	FDI	**-0.030****	**0.003**	-0.032*	-0.016	**-0.025***	**-0.003**	-0.011	-0.017	-0.011	-0.015	**-0.04*****	**-0.006**
	FDI*(INST≤ γ)	**-1.84*****	**0.977**	-1.162**	-0.90***	**-0.184**	**-0.200**	1.564	0.136	-0.89***	-0.817	**0.209**	**-0.537***
	FDI*(INST> γ)	**0.019*****	**0.011***	0.027	0.008	**0.0145***	**0.014****	-0.002	-0.012	0.001	0.011	**0.022*****	**0.011***
EUROPE	FDI	0.068***	**0.019**	0.078***	0.107***	**0.171*****	0.044***	0.056***	0.049***	**0.055*****	0.042***	**-0.005**	**0.028****
	FDI*(INST≤ γ)	-0.22***	**-0.005**	0.055	-0.14***	**-0.28*****	0.118	0.009	0.0231	**-0.032**	-0.056	**0.014**	**0.079**
	FDI*(INST> γ)	0.006	**0.022****	-0.001	0.032	**0.034*****	0.002	0.004	0.009	**0.014***	0.017	**0.009*****	**0.015*****

** Values in bold indicate the most significant institutional mechanisms that condition the positive impact of FDI on growth. Standard errors *** p<0.01, ** p<0.05, * p<0.1.*

Socio-economic condition can be also a mechanism through which FDI impacts growth. In this case, pressures at work and social dissatisfaction could restrain the activity of the foreign investors. In some cases it could even stop for a few months the project so government cannot profit from this investment. Results of Table 5 indicate that the effect of FDI on growth is higher in the Europe group than in the MENA region and the SSA group when they are above the critical value of socioeconomic conditions of 0.37, 0.35 and 0.11 respectively (column 2). We note that the level of socioeconomic conditions is the highest in the Europe group.

For control of corruption, FDI has a negative effect on growth in the MENA region (Table 5, column 6). But, the additional effect of fighting against corruption makes the impact of FDI on growth positive and significant when the level of corruption is higher than 0.30. It is the same case in the SSA group when corruption is higher than 0.15. Ajide et al., (2014) find a threshold level of corruption for 27 countries of SSA above which FDI impacts positively growth. We highlight that the effect on growth is higher in the MENA region than in the SSA group when they are above the threshold of 0.30 and 0.15 respectively. McCloud and Kumbhakar (2012) find evidence that controlling for corruption reduces the magnitude of unobserved heterogeneity in the FDI–growth relationship. Indeed, developing countries have not the same threshold above which control of corruption has a positive effect on FDI-growth. Results highlight the threshold effect of corruption in explaining these ambiguous outcomes. In case of corruption, the benefits of FDI are diverted for the profit of specific groups (Oligarchy). Meisel and Aoudia (2007) describe this group of insider or interest group. In this case the benefit of FDI will not reach growth.

The effect of FDI on growth becomes positive in case of the variable Law and Order (column 9). The strength and impartiality of the legal system prevent the misappropriation of funds by the group of insiders. They act as a guarantee for the foreign investors as they favor the application of the clauses stated in the contract. They form together a mechanism for growth to benefit easily from FDI. This effect is confirmed if the level of Law and Order is above the threshold of 0.25 for the MENA region, 0.20 for the America group and 0.28 for the Europe group. A one percent improve in FDI will have an additional effect on growth by 0.002 percent in the MENA region (if Law and Order is higher than 0.25), 0.014 in the Europe group (if Law and Order is higher than 0.5) and the highest improve is in the America group by 0.029 percent (if Law and Order is higher than 0.20). However, if the level of Law and Order is weak in the MENA region (below 0.25) and in the America group (below 0.20), FDI impacts negatively growth. In fact, Busse and Groizard (2008), clarify that restrictive employment laws (hiring and firing of employees) create a weak labor market turnover that limits domestic firms gains from technology spillovers. Other type of government regulation can lead to the same results. For example ensuring creditor rights and enforcement of contracts are hard to apply due to high uncertainty, long periods of investment and great expenses. This result may reduce investment in the host country, which lower productivity related to the exploitation of technology spillovers from FDI inflows.

Bureaucracy mitigates the negative effect of FDI on growth for the MENA region and the SSA group when the level of bureaucracy is higher than respectively 0.26 and 0.2 (column 12). For the Europe group, improving the quality of bureaucracy, raise the positive effect of FDI on growth from 0.028 to 0.045. Indeed, this institutional variable measures the ability of bureaucracy to resist to political change that is the stability of administrative procedures. The more the government is stable despite the political changes and the less FDI will be impacted. In contrary, the instability of bureaucracy exposes investors to downturns and often changes in the administrative procedures. This result in an additional cost for investors and limit the achievement of targets set by the foreign investors. So, the impact on growth will be limited (less tax payment). If doing business is subject to many bureaucratic procedures (requiring time and resources), then FDI flows can be prevented from being reallocated to the most productive sectors (Busse and Groizard, 2008).

Aidt and Gassebner (2010) point that democracy is associated with more trade liberalization. The latter leads to a more competitive environment on local market. Higher competitiveness between domestic firms improves their resource allocation and upper efficiency. Indeed, democracy guarantees an enforcement of property rights and the risk of expropriation for foreign investor (Harms and Ursprung, 2002; Jensen, 2008; Jensen, 2003). Our results point that democracy is an important mechanism through which FDI impacts growth for the Asia, and the Europe group (column 12). These results are confirmed if the level of democracy is higher than the threshold of 0.5 for the Asia group, 0.17 for the SSA group and 0.48 for the Europe group. Once the SSA and the Europe group are above their critical values of democracy, the effect of FDI on growth is higher in the middle income than in the high income group.

Results show that for the MENA region, above the threshold of the institutional variables like government stability, fighting against corruption, the respect of law and order and less bureaucracy enable the country to benefit from FDI . As opposite to the America group in which to draw advantage from FDI they should improve government stability, ethnic tension and law and order. It is government stability and democracy that matter most for the SSA group, external conflict and democracy for the Asia group, socioeconomic conditions, law and order and bureaucracy for the Europe group. Values in bold in Table 5 indicates that, the five variables such as: government stability, socioeconomic conditions, law and order, democratic accountability and bureaucracy quality, are the most important institutional variables to benefit from FDI for the 3 groups out of five in this study. Our results confirm the work of Júlio, Pinheiro-Alves, and Tavares (2013). They also find that these variables are important to benefit from FDI.

5. CONCLUSION

The aim of this paper is to test the indirect effect of FDI on growth through institutions for the 5 groups: MENA, Europe, America, Asia and SSA divided into high, middle and low income countries. Our main conclusion is that institutional quality differently modulates the effect of FDI on economic growth for the five groups. This difference is due to the institutional level and to the level of income of each group. It depends also if the group has reached the institutional threshold. Furthermore, the magnitude of the indirect effect of FDI on growth through institutions depends on the level of income.

The global effect of the interaction between FDI and institutions can hide specific effect of FDI on growth for countries that are below and above the steady state. The method of Caner and Hansen (2004) allows us to divide the region into countries that are above and below the critical-value. Our results highlight the importance of taking into consideration countries that are below and above the threshold level of institutions as it gives a clear idea beyond which level of institutions FDI impacts positively growth.

The magnitudes of the effect of FDI nexus institutions on growth are non-uniform across country groups. The critical value of institutions explains the difference between the groups. A minimum level of institutions is required for the positive impact of FDI on growth. It is found that FDI enhances growth through government stability, socioeconomic conditions, law and order, democratic accountability and bureaucracy quality for three out of the five groups.

Furthermore, a group of countries can be above the institutional threshold level but belongs to different level of income. Results highlight that even if countries are above the institutional threshold, the effect of FDI on growth can be different. This difference is due to the income level of countries. Indeed, above the global institutional level, the positive impact of FDI on growth is more important in the middle income countries than in the high income countries (Nawaz, 2015). However, this result is different depending on the institutional variable. For example, for countries of the MENA region and the Europe group, which have a level of bureaucracy above the threshold, the positive impact of FDI on growth is greater in the middle income countries than in the high income. Nevertheless, above the steady state of the variable corruption, the positive impact of FDI on growth in the MENA region and the Asia group is more important in the high income countries.

Furthermore, we point that some features of institutional quality could pay-off faster in terms of marginal effect of FDI on growth. Therefore, priority should be given to these specific features, as further institutional complementarities would eventually lead to an incremental effect on FDI and growth.

The estimation of a threshold level of institutional quality that conditions the positive effect of FDI on growth highlight that policies will have no benefit for host countries unless there is an improvement of their institutional framework. The finding of "better institutions (above threshold) attract more FDI" should also encourage policy makers to upgrade the local institutional environment before engaging in FDI attraction policies.

APPENDIX 1

Table 1A. Matrix of correlation

	Yit-1	G	GFCF	INFRA	CREATION	HK	TRADE	INST	FDI
Yit-1	1.000								
G	0.073	1.000							
GFCF	0.101	0.133	1.000						
INFRA	0.111	0.022	-0.037	1.000					
CREATION	0.496	0.376	0.179	0.044	1.000				
HK	0.307	0.214	0.219	-0.282	0.503	1.000			
TRADE	-0.101	0.134	0.160	-0.089	0.133	0.226	1.000		
INST	0.471	0.239	0.254	-0.044	0.630	0.433	0.149	1.000	
FDI	0.025	0.024	0.069	-0.031	0.205	0.200	0.264	0.212	1.000

Table 1B. Variance Inflation Factor (VIF)

Variable	VIF	1/VIF
CREATION	2.15	0.46
INST	1.79	0.55
HK	1.51	0.66
G	1.19	0.83
TRADE	1.17	0.85
FDI	1.16	0.86
GFCF	1.10	0.91
INFRA	1.09	0.91
Mean VIF	1.39	

Table 1C. List of countries

Group	Level of income	List of countries
MENA	High income	Bahrain, Israel, Kuwait, Oman, Qatar, Saudi Arabia, United Arab Emirates
	Middle income	Algeria, Egypt, Iran, Iraq, Jordan, Lebanon, Libya, Morocco, Syria, Tunisia, West Bank and Gaza, Yemen
Europe	High income	Austria, Belgium, Croatia, Cyprus, Czech Republic, Denmark, Estonia, Finland, France, Germany, Greece, Iceland, Italy, Latvia, Lithuania, Luxembourg, Malta, Netherlands, Norway, Poland, Portugal, Slovakia, Slovenia, Spain, Sweden, Switzerland, United Kingdom
	Middle income:	Albania, Armenia, Azerbaijan, Belarus, Bosnia and Herzegovina, Bulgaria, Georgia, Hungary, Macedonia, Moldova, Romania, Serbia, Turkey, Ukraine
America	High income	Canada, Chile, Puerto Rico, St. Kitts and Nevis, Trinidad and Tobago, United States, Uruguay
	Middle income	Argentina, Bolivia, Brazil, Colombia, Costa Rica, Cuba, Dominica, Dominican Rep., Ecuador, El Salvador, Guatemala, Guyana, Honduras, Jamaica, Mexico, Nicaragua, Panama, Paraguay, Peru, St. Lucia, St. Vincent and the Grenadines, Suriname, Venezuela
Asia	High income	Australia, Brunei Darussalam, Hong Kong, Ireland, Japan, Korea, New Zealand, Russia, Singapore
	Middle income	China, India, Indonesia, Kazakhstan, Kyrgyz Republic, Malaysia, Maldives, Mongolia, Pakistan, Papua New Guinea, Philippines, Solomon Islands, Sri Lanka, Thailand, Timor-Leste, Tonga, Turkmenistan, Uzbekistan, Vanuatu, Vietnam
	Low Income	Bangladesh, Cambodia, Nepal, Myanmar, Tajikistan
SSA	Middle income	Botswana, Cameroon, Gabon, Ghana, Mauritania, Mauritius, Namibia, Nigeria, Senegal, Seychelles, South Africa, Sudan, Swaziland, Zambia
	Low Income	Burkina Faso, Central African Republic, Ethiopia, Guinea, Guinea-Bissau, Kenya, Liberia, Madagascar, Malawi, Mali, Mozambique, Niger, Rwanda, Sierra Leone, Tanzania, Togo, Uganda, Zimbabwe

APPENDIX 2

Table 2A. The effect of threshold of institutions by income on FDI and growth by region

VARIABLES	MENA (1)	America (2)	Asia (3)	Europe (4)	SSA (5)
Y_{it-1}	0.730***	0.986***	0.930***	0.832***	0.855***
	(0.0624)	(0.352)	(0.0472)	(0.0162)	(0.0151)
G	0.262*	0.0233	0.687*	-0.133	-0.176***
	(0.139)	(0.519)	(0.385)	(0.0873)	(0.0606)
GFCF	-0.149	0.625	1.110**	0.136	0.0560
	(0.220)	(1.672)	(0.485)	(0.0905)	(0.0436)
INFRA	1.740***	0.144	1.110*	0.507**	-0.005
	(0.459)	(0.830)	(0.632)	(0.203)	(0.0158)
CREATION	-0.0196	-0.375	-0.153	0.0980***	-0.0692***
	(0.0354)	(0.677)	(0.147)	(0.0370)	(0.0259)
HK	-0.899**	3.104	-1.122	0.736**	-0.00824
	(0.401)	(5.921)	(0.826)	(0.339)	(0.0651)
TRADE	-0.142	-0.199	-0.126	0.460***	-0.235***
	(0.235)	(0.618)	(0.106)	(0.0587)	(0.0538)
FDI	-0.112	0.490	0.488**	-0.002	-0.0325
	(0.129)	(0.285)	(0.606)	(0.0453)	(0.028)
FDI*(INST<= ɣ)_high income			-		
FDI*(INST>ɣ)_high income			0.979**		
			(0.790)		
FDI*(INST<= ɣ)_middle income	0.070	-0.725	-0.809**	-0.0107	1.646
	(0.482)	(0.934)	(0.552)	(0.146)	(0.110)
FDI*(INST>ɣ)_middle income	0.241*	0.564**	0.327*	0.572**	0.266***
	(0.377)	(0.753)	(0.779)	(0.267)	(0.0840)
δ_1	-0.276**	-0.861	-1.801	-0.142	-0.905**
	(0.107)	(1.464)	(1.160)	(0.262)	(1.989)
Constant	0.459*	0.417*	1.448***	0.862***	0.245**
	(0.269)	(0.590)	(0.391)	(0.434)	(0.314)
Observations	608	992	1,065	1,312	1,024
Number of id	19	31	34	41	32
AR(2) P-value	0.177	0.171	0.142	0.211	0.159
Sargan P-value	0.157	0.160	0.156	0.131	0.216

*Standard errors in parentheses *** p<0.01, ** p<0.05, * p<0.1*

Table 2B. The effect of FDI nexus institutions on growth for the MENA region

Institutional Variables	Govern-ment Stability	Socio-economic Condi-tions	Internal Conflict	External Conflict	Invest-ment profile	Corrup-tion	Military in Politics	Religious Tensions	Law and Order	Ethnic Tensions	Demo-cratic Ac-counta-bility	Bureau-cracy Quality
	(1)	(2)	(3)	(4)	(5)	(6)	(7)	(8)	(9)	(10)	(11)	(12)
Y_{it-1}	0.975***	0.951***	0.944***	0.903***	0.963***	0.952***	0.948***	0.958***	0.952***	0.935***	0.974***	0.922***
	(0.0299)	(0.0227)	(0.0368)	(0.0276)	(0.0207)	(0.0251)	(0.0237)	(0.0332)	(0.0321)	(0.0347)	(0.0333)	(0.0269)
G	0.00686	0.0930	0.114	0.226**	0.0358	0.147	0.145	0.0400	0.0387	0.177	-0.0490	0.191**
	(0.109)	(0.0868)	(0.118)	(0.107)	(0.0937)	(0.108)	(0.105)	(0.112)	(0.126)	(0.110)	(0.137)	(0.0969)
GFCF	0.0220	-0.0414	-0.166**	-0.150*	0.0260	-0.0685	-0.0758	0.0317	-0.208**	-0.0547	-0.158	-0.123
	(0.0738)	(0.0782)	(0.0758)	(0.0882)	(0.0570)	(0.0911)	(0.0851)	(0.0685)	(0.0944)	(0.0816)	(0.106)	(0.104)
INFRA	0.234	0.362**	0.552**	0.730***	0.275*	0.467***	0.381**	0.307*	0.476**	0.637***	0.453**	0.655***
	(0.199)	(0.141)	(0.227)	(0.197)	(0.147)	(0.174)	(0.150)	(0.158)	(0.213)	(0.232)	(0.230)	(0.182)
CREATION	0.000179	-0.0220	-0.00447	-0.00250	-0.0195	-0.0294	-0.0243	-0.00951	0.00545	-0.0178	0.0135	-0.0186
	(0.0159)	(0.0165)	(0.0136)	(0.0153)	(0.0255)	(0.0200)	(0.0203)	(0.0204)	(0.0175)	(0.0141)	(0.0191)	(0.0179)
HK	-0.264*	-0.289**	-0.50***	-0.45***	-0.261**	-0.380**	-0.249	-0.28***	-0.45***	-0.53***	-0.54***	-0.499***
	(0.145)	(0.132)	(0.186)	(0.159)	(0.130)	(0.149)	(0.158)	(0.107)	(0.161)	(0.174)	(0.193)	(0.157)
TRADE	0.0424	0.0782	0.0609	0.133	0.0876	0.0912	-0.0186	0.0706	0.120*	0.0707	0.0734	0.109
	(0.0649)	(0.0625)	(0.0977)	(0.0828)	(0.0748)	(0.0675)	(0.0466)	(0.0875)	(0.0691)	(0.0819)	(0.0640)	(0.0675)
FDI	-0.0263	-0.0272	-0.0542*	-0.055**	-0.0181	-0.0176	-0.0135	-0.00034	-0.0514*	-0.0178	-0.0389	-0.0498*
	(0.0227)	(0.0192)	(0.0293)	(0.0253)	(0.0209)	(0.0192)	(0.0165)	(0.0258)	(0.0286)	(0.0360)	(0.0245)	(0.0266)
FDI*(INST≤ γ)	-0.911*	0.603	0.380	-0.359	1.605	0.0607	0.486	-0.132	-0.271*	0.160	-0.472	-0.233*
	(0.516)	(0.749)	(0.464)	(0.349)	(0.979)	(0.286)	(0.303)	(0.168)	(0.373)	(0.248)	(0.361)	(0.169)
FDI*(INST>γ)	0.243*	0.0157*	0.0275	0.0147	-0.0153	0.0267*	0.0183	0.000133	0.034*	-0.00449	0.0144	0.0216*
	(0.0189)	(0.0252)	(0.0226)	(0.0159)	(0.0212)	(0.0162)	(0.0130)	(0.0192)	(0.0250)	(0.0289)	(0.0193)	(0.0196)
δ_1	0.473	-0.265	-0.793	0.843	-0.347*	-0.145	-1.362	0.420	-0.777	-0.320	1.274	-0.349
	(0.655)	(1.075)	(0.137)	(0.989)	(0.868)	(0.876)	(0.981)	(0.480)	(0.855)	(0.620)	(1.050)	(0.398)
Threshold γ	0.42	0.35	0.26	0.28	0.20	0.30	0.22	0.34	0.25	0.38	0.25	0.26
Constant	0.0457	0.0203	0.604*	0.447	-0.183	-0.127	0.401	-0.121	0.690*	0.0669	0.721*	0.260
	(0.313)	(0.420)	(0.354)	(0.327)	(0.361)	(0.292)	(0.342)	(0.430)	(0.370)	(0.393)	(0.431)	(0.364)
Observations	608	608	608	608	608	608	608	608	608	608	608	608
Number of id	19	19	19	19	19	19	19	19	19	19	19	19
AR(2) P-value	0.126	0.147	0.246	0.172	0.256	0.125	0.163	0.201	0.273	0.139	0.166	0.141
Sargan P-value	0.316	0.449	0.166	0.427	0.195	0.529	0.605	0.693	0.485	0.153	0.290	0.298

Table 2C. The effect of FDI nexus institutions on growth for the Europe group

Institutional Variables	Govern-ment Stability	Socio-eco. Condi-tions	Internal Conflict	External Conflict	Invest-ment profile	Corrup-tion	Military in Politics	Religious Tensions	Law and Order	Ethnic Tensions	Demo-cratic Accounta-bility	Bureau-cracy Quality
	(1)	(2)	(3)	(4)	(5)	(6)	(7)	(8)	(9)	(10)	(11)	(12)
Yit-1	0.965***	0.990***	1.018***	0.996***	1.052***	0.988***	1.016***	0.981***	1.027***	1.017***	1.005***	1.027***
	(0.03)	(0.0167)	(0.0129)	(0.0157)	(0.0279)	(0.0140)	(0.0189)	(0.0142)	(0.0142)	(0.0171)	(0.0180)	(0.0144)
G	-0.0093	-0.0279	0.119	0.101	0.0694	-0.21***	0.0145	-0.0618	0.0190	-0.0136	-0.128	-0.0790
	(0.0975)	(0.0525)	(0.0780)	(0.0805)	(0.0983)	(0.0558)	(0.0614)	(0.0709)	(0.0733)	(0.0562)	(0.0804)	(0.0569)
GFCF	0.133***	0.106***	0.0712**	0.0505	-0.0277	0.118***	0.106***	0.0971***	0.0560*	0.136***	0.0596	0.0719**
	(0.0457)	(0.0289)	(0.0338)	(0.0310)	(0.0462)	(0.0309)	(0.0372)	(0.0331)	(0.0299)	(0.0320)	(0.0379)	(0.0294)
INFRA	-0.0525	-0.105	-0.0315	-0.215**	-0.300**	-0.0595	-0.0162	-0.0870	-0.206**	0.0283	-0.0370	-0.129*
	(0.106)	(0.0936)	(0.093)	(0.0837)	(0.133)	(0.0809)	(0.0922)	(0.0996)	(0.0819)	(0.0907)	(0.0960)	(0.0782)
CREATION	0.0258	0.0129	-0.034**	0.00860	-0.0412	0.0277**	-0.0250	0.0195	-0.0200	-0.0244	-0.0055	-0.0149
	(0.0318)	(0.0140)	(0.0137)	(0.0163)	(0.0259)	(0.0113)	(0.0192)	(0.0152)	(0.0161)	(0.0160)	(0.0186)	(0.0122)
HK	-0.253	-0.0673	-0.228*	-0.0051	-0.299	-0.0732	-0.172	-0.0972	0.139	-0.240*	-0.152	0.106
	(0.161)	(0.124)	(0.135)	(0.117)	(0.209)	(0.118)	(0.130)	(0.151)	(0.101)	(0.138)	(0.138)	(0.110)
TRADE	-0.11***	-0.0170	-0.11***	-0.09***	-0.069**	-0.10***	-0.09***	-0.099***	-0.066***	-0.072**	-0.0058	-0.0351
	(0.0381)	(0.0239)	(0.0317)	(0.0238)	(0.0349)	(0.0280)	(0.0287)	(0.0313)	(0.0198)	(0.0297)	(0.0271)	(0.0324)
FDI	0.068***	0.0198	0.078***	0.107***	0.171***	0.045***	0.056***	0.0495***	0.0551***	0.042***	-0.0006	0.0283**
	(0.025)	(0.0184)	(0.0151)	(0.0128)	(0.0262)	(0.0088)	(0.0091)	(0.0135)	(0.0125)	(0.0140)	(0.0187)	(0.0133)
FDI*(INST≤ γ)	-0.22***	-0.0053	0.0550	-0.14***	-0.28***	0.118	0.00921	0.0231	-0.0321	-0.0564	0.0147	0.0792
	(0.0781)	(0.0540)	(0.0574)	(0.0863)	(0.105)	(0.0827)	(0.0422)	(0.0314)	(0.169)	(0.0359)	(0.0311)	(0.0825)
FDI*(INST>γ)	0.00631	0.0224**	-0.0015	0.032	0.034***	0.00287	0.00425	0.00982	0.0143*	0.0174	0.04***	0.015***
	(0.0125)	(0.0111)	(0.0104)	(0.0104)	(0.0099)	(0.0056)	(0.0049)	(0.0114)	(0.00737)	(0.0091)	(0.0105)	(0.0058)
δ1	0.565	-0.133*	-0.221	0.0465	0.416	-0.303	-0.0188	-0.0257	-0.0764*	0.30	-0.185**	-0.0198
	(0.231)	(0.109)	(0.201)	(0.304)	(0.284)	(0.260)	(0.150)	(0.162)	(0.525)	(0.120)	(0.0905)	(0.250)
Threshold γ	0.40	0.37	0.48	0.54	0.39	0.3	0.41	0.48	0.28	0.5	0.48	0.3
Constant	0.216	-0.186	-0.617*	-0.323	-1.013**	0.726***	-0.370	0.329	-0.490	-0.467*	0.0151	-0.272
	(0.575)	(0.303)	(0.338)	(0.353)	(0.469)	(0.260)	(0.369)	(0.334)	(0.334)	(0.272)	(0.366)	(0.384)
Observations	1,312	1,312	1,312	1,312	1,312	1,312	1,312	1,312	1,312	1,312	1,312	1,312
Number of id	41	41	41	41	41	41	41	41	41	41	41	41
AR(2) P-value	0.147	0.440	0.257	0.147	0.263	0.432	0.452	0.328	0.337	0.256	0.242	0.442
Sargan P-value	0.264	0.327	0.359	0.173	0.259	0.487	0.345	0.272	0.126	0.201	0.285	0.378

*Standard errors in parentheses *** p<0.01, ** p<0.05, * p<0.1.*

Table 2D. The effect of FDI nexus institutions on growth for America group

Institutional Variables	Government Stability	Socio-economic Conditions	Internal Conflict	External Conflict	Investment profile	Corruption	Military in Politics	Religious Tensions	Law and Order	Ethnic Tensions	Democratic Accountability	Bureaucracy Quality
	(1)	(2)	(3)	(4)	(5)	(6)	(7)	(8)	(9)	(10)	(11)	(12)
Y_{it-1}	1.027***	1.00***	1.001***	1.017***	1.018***	1.026***	1.005***	1.026***	1.009***	1.024***	1.012***	1.002***
	(0.0120)	(0.0137)	(0.0132)	(0.0122)	(0.0159)	(0.0143)	(0.0120)	(0.0158)	(0.0118)	(0.0123)	(0.0118)	(0.0109)
G	-0.06***	-0.08***	-0.10***	-0.09***	-0.09***	-0.056**	-0.092***	-0.0494**	-0.0359	-0.081***	-0.07***	-0.0437**
	(0.0204)	(0.0231)	(0.0217)	(0.0256)	(0.0215)	(0.0235)	(0.0217)	(0.0209)	(0.0251)	(0.0192)	(0.0236)	(0.0215)
GFCF	0.0765**	-0.0255	-0.0292	-0.115**	0.0739**	-0.0888*	-0.076**	-0.0346	-0.0331	-0.0174	0.0604	0.00165
	(0.0349)	(0.0418)	(0.0456)	(0.0529)	(0.0333)	(0.0496)	(0.0365)	(0.0574)	(0.0465)	(0.0405)	(0.0434)	(0.0411)
INFRA	0.0401	-0.140*	0.0745	0.0272	0.0741	0.0550	0.0241	-0.0308	0.0621	-0.0731	0.00195	-0.0144
	(0.0844)	(0.0724)	(0.0601)	(0.0561)	(0.0785)	(0.0592)	(0.0619)	(0.0507)	(0.0651)	(0.0556)	(0.0568)	(0.0603)
CREATION	-0.02***	0.00231	0.0105	0.00124	-0.00585	-0.00805	-0.00158	-0.00730	0.00157	-0.00858	-0.00258	-0.00210
	(0.00761)	(0.0078)	(0.00754)	(0.00710)	(0.0101)	(0.00794)	(0.00682)	(0.00861)	(0.00722)	(0.00638)	(0.00720)	(0.00636)
HK	-0.0925	0.219**	-0.137**	-0.0556	-0.0759	-0.0671	0.0247	-0.0668	-0.0924	0.0618	-0.0767	-1.12e-05
	(0.106)	(0.111)	(0.0690)	(0.0725)	(0.102)	(0.0852)	(0.0890)	(0.0740)	(0.0843)	(0.0688)	(0.0734)	(0.0652)
TRADE	-0.0220	0.0466**	0.0421**	0.063***	0.0256	0.0661**	0.0407**	0.0334	0.0715**	0.0209	0.00304	0.0129
	(0.0253)	(0.0226)	(0.0200)	(0.0226)	(0.0193)	(0.0262)	(0.0206)	(0.0262)	(0.0301)	(0.0210)	(0.0213)	(0.0213)
FDI	0.0226	0.0166	0.00488	-0.00521	0.0102	-0.0157	-0.0103	0.0202*	0.021	0.0177	0.0206*	0.0101
	(0.0132)	(0.0113)	(0.0111)	(0.0111)	(0.00999)	(0.0111)	(0.0104)	(0.0114)	(0.0137)	(0.0117)	(0.0124)	(0.0119)
FDI*(INST≤ ɣ)	0.00647	-0.0253	-0.0614	-0.00693	-0.23***	0.0566	0.0412	0.241***	-0.95***	0.0348	-0.0339	0.272
	(0.0928)	(0.0433)	(0.0722)	(0.0725)	(0.0812)	(0.0913)	(0.0345)	(0.0780)	(0.224)	(0.0696)	(0.0378)	(0.455)
FDI*(INST>ɣ)	0.0111*	0.00110	-0.00617	0.00149	-0.00605	-0.00150	0.00575	-0.0104	0.0293*	0.0839*	-0.00522	0.00527
	(0.006)	(0.0094)	(0.0059)	(0.0065)	(0.0047)	(0.0054)	(0.0036)	(0.0072)	(0.0072)	(0.0045)	(0.0049)	(0.0046)
δ_1	-0.126	0.0649	0.137	0.0433	-0.65***	-0.207	-0.126	-0.95***	2.414	-0.196	0.0579	-0.844
	(0.258)	(0.0994)	(0.192)	(0.228)	(0.244)	(0.347)	(0.110)	(0.326)	(0.587)	(0.248)	(0.117)	(1.388)
Threshold ɣ	0.38	0.38	0.42	0.51	0.35	0.33	0.41	0.51	0.20	0.40	0.45	0.24
Constant	-0.329*	0.00788	0.242	0.212	-0.239	-0.0282	0.315	-0.212	-0.151	-0.104	-0.162	-0.00772
	(0.182)	(0.161)	(0.177)	(0.189)	(0.234)	(0.183)	(0.194)	(0.187)	(0.186)	(0.184)	(0.191)	(0.181)
Observations	992	992	992	992	992	992	992	992	992	992	992	992
Number of id	31	31	31	31	31	31	31	31	31	31	31	31
AR(2) P-value	0.281	0.247	0.353	0.263	0.275	0.153	0.147	0.380	0.281	0.350	0.241	0.132
Sargan P-value	0.260	0.175	0.196	0.186	0.174	0.456	0.325	0.197	0.182	0.196	0.166	0.272

Table 2E. The effect of FDI nexus institutions on growth for Asia group

Institutional Variables	Government Stability	Socio-economic Conditions	Internal Conflict	External Conflict	Investment profile	Corruption	Military in Politics	Religious Tensions	Law and Order	Ethnic Tensions	Democratic Accountability	Bureaucracy Quality
	(1)	(2)	(3)	(4)	(5)	(6)	(7)	(8)	(9)	(10)	(11)	(12)
Y_{it-1}	0.704***	0.737***	0.561***	0.634***	0.560***	0.724***	0.754***	0.669***	0.65***	0.91***	0.82***	0.752***
	(0.111)	(0.124)	(0.0773)	(0.0887)	(0.0797)	(0.115)	(0.120)	(0.109)	(0.111)	(0.128)	(0.120)	(0.148)
G	0.0177	0.455	-0.215	0.307	0.577*	-0.145	0.0650	-0.0835	0.0663	0.261	-0.0841	0.436
	(0.436)	(0.350)	(0.272)	(0.394)	(0.300)	(0.409)	(0.350)	(0.395)	(0.377)	(0.454)	(0.457)	(0.478)
GFCF	-0.549	-0.344	-0.986***	-0.668*	-0.613	-0.384	-0.293	-0.679	-0.938*	-0.191	-0.130	-0.187
	(0.621)	(0.414)	(0.328)	(0.356)	(0.388)	(0.495)	(0.416)	(0.490)	(0.514)	(0.430)	(0.427)	(0.304)
INFRA	-0.0203*	-0.0181	-0.0229**	-0.040***	-0.02***	-0.0158	-0.0145	-0.0304**	-0.029**	-0.0145	-0.0128	-0.0241
	(0.0116)	(0.0141)	(0.0100)	(0.0150)	(0.0103)	(0.0144)	(0.0160)	(0.0148)	(0.0141)	(0.015)	(0.0160)	(0.0150)
CREATION	0.255*	0.166	0.379***	0.329***	0.279***	0.225*	0.217*	0.289***	0.318**	0.0528	0.168	0.128
	(0.135)	(0.118)	(0.0844)	(0.0933)	(0.0891)	(0.134)	(0.125)	(0.111)	(0.126)	(0.135)	(0.124)	(0.133)
HK	-0.0639	-0.571	0.336	-0.680	-0.172	-0.0365	-0.351	-0.235	-0.422	-0.218	-0.485	-0.274
	(0.530)	(0.616)	(0.478)	(0.647)	(0.418)	(0.713)	(0.696)	(0.581)	(0.671)	(0.704)	(0.667)	(0.672)
TRADE	0.0312	0.0543	0.104**	0.0840	0.0693	-0.0283	-0.0815	-0.138	-0.0221	-0.0238	0.0868	-0.0860
	(0.0770)	(0.0806)	(0.0426)	(0.128)	(0.0546)	(0.0988)	(0.126)	(0.110)	(0.133)	(0.142)	(0.146)	(0.0765)
FDI	0.0152	0.184	-0.0178	-0.0181	0.272***	0.0754	-0.200*	0.102	0.0949	0.0516	-0.0380	0.288
	(0.217)	(0.135)	(0.124)	(0.129)	(0.0921)	(0.126)	(0.140)	(0.152)	(0.197)	(0.192)	(0.178)	(0.195)
FDI*(INST≤ ɣ)	0.129	0.748	-0.271	1.328	-0.128	0.057	-0.0807*	0.799	0.534	0.071	-0.0899	-0.386
	(0.316)	(0.705)	(0.818)	(0.803)	(0.543)	(1.121)	(0.786)	(1.157)	(1.227)	(0.135)	(0.565)	(1.099)
FDI*(INST>ɣ)	0.00720	0.124	0.0537	0.110*	0.0309	0.0226	0.0445*	0.0314	0.00914	0.0273	0.0702*	-0.0177
	(0.076)	(0.106)	(0.079)	(0.093)	(0.062)	(0.095)	(0.061)	(0.063)	(0.12)	(0.076)	(0.066)	(0.073)
δ_1	-0.526*	-0.879	0.121	-0.007	0.579	-0.572*	-0.254	-0.243	-0.117	-0.468	0.851	0.638
	(0.97)	(1.363)	(0.331)	(0.374)	(1.781)	(3.924)	(0.455)	(0.531)	(1.918)	(0.657)	(1.848)	(0.273)
Threshold ɣ	0.80	0.31	0.29	0.40	0.36	0.28	0.33	0.30	0.26	0.19	0.5	0.29
Constant	1.101	1.619	0.495***	0.922**	0.040**	1.707	0.491*	0.498**	0.670**	0.777	1.991	0.552
	(0.772)	(0.584)	(0.845)	(0.403)	(0.914)	(0.412)	(0.052)	(0.788)	(0.883)	(0.779)	(0.681)	(0.767)
Observations	1,088	1,088	1,088	1,088	1,088	1,088	1,088	1,088	1,088	1,088	1,088	1,088
Number of id	34	34	34	34	34	34	34	34	34	34	34	34
AR(2) P-value	0.186	0.190	0.262	0.188	0.182	0.155	0.308	0.165	0.192	0.141	0.287	0.432
Sargan P-value	0.475	0.518	0.442	0.448	0.429	0.504	0.562	0.531	0.502	0.562	0.539	0.532

*Standard errors in parentheses *** $p<0.01$, ** $p<0.05$, * $p<0.1$.*

Table 2F. The effect of FDI nexus institutions on growth for SSA group

Institutional Variables	Government Stability	Socio-economic Conditions	Internal Conflict	External Conflict	Investment profile	Corruption	Military in Politics	Religious Tensions	Law and Order	Ethnic Tensions	Democratic Accountability	Bureaucracy Quality
	(1)	(2)	(3)	(4)	(5)	(6)	(7)	(8)	(9)	(10)	(11)	(12)
Y_{it-1}	0.952***	1.020***	0.907***	0.992***	0.976***	1.027***	1.001***	1.00***	1.027***	0.976***	0.959***	0.998***
	(0.0231)	(0.0198)	(0.0227)	(0.0222)	(0.0200)	(0.0214)	(0.0188)	(0.0195)	(0.0257)	(0.0199)	(0.0169)	(0.0174)
G	0.0540	-0.0284	0.0588	0.00811	0.0224	-0.0243	-0.0354	-0.0692*	-0.0564*	-0.00305	0.00797	-0.0205
	(0.0436)	(0.0408)	(0.0393)	(0.0392)	(0.0415)	(0.0421)	(0.0364)	(0.0381)	(0.0327)	(0.0379)	(0.0336)	(0.0434)
GFCF	-0.0660**	-0.0191	0.0376	-0.00218	-0.0395	0.0298	0.0591**	0.0558	0.0783**	0.0390	-0.0106	-0.00023
	(0.0312)	(0.0335)	(0.0348)	(0.0417)	(0.0440)	(0.0479)	(0.0275)	(0.0354)	(0.0362)	(0.0349)	(0.0355)	(0.0317)
INFRA	0.025***	-0.00344	0.00907*	0.00745	0.00604	-0.00222	0.000819	-0.0153*	0.0171**	-0.00134	0.00222	-0.00946
	(0.00534)	(0.00607)	(0.00477)	(0.00776)	(0.00567)	(0.00981)	(0.00747)	(0.0088)	(0.0070)	(0.00496)	(0.006)	(0.00754)
CREATION	-0.00521	-0.0163	0.0290	-0.0376	-0.0256	-0.0421**	-0.00694	-0.00607	-0.0190	-0.034**	0.0111	-0.00725
	(0.0220)	(0.0136)	(0.0212)	(0.0229)	(0.0207)	(0.0190)	(0.0145)	(0.0135)	(0.0199)	(0.0166)	(0.0171)	(0.0138)
HK	-0.00368	0.0754*	0.0121	0.107*	0.124**	0.0222	0.0793	0.15***	0.0466	0.155***	0.0155	0.0488
	(0.0356)	(0.0432)	(0.0518)	(0.0552)	(0.0542)	(0.0428)	(0.0647)	(0.0478)	(0.0525)	(0.0491)	(0.0389)	(0.0436)
TRADE	0.173***	0.00543	0.136***	0.0708	0.0697*	0.0467	-0.00371	-0.0107	-0.0553*	0.0490	0.0752**	0.0216
	(0.0312)	(0.0371)	(0.0393)	(0.0481)	(0.0378)	(0.0427)	(0.0352)	(0.0407)	(0.0328)	(0.0310)	(0.0316)	(0.0329)
FDI	-0.0300**	0.00365	-0.0322*	-0.0164	-0.0252*	-0.00326	-0.0118	-0.0176	-0.0111	-0.0158	-0.04***	-0.00670
	(0.0140)	(0.0171)	(0.0165)	(0.0129)	(0.0131)	(0.0129)	(0.0148)	(0.0128)	(0.0187)	(0.0184)	(0.0137)	(0.0181)
FDI*(INST≤ γ)	-1.841***	0.977***	-1.162**	-0.903***	-0.184	-0.200	1.564	0.136	-0.889***	-0.817	0.209	0.537*
	(0.345)	(0.376)	(0.489)	(0.302)	(0.186)	(0.580)	(0.349)	(0.235)	(0.259)	(0.583)	(0.134)	(0.280)
FDI*(INST>γ)	0.119***	0.0170	0.000270	0.00860	0.0145*	0.0143**	-0.00227	-0.0126*	0.00100	0.0112	0.022***	0.0119*
	(0.0069)	(0.011)	(0.010)	(0.012)	(0.0083)	(0.0069)	(0.0058)	(0.007)	(0.0107)	(0.0091)	(0.0075)	(0.0061)
δ_1	-0.059***	-0.42***	0.832	-1.494**	0.298	0.890	-0.083	-0.643	-0.997**	0.387	-0.697	-1.670*
	(1.658)	(1.384)	(0.445)	(1.439)	(0.839)	(1.682)	(0.072)	(0.837)	(0.981)	(2.574)	(0.502)	(0.938)
Threshold γ	0.15	0.11	0.15	0.3	0.2	0.15	0.12	0.2	0.17	0.15	0.17	0.2
Constant	-0.287	-0.0937	0.0736	-0.362	-0.0761	-0.625**	-0.0100	0.202	-0.0489	-0.213	0.144	-0.0244
	(0.320)	(0.222)	(0.251)	(0.302)	(0.275)	(0.277)	(0.204)	(0.223)	(0.272)	(0.221)	(0.260)	(0.236)
Observations	1,024	1,024	1,024	1,024	1,024	1,024	1,024	1,024	1,024	1,024	1,024	1,024
Number of id	32	32	32	32	32	32	32	32	32	32	32	32
AR(2) P-value	0.526	0.522	0.568	0.156	0.143	0.348	0.217	0.264	0.129	0.248	0.295	0.161
Sargan P-value	0.172	0.154	0.172	0.178	0.162	0.274	0.255	0.267	0.265	0.264	0.262	0.161

*Standard errors in parentheses. *** p<0.01, ** p<0.05, * p<0.10.*

REFERENCES

Acemoglu, D., Johnson, S., Robinson, J.A. (2002). Reversal of fortune: Geography and institutions in the making of the modern world income distribution. *Quarterly Journal of Economics*, 118, 1231–1294.

Acemoglu, D., Johnson, S., Robinson, J.A. (2005). *Institutions as a fundamental cause of long-run growth*. Handbook of Economic Growth, 1, 385–472.

Aidt, T.S., Gassebner, M. (2010). Do autocratic states trade less? *The World Bank Economic Review*, 24(1), 38–76.

Ajide, K., Adeniyi, O., Raheem, I. (2014). Does Governance Impact on the Foreign Direct Investment-Growth Nexus in Sub-Saharan Africa? *Zagreb International Review of Economics and Business*, 17(2), 71–81.

Alfaro, L., Chanda, A., Kalemli-Ozcan, S., Sayek, S. (2004). FDI and economic growth: the role of local financial markets. *Journal of International Economics*, 64(1), 89–112.

Ali, F.A., Fiess, N., MacDonald, R. (2010). Do institutions matter for foreign direct investment? *Open Economies Review*, 21(2), 201–219.

Alonso-Borrego, C., Arellano, M. (1999). Symmetrically normalized instrumental-variable estimation using panel data. *Journal of Business & Economic Statistics*, 17(1), 36–49.

Arellano, M., Bond, S. (1991). Some tests of specification for panel data: Monte Carlo evidence and an application to employment equations. *The Review of Economic Studies*, 58(2), 277–297.

Arellano, M., Bover, O. (1995). Another look at the instrumental variable estimation of error-components models. *Journal of Econometrics*, 68(1), 29–51.

Ayadi, R., Arbak, E., Naceur, S. B., & De Groen, W. P. (2015). Financial Development, Bank Efficiency, and Economic Growth Across the Mediterranean. In Ayadi R., Dabrowski M., De Wulf L. (Eds.) *Economic and Social Development of the Southern and Eastern Mediterranean Countries*, Springer, 219–233.

Aykut, D., Sayek, S. (2007). The role of the sectoral composition of foreign direct investment on growth. In L. Piscitello and G. D. Santangelo (eds.), *Do Multinationals Feed Local Development and Growth?,* Amsterdam: Elsevier.

Azman-Saini, W.N.W., Baharumshah, A.Z., Law, S.H. (2010). Foreign direct investment, economic freedom and economic growth: International evidence. *Economic Modelling*, 27(5), 1079–1089.

Bick, A. (2010). Threshold effects of inflation on economic growth in developing countries. *Economics Letters*, 108(2), 126–129.

Blomström, M., Kokko, A., Mucchielli, J.-L. (2003). *The economics of foreign direct investment incentives*. Springer.

Blundell, R., Bond, S. (1998). Initial conditions and moment restrictions in dynamic panel data models. *Journal of Econometrics*, 87(1), 115–143.

Borensztein, E., De Gregorio, J., Lee, J.-W. (1998). How does foreign direct investment affect economic growth? *Journal of International Economics*, 45(1), 115–135.

Brahim, M., Rachdi, H. (2014). Foreign Direct Investment, Institutions and Economic Growth: Evidence from the MENA Region. *Journal of Reviews on Global Economics*, 3, 328–339.

Bruno, R.L., Campos, N.F. (2013). Reexamining the conditional effect of foreign direct investment, IZA Discussion Paper No. 7458.

Busse, M., Groizard, J.L. (2008). Foreign direct investment, regulations and growth. *The World Economy*, 31(7), 861–886.

Busse, M., Hefeker, C. (2007). Political risk, institutions and foreign direct investment. *European Journal of Political Economy*, 23(2), 397–415.

Caner, M., Hansen, B.E. (2004). Instrumental variable estimation of a threshold model. *Econometric Theory*, 20(5), 813–843.

Cantwell, J., Dunning, J.H., Lundan, S.M. (2010). An evolutionary approach to understanding international business activity: The co-evolution of MNEs and the institutional environment. *Journal of International Business Studies*, 41(4), 567–586.

Carkovic, M.V., Levine, R. (2002). Does foreign direct investment accelerate economic growth? University of Minnesota Department of Finance Working Paper.

De Mello, L.R., Sinclair, M.T. (1995). Foreign Direct Investment, Joint Ventures, and Endogenous Growth', Department of Economics, University of Kent. UK, mimeo.

De Mello Jr, L.R. (1997). Foreign direct investment in developing countries and growth: A selective survey. *The Journal of Development Studies*, 34(1), 1–34.

Dunning, J.H., Lundan, S.M. (2008). Institutions and the OLI paradigm of the multinational enterprise. *Asia Pacific Journal of Management*, 25(4), 573–593.

Durham, J.B. (2004). Economic growth and institutions: some sensitivity analyses, 1961-2000. *International Organization*, 58(3), 485–529.

El Khoury, A.C., Savvides, A. (2006). Openness in services trade and economic growth. *Economics Letters*, 92(2), 277–283.

Falvey, R., Foster, N., Greenaway, D. (2007). Relative backwardness, absorptive capacity and knowledge spillovers. *Economics Letters*, 97(3), 230–234.

Ford, T.C., Rork, J.C., Elmslie, B.T. (2008). Foreign Direct Investment, Economic Growth, and the Human Capital Threshold: Evidence from US States. *Review of International Economics*, 16(1), 96–113.

Globerman, S., Shapiro, D. (2002). Global foreign direct investment flows: The role of governance infrastructure. *World Development*, 30(11), 1899–1919.

Greenaway, D., Kneller, R. (2007). Firm heterogeneity, exporting and foreign direct investment. *The Economic Journal*, 117(517), 134–161.

Hansen, B.E. (1999). Threshold effects in non-dynamic panels: Estimation, testing, and inference. *Journal of Econometrics*, 93(2), 345–368.

Hansen, B.E. (2000). Testing for structural change in conditional models. *Journal of Econometrics*, 97(1), 93–115.

Hansen, H., Rand, J. (2006). On the causal links between FDI and growth in developing countries. *The World Economy*, 29(1), 21–41.

Harms, P., Ursprung, H.W., (2002). Do civil and political repression really boost foreign direct investments? *Economic Inquiry*, 40(4), 651–663.

Jensen, N. (2008). Political risk, democratic institutions, and foreign direct investment. *The Journal of Politics*, 70(4), 1040–1052.

Jensen, N.M. (2003). Democratic governance and multinational corporations: Political regimes and inflows of foreign direct investment. *International Organization*, 57(3), 587–616.

Jude, C., Levieuge, G. (2013). Growth effect of FDI in developing economies: The role of institutional quality. MPRA Working Paper.

Júlio, P., Pinheiro-Alves, R., Tavares, J. (2013). Foreign direct investment and institutional reform: evidence and an application to Portugal. *Portuguese Economic Journal*, 12(3), 215–250.

Kaufmann, D., Kraay, A., Zoido, P. (1999). Aggregating governance indicators. *World Bank Policy Research Working Paper*, 2195.

Kremer, S., Bick, A., Nautz, D. (2013). Inflation and growth: new evidence from a dynamic panel threshold analysis. *Empirical Economics*, 44(2), 861–878.

Lewbel, A. (2012). Using heteroscedasticity to identify and estimate mismeasured and endogenous regressor models. *Journal of Business & Economic Statistics*, 30(1), 67–80.

Lim, M.E.-G. (2001). *Determinants of, and the relation between, foreign direct investment and growth: a summary of the recent literature*. International Monetary Fund.

McCloud, N., Kumbhakar, S.C. (2012). Institutions, foreign direct investment and growth: a hierarchical Bayesian approach. *Journal of the Royal Statistical Society*: Series A (Statistics in Society), 175(1), 83–105.

Meisel, N., Aoudia, J.O. (2007). Une nouvelle base de données institutionnelles : Profils Institutionnels 2006. *Les Cahiers de La DGTPE*, 9, 1–32.

Mencinger, J. (2003). Does foreign direct investment always enhance economic growth? *Kyklos*, 56(4), 491–508.

Meyer, K., Bevan, A.A., Estrin, S. (2004). Foreign investment location and institutional development in transition economies (was institution building and the integration of Eastern Europe in international production). *International Business Review*, 13(1), 43–64.

Meyer, K.E. (2004). Perspectives on multinational enterprises in emerging economies. *Journal of International Business Studies*, 35(4), 259–276.

Meyer, K.E., Sinani, E. (2009). When and where does foreign direct investment generate positive spillovers? A meta-analysis. *Journal of International Business Studies*, 40(7), 1075–1094.

Minea, A., Villieu, P., (2010). Développement financier, qualité institutionnelle et croissance: un modèle simple avec effets de seuil. *Région et Développement*, 32, 31–58.

Moran, T.H., Graham, E.M., Blomström, M. (eds.) (2005). *Does Foreign Direct Investment Promote Development?* Institute for International Economics Monograph Titles.

Nawaz, S. (2015). Growth effects of institutions: A disaggregated analysis. *Economic Modelling*, 45, 118–126.

North, D.C. (2005). Institutions and the process of economic change. *Management International*, 9(3), 1–7.

Sen, H. (1998). Different arguments for and against the role and impact of foreign direct investment on the development potentials of developing countries: an overview. *Journal of Economics and Administrative Sciences*, 13(1), 181–190.

Stein, E., Daude, C. (2001). Institutions, integration and the location of foreign direct investment. Inter-American Development Bank, Research Department, Washington, DC, Mimeographed document.

Sylwester, K. (2005). Foreign direct investment, growth and income inequality in less developed countries. *International Review of Applied Economics*, 19(3), 289–300.

Vissak, T., Roolaht, T. (2005). The negative impact of foreign direct investment on the Estonian economy. *Problems of Economic Transition*, 48(2), 43–66.

Wang, D.T., Gu, F.F., David, K.T., Yim, C.K.B. (2013). When does FDI matter? The roles of local institutions and ethnic origins of FDI. *International Business Review*, 22(2), 450–465.

Wei, S.-J. (2000). How Taxing is Corruption on International Investors? *Review of Economics and Statistics*, 82(1), 1–11.

Wu, J.-Y., Hsu, C.-C. (2012). Foreign direct investment and income inequality: Does the relationship vary with absorptive capacity? *Economic Modelling*, 29(6), 2183–2189.

L'EFFET DES INVESTISSEMENTS DIRECT ETRANGERS SUR LA CROISSANCE : L'EXISTENCE DE SEUILS INSTITUTIONNELS

Résumé **-** *Cet article analyse l'effet des investissements directs étrangers (IDE) sur la croissance économique et montre le rôle joué par la qualité des institutions dans cinq régions (Afrique subsaharienne, MENA, Europe, Asie et Amérique) pour la période 1984-2013. En utilisant la méthode de GMM en système, les résultats du modèle mettent en évidence le rôle du développement institutionnel dans la relation IDE-croissance et révèlent l'existence d'un seuil institutionnel, calculé selon la méthode de Caner et Hansen (2004), pour chaque groupe (excepté l'Amérique) au-delà duquel les IDE impactent positivement la croissance. L'analyse détaillée des indicateurs institutionnels fait apparaître que la stabilité politique et le respect des lois sont les composantes clés à travers lesquelles les IDE tendent à affecter la croissance.*

Mots-clés - INVESTISSEMENT DIRECT ETRANGER, CROISSANCE, EFFET DE SEUIL, INSTITUTIONS

THE EFFECT OF ECONOMIC FREEDOM ON BUSINESS CYCLE VOLATILITY: CASE OF DEVELOPING COUNTRIES

Nabil ALIMI*

Abstract **-** *Few studies have analyzed the effect of economic freedom on business cycle volatility. The objective of this paper is to examine the relationship between economic freedom and volatility cycles of 109 developing countries over the period 1995-2012. Using Generalized Method of Moments (GMM) estimators we prove that greater economic freedom leads to less business cycle volatility. Yet, this link is not statistically significant for all different income level groups.*

Key-words **-** ECONOMIC FREEDOM, DEVELOPING COUNTRIES, BUSINESS CYCLE FLUCTUATIONS

JEL Classification **-** E32, O5, O17

The author is grateful to the reviewer's comments and suggestions that enriched and improved the quality of the manuscript.

* Université de Tunis El Manar, Faculté des sciences économiques et de gestion de Tunis ; nabil.alimi@fsegt.rnu.tn

1. INTRODUCTION

In spite of an abundant literature on the determinants of economic growth and the relationship between economic growth and volatility, few studies have focused on the question of business cycle volatility and their causes. The scarcity of studies on this topic is mainly due to the fact that until the 1980s business cycles and economic growth theories were considered two independent streams of economic theory. Three main papers published in the early 1980s put the long believed evidence into question. The first is Nelson and Plosser (1982) showed that the movements of gross domestic product (GDP) tend to be permanent. Second, joining Schumpeter (1911), who argued that the main cause of business cycle volatility is the adoption of new technology, Kydland and Prescott (1982), and Long and Plosser (1983) provided new models for which they incorporated the growth and business cycles theories for analyzing economic fluctuations[1]. According to these authors the main cause of output fluctuations is the stochastic variations in technology. In the third study, by incorporating endogenous growth theory in business cycle model, King et al. (1988) showed that temporary disruptions in production can affect the trend of the output.

These papers have shaken the basic beliefs of Real Business Cycles (RBC) literature and re-established the relationship between business cycle and economic growth. Therefore, it would then be unsafe to hold the view that economic fluctuation and economic growth theories are disconnected. The live debate about the relationship between business cycle volatility and growth dates back to the early 1990s. That it is positive or negative depends on the operating mechanisms (Imbs, 2002). Yet it seems that most papers on this topic tend to find a strong connection between business cycle fluctuation and long-run growth (Caballero and Hammour, 1994; Ramey and Ramey, 1995; Aghion and Saint-Paul 1998; Martin and Rogers, 2000; Kroft and Lloyd-Ellis, 2002; Fatás, 2002; Serven, 2003; etc.).

The importance of the above mentioned debate is certainly undeniable, yet what is more important for us is to trace the possible causes of the volatility of economic growth as determining them is in the very heart of controlling the level of growth volatility. This question is of paramount importance for developing economies since some research on business cycle volatility proves that, in the major developed market economies, the business cycle has become less volatile (Altman, 1992; Balke and Gordon, 1989; Boltho, 1989) while developing countries encountered larger volatility (Loayza et al., 2007).

It is commonly admitted that there are three main resources of macroeconomic volatility in developing countries. The most immediate one is that developing countries receive bigger exogenous shocks because of their higher trade and financial openness degree. Head (1995) demonstrated that the higher output variance of smaller countries is due to their greater openness and susceptibility

[1] We should point out here that the RBC considers technical progress as a purely random shock. It produces no break, contrary to what one can say of Schumpeter.

to exogenous shocks. Loayza and al. (2007)[2] and Carmignani and al. (2007) stressed the importance of trade openness as an essential source of volatility. In countries with less-diversified economic structures trade openness may enhance output volatility[3] (Easterly, Islam, and Stiglitz, 2000, Giovanni and Levchenko, 2008). In addition, sudden stops or speculative attacks can be a source of exogenous shocks. Second, developing economies are more likely to experience more domestic shocks, generated by; intrinsic instability of the development process, volatile fiscal policy (Fatás and Mihov, 2006), social conflict, economic mismanagement and political instability (Raddatz, 2007). Third, financial markets and the macroeconomic stabilization policies identified by literature as shock absorber are weak and inefficient in developing countries, so they often amplify volatility. Kharroubi (2006) proved that the negative relationship between volatility and economic growth observed in developing countries is based on the weaknesses of their financial systems.

In economic growth literature many studies evaluated the impact of economic freedom[4] on growth and development and most of them have supported a positive link between economic freedom and growth[5]. For example, Gwartney and al. (1996) note that the countries with the highest economic freedom scores have an average annual growth rate of per capita real GDP of 2.4% while those with the lowest economic freedom scores have an average of negative 1.3% for 1980-1994. Nevertheless, economic freedom as determining factor of economic fluctuations has received little attention in the literature. It was not until recent years that economists have just begun to assess the effects of economic freedom on economic performance (Lipford, 2007). This analysis can be viewed as an attempt to fill this gap and a contribution to the literature attempting to understand how economic freedom matters for economic volatility.

The effect of economic freedom on the volatility cycles, which until now has never been studied, is ambiguous and the economic theory does not give an adequate answer. On one hand, economic freedom can increase volatility through business, financial and trade freedoms that can contribute to the failure of many businesses. On the other hand, economic freedom can serve as catalyst for stability. Freedom of wages, contracts and prices can absorb economic shocks (Campell and Snyder, 2012). Freedom of property and the accessibility to sound money can also guarantee a safe and stable economic environment.

---

[2] Loayza and al. (2007) demonstrated that over each of four decades in 1960-2000, developing countries (except East Asia developing countries) encountered terms of trade volatility at least three times larger than the industrial economies.

[3] If trade openness leads to industrial specialization, a specific sector shock transform into whole economic shock. In this case trade openness may enhance volatility. For a detail overview of the effect of trade on specialization see Alimi (2015).

[4] Berggren (2003) defined economic freedom as "the degree to which an economy is a market economy – that is, the degree to which it entails the possibility of entering into voluntary contracts within the framework of a stable and predictable rule of law that upholds contracts and protects private property, with a limited degree of interventionism in the form of government ownership, regulations, and taxes".

[5] For empirical studies review, see De Haan et al. (2006).

Hence, the main objective of this paper is to demonstrate empirically whether economic freedom is a stabilizing factor of business cycle in 109 developing countries[6] or rather a destabilizing one and if the effect of economic freedom changes according to the income level, after controlling this effect by other important characteristics of these countries.

To set the stage for this analysis, we shall focus our attention on the relationship between business cycle volatility and economic growth (section 2) which will itself pave the way to developing an econometric model that allows us to study the relationship between business cycle fluctuation and economic freedom (section 3). Our research will be accentuated with the empirical results (Section 4). Last but not least we will highlight our findings in a fifth section offering concluding results.

2. BUSINESS CYCLE VOLATILITY AND ECONOMIC GROWTH: A BRIEF OVERVIEW

As far as we know, most of the published studies on this topic recognize a relationship between economic growth and business cycle volatility. While some theoretical and empirical approaches predict a positive relationship, others predict a negative one. To highlight this debate and without immersing ourselves into details and without the intention of being exhaustive, we would mention a few studies below.

Schumpeter (1911) argued that technological innovation which contributes to long-run growth can cause cyclical fluctuations. In turn, Kuznets (1967) and the partisans of real business cycle theory (Kydland and Prescott, 1982, Long and Plosser, 1983...) demonstrated a positive relationship between fluctuations and economic growth. This result was confirmed by Komendi and Meguire (1985) and Grier and Tullock (1989) who find a positive relationship between mean growth and its standard deviation. So, if business cycle volatility is reduced, we would expect lower rate of economic growth and vice versa. This means that there is a tradeoff between economic growth and cyclical volatility.

After losing the momentum for several years, debate about volatility-growth relationship has prompted a resurgence of interest particularly since Ramey and Ramey (1995) uncovered a strong negative link between volatility and growth in 92 less-developed[7]. However, positive impact did manifest in the OECD countries.

In the same spirit of Ramey and Ramey (1995) and along their lines, some other empirical papers further lend credence to the strong correlation between

[6] See appendix 1 for the list of developing countries and the different income level groups.

[7] Ramey and Ramey (1995) showed that the standard dichotomy in macroeconomics between growth and the volatility of economics fluctuations is not supported by the data. Ramey and Ramey explained the real business cycle theory and Lucas's (1987) questionable conclusions by the assumption of the absence of any interaction. They added: "by assuming no interaction between volatility and growth, the theoretical business cycle and growth literatures omit important elements" (p. 1148).

real business cycle and economic growth and supporting Ramey and Ramey findings (Kharroubi, 2006; Aghion and al., 2005; Fatás, 2002; Aghion and St Paul, 1998; Kroft and Huw, 2002 and Faruk, 2006).

Using Spearman correlation coefficient for the shorter and longer time-frames Altman (1995) found that over time per-capita economic growth is inversely related to business cycle volatility, quite contrary to what one would expect from the Schumpeter-Kuznets and real business cycle analyses. However, this negative relationship is not a strong one, so it is difficult to discern any clear relationship between increases in growth and a dampening of the business cycle. According to Altman there is no support for the view that there is a tradeoff between economic growth and cyclical volatility. He adds that high levels of cyclical volatility are not a necessary condition for high rates of economic growth. For this reason, one cannot argue that dampening the business cycle will result in less economic growth and business cycle volatility should result in a fall in the rate of economic growth.

Mills (2000) reworked the Altman analysis by using different statistical techniques (graphical, linear regression, rank correlation, and exploratory data analysis) over 1870-1994, to assess the robustness of the Altman's results. He concluded that a tight relationship between volatility and growth has not existed over the complete period and there is little evidence of a positive relationship between growth and volatility[8]. Mills added that the nature of the relationship changes through periods and methods. Using the linear trend estimate of volatility for the sample period 1870-1908, the author showed that the relationship is essentially flat for low levels of volatility, but positive for the countries with the highest cyclical volatility. However by using the linear trend measure Mills demonstrated a positive relationship for low levels of volatility but negative relationship for high levels. These relationships would disappear if the sample period was extended to 1928. All estimates suggest no relationship for low levels of volatility, but the two linear (BK and HP) filters estimates indicate a positive relationship for high levels of volatility. For the period 1954-1972 all measures used by Mills (2000) showed a positive relationship between low levels of volatility and growth.

3. DATA, METHODOLOGY AND EMPIRICAL MODEL

The empirical methodology used in this study is cross-country regression analysis. We examine the relationship between business cycle fluctuation and economic freedom using a large data set that includes 109 developing countries from different regions in the first step. In the second step we subdivide the total sample into sub-samples according the income level.

Several methods have been proposed to measure the volatility of the variables. Cariolle (2012) classified them into three approaches: economic volatility as the standard deviation of the growth rate of a variable (Ramey and Ramey, 1995; Servén, 1997; Acemoglu et al., 2003; Di Giovanni and Levchenko, 2010;

[8] Only for Japan, Korea and Taiwan, structural volatility estimate show a nonlinear but positive relationship between volatility and growth over the period 1870-1994.

Van der Ploeg and Poelhekke, 2009 and Raddatz, 2007…etc.), economic volatility as the standard deviation of the residual of an econometric regression (Servén, 1998; Pritchett, 2000; Combes and Guillaumont, 2002; …etc) and economic volatility as the standard deviation of the cycle isolated by a statistical filter (Altman, 1995; Dawe, 1996 ; Becker and Mauro, 2006; Chauvet and Guillaumont, 2009; Afonso and Furceri, 2010). While the first and the second approaches put forward restrictive hypotheses, the third approach does not formulate the behavior of a series in advance. Thus, we choose the latter approach as a measure of volatility and business cycle volatility, the dependent variable in the analysis, is the standard deviation of the cyclical component of real GDP isolated using Hodrick-Prescott (1997) filter[9].

All explanatory variables considered in the empirical analysis are briefly discussed below.

EFI is the economic freedom index and it is our variable of interest. We use the economic freedom index published by The Wall Street Journal and The Heritage Foundation. The index is scaled from 0 to 100, where 0 represents the least free and 100 represents the most free.

The control variables considered for the volatility regressions represent the foremost causes of macroeconomic fluctuations as described in the literature. These include the average of opening rate ([exports + imports] / GDP) (OPEN) calculated at the beginning and ending of the period – as a proxy for economic diversification (Lipford, 2007), the standard deviation of the annual growth rate of terms of trade (SDTTG) – as a measure of terms of trade shocks[10], the frequency of financial crises (FFC) – measured as the fraction of years in the sample period during which a country experienced a financial crises, the standard deviation of inflation rate (SDINF), and an indicator of financial openness (KAOPEN). Capital movement's liberalization is a double-edged sword. On the one hand, the easing of restrictions on capital movements can promote the development of financial system. This can reduce economic volatility due to improved efficiency in the allocation of productive resources and adjustment to shocks. On the other hand, financial liberalization imposes constraints on the conduct of economic policy and may make economies more sensitive to disturbances affecting them (Dornbusch and Giovannini, 1990). Moreover, capital flows are also a propagation mechanism of financial and currency crises (Calvo and Mendoza, 2000; Calvo, 2000) that make the most unstable growth (Combes and al., 2000).

---

[9] To extract cyclical component from macroeconomic aggregate different measures have been proposed (Altman, 1995; Harvey, 1985; Baxter and King (BK), 1995; Hodrick and Prescott (HP), 1997, etc.). Among these filters, HP filters was been extensively used in business cycle research.

[10] Terms of trade shocks have the potential to affect economic volatility and it is likely to have a greater effect in countries more open to international trade (Andrews and Rees, 2009; Mendoza, 1995; Kose, 2002).

In addition, using the Exchange Rate Regime Reinhart and Rogoff[11] we define a dummy variable for the change in exchange rate regime (CHERR) that take one if over the period 1995-2012 country adopt more than one exchange rate regime and zero otherwise.

Underlying data on real GDP, inflation rates, openness degree, population and terms of trade are from the World Bank's World Development Indicators database. Data on financial crises are from Laeven and Valencia (2008). As noted above, the EF index is from Wall Street Journal and The Heritage Foundation (2013). The measure of financial openness is the Chinn & Ito index for financial openness (KAOPEN)[12].

To perform analysis on the effect of economic freedom on economic cycle volatility we investigate the model adopted by Lipford (2007) and Dawson (2010). However, we should mention that there is a difference between the methods that were used. While Lipford (2007) and Dawson (2010) used the ordinary least squares (OLS)[13], we will use the GMM estimators. We chose this method to take in consideration the possibility of endogeneity of economic freedom. Thus, the following model will be estimated considering 109 developing countries and four different income level groups during the period 1995-2012:

$$\sigma_i = \alpha_0 + \alpha_1 EFI_i + \alpha_2 Z_i + \varepsilon_i$$

σ_i is a measure of business cycle volatility. Z_i is a vector of control variables as defined previously.

The linear regression Eq. (1) raises the challenge of endogeneity: the possibility that economic freedom is endogenous. That is, economic freedom itself may be determined to some extent by the underlying macroeconomic environment, in particular the volatility of the business cycle. Similarly, fluctuations of the business cycle may prompt various other policy changes that affect the degree of economic freedom (Dawson, 2010). To control this problem, we use the Generalized Method of Moments (GMM) estimators suggested by Arellano and Bond (1991). To isolate the exogenous variation in economic freedom instrumental variables were used such as the initial level of real GDP, standard deviation of terms of trade, openness, frequency of financial crises and the standard deviation of inflation rates (Hall and Jones, 1999; Dollar and Kraay, 2003; Dawson, 2010). Table 3.1 provides summary statistics for all variables for the total sample and tables 3.2, 3.3, 3.4 and 3.5 for different income level groups[14] (appendix 3).

In addition due to the risk of multicollinearity it is necessary before estimation to look closely at the correlation coefficients between independent varia-

---

[11] http://www.carmenreinhart.com/data/browse-by-topic/topics/11/

[12] Web.pdx.edu./~ito/Chinn-Ito_website.htm

[13] Dawson (2010) used the two-stage least squares for the instrumental variables analysis.

[14] The variables, Economic freedom index (EFI), open and the GDP are expressed in their natural logarithmic form.

bles. Tables 4.1[15] (appendix 4) details results of correlation test. As we can see some independent variables suffer from multicollinearity. For example, the simple coefficient correlation between economic freedom index (EFI) on one hand and the measure of financial liberalization (KAOPEN), the standard deviation of inflation (SDINF) and the standard deviation of terms of trade growth rate (SDTTG), on the other hand, are approximately 0.5, 0.30 and 0.28, respectively[16]. This result is not surprising since business freedom, monetary freedom and trade freedom are some components of economic freedom. To avoid correlation between these explanatory variables, the EFI is adjusted to exclude business freedom, monetary freedom and trade freedom from the measure of overall economic freedom. These adjusted measures of the EFI are used in the analysis that follows. To take these collinear relationships into consideration, the reported regressions contain combinations of the independent variables that minimize the inclusion of collinear variables.

4. EMPIRICAL RESULTS

Table 1 presents empirical findings. Columns 2 and 3 present the results for the total sample and columns 4 to 10 report the results of estimates for different income level groups. For all regressions, the model is globally significant.

Even though, standard deviation of inflation (SDINF), the change in exchange rate regime (CHERR) and the measure of financial openness (KAOPEN) were consistently found to be statistically insignificant in explaining volatility across countries in regressions for total sample they are theoretically valid and likely to be correlated with other explanatory variables. Since excluding these variables would violate one of the classical assumptions of the linear regression model and cause bias in the coefficient estimates, they are not excluded from the analysis (Dawson, 2010).

In addition we point out that economic freedom loses its statistical significance when we introduce the change in exchange rate regime, but the volatility of terms of trade keep their significance and expected signs in all regressions.

As to the key interest variable (EFI), regressions 1(a) and 1(b) support the hypothesis that economic freedom contribute to more stable economic cycles in developing economies. Economic freedom evidently improves an economy's capacity to adjust to any shock, whether from policy or external causes. The estimated impact of an increase of one standard deviation in economic freedom in reducing volatility over 18-year period is 0.1%.

As for the control variables the coefficient of openness (OPEN) is positive and statistically significant (1(a), 1(b)). This means that trade increase the volatility of business cycle via the transfer of external shocks. The coefficient of standard deviation of terms of trade growth rate (SDTTG) is statistically significant and positive (1(a), 1(b)), as expected.

---

[15] Table 4.1 report the result of coefficient correlation between variables of the total sample. See tables 4.2, 4.3, 4.4 and 4.5 for the coefficient correlation between variables of different income level groups (appendix 4).

[16] These correlation coefficients are significant at 5% risk level.

Table 1. Business cycle volatility and economic freedom, 1995-2012 general moment method (GMM) estimation

Variable	Total sample (1)		Low Income (2)	Lower middle income (3)		Upper lower income (4)		High income (5)	
	Regression (a)	Regression (b)	Regression (a)	Regression (a)	Regression (b)	Regression (a)	Regression (b)	Regression (a)	Regression (b)
EFI	-0.013** (-2.306)	-0.010** (-1.944)	-0.007 (-0.885)	-0.004 (-0.760)	-0.006 (-1.330)	-0.016 (-1.586)	0.002 (0.297)	-0.006 (-0.607)	-0.020** (-2.685)
FFC	0.098* (1.675)		0.213*** (3.482)	-0.028 (-1.588)		0.284** (2.136)			0.137* (2.210)
CHERR		0.001 (0.150)	-0.004 (-0.685)		0.011** (2.318)		-0.014 (-0.869)	0.035*** (4.601)	
KAOPEN	0.0002 (0.022)	0.004 (0.632)	-0.030** (-2.086)				0.010 (1.391)	-0.024 (-1.443)	0.0003 (0.029)
OPEN	0.017*** (2.860)	0.014*** (2.714)	0.013 (1.566)	0.005 (0.883)	0.011** (2.302)	0.023* (1.902)		0.010 (1.252)	0.021*** (3.315)
SDINF	0.0002 (1.072)		0.0004 (0.960)	0.0007*** (7.047)				-0.0006** (-2.713)	
SDTTG	0.049** (2.276)	0.061*** (3.504)	0.029* (1.777)	0.094*** (4.247)		-0.040 (-0.440)	-0.001 (-0.013)	0.220*** (5.875)	0.204*** (4.294)
J-statistic	0.005	0.010	0.004	0.017	0.020	0.032	0.001	0.070	0.0004
Ajusted - R2	0.102	0.032	0.572	0.566	0.193	0.02	0.069	0.688	0.48
Obs	109	109	23	35	35	36	36	15	15

Estimation is by GMM. T-student is shown in parentheses. ***, **, and * indicate significance at the 1%, 5%, and 10% levels, respectively.

This result is in accordance with the ones of Dawson (2010) and Andrews and Rees (2009) who demonstrated that terms of trade volatility has a significant and positive impact on the volatility of output growth. It is also in accordance with the result of Kose (2002) and Mendoza (1995). Indeed Kose confirmed that the terms of trade shocks can explain almost all of the variance in output in small open developing economies and Mendoza estimated that roughly one-half of the variation in aggregate output in a sample of G7 and 23 developing countries can be attributed to the terms of trade shocks. The coefficient of financial crises frequency is significant and positive (1(a), 2(a), 4(a), 5(b)), as expected.

Looked closely to these coefficients we estimate that an increase of one standard deviation in the volatility of terms of trade and openness leads to an increase by 0.7% and 0.76% in business cycle volatility, respectively.

As it was mentioned earlier, to answer the question if the effect of economic freedom on business cycle differs according to the income group, we estimate equation 1 for four different income level groups.

For the whole sample considered (109 developing countries) economic freedom has a negative and statistically significant effect on business cycle volatility as it was pointed out earlier. However, the estimation findings by income level groups suggest the absence of a significant relationship between these two variables, except in the case of developing high income countries (regression 5b). This finding leaves us to think about the presence of a development threshold from which economic freedom starts to affect volatility. We particularly see that high income group have the highest average degree of economic freedom while the low income countries have the lowest degree of economic freedom (table 2, appendix 2).

Openness (3(b), 4(a) and 5(b)) and terms of trade shocks (2(a), 3(a), 5(a) and 5(b)) preserve their significances in most of the cases and they are more significant in high income group where a fall of one standard deviation in openness and the volatility of terms of trade lead to a decrease in business cycle volatility by 8.75% and 2.22%, respectively.

The coefficient of frequency of financial crises (FFC) is statistically significant and positive in the case of low income group, upper middle income group and high income group, and it is higher in the case of low income group where the frequency of financial crises is the highest. The measure of financial openness (KAOPEN) is statistically significant and negative only in low income group where an increase in KAOPEN score of one standard deviation contributes to a decrease in business cycle volatility by 1%. This conclusion confirms the benefit of financial openness on growth and volatility widely discussed in economic literature.

Volatility of inflation rate increase business cycle volatility in lower middle income group and decrease it in high income group.

5. CONCLUSION

Studies that have examined the relationship between economic freedom and volatility have been relatively thin. Three exceptions are the studies by Lipford (2007), Dawson (2010) and Campbell and Snyder (2012). The purpose of this paper was a careful analysis to examine whether there is in fact a close and robust relationship between economic freedom and business cycle volatility for 109 developing countries in a first step and for different income level groups, in a second step, over the period 1995-2012.

Three main results emerge from this study. First, our findings suggest that economic freedom foster economic stability in developing countries, even after controlling for other determinants of volatility and accounting for possible endogeneity of economic freedom. Yet this effect differs from one income level group to another. In other words, our findings imply that economic freedom is a stabilizing factor in high income countries nevertheless its effect in the other groups is not significant. Second, changes in exchange rate regime stimulate volatility in lower middle income level group and high income level group. Third, financial openness weakens business cycle volatility in low income countries. This result can be considered as an argument to prod these countries to restructuring their financial systems into benefit from international capital.

This result can be considered as an argument to encourage these countries to restructure their financial systems before liberalization to benefit from international capital.

As expected and in concordance with many other studies, an increase in openness, volatility of terms of trade and the frequency of financial crises is associated with an increase in business cycle volatility in developing countries.

REFERENCES

Acemoglu, D., Johnson, S., Robinson, J., Thaicharoen, Y., 2003, "Institutional causes, macroeconomic symptoms: volatility, crises and growth", *Journal of Monetary Economics*, 50(1), 49-123.

Afonso, A., Furceri, D., 2010, "Government size, composition, volatility and economic growth", *European Journal of Political Economy*, 26(4), pp. 517-532.

Aghion, P., Bloom, N., Blundell, R., Griffith, R., Howitt, P., 2005, "Competition and Innovation: An Inverted-U Relationship", *Quarterly Journal of Economics*, 120(2), 701-728.

Aghion, P., Saint-Paul, G., 1998, "Virtues of Bad Times: Interaction between Productivity Growth and Economic Fluctuations", *Macroeconomic Dynamics*, 2 (3), 322-344.

Alimi, N., 2015, "The Effect of Trade, Specialization and Financial Integration on Business Cycles Synchronization in Some Mediterranean Countries", *Asian Economic and Financial Review*, 5(1), 110-118.

Altman, M., 1992, "Business Cycle Volatility in Developed Market Economies", 1870-1986: Revisions and Conjectures", *Eastern Economic Journal, 18(3),* 259-275.

Altman, M., 1995, "Business Cycle Volatility and Economic Growth: the Historical Record, 1870-1986", *Journal of Post Keynesian Economics*, 17, 561-577.

Andrews, D., Rees, D., 2009, "Macroeconomic Volatility and Terms of Trade Shocks", *Reserve Bank of Australia Research Discussion Paper 2009-05*, p. 45.

Balke, N. S., Gordon, R. J., 1989, "The Estimation of Prewar Gross National Product: Methodology and New Evidence", *Journal of Political Economy*, 97, 38-92.

Baxter, M., King, R.G., 1999, "Measuring Business Cycles: Approximate Band-Pass Filters for Economic Time Series", *The Review of Economics and Statistics,* 81, 575-593.

Baxter, M., Stockman, A. C., 1989, "Business Cycles and the Exchange Rate Regime: Some International Evidence", *Journal of Monetary Economics*, 23(3), 377-400.

Becker, T., Mauro, P., 2006, "Output drops and the Shocks that Matter", *IMF Working Paper* 06/172, International Monetary Fund.

Berggren, N., 2003, "The Benefits of Economic Freedom: A Survey", *Independent Review,* 8, 193-211.

Boltho, A., 1989, "Did activism policy work?", *European Economic Review*, 33(9), 1709-1726.

Caballero, R. J., Hammour, M. L., 1994, "The Cleansing Effect of Recessions", The *American Economic Review*, 84 (5), 1350-1368.

Calvo, G. A., 2000, "The Case for Hard Pegs in the Brave New World of Global Finance ", *in Don't Fix, Don't Float, (Eds.), J. Braga de Macedo, D. Cohen, and H. Reisen, OECD Development Centre Studies*, Paris, 77-83.

Calvo, G. A., Mendoza, E. G., 2000, "Capital Markets Crises and Economic Collapse in Emerging Markets: An Informational-Frictions Approach", *American Economic Review*, 90(2), 59-64.

Campbell, N., Snyder, T., 2012, "Economic Freedom and Economic Volatility", *Journal of International and Global Economic Studies*, December 2012, 60-76.

Cariolle, J., 2012, "Measuring Macroeconomic Volatility Applications to Export Revenue Data, 1970-2005", *foundation pour les études et recherches sur le développement international, Working paper n°I14*, March.

Carmignani, F., Colombo, E., Tirelli, P., 2007, "Public Expenditure and Growth Volatility: Do Globalisation and Institution Matter?", *Working Paper Series*, No. 116/2007, Department of Economics, University of Milan-Bicocca.

Chauvet, L., Guillaumont, P., 2009, "Aid, Volatility, and Growth Again: When Aid Volatility Matters and When it Does Not", *Review of Development Economics*, 13(3), 452-463.

Combes, J.L., Guillaumont, P., 2002, "Commodity Price Volatility, Vulnerability and Development", *Development Policy Review*, 20(1), 25-39.

Combes, J.L., Guillaumont, P., Jeanneney, S. G., Combes, P.M., 2000, « Ouverture sur l'extérieur et instabilité des taux de croissance », *Revue Française d'Economie*, 15(1), 3-33.

Dawe, D., 1996, "A New Look at the Effects of Export Volatility on Investment and Growth", *World Development*, 24(12), 1905-1914.

Dawson, J. W., 2010, "Macroeconomic Volatility and Economic Freedom – a Preliminary Analysis", chapter 4, in *Economic Freedom of the World: 2010 Annual Report*, 175-185.

De Haan, J., Lundstrom, S., Sturm, J.E., 2006, "Market-Oriented Institutions and Policies and Economic Growth: A Critical Survey", *Journal of Economic Surveys*, 20(2), 157-191.

Di Giovanni, J., Levchenko, A., 2008, "Trade Openness and Volatility", *The Review of Economics and Statistics*, 91(3), 558-585.

Di Giovanni, J., Levchenko, A. A., 2010, "The Risk Content of Exports: a Portfolio view of International trade", *NBER Working Paper Series*, No. 16005.

Dollar, D., Kraay, A., 2003, "Institutions, trade, and growth", *Journal of Monetary Economics*, 50(1), 133-162

Dornbusch, R., Giovannini, A., 1990, "Monetary Policy in the Open Economy", in "Handbook of Monetary Economics", *Vol. II, (Eds), Friedman M. Benjamin and Frank H. Hahn, Edition 1*, Vol. 2, Chapter 23, 1231-1303, Elsiever.

Easterly, W., Islam, R., Stiglitz, J.E., 2000, "Explaining growth volatility," *Annual World Bank Conference on Development Economics*, January. Available at: http://www.worldbank.org/research/growth/growth%20volatility%20jan%202000.html

Fatás, A., 2002, "The Effects of Business Cycles on Growth", *Central Bank of Chile Working Papers*, no 156.

Fatas, A., Mihov, I., 2006, "The Macroeconomic Effects of Fiscal Rules in the US States", *Journal of Public Economics*, 90(1), 101-117.

Grier, K., Tullock, G., 1989, "An Empirical Analysis of Cross-National Economic Growth, 1951- 1980", *Journal of Monetary Economics*, 24(1), 259-276.

Gwartney, J., Lawson, R., Block, W., 1996, "Economic Freedom of the World: 1975-1995", *The Fraser Institute*, Vancouver.

Hall, R. E., Jones, C. I., 1999, "Why Do Some Countries Produce So Much More Output Than Others?", *Quarterly Journal of Economics*, 114(1), 83-116.

Harvey, A. C., 1985, "Trends and Cycles in Macroeconomic Time Series", *Journal of Business and Economic Statistics*, 3(3), 216-27.

Head, A.C., 1995, "Country size, aggregate fluctuations, and international risk sharing", *The Canadian Journal of Economics*, 28 (4b), 1096-1119.

Hodrick, R.J., Prescott, E.C., 1997, "Postwar U.S. Business Cycles: An Empirical Investigation", *Journal of Money, Credit and Banking*, 29(1), 1-16.

Imbs, J., 2002, "Why the Link Between Volatility and Growth is Both Positive and Negative", *CEPR Discussion Papers*, no 3561.

Kharroubi, E., 2006, "Illiquidity, Financial Development and Growth-Volatility Relationship", *Banque de France, Working Paper No. 139*, p.50

King, R., Plosser, C., Rebelo, S., 1988, "Production, Growth and Business Cycles: I. the Basic Neoclassical Model", *Journal of Monetary Economics*, 21(2-3), 195-232.

Kose, M. A., 2002, "Explaining Business Cycles in Small Open Economies: How Much Do World Prices Matter?", *Journal of International Economics*, 56 (2), 299-327.

Kroft, K., Lloyd-Ellis, H., 2002, "Further Cross-Country Evidence on the Linkage Between Growth, Volatility and Business Cycles", *University of California, Berkeley and Queen's university, Working Paper Series in Economics*.

Kuznets, S., 1967, "Population and Economic Growth", *Proceedings of the American Philosophical Society,* 111(3), 170-93.

Kydland, F. E., Prescott, E.C., 1982, "Time to Build and Aggregate Fluctuations", *Econometrica*, 50(6), 1345-1370.

Laeven, L., Valencia, F., 2012, "Systemic Banking Crises Database: An Update", *IMF WP/12/163*.

Lipford, J. W., 2007, "Short Run Macroeconomic Performance and Economic Freedom: Can Economic Growth Rates be Higher and More Stable?", *Journal of Private Enterprise*, 23(1), 3-29.

Loayza, N.V., Rancière, R., Servén, L., Vantura, J., 2007, "Macroeconomic Volatility and Welfare in Developing Economies", *World Bank Economic Review*, 21(3), 343-357.

Long, J., Plosser, C., 1983, "Real Business Cycles," *Journal of Political Economy*, 91(1), 39-69.

Lucas, R., 1987, *Models of Business Cycles*, Oxford: Blackwell.

Martin, P., Rogers, C. A., 2000, "Long-Term Growth and Short-Term Economic Instability", *European Economic Review*, 44(2), 359-81.

Mendoza, E.G., 1995, "The Terms of Trade, The Real Exchange Rate, and Economic Fluctuations", *International Economic Review*, 36(1), 101-137.

Mills, T.C., 2000, "Business Cycle Volatility and Economic Growth: a Reassessment", *Journal of Post Keynesian Economics*, 23(1), 107-116.

Nelson, C., Plosser, C., 1982, "Trends and Random Walks in Macroeconomic Time Series: Some Evidence and Implications", *Journal of Monetary Economics*, 10(2), 139-162.

Pritchett, L., 2000, "Understanding Patterns of Economic Growth: Searching for Hills among Plateaus, Mountains, and Plains", *The World Bank Economic Review*, 14(2), 221-250.

Raddatz, C., 2007, "Are External Shocks Responsible For The Instability of Output in Low Income Countries?", *Journal of Development Economics*, 84(1), 155-187.

Ramey, G., Ramey, V.A., 1995, "Cross-Country Evidence on The Link Between Volatility and Growth", *The American Economic Review*, 85(5), 1138-1151.

Rancière, R., Tornell, A., Westermann, F., 2008, "Systemic Crises and Growth", *Quarterly Journal of Economics*, 123(1), 359-406.

Schumpeter, J. A., 1911, *The Theory of Economic Development*, Harvard Economic Studies, 46, 255p.

Serven, L., 1997, "Uncertainty, Volatility, and Irreversible Investment: Theory, Evidence, and Lessons for Africa", *Journal of African Economies*, 6(3), 229-268.

Serven, L., 1998, "Macroeconomic Uncertainty and Private Investment in Developing Countries: An Empirical Investigation", *Policy Research Working Paper 2035,* The World Bank.

Serven, L., 2003, "Real-Exchange-Rate Uncertainty and Private Investment in LDCs", *Review of Economics and Statistics*, 85 (1), 212-218.

Van der Ploeg, F., Poelhekke, S., 2009, "Volatility and the natural resource curse", *Oxford Economic Papers,* 61(4), 727-760.

APPENDIX 1

List of developing countries: different income level groups

LOW INCOME	LOWER MIDDLE INCOME	UPPER MIDDLE INCOME	HIGH INCOME
Bangladesh	Armenia	Albania	Bahamas
Benin	Bolivia	Algeria	Bahrain
Burkina-Faso	Cameroon	Angola	Chile
Cambodia	Côte-d'Ivoire	Azerbaijan	Emirates U.A
Chad	Egypt	Belarus	Croatia
Ethiopia	El Salvador	Belize	Equatorial-Guinee
Guinea	Georgia	Bosnia & Herzegovina	Kuwait
Guinea-Bissau	Ghana	Botswana	Latvia
Haiti	Guatemala	Brazil	Lithuania
Kenya	Guyana	Bulgaria	Oman
Madagascar	Honduras	China	Poland
Malawi	India	Colombia	Russia
Mali	Indonesia	Costa-Rica	Saudi A.
Mozambique	Kyrgyz	Dominican R.	Trinidad & Tobago
Nepal	Lao	Ecuador	Uruguay
Niger	Lesotho	Fiji	
Rwanda	Mauritania	Gabon	
Sierra Leone	Moldova	Hungary	
Tajikistan	Mongolia	Jordan	
Tanzania	Morocco	Kazakhstan	
Togo	Nicaragua	Lebanon	
Uganda	Nigeria	Macedonia	
Zimbabwe	Pakistan	Malaysia	
	Paraguay	Malta	
	Philippines	Mauritius	
	Senegal	Mexico	
	Sri Lanka	Namibia	
	Swaziland	Panama	
	Syrian A. R.	Peru	
	Ukraine	Romania	
	Uzbekistan	South Africa	
	Vietnam	Suriname	
	Yemen	Thailand	
	Zambia	Tunisia	
		Turkey	
		Turkmenistan	
		Venezuela	

APPENDIX 2

Table 2. Average of economic freedom index and business cycle volatility

Countries	Economic freedom index*	Business cycle volatility (%)
Low income (N=23)	3.95	3.51
Lower middle income (N=34)	4.00	4.78
Upper middle income (N=37)	4.05	4.69
High income (N=15)	4.16	2.76

* The average of neperian logarithm of economic freedom index.
N = number of countries.

APPENDIX 3

Table 3.1. Summary statistics (total sample)

	Mean	Median	Maximum	Minimum	Std. Dev.
BCV	0.039	0.028	0.379	0.006	0.042
EFI	4.034	4.054	4.317	3.580	0.136
FFC	0.056	0.056	0.278	0.000	0.071
KAOPEN	0.432	0.293	1.557	0.000	0.327
OPEN	4.294	4.304	5.357	3.058	0.451
SDINF	11.922	4.672	169.075	0.738	21.982
SDTTG	0.196	0.165	1.138	0.068	0.141

Table 3.2. Summary statistics (low income)

	Mean	Median	Maximum	Minimum	Std. Dev.
BCV	0.035	0.024	0.101	0.006	0.027
EFI	3.951	3.954	4.140	3.580	0.120
FFC	0.043	0.000	0.278	0.000	0.078
KAOPEN	0.295	0.177	1.557	0.081	0.332
OPEN	4.098	4.037	5.357	3.235	0.470
SDINF	7.199	5.538	19.103	0.738	4.977
SDTTG	0.286	0.223	1.137	0.073	0.246

Table 3.3. Summary statistics (lower middle income group)

	Mean	Median	Maximum	Minimum	Std. Dev.
BCV	0.028	0.021	0.080	0.009	0.018
EFI	4.016	4.047	4.258	3.768	0.106
FFC	0.066	0.056	0.222	0.000	0.077
KAOPEN	0.434	0.252	0.947	0.000	0.317
OPEN	4.313	4.321	5.005	3.544	0.367
SDINF	11.701	5.417	86.735	1.415	16.933
SDTTG	0.179	0.171	0.382	0.083	0.070

Table 3.4. Summary statistics (upper middle income group)

	Mean	Median	Maximum	Minimum	Std. Dev.
BCV	0.047	0.029	0.378	0.015	0.063
EFI	4.060	4.073	4.254	3.614	0.139
FFC	0.067	0.055	0.222	0,000	0.065
KAOPEN	0.421	0.347	1,000	0.036	0.280
OPEN	4.350	4.446	5.292	3.058	0.498
SDINF	17.144	4.408	169.075	1.105	33.223
SDTTG	0.160	0.143	0.433	0.068	0.072

Table 3.5. Summary statistics (high income group)

	Mean	Median	Maximum	Minimum	Std. Dev.
BCV	0.051	0.052	0.134	0.020	0.031
EFI	4.164	4.195	4.335	3.889	0.132
FFC	0.038	0.000	0.167	0.000	0.057
KAOPEN	0.676	0.746	1.000	0.014	0.343
OPEN	4.456	4.547	5.072	3.640	0.417
SDINF	7.791	4.008	46.057	0.921	11.900
SDTTG	0.179	0.164	0.441	0.090	0.101

APPENDIX 4

Table 4.1. Correlation coefficients (total sample)

	BCV	CHERR	CRISES	EFI	KAOPEN	OPEN	SDINF	SDTTG
BCV	1,000							
CRC	-0,030	1,000						
CRISES	0,211**	0,358***	1,000					
EFI	-0,201**	-0,141	-0,278	1,000				
KAOPEN	-0,052	0,087	0,133	0,500***	1,000			
OPEN	0,189**	0,063	-0,089	0,116	0,057	1,000		
SDINF	0,222**	0,227**	0,176*	-0,302***	-0,140	0,048	1,000	
SDTTG	0,193**	0,012	0,122	-0,280***	-0,072	0,104	-0,039	1,000

***, **, and * indicate significance at the 1%, 5%, and 10% levels, respectively.

Table 4.2. Correlation coefficients (low income economies)

	BCV	CHERR	CRISES	EFI	KAOPEN	OPEN	SDINF	SDTTG
BCV	1.000							
CHERR	-0.052	1.000						
CRISES	0.564***	0.164	1.000					
EFI	-0.720***	-0.064	-0.705***	1.000				
KAOPEN	-0.188	0.282	0.434**	0.158	1.000			
OPEN	0.273*	0.305	-0.047	-0.028	-0.145	1.000		
SDINF	0.113	0.093	0.080	0.045	-0.005	-0.151	1.000	
SDTTG	0.595***	-0.088	0.369*	-0.352*	-0.052	0.222	0.078	1.000

***, **, and * indicate significance at the 1%, 5%, and 10% levels, respectively.

Table 4.3. Correlation coefficients (lower middle income economies)

	BCV	CHERR	CRISES	EFI	KAOPEN	OPEN	SDINF	SDTTG
BCV	1							
CHERR	0.386**	1						
CRISES	0.023	0.307*	1,000					
EFI	-0.062	0.105	0.058	1,000				
KAOPEN	0.013	0.148	0.120	0.573***	1,000			
OPEN	0.422**	0.354**	0.104	-0.011	-0.210	1,000		
SDINF	0,677***	0.362**	0.129	-0.259	-0.037	0.304*	1,000	
SDTTG	0.401**	0.416**	0.073	-0.183	-0.045	0.303*	-0.009	1

***, **, and * indicate significance at the 1%, 5%, and 10% levels, respectively.

Table 4.4. Correlation coefficients (lower middle income economies)

	BCV	CHERR	CRISES	EFI	KAOPEN	OPEN	SDINF	SDTTG
BCV	1.000							
CHERR	-0.156	1.000						
CRISES	0.271	0.494***	1.000					
EFI	-0.262	-0.332*	-0.397*	1.000				
KAOPEN	-0.124	-0.144	-0.094	0.483***	1.000			
OPEN	0.088	-0.147	-0.206	0.033	0.248	1.000		
SDINF	0.180	0.208	0.190	-0.503***	-0.292*	0.003	1.000	
SDTTG	0.007	-0.071	0.039	-0.023	0.268	0.161	0.022	1.000

***, **, and * indicate significance at the 1%, 5%, and 10% levels, respectively.

Table 4.5. Correlation coefficients (high income economies)

	BCV	CHERR	CRISES	EFI	KAOPEN	OPEN	SDINF	SDTTG
BCV	1.000							
CHERR	0.281	1.000						
CRISES	0.064	0.564**	1.000					
EFI	-0.514*	-0.024	-0.275	1.000				
KAOPEN	-0.101	0.286	0.133	0.529*	1.000			
OPEN	0.377	-0.229	-0.575**	0.065	-0.083	1.000		
SDINF	0.052	0.499*	0.483*	-0.466	-0.169	-0.444	1.000	
SDTTG	0.774***	-0.123	-0.094	-0.311	-0.101	0.374	-0.013	1.000

***, **, and * indicate significance at the 1%, 5%, and 10% levels, respectively.

L'EFFET DE LA LIBERTÉ ÉCONOMIQUE SUR LA VOLATILITÉ DES CYCLES DANS LES PAYS EN DÉVELOPPEMENT

Résumé - *Très peu d'études ont étudié l'effet de la liberté économique sur la volatilité des cycles économiques. L'objectif de cet article est de vérifier si ce lien existe en considérant 109 pays en développement sur la période 1995-2012. En utilisant la méthode des moments généralisés (GMM), nous montrons que de manière générale les pays qui disposent d'une plus grande liberté économique connaissent des cycles moins volatils. Toutefois, ce résultat n'est pas vérifié dans tous les cas si l'on envisage des groupes de pays particuliers selon leur niveau de revenu.*

Mots-clés - LIBERTÉ ÉCONOMIQUE, PAYS EN DÉVELOPPEMENT, VOLATILITÉ DES CYCLES ÉCONOMIQUES

DÉTERMINANTS DE L'ADOPTION DES TIC DANS UN PAYS EN DÉVELOPPEMENT : UNE ANALYSE ÉCONOMÉTRIQUE SUR LES ENTREPRISES INDUSTRIELLES AU CAMEROUN

Ariel Herbert FAMBEU*

Résumé - *L'objectif de ce travail est d'analyser les facteurs responsables de l'adoption des Technologies de l'Information et de la Communication (TIC) dans un pays en développement. Pour cela, nous estimons un modèle probit ordonné bivarié sur un échantillon de 1008 entreprises industrielles au Cameroun. En plus des déterminants traditionnels cités par les modèles de diffusion technologique et de profitabilité attendue (effets de rang, de stock-ordre et épidémiques), nous mettons en évidence le facteur de « complémentarité des pratiques organisationnelles » proposé par la théorie de la supermodularité, d'une part, et les caractéristiques des dirigeants, d'autre part. Nos résultats économétriques montrent que l'adoption des TIC par les entreprises dépend principalement des pratiques organisationnelles, de la taille, du statut juridique, du capital humain du dirigeant et de l'adoption par les autres entreprises du secteur ou de la région. Nous trouvons ainsi qu'il existe un lien de complémentarité entre l'adoption des TIC et le niveau de pratiques organisationnelles. Ce travail met également en évidence l'importance du dirigeant, notamment dans les petites et moyennes entreprises, rôle souvent négligé dans la littérature sur l'adoption des TIC.*

Mots-clés - ADOPTION DES TECHNOLOGIES DE L'INFORMATION ET DE LA COMMUNICATION, CAMEROUN, PROBIT ORDONNÉ BIVARIÉ, COMPLÉMENTARITÉ DES PRATIQUES ORGANISATIONNELLES

Classification JEL - L6, L7, O33

L'auteur remercie le rapporteur anonyme pour ses précieuses remarques et suggestions. Nous remercions également les participants au séminaire sur l'économie numérique à Montréal (Canada) en octobre 2015 pour leurs commentaires.

* Groupe de Recherche en Economie Théorique et Appliquée (GRETA), FSEGA, Université de Douala (Cameroun) ; Mail : afambeu@yahoo.fr

1. INTRODUCTION

Les Technologies de l'Information et de la Communication (TIC) sont au cœur de la « nouvelle » économie fondée sur la connaissance. De nombreux travaux ont pu montrer que les TIC, l'innovation et le changement technologique sont des déterminants importants de la productivité et de la croissance des pays (Jorgenson et Stiroh, 2000 ; Oliner et Sichel, 2000 ; Brynjolfsson et Hitt, 2000 ; Bassanini et Scarpetta, 2002; OCDE, 2004 ; Timmer et van Ark, 2005 ; Holt et Jamison, 2009 ; Kretschmer, 2012 ; Biagi, 2013...).

L'impact des investissements en TIC sur la productivité et la croissance s'avère supérieur au niveau de l'entreprise par rapport à l'industrie et au pays (Lehr et Lichtenberg, 1999 ; Brynjolfsson et Hitt, 2000, 2003 ; Matteucci et al., 2005). Pour les entreprises, l'utilisation des TIC conduit à des améliorations dans la conception des produits, le marketing, la production, le financement et l'organisation (Hollenstein, 2004 ; Bloom et al., 2012). En outre, les TIC sont souvent un moteur de l'innovation en facilitant la création de nouveaux produits et services (Becchetti et al., 2003 ; Carlsson, 2004 ; Hollenstein, 2004).

Il est loisible de constater aujourd'hui que l'investissement en TIC a un effet sur la performance des entreprises dans les pays développés, d'autant si cet investissement en TIC est accompagné par d'autres types d'investissements, surtout en matière de changements organisationnels et de capital humain (Milgrom et Robert, 1995 ; Greenan et al., 2001 ; OCDE 2003 ; Bloom et al., 2012 ; World Bank, 2016). Selon un nouveau rapport de la Banque mondiale, les TIC se diffusent rapidement à travers le monde en développement, mais leur adoption est encore insuffisante et les dividendes escomptés (productivité, croissance, emploi, etc.) ne sont pas à la hauteur des attentes (World Bank, 2016). Ce rapport confirme la nécessité pour les entreprises aussi bien du Nord que du Sud à investir en capital humain et changements organisationnels pour bénéficier pleinement de l'adoption des TIC. Différents travaux ont pu montrer que les TIC présentent une opportunité pour les pays en développement (PED) en permettant d'améliorer leur compétitivité et d'entrer dans l'économie de la connaissance (Steinmueller, 2001 ; Lal, 2004 ; Basant et al., 2011 ; Tello, 2011 ; Calza et Rovira, 2011 ; Gutiérrez, 2011 ; Akomea-Bonsu, 2012).

Si la diffusion des TIC est largement expliquée dans les pays développés, elle reste très peu étudiée dans les pays en développement. Dans les PED, les TIC présentent un caractère systémique, puisque leur adoption est conditionnée par un contexte environnant différent de celui des pays développés. Ces différences sont entre autres les infrastructures disponibles, la qualité et la disponibilité de personnel qualifié, la taille du marché national, l'ouverture du marché, la capacité d'adaptation des schémas organisationnels et productifs, la taille des entreprises et le profil du dirigeant. Les PED sont en effet caractérisés par une prédominance des petites et moyennes entreprises (PME) et des très petites entreprises (TPE), et celles-ci ne bénéficient pas aisément des sources de financement nécessaires à leur extension ou à leur modernisation. De plus, ces TPE et PME sont très souvent dirigées par leur promoteur (ou créateur de l'entreprise) dont l'investissement en TIC dépend fortement.

Cette étude qui est une première au Cameroun utilise les données d'une enquête originale faite par l'Institut National de la Statistique (INS) en 2009. Une analyse multivariée ordonnée est réalisée pour contrôler le lien de complémentarité qui pourrait exister entre l'adoption des TIC et les pratiques organisationnelles de l'entreprise. En plus des déterminants traditionnels cités par les modèles de diffusion technologique et de profitabilité attendue (effets de rang, de stock-ordre et épidémiques), nous mettons en évidence d'une part la complémentarité des pratiques organisationnelles et d'autre part les caractéristiques des dirigeants.

L'article est organisé de la manière suivante. La section 2 est consacrée à une revue de la littérature théorique et empirique se rapportant à l'adoption des TIC. La section 3 présente la méthodologie retenue. Les résultats sont discutés dans la section 4 et conduisent aux principales conclusions et recommandations dans la cinquième section.

2. REVUE DE LA LITTERATURE DE L'ADOPTION DES TIC DANS LES ENTREPRISES

2.1. Cadre théorique

La littérature qui analyse les déterminants de l'adoption des TIC en propose deux grands types. Le premier est constitué de facteurs qui affectent directement les coûts et les bénéfices de l'adoption d'une nouvelle technologie. Dans cette approche, quatre effets sont habituellement mis en avant : les effets de rang, les effets de stock, les effets d'ordre et les effets épidémiques (Karshenas et Stoneman, 1993). Le second type est issu d'une approche qui porte l'accent sur la complémentarité entre les TIC et certaines pratiques organisationnelles et les gains d'efficacité associés (Milgrom et Roberts, 1990). Aux différents facteurs évoqués par ces deux approches, Bocquet et Brossard (2007) ajoutent deux autres facteurs : la capacité d'apprentissage des entreprises et leurs capacités (capabilités) technologiques. Dans ce travail, nous mettons également en évidence le profil du dirigeant de l'entreprise comme un troisième type de déterminant.

2.1.1. Modèles d'adoption des innovations et profitabilité attendue

Ces modèles sont constitués de facteurs qui affectent directement les coûts et les bénéfices de l'adoption d'une nouvelle technologie : les modèles épidémiques, de rang, de stock, et d'ordre.

Les modèles épidémiques ou de diffusion par contagion, inspirés des travaux de Mansfield (1961), considèrent que l'information relative à une innovation est déterminante pour son adoption et qu'elle est coûteuse. Chaque adoptant génère ainsi une externalité positive en transférant de l'information aux autres adoptants potentiels. Tout en reconnaissant leur validité dans de nombreuses études empiriques, ces modèles ont été critiqués en raison notamment du traitement uniforme des firmes qui sont supposées avoir une probabilité identique d'être contaminées. Ces modèles s'intéressent essentiellement au comportement agrégé des firmes en ignorant quasiment le processus décisionnel au niveau individuel (Grolleau, 2001). Or toutes les entreprises ne disposent pas de la même information, en quantité identique, au même moment. L'influence de la proximité géographique a notamment été examinée dans la littérature économique portant sur les déterminants spatiaux de l'adoption et de la diffusion technologique. L'idée générale est que l'environnement dans lequel la firme est localisée influence sa capacité à innover et notamment sa capacité à adopter de nouvelles technologies (Galliano et Roux, 2006). Bocquet et Brossard (2008) se sont également intéressés à la notion de proximité « épistémique ». Il existe selon eux, une proximité épistémique entre deux firmes si celles-ci partagent des problèmes communs et des représentations partagées. Cette proximité épistémique serait de nature à renforcer les échanges de connaissances entre des entreprises localisées à proximité et partageant les mêmes caractéristiques productives et technologiques.

Les modèles de rang ou modèles probit sont associés à l'hétérogénéité des entreprises et supposent que l'adoption de la technologie, à un moment donné, génère des profits différents du fait de caractéristiques inhérentes à chaque firme. Les décisions d'adoption sont avant tout déterminées par un arbitrage entre les profits supplémentaires espérés grâce à l'adoption et les coûts du changement de technologie. Or les coûts et les bénéfices du changement technologique des firmes dépendent d'un plus ou moins grand nombre de variables : la taille, l'âge, le capital humain, les politiques de prix et de services des fournisseurs, le statut juridique de l'entreprise, ses capacités d'apprentissage, d'absorption et de changement, la nature de son environnement concurrentiel, etc. Ainsi, les firmes peuvent être rangées ou classées en fonction du profit généré par l'adoption à une période donnée (Baldwin et Rafiquzzaman, 1998). L'attractivité de l'innovation, représentée par le profit généré par l'adoption, est censée croître avec le temps du fait d'économies d'échelle externes, du « learning by doing » et de la diminution des coûts de recherche, entre autres. Par exemple, les premiers adoptants permettent de diminuer les coûts de recherche pour les suivants en rendant l'innovation et ses conséquences plus transparentes. La profitabilité augmentant, le seuil critique déterminant la décision d'adopter s'abaisse permettant ainsi à d'autres firmes d'adopter l'innovation. Ainsi, les firmes adoptent à des moments différents parce qu'elles diffèrent sur des caractéristiques qui affectent le profit généré par l'adoption, cette profitabilité étant elle-même variable en fonction du nombre d'adoptants.

L'intensité concurrentielle est considérée comme une caractéristique liée à l'industrie et faisant partie de ce fait des modèles de *rang*. L'intensité concurrentielle est généralement liée au degré de concentration du secteur et à la capacité des concurrents à ériger des barrières à la mobilité (Porter, 1980). Pour les entreprises qui opèrent sur des marchés très concurrentiels, l'adoption d'une innovation peut être nécessaire au maintien de sa position sur le marché ; elle peut permettre de construire ou de maintenir des barrières à l'entrée (Robertson et Gatignon, 1986). Dans un tel environnement, le fait de ne pas procéder à une innovation déjà adoptée par les autres concurrents peut constituer un désavantage compétitif. Ceci dépend de l'importance stratégique de l'innovation et de ses implications potentielles sur l'efficacité et l'efficience des activités de l'entreprise (Frambach et Schilleweart, 2002). La littérature a mis en évidence différents types de relations entre le degré de concurrence du secteur et l'adoption technologique. Dans la littérature s'intéressant aux organisations industrielles, un impact positif a pu être montré à la fois pour des firmes opérant dans des secteurs très concurrentiels mais aussi pour des firmes confrontées à une pression concurrentielle beaucoup plus faible (Gatignon et Robertson, 1989 ; Kamien et Schwartz, 1982 ; Baldwin et Scott, 1987 ; Majumdar et Venkataraman, 1992).

Les modèles de stock-ordre expriment l'influence ambigüe de la concurrence sur le processus de diffusion des technologies. Ils ont fait l'objet d'analyses à partir de la théorie des jeux développée par Reinganum (1981), Fudenberg et Tirole (1985), Dasgupta (1986) et Quirmbath (1986). Les théoriciens des jeux suggèrent que la rentabilité des nouvelles technologies pour l'utilisateur, combinée à des pressions incessantes de leurs concurrents afin de réduire les coûts, permet de déterminer le temps d'adoption pour l'entreprise et de savoir qui sera leader ou suiveur[1]. *Les modèles d'ordre* sont basés sur l'idée que l'ordre dans lequel les firmes adoptent la nouvelle technologie détermine le profit qu'elles peuvent en obtenir. Le profit de l'adoption est plus important pour les firmes qui sont les toutes premières à adopter la nouvelle technologie (les first-movers). Cela peut être dû au fait qu'elles sont alors en position de préempter les surprofits (Fudenberg et Tirole, 1985), de prendre place sur les sites géographiques les plus avantageux, ou d'être les premières à avoir accès à une main-d'œuvre qualifiée disponible seulement en quantité limitée (Ireland et Stoneman, 1985). *Les modèles de stock* reposent sur l'idée que le profit généré par l'adoption d'une innovation est fonction du nombre total de firmes ayant déjà adopté l'innovation. Les bénéfices liés à l'adoption pour l'adoptant marginal diminuent avec l'augmentation du nombre de firmes ayant déjà adopté l'innovation (Karshenas et Stoneman, 1993). Ces deux modèles impliquent que la probabilité d'adoption sera d'autant plus élevée que le nombre d'adoptants et/ou le stock de la nouvelle technologie déjà installée sont faibles. Les modèles de stock se concentrent sur le nombre d'adoptants à l'équilibre et sur la moindre profitabilité de l'adoption, donc sur une moindre probabilité d'adoption supplémentaire. A l'inverse, les modèles d'ordre se focalisent sur l'anticipation des adoptions suivantes. Ainsi, l'ordre a un impact positif sur la probabilité d'adoption tandis que l'effet stock a un impact négatif. Cependant, lorsqu'il y a une

[1] Néanmoins, la préoccupation des théoriciens des jeux a été mise sur le temps d'adoption d'une nouvelle technologie. Leurs modèles se concentrent sur la rentabilité de l'innovation pour l'utilisateur et considèrent le moment exact de l'adoption dans des conditions de duopole ou d'oligopole. Les principales conclusions sont que, même lorsque les entreprises disposent d'une information identique et parfaite sur une technologie, le comportement stratégique peut conduire à un équilibre de Nash avec différentes dates d'adoption. Reinganum (1981) montre que le premier entrant ou adoptant moissonne tous les avantages de la nouvelle technologie et donc il y a une course pour être un leader plutôt que suiveur. Ces modèles n'évoquent toutefois pas la possibilité d'un comportement préventif de la part des entreprises rivales. En supposant que le comportement de préemption puisse survenir en raison des incitations des entreprises, Fudenberg et Tirole (1985) démontrent que la date d'adoption sera différente.

forte incertitude sur les bénéfices futurs de la nouvelle technologie, ou bien lorsque l'on est confronté à des technologies à effets de réseau, ces effets peuvent être totalement inversés (Bocquet et Brossard, 2008).

Bocquet et al. (2007) critiquent ces approches de la diffusion en insistant sur la complexité du phénomène d'adoption. D'une part, avant d'investir dans les TIC, les adopteurs potentiels ont en effet besoin d'acquérir des connaissances sur les technologies disponibles de manière à pouvoir sélectionner les plus profitables. D'autre part, s'il est vrai que les TIC n'exigent pas forcement l'acquisition de savoirs nouveaux à l'échelle de la firme, leur mise en œuvre demeure un processus complexe au plan organisationnel.

2.1.2. Théorie de la supermodularité

Même si les facteurs identifiés par l'approche de la diffusion sont importants, Milgrom et Roberts (1990, 1995) fondateurs de la théorie de la supermodularité, suggèrent que les firmes ne s'intéressent pas à l'adoption des TIC si elles n'ont pas adopté des pratiques stratégiques et organisationnelles relatives au nouveau système de production flexible. Ils traduisent mathématiquement la complémentarité entre ces facteurs de propriété de *supermodularité* : l'efficacité marginale d'un facteur, ici les TIC, croît avec le niveau d'un autre facteur, en l'occurrence le niveau de diffusion des pratiques innovantes[2]. La théorie de la supermodularité défend l'idée de complémentarité dans une approche systémique (*i.e.* combinaison d'un ensemble d'éléments multiples) plus qu'interactive (*i.e.* qui se focalise sur des effets d'interaction entre un nombre limité de facteurs) (Ennen et Richter, 2010). L' « effet système » est notamment envisagé entre les pratiques organisationnelles, stratégiques, et les technologies de l'information, dans le cadre de la firme moderne et flexible. Leur adoption conjointe est source d'une efficacité supérieure à la somme des gains qu'elles pourraient générer isolément. Dans le domaine de la stratégie, la notion de complémentarité est largement utilisée en synonyme de « *fit* » ou de « *congruence* » (Miller, 1986 ; Ennen et Richter, 2010). L'idée centrale de cette approche est qu'une entreprise qui ajuste mutuellement des facteurs contextuels, stratégiques et organisationnels, est susceptible de bénéficier d'un avantage supérieur par rapport aux entreprises où un tel ajustement (« *fit* ») fait défaut.

Les recherches qui se réclament de la théorie de la supermodularité utilisent deux principales approches que Galia et al. (2013) nomment « complémentarités dans l'usage » (*complementarities-in-use*) et « complémentarités en performance » (*complementarities-in-performance*). La première porte sur les liens entre des ensembles d'activités : on regarde si ces activités sont dépendantes et s'il y a un bon ajustement entre elles, suggérant une interaction mutuelle bénéfique. La seconde, plus fine et peut-être plus fidèle à la modélisation de Milgrom et Roberts (1990), explore plus précisément les effets de la combinaison d'activités ou pratiques sur la performance économique des entreprises. Puisque dans ce travail l'objectif est d'identifier les facteurs favorisant ou non l'adoption

---

[2] Pour des profits deux fois dérivables, la supermodularité est équivalente à la positivité de toutes les dérivées partielles croisées de Schwarz.

des TIC par les entreprises en prenant en compte les relations de complémentarité avec les pratiques organisationnelles, nous nous situons plutôt dans l'approche de la « complémentarité dans l'usage ».

Selon Athey et Stern (1998), la fonction de production classique doit être augmentée d'une fonction de production de « *design organisationnel* » qui résume les choix discrets que l'entreprise réalise dans les domaines stratégiques. En effet, dans une fonction de production classique, l'entreprise choisit essentiellement ses quantités de facteurs de production. A ces choix opérationnels, la théorie de la supermodularité ajoute une série de choix stratégiques : choix de produits, d'équipements, de pratiques organisationnelles. Si des variables complémentaires d'une fonction de production augmentent simultanément, alors la productivité augmente plus que si l'on sommait la valeur des changements induits par l'augmentation de chacune des variables prises isolément. Si les firmes choisissent leurs technologies et leurs pratiques par optimisation, et s'il y a des complémentarités entre ces dernières, l'adoption des TIC devrait être positivement influencée par l'adoption de pratiques organisationnelles et stratégies complémentaires. Une seconde approche consiste à estimer dans une fonction de production les paramètres associés à des termes d'interaction entre variables technologiques et organisationnelles. Athey et Stern (1998) montrent, en travaillant sur différentes configurations d'erreurs dans la mesure des variables, qu'aucune de ces approches n'est pleinement satisfaisante et que chacune ne mesure que des « présomptions » de complémentarité.

Bocquet et Brossard (2007) mentionnent que les connaissances limitées et les compétences insuffisantes inhibent l'adoption des TIC, mais elles sont considérées comme des facteurs exogènes, les conséquences d'un possible apprentissage endogène sont ignorées. A l'inverse, Dosi (1988) propose une conception dynamique d'apprentissage, où les firmes aux connaissances limitées peuvent à un certain moment les accroitre. L'apprentissage est une capacité adaptative qui augmente l'habileté à sélectionner les technologies requises. Le point important est que le processus ne nécessite pas systématiquement l'adoption de tout le menu TIC mais de sélectionner seulement les technologies les plus importantes. Cette capacité dépend, entre autres, du niveau du capital humain, de l'expérience dans les anciennes technologies, de la capacité à l'exportation, de la R&D ainsi que de l'âge de l'entreprise.

2.1.3. Le rôle du dirigeant

Le rôle du dirigeant de l'entreprise est important dans l'adoption des TIC dans les PED, caractérisés par une prédominance des TPE et PME. Dans les PME les dirigeants prennent les décisions d'adoption des TIC à partir de la phase de planification jusqu'à la mise en œuvre et dans les étapes de mise à niveau du système (Bruque et Moyano, 2007 ; Nguyen, 2009). En effet, les PME sont généralement des structures simples et très centralisées avec un chef d'entreprise, où dans la plupart des cas le propriétaire et le dirigeant sont une seule et même personne (Ghobakhloo et al., 2011a). Un certain nombre d'études ont révélé que dans les PME, les décisions du chef d'entreprise (dirigeant /propriétaire) influent sur l'orientation stratégique et l'organisation des différentes activités de l'entreprise, tant en cours qu'à l'avenir (Fuller-Love, 2006; Smith, 2007).

Selon la littérature, les décisions d'adoption technologique sont principalement liées à plusieurs caractéristiques du dirigeant : sa compétence basée sur son niveau d'éducation et son expérience personnelle (Riemenschneider et Mykytyn, 2000 ; Raymond et St-Pierre, 2005 ; Ghobakhloo et al., 2011a), sa connaissance des TIC et une attitude positive envers ces technologies (Thong et Yap, 1995 ; Foong, 1999 ; Thong, 1999 ; Kutlu et Özturan, 2008 ; Ghobakhloo et al., 2010), sa volonté de croissance de l'entreprise (Jeffcoate et al., 2002 ; Drew, 2003 ; Tseng et al., 2004 ; Ghobakhloo et al., 2011b) et de développement à l'international (Jeffcoate et al., 2002 ; Raymond et St-Pierre, 2005). En s'appuyant sur la théorie basée sur les ressources, Caldeira et Ward (2003) et Ghobakhloo et al. (2011b) ont montré que le soutien de la direction entre de manière significative dans le succès d'adoption des TIC au sein des PME.

2.2. Littérature empirique

La littérature a largement analysé les divers facteurs inhérents à l'adoption des TIC par une entreprise, aussi bien dans les pays développés que dans les pays en développement.

Dans les pays développés, Hollenstein et Woerter (2008) ont étudié les déterminants de l'adoption et de la diffusion des TIC dans les entreprises en Suisse et ont montré que l'adoption des TIC était liée aux avantages attendus, aux coûts d'adoption, aux possibilités technologiques, à l'état de la concurrence et à la taille de l'entreprise, mais également au pourcentage des firmes qui l'ont adopté dans le secteur (effet épidémique). Haller et Siedschlag (2011) ont constaté que l'adoption des TIC dans les entreprises manufacturières irlandaises a été inégale selon les entreprises, les industries et l'espace. Selon leurs calculs, les entreprises ayant plus de travailleurs qualifiés, opérant dans les secteurs producteurs et utilisateurs de TIC et situées dans la région de Dublin (la capitale) ont eu relativement plus de succès dans l'adoption et l'utilisation des TIC. Bayo-Moriones et Lera-López (2007) montrent que la taille des entreprises et une main-d'œuvre hautement qualifiée sont positivement associées à l'adoption des TIC dans un échantillon d'entreprises espagnoles.

Fabiani et al. (2005) mettent en évidence que dans le secteur manufacturier italien l'adoption des TIC est associée à la taille de l'entreprise, au capital humain, à la présence de grandes entreprises dans le secteur et aux changements dans les structures organisationnelles. Hur et al. (2005) ont montré l'existence de complémentarité entre l'adoption des TIC et la présence de main-d'œuvre qualifiée dans le secteur manufacturier coréen. Dans une étude sur les entreprises allemandes, Hempell (2003) a souligné que les TIC nécessitent plus d'investissements en capital humain fourni par l'éducation formelle, avant même la formation en entreprise. En étudiant des entreprises suisses, Hollenstein (2004) trouve des résultats similaires ainsi que des effets de la pression concurrentielle (et plus largement des effets de rang) et de l'effet épidémique sur l'adoption des TIC. C'est aussi le cas dans l'étude de Bartoloni et Baussola

(2001) sur l'industrie manufacturière italienne où les auteurs mesurent l'effet épidémique par le nombre d'adoptants courants.

Battisti et al. (2004) montrent que les premiers adoptants de logiciels de conception informatisée bénéficient de profits plus élevés que les adoptants plus tardifs (effet d'ordre) et qu'il se produit aussi un effet de contagion lié au nombre croissant d'utilisateurs de ces technologies (effet épidémique). Cet effet épidémique ne fonctionne pas, dans leur échantillon, lorsqu'il s'agit de la diffusion non pas d'une technologie mais d'une pratique organisationnelle (la mise en place d'équipes de conception entre clients et fournisseurs). Caselli et Coleman (2001) ont étudié 89 pays où il apparaît que la valeur des importations de matériel informatique – un indicateur de l'investissement en TIC – a été significativement associée à la scolarité et à l'ouverture commerciale mesurée par l'intensité des importations. En France, Bocquet et Brossard (2008) ont montré l'influence positive de la proximité géographique sur l'adoption d'un progiciel de gestion (ERP). Bocquet et Brossard (2008) se sont également intéressés à la notion de proximité « épistémique », c'est à dire la combinaison de l'environnement géographique et sectoriel. Leur étude empirique montre un impact positif de la proximité « épistémique » sur l'adoption d'un ERP. Canepa et Stoneman (2004) proposent une comparaison internationale des dynamiques de diffusion des nouvelles technologies de production et indiquent que, dans la plupart des pays étudiés, les deux déterminants principaux de l'adoption sont les effets de rang et les effets épidémiques.

Une des toutes premières études à prendre en compte l'hypothèse de complémentarité de Milgrom et Roberts a été menée par Arora et Gambardella (1990) à partir de 81 firmes de l'industrie chimique et pharmaceutique situées aux Etats-Unis, en Europe et au Japon. Leur étude a mis en évidence l'existence d'une complémentarité entre les différentes pratiques de partenariat externe. Cependant, le nombre trop réduit de variables de contrôle ne permet pas de traiter correctement le biais d'hétérogénéité propre à ce type de test. Stoneman et Kwon (1994) ont approfondi les résultats de Karshenas et Stoneman (1993) en montrant que la décision d'adopter dépend des effets de complémentarité entre technologies. Ils ont ainsi montré que les caractéristiques et le processus de diffusion d'une technologie particulière peuvent avoir un impact important sur la diffusion d'une autre technologie. Hollenstein (2004) teste la possibilité d'une causalité inverse selon laquelle les pratiques organisationnelles nouvelles seraient mises en place du fait de l'adoption des TIC. Cette hypothèse est vérifiée dans le cadre des entreprises suisses étudiées, mais il montre que les pratiques organisationnelles mettent plus de temps à s'ajuster que l'équipement en TIC. Bayo-Morionesa et Lera-Lopez (2007) montrent sur les entreprises espagnoles que l'adoption des ordinateurs et de l'intranet dépend positivement de l'application des normes ISO 9000 et de la poursuite d'une stratégie de différenciation. Les résultats de Bocquet et Brossard (2008) suggèrent que la supermodularité ne signifie pas plus de TIC avec plus de pratiques stratégiques et organisationnelles innovantes. En effet, sur une base de 136 entreprises en France, les auteurs montrent que seulement certains dispositifs organisationnels et certains choix stratégiques sont complémentaires. Ces conclusions viennent ainsi confirmer les travaux de Bocquet et al. (2007) selon lesquels les pratiques « innovantes » ne sont pas forcément complémentaires à tous les types de TIC.

Dans les pays en développement, les études sont plus récentes du fait de l'absence de données microéconomiques fiables sur plusieurs années.

Nour (2011) a étudié l'adoption et l'impact des TIC dans les pays arabes du Golfe. Au niveau microéconomique, l'adoption des TIC augmente avec la taille des entreprises et de l'industrie. Gallego et al. (2015) ont mené une étude sur 3759 entreprises manufacturières colombiennes afin d'identifier les facteurs d'adoption des TIC par les entreprises. Selon leur étude, l'adoption est facilitée quand une entreprise est relativement grande, possède un capital humain assez large et s'engage dans des activités innovantes. Ses déterminants sont plus significatifs pour les PME que pour les grandes entreprises. Machikita et al. (2010) ont examiné l'adoption des TIC dans quatre pays de l'Asean (Indonésie, Philippines, Thaïlande et Vietnam) et ont montré que la taille de l'entreprise influe positivement sur la probabilité d'adoption des TIC. Mughal et Diawara (2011) ont étudié l'impact du capital humain sur l'adoption et la diffusion des TIC dans les entreprises pakistanaises. Ils ont conclu que le niveau de formation, le niveau de qualification des dirigeants et le niveau d'éducation des salariés sont associés à l'adoption des TIC.

Kossaï et al. (2010) ont montré que l'investissement dans le capital humain est le principal déterminant de l'adoption des TIC des PME tunisiennes du secteur électrique et électronique. Dans une étude auprès de 625 PME sénégalaises, Diawara et Mughal (2014) ont montré que le capital humain était important dans la décision des entreprises d'adopter ou pas les TIC. La formation des dirigeants et le niveau d'éducation des salariés étaient les déterminants les plus significatifs. Lal (2007), dans une étude sur les entreprises manufacturières nigérianes, a mis en évidence que la capacité d'absorption des employés, mesurée par le nombre de techniciens, a joué un rôle important dans l'adoption des TIC. Il a également constaté que les PME adoptent les TIC pour obtenir des informations appropriées et plus précises en termes de spécification des produits, sur les technologies de production nouvelles et en matière commerciale. Le rôle positif de la capacité d'absorption des entreprises est confirmé par Ndiege et al. (2014) sur les petites et moyennes entreprises du Kenya. Dans une étude sur les PME en Ouganda, Ssewanyana et Busler (2007) ont relevé le retard enregistré par rapport aux pays développés. La faible adoption des TIC est liée au coût élevé des investissements nécessaires, au manque de connaissances et de compétences des employés. Leurs résultats suggèrent qu'il est nécessaire d'élargir la formation à l'usage des TIC pour les employés, afin de permettre aux entrepreneurs de tirer profit des opportunités liées aux TIC et de réduire leur coût d'acquisition (coûts élevés du matériel, des logiciels et des services internet).

De même que Gallego et al. (2015) en Colombie, un lien entre innovations organisationnelles et intensité d'adoption des TIC est trouvé par Ben Khalifa (2014) sur 145 firmes tunisiennes. Sur 1000 entreprises au Brésil et en Inde, Basant et al. (2011) ont montré qu'il existe une plus forte productivité lorsque l'entreprise adopte les TIC et effectue simultanément des changements organisationnels. Cependant, cette complémentarité ne s'opère que pour les entreprises fortement dotées en TIC. Sur données d'entreprises béninoises, Gnansounou (2010) a identifié la localisation géographique, l'âge, la taille, mais aussi les caractéristiques des principaux actionnaires (niveau d'instruction et niveau de connaissance de l'utilisation de l'outil informatique) comme étant des déterminants significatifs de l'adoption des TIC.

Les études réalisées sur 166 petites entreprises à Singapour par Thong (1999) et Thong et al. (1995) ont montré que les dirigeants les mieux formés et disposant de meilleures connaissances permettent de réduire le degré d'incertitude et le risque d'où une plus forte probabilité d'adoption des TIC. Raymond et StPierre (2005) mettent en évidence sur 248 PME manufacturières canadiennes que le niveau d'éducation et l'expérience du dirigeant de la PME influencent l'adoption de systèmes de production technologiques sophistiqués basés et construits autour des TIC. Par ailleurs, Correa et al. (2010), ont constaté que les PME d'Europe de l'Est et d'Asie centrale dirigées par des dirigeants ayant un diplôme universitaire ou de troisième cycle sont 23 pour cent plus susceptibles d'adopter des TIC. Sur un échantillon de 121 PME iraniennes Ghobakhloo et al. (2011b) montrent également que l'adoption des TIC est influencée non seulement par les caractéristiques du personnel, mais aussi par ceux du dirigeant (notamment la volonté du dirigeant à fournir des ressources pour l'implémentation des TIC). Dans une étude auprès de 625 PME sénégalaises, Diawara et Mughal (2014) ont montré que le capital humain était important dans la décision des entreprises d'adopter ou pas les TIC. La formation des dirigeants et le niveau d'éducation des salariés étaient les déterminants les plus significatifs. Oyelaran-Oyeyinka et Lal (2004) ont mené une enquête auprès des PME ougandaises, nigérianes et indiennes et font apparaître l'existence d'une corrélation entre les entreprises utilisant des technologies avancées et le niveau d'éducation des entrepreneurs ainsi qu'entre les différents modes d'apprentissage et la complexité d'utilisation des TIC. De même, Kapurubandara et Lawson (2006) montrent que les caractéristiques du dirigeant peuvent être un frein au développement des TIC dans les PME au Sri Lanka.

Les travaux analysant l'adoption des TIC par les entreprises au Cameroun restent quasi-inexistants. En effet, la quasi-totalité des travaux sur les TIC au niveau microéconomique porte sur leur adoption et leurs usages par des individus et des ménages (Mukoko, 2012 ; Tamokwé, 2013 ; Fambeu et Bakehe, 2015).

3. MÉTHODOLOGIE

3.1. Données

Notre analyse empirique est basée sur les données d'entreprises industrielles issues du Recensement Général des Entreprises (RGE) réalisé au cours de la période août-novembre 2009 par l'Institut National de la Statistique (INS), selon la classification en très petites entreprises (TPE), petites entreprises (PE), moyennes entreprises (ME) et grandes entreprises (GE) en fonction de l'importance du chiffre d'affaires et des effectifs employés. 11 685 entreprises industrielles en activité (soit 12,43% des entreprises totales, avec 86,5% pour le tertiaire et 1,07 pour le primaire) ont été recensées, parmi lesquelles 6 906 exercent dans les deux principales métropoles du pays, Douala et Yaoundé, ce qui représente 59% du total. Ces deux agglomérations sont les lieux privilégiés de localisation des ME (80,6% de l'ensemble) et des GE (78,5%). Ensuite, pour ce qui concerne les questionnaires de structure, l'INS a retenu 1008 entreprises industrielles à l'issue des opérations d'apurement de la base de données de la population mère (soit 12,55% de l'échantillon), afin d'assurer la représentativité du secteur industriel. Ces questionnaires de structure contiennent les informations sur le chiffre d'affaires, l'effectif employé, la valeur ajoutée, les exportations, l'âge de l'entreprise, l'environnement des affaires, les investissements (R&D, immobilier, etc.), les innovations technologiques, la certification ISO, la formation du personnel, l'utilisation des TIC, etc. Conformément à la nomenclature d'activités du Cameroun (NACAM), le secteur industriel est subdivisé en 5 sous-secteurs : l'extraction (contenant 2 branches), les industries alimentaires (7 branches), les autres industries manufacturières (14 branches), l'électricité-eau-gaz (1 branche) et la construction (1 branche). Cette nomenclature du Cameroun est une adaptation de la Nomenclature des Activités des Etats Membres d'AFRISTAT (NAEMA) inspirée de la classification internationale type, par industrie, de toutes les branches d'activité économique (CITI rév. 3.1).

Comme le montrent les tableaux 1 et 2 (en annexe), notre échantillon n'est pas parfaitement représentatif des entreprises industrielles au Cameroun. Cela est dû au fait que la phase d'épuration de la base de données a conduit à éliminer environ 95% des TPE, entreprises pourtant les plus représentées dans la population mère (84%). Par conséquent, du fait de la surreprésentation des TPE dans les « autres industries manufacturières » (tableau 3 en annexe), l'élimination de celles-ci entraine automatiquement une réduction du poids de ce secteur et augmente le poids des autres types d'entreprises et des autres secteurs. Toutefois, les TPE et le sous-secteur « autres industries manufacturières » restent toujours fortement représentés dans l'échantillon (tableaux 3 et 4 en annexe) comme c'est le cas dans la population mère. Bien que cet échantillon ne soit pas parfaitement représentatif des entreprises industrielles et qu'il convient donc de rester prudent sur les résultats obtenus, l'utilisation de cette base de données originale peut nous permettre de tirer des enseignements sur les conditions d'utilisation des TIC par les entreprises au Cameroun.

3.2. Modèle économétrique

L'adoption simultanée des TIC (Y_1) et des pratiques organisationnelles (Y_2) dans une entreprise est décrite par le système d'équations suivant :

$$\begin{cases} Y_1^* = \beta_1 X_1 + \varepsilon_1 & (1) \\ Y_2^* = \beta_2 X_2 + \varepsilon_2 & (2) \end{cases}$$

où les erreurs ε_{1i} et ε_{2i} suivent une loi normale bivariée :

$$\begin{pmatrix} \varepsilon_1 \\ \varepsilon_2 \end{pmatrix} \sim i.i.d.N \left(\begin{pmatrix} 0 \\ 0 \end{pmatrix}, \begin{pmatrix} \sigma^2 & \rho \\ \rho & \sigma^2 \end{pmatrix} \right)$$

X_i représente le vecteur des variables explicatives, β_1 et β_2 sont les vecteurs des paramètres à estimer.

Y_1^* et Y_2^* sont les variables latentes représentant respectivement les profits nets pour une firme d'adopter au moins une TIC et une pratique organisationnelle. Toutefois, nous n'observons pas ces deux variables latentes, mais les variables catégorielles Y_1(cinq modalités) et Y_2 (cinq modalités) telles que :

$$Y_1 = \begin{cases} 0 & si\ Y_1^* < c_{11} \\ 1 & si\ c_{11} \leq Y_1^* \leq c_{12} \\ 2 & si\ c_{12} \leq Y_1^* \leq c_{13} \\ 3 & si\ c_{13} \leq Y_1^* \leq c_{14} \\ 4 & si\ Y_1^* > c_{14} \end{cases} \qquad Y_2 = \begin{cases} 0 & si\ Y_2^* < c_{21} \\ 1 & si\ c_{21} \leq Y_2^* \leq c_{22} \\ 2 & si\ c_{22} \leq Y_2^* \leq c_{23} \\ 3 & si\ c_{23} \leq Y_2^* \leq c_{24} \\ 4 & si\ Y_2^* > c_{24} \end{cases} \qquad (3)$$

où les c_{ij} ($c_{ij} \in R$) sont les points limites estimés à partir d'autres paramètres du modèle. Ces points limites doivent satisfaire les conditions suivantes : $c_{11} < c_{12} < c_{13} < c_{14}$; $c_{21} < c_{22} < c_{23} < c_{24}$. Les paramètres de ce système d'équations ((1) et (2)) sont identifiés uniquement en imposant une restriction d'exclusion sur les vecteurs X_1 ou X_2 *i.e.* au moins un élément de X_1 ne doit pas être présent dans X_2 (Sajaia, 2008).

Dans ce travail, nous analysons les déterminants de l'adoption des TIC tout en contrôlant la complémentarité des pratiques organisationnelles. Ces deux variables expliquées sont discrètes et ordonnées. En effet, dans le questionnaire, il a été demandé à l'entreprise si elle disposait d'au moins un ordinateur fonctionnel, d'un réseau intranet, d'une connexion à internet et si elle effectue des opérations d'affaires par internet. Ainsi, nous affectons un score de 0 à une entreprise si elle n'a adopté aucune TIC, 1 si elle a au moins un ordinateur fonctionnel, 2 si en plus de l'ordinateur elle dispose d'un réseau intranet ou d'une connexion internet (toutes les entreprises qui disposent d'une connexion internet et/ou d'un réseau intranet disposent déjà d'au moins un ordinateur), 3 si en plus de l'ordinateur elle dispose d'une connexion internet et du réseau intranet ou d'une connexion internet et fait des opérations d'affaires via internet (toutes les entreprises qui pratiquent le e-business disposent déjà d'au moins un ordinateur et une connexion à internet), 4 si en plus de l'ordinateur elle dispose d'une connexion internet, d'un réseau intranet et fait des opérations d'affaires via internet.

Les données permettent également d'appréhender quelques dispositifs organisationnels mis en place par l'entreprise tels que la formation du personnel liée aux technologies, une gestion informatisée, la certification ISO, les prestations sociales autres que indemnités de transport et de logement et cotisations CNPS dans le but de motiver les salariés.

Ces informations nous permettent de construire une variable représentative du niveau d'adoption des TIC (NTIC) et une autre du niveau de pratiques organisationnelles (NPO) :

$$NATIC = \begin{cases} 0 & si\ pas\ de\ TIC \\ 1 & si\ une\ TIC \\ 2 & si\ deux\ TIC \\ 3 & si\ trois\ TIC \\ 4 & si\ quatre\ TIC \end{cases} \qquad NPO = \begin{cases} 0 & si\ aucune\ pratique \\ 1 & si\ une\ pratique \\ 2 & si\ deux\ pratiques \\ 3 & si\ trois\ pratiques \\ 4 & si\ quatre\ pratiques \end{cases}$$

Les variables explicatives sont quant à elles[3] :

- *Les effets de rang* liés à l'entreprise qui contiennent l'âge, la taille, le capital humain, la recherche et développement, la propriété du capital (IDE), l'appartenance à un groupe, le statut juridique, le degré de concurrence (indice d'Herfindahl) et l'ouverture commerciale (exportations) ;
- *L'effet de stock-ordre* mesuré par la moyenne d'adoption des TIC ou des pratiques organisationnelles des entreprises autour d'une firme i opérant dans le même secteur d'activité j. Cette mesure a été choisie parce qu'il n'existe pas d'informations sur le délai d'adoption nous permettant ainsi de différencier les deux effets. Nous avons donc utilisé la formule suivante :

$$\bar{y}_i = \frac{\sum_{i \in N_j} y_{ji} - y_i}{N_j - 1} \quad (4)$$

- *L'effet épidémique* qui mesure le niveau moyen d'adoption des entreprises dans un voisinage géographique donné. Dans ce travail, nous utilisons la région de recensement comme voisinage géographique. La formule utilisée est la même que celle de l'effet de stock-ordre, mais en remplaçant le secteur j par la région r.
- *Les caractéristiques du dirigeant* mesurées par son genre, sa nationalité et son diplôme.

3.3. Traitement des données et estimation du modèle

En amont de l'estimation du modèle, il est primordial de considérer les données incomplètes ou manquantes. Si le pourcentage de non-réponse est faible (5% ou moins), l'élimination de ces observations peut être une solution raisonnable au problème. Cependant, dans un ensemble multivarié où plusieurs variables peuvent avoir des valeurs manquantes, les observations ayant au moins une donnée manquante représentent une proportion importante de la base de données. Dans ce travail, comme le montre le tableau 6 (en annexe), il existe des données manquantes partielles allant de 6,7% à 58,3% selon les variables. Dans ce cas, ne pas tenir compte des données manquantes conduirait à une perte d'efficacité car une partie importante de l'information est ignorée.

Il existe deux techniques de correction de la non-réponse : la repondération (principalement utilisée pour compenser la non-réponse totale) et l'imputation (principalement utilisée pour prédire la non-réponse partielle). Cette deuxième technique est utilisée ici puisque nos données sont partiellement absentes. Les réponses manquantes sont remplacées par une (ou plusieurs) valeur(s) « plausible(s) » qui est (sont) en général issue (s) ou estimée (s) à partir de la distribution des répondants.

Pendant longtemps, les recherches ont été conduites en remplaçant chaque donnée manquante par une donnée prédite ou simulée (imputation simple). Cependant, cette méthode présente des limites, notamment parce qu'elle sous-

[3] Elles sont définies en détail dans le tableau 5 en annexe.

estime l'incertitude en considérant les valeurs imputées comme vraies. D'autre part, cette méthode nécessite que les données soient complètes et connues pour l'ensemble des variables prises en compte dans le modèle d'imputation, mais cette limite est peu évoquée dans la littérature.

Dans le cadre de ce travail, nous avons appliqué une procédure d'imputation multiple (IM). Cette méthode consiste à créer plusieurs valeurs possibles d'une valeur manquante. Le principe et les techniques d'imputation multiple ont été développés par Rubin (1978 ; 1987). En plus de considérer simultanément tous les individus et toutes les variables (avec et sans données manquantes), cette méthode permet de prendre en compte l'incertitude sur la prédiction de la valeur de remplacement. L'idée principale de l'IM est de produire *m* bases de données imputées. Dans chaque base imputée, chaque valeur absente est remplacée au bout d'un processus itératif par une estimation. L'objectif de cette technique n'est pas de prédire au mieux les valeurs manquantes, mais bien de prendre en compte et refléter l'incertitude liée aux données manquantes. Un autre avantage de l'IM est qu'elle a un haut degré d'efficacité même si le nombre d'imputation (*m*) est petit. Rubin (1987) montre qu'avec seulement 3 à 5 imputations, on peut obtenir d'excellents résultats ; donc il n'est pas nécessaire que *m* soit très grand pour gagner en efficacité (dans ce travail, m=10). Plusieurs formulations de cette méthode existent et diffèrent par les modèles spécifiés, leurs hypothèses et la façon de générer les imputations. En faisant l'hypothèse d'une situation de données manquantes aléatoirement (MAR), nous avons mis en place une procédure d'imputation multi-variable par équations enchaînées ou *Multivariate Imputation by Chained Equations* (*MICE*). Cette procédure permet d'estimer les paramètres sur chacun des *m* échantillons ainsi imputés, puis les estimations du modèle final par une combinaison de ces *m* estimations (Rubin, 1987). L'utilisateur de cette méthode spécifie la distribution conditionnelle pour les données manquantes de chaque variable contenant ces dernières (Royston, 2004). Cette méthode à l'avantage de combiner les imputations de variables de toutes natures (continues, binaires et catégorielles à plus de deux modalités).

4. RÉSULTATS

L'estimation du modèle s'est faite à partir d'un probit ordonné bivarié (tableau 7) afin de tenir compte d'un lien potentiel de complémentarité entre les TIC et les pratiques organisationnelles. Greene et Hensher (2010) préconisent d'interpréter les coefficients obtenus du modèle probit ordonné avec précaution.

La valeur absolue prise par les coefficients estimés ne peut pas faire l'objet d'une interprétation directe en termes de dérivées partielles, ou d'élasticités, de la variable expliquée par rapport aux variables explicatives. Ce qui est important dans ces résultats est moins la valeur absolue des coefficients que le signe et le degré de significativité de ceux-ci.

Conformément à la théorie de la supermodularité, un premier résultat indique que l'adoption des TIC par les entreprises est influencée par leur niveau de pratiques organisationnelles (*rho* positif et significatif). Plus l'entreprise adopte les pratiques organisationnelles, plus elle adopte les TIC et inversement.

En d'autres termes, il existe un lien de complémentarité entre l'adoption des TIC et les changements organisationnels. Ce lien de complémentarité trouvé au Cameroun est en accord avec d'autres travaux réalisés dans les pays en développement, notamment en Afrique du Sud (Cloete et al., 2002), en Colombie (Gallego et al., 2015) et en Tunisie (Ben Kalifa, 2014).

Tableau 7. Estimation du modèle probit ordonné bivarié

Variables	NATIC	NPO
Age	-0.048 (0.063)	0.039 (0.053)
Taille	0.272*** (0.044)	0.138*** (0.040)
Salaire	0.072 (0.049)	0.042 (0.038)
Rd	0.223 (0.211)	-0.014 (0.201)
Groupe	0.055 (0.123)	-
Ide	-0.072 (0.285)	-0.361 (0.311)
Si	-0.265** (0.131)	-0.0001 (0.199)
Sa	0.521*** (0.126)	0.186 (0.132)
Export	0.965 (0.191)	-0.098 (0.177)
Hhi	-0.00007 (0.00004)	-8.1e-06 (0.00006)
Homme	0.022 (0.191)	-0.045 (0.181)
Cameroun	-0.182 (0.166)	-0.072 (0.121)
France	0.161 (0.229)	0.763*** (0.193)
Eurhorsfce	-0.277 (0.262)	0.231 (0.227)
Secondaire	0.093 (0.156)	0.732*** (0.127)
Bac	0.431** (0.182)	0.764*** (0.121)
Bacplus	0.687*** (0.122)	1.41*** (0.087)
Epidemique	0.577*** (0.076)	1.03*** (0.168)
Stockordre	0.671*** (0.166)	0.545 (0.432)

Rho	0.392*** (0.0791)
N	1008
Athrho	0.503*** (0.078)
cut11	1.057*** (0.443)
cut12	2.435*** (0.492)
cut13	3.121*** (0.536)
cut14	3.792*** (0.610)
cut21	1.155*** (0.724)
cut22	1.733*** (0.755)
cut23	2.992*** (0.712)
cut24	3.782*** (0.777)

*Ecarts-types entre parenthèses : * significatif à 10%; **significatif à 5%; ***significatif à 1%. Source : auteur.*

Il apparait que l'adoption des TIC et celles des pratiques organisationnelles n'ont pas forcément les mêmes déterminants. En effet, si la taille, la proximité géographique et le capital humain du dirigeant sont les déterminants communs des TIC et des pratiques organisationnelles, le statut juridique et l'environnement sectoriel influencent seulement l'adoption des TIC, alors que la nationalité du dirigeant influence seulement les pratiques organisationnelles de l'entreprise.

En ce qui concerne les *effets de rang*, la taille des entreprises influence significativement l'adoption des TIC. Malgré la baisse spectaculaire des coûts du matériel et des composants informatiques ainsi que du traitement de l'information et des communications ces trente dernières années, l'adoption des TIC est toujours faible dans les petites entreprises, disposant de capacités financières moins importantes. Selon Mansfield (1968), les dirigeants de PME ont tendance à avoir une aversion pour le risque, or investir dans les nouvelles technologies comporte forcément un risque. Ceci confirme le lien positif entre la taille de l'entreprise et la probabilité d'adopter les TIC. Une autre explication viendrait du fait que les petites et les très petites entreprises n'ont pas initié des stratégies et des pratiques organisationnelles leur permettant d'adopter les nouvelles technologies. Cette influence de la taille de l'entreprise a été retrouvée, notamment dans les travaux de Machikita et al. (2010). Nos résultats montrent aussi que les entreprises individuelles adoptent moins les TIC que les sociétés anonymes, qui sont généralement plus grandes. L'influence du capital humain des employés de l'entreprise est (positive mais) non significative. Ce résultat étonnant peut trouver une explication dans le fait qu'au Cameroun le salaire serait un indicateur peu précis du capital humain des employés. En effet, au Cameroun et globalement dans les pays en développement, les salariés sont rémunérés à un montant nettement inférieur à leur niveau de qualification ou de compétence. Une appréciation de la qualification des employés par le salaire sous-estime ainsi le niveau réel de qualification dans l'entreprise.

Par contre, le capital humain du dirigeant est positivement lié à l'adoption des TIC. Sachant qu'au Cameroun plus de 90% des entreprises sont des PME et des TPE, le capital humain du dirigeant est fondamental. Les TPE et les PME sont principalement des structures simples et très centralisées avec un chef d'entreprise où, dans la plupart des cas, le propriétaire et le dirigeant sont une seule et même personne. Un certain nombre d'études ont révélé que dans les PME, le rôle du chef d'entreprise (dirigeant/propriétaire) est au cœur de l'entreprise concernant l'orientation stratégique et l'organisation des activités (Fuller-Love, 2006 ; Smith, 2007 ; Ghobakhloo et al., 2011b), particulièrement en ce qui concerne l'adoption des TIC (Bruque et Moyano, 2007; Nguyen, 2009) et qui dépend souvent de son niveau d'éducation (Kossai et al., 2010; Diawara et Mughal, 2014; Oyelaran Oyeyinka et Lal, 2004).

L'effet de *stock-ordre* est positif et significatif : une entreprise tend d'autant plus à adopter des TIC qu'elle appartient à un secteur où le niveau d'utilisation des TIC est élevé. Nous obtenons ici le même résultat que Karshenas et Stoneman (1993) et Bocquet et Brossard (2008) qui n'ont jamais obtenu l'effet attendu (signe négatif). Conformément aux arguments théoriques évoqués plus haut (section 2.1.), cette inversion de signe peut traduire un comportement de *second mover* de la part des entreprises étudiées. Lorsqu'il y a une forte incertitude sur les bénéfices futurs d'une nouvelle technologie, ou bien lorsque l'on est confronté à des technologies à effets de réseau, les prédictions de l'effet de stock-ordre peuvent être totalement inversées (Bocquet et Brossard, 2008) ou alors absorbées par les effets de proximité.

L'effet de la variable *épidémique* montre que les entreprises tendent à adopter les TIC à mesure que leurs voisins le font, rejoignant les conclusions de Gallego et al. (2015) en Colombie et de Ben Khalifa (2014) en Tunisie.

5. CONCLUSION

Dans cet article, nous avons examiné les facteurs qui conduisent à l'adoption des TIC par les entreprises au Cameroun. Afin de vérifier le lien de complémentarité entre les TIC et les pratiques organisationnelles, nous avons estimé un modèle probit ordonné bivarié sur un échantillon de 1008 entreprises industrielles.

Les résultats confirment la théorie de la supermodularité suggérée par Milgrom et Roberts (1990) qui met en évidence la complémentarité entre l'adoption des TIC et les changements organisationnels. Nous trouvons que les entreprises adoptent davantage les TIC si elles ont adopté des pratiques organisationnelles et inversement. Même si plusieurs travaux aussi bien dans les pays développés qu'en développement confirment ce lien de complémentarité, Bocquet et Brossard (2008) relèvent que cette relation reste complexe. Nous avons montré que la taille et le statut juridique de l'entreprise sont des facteurs décisifs de l'adoption des TIC. Ce résultat révèle que la baisse des prix des TIC ne suffit pas à en assurer une large diffusion auprès des entreprises. Autrement dit, d'autres facteurs complémentaires tels que les changements organisationnels et/ou le capital humain sont nécessaires pour une adoption efficace. Par ailleurs, nous trouvons que le capital humain du dirigeant est plus important que le capital humain des employés dans le processus d'adoption des TIC. Ce résultat nous interpelle sur l'importance du dirigeant dans les entreprises des pays en développement, quand on sait que la grande majorité de ces entreprises sont des TPE et des PME. En ce qui concerne les effets épidémiques et de stock-ordre, nous avons trouvé, en accord avec la majorité des travaux, que l'adoption des TIC est facilitée par le comportement des autres entreprises. Une entreprise est d'autant plus encouragée à adopter des TIC qu'elle est entourée par des entreprises qui les utilisent déjà dans la région ou dans le secteur.

Toutefois, nos résultats doivent être considérés avec prudence car l'échantillon utilisé, bien que contenant des informations originales, n'est pas parfaitement représentatif des entreprises industrielles au Cameroun. Néanmoins, nous pouvons tirer quelques enseignements pour l'élaboration d'une politique de diffusion des TIC. Ainsi, en matière de politique industrielle, pour pouvoir élargir la diffusion des TIC dans le tissu économique camerounais et gagner en compétitivité, il est indispensable de promouvoir les changements organisationnels dans les entreprises. L'amélioration de la qualité des enseignements et de la formation reste indispensable, mais surtout des formations spécifiques aux promoteurs ou dirigeants de faible niveau d'instruction. Il s'agira ici de leur ouvrir des fenêtres sur les possibilités offertes par les TIC afin de leur faire percevoir l'importance de ces technologies dans l'entreprise. Enfin, la dotation d'équipements et d'infrastructures (électricité, connexion internet à haut débit, etc.) facilitant l'adoption des TIC dans les zones géographiques isolées, associée à la promotion de l'utilisation des TIC dans les branches d'activités moins utilisatrices des TIC permettraient non seulement une réduction de la fracture numérique au sein des entreprises, mais également un rattrapage technologique sur les régions et les pays plus avancés.

REFERENCES

Akomea-Bonsu, C., 2012, "The impact of Information and Communication Technologies (ICT) on Small and Medium Scale Enterprises (SMEs) in the Kumasi Metropolis, Ghana, West Africa", *European Journal of Business and Management,* 4(20), 152-158.

Arora, A., Gambardella, A., 1990, « Complementarity and External Linkages: The Strategies of the Large Firms in Biotechnology », *Journal of Industrial Economics*, 38(4), 361-379.

Athey, S., Stern, S., 1998, "An empirical Framework for Testing Theories about Complementarity in Organizational Design", *National Bureau of Economic Research, WP* 6600.

Baldwin, J.R., Rafiquzzaman, M., 1998, "The Determinants of the Adoption Lag for Advanced Manufacturing Technologies", *Research Paper Series*, 117, Statistique Canada.

Baldwin, W.L., Scott, J.T., 1987, "Market structure and technological change", *Chur, Switzerland: Harwood Academic Publishers*, 1987.

Bartoloni, E., Baussola, M., 2001, "The Determinants of Technology Adoption in Italian Manufacturing Industries", *Review of Industrial Organization*, 19(3), 305-328.

Basant, R., Commander, S., Harrison, R., Menezes-Filhon, N., 2011, ICT and Productivity in Developing Countries: New Firm Level Evidence from Brazil and India, *IZA Discussion Paper* No. 2294.

Bassanini, A., Scarpetta, S., 2002, "Growth, Technological Change, and ICT Diffusion: Recent Evidence from OECD Countries", *Oxford Review of Economic Policy*, 18(3), 324-344.

Battisti, G., Canepa, A., Stoneman, P., 2004, "Profitability, Externalities and Policy in the Inter and Intra Firm Adoption of New Technology: The Example of E-Business Activities in the UK", *Paper Presented at the 8th Conference of the European Network on Industrial Policy* (EUNIP), Birmingham, December.

Bayo-Moriones, A., Lera-López, F., 2007, "A Firm Level Analysis of Determinants of ICT Adoption in Spain", *Technovation*, 27(6-7), 352-366.

Beccheti, L., D.A., Londono Bedoya, L., Paganetto, L., 2003, "ICT Investment, Productivity and Efficiency: Evidence at Firm Level using a Stochastic Frontier Approach", *Journal of Productivity Analysis,* 20(2), 143-167.

Ben Khalifa, A., 2014, « Déterminants de la diffusion des TIC dans les pays Sud-Méditerranéens : Cas de la Tunisie », International Conference on Business, Economics, Marketing & Management Research (BEMM'13) Volume Book: Economics & Strategic Management of Business Process (ESMB) Copyright – IPCO Vol.2, 185-190.

Biagi, F., 2013, "ICT and productivity: A review of a literature", *Working Paper*, Institute for Prospective Technological Studies Digital Economy.

Bloom, N., Sadun, R., Van Reenen, J., 2012, "Americans Do IT Better: US Multinationals and the Productivity Miracle", *American Economic Review*, 102(1), 167-201.

Bocquet, R., Brossard, O., 2008, « Adoption des TIC, proximité et diffusion localisée des connaissances », *Revue d'économie régionale et urbaine*, n°3.

Bocquet, R., Brossard, O., Sabatier, M., 2007, "Complementarities in organizational design and the diffusion of information technologies: An empirical analysis", *Research Policy*, 36, 367-386.

Bocquet, R., Brossard, O., 2007, « The Variety of ICT Adopters in the Intra-Firm Diffusion Process : Theoretical Arguments and Empirical Evidence », *Structural Change and Economic Dynamics*, 18(4), 409-437.

Bruque, S., Moyano, J., 2007, "Organisational determinants of information technology adoption and implementation in SMEs: The case of family and cooperative firms», *Technovation*, 27(5), 241-253.

Brynjolfsson, E., Hitt, L., 2000, "Beyond Computation: Information technology, Organizational Transformation and Business Performance", *Journal of Economic Perspectives,* 14, 23-48.

Brynjolfsson, E., Hitt, L., 2003, "Computing Productivity: Firm Level Evidence", *The Review of Economics and Statistics*, 85(4), 793-808.

Caldeira, M. M., Ward, J. M. 2003, "Using resource-based theory to interpret the successful adoption and use of information systems and technology in manufacturing small and medium-sized enterprises". *European Journal of Information Systems*, 12(2), 127-141.

Calza, E., Rovira, S., 2011, "ICT, organizational change and firm performance: evidence from Argentina", Vergara, S., Rovira, S. and Balboni, M. "ICT in Latin America: A Microdata Analysis", ECLAC - United Nations, No. 34598, 203-237. LC/R.2172.

Canepa A., Stoneman P., 2004, "Comparative International Diffusion: Patterns, Determinants and Policies", *Economics of Innovation and New Technology*, 13(3), 279-98.

Carlsson, B., 2004, "The Digital Economy: What is New and What is Not?", *Structural Change and Economic Dynamics*, 15(3), 245-264.

Carson, D., Gilmore, A. 2000, "SME marketing management competencies», *International Business Review*, 9(3), 363-382.

Caselli, F., Coleman, II. W. J., 2001, "Cross-country technology diffusion: The case of computers", *American Economic Re*view, 91(2), 328-335.

Cloete, E., Courtney, S., Fintz, J., 2002, « Small business acceptance and adoption of ecommerce in the Western Cape Province of South Africa », *Electronic Journal on information systems in Developing countries*, 10(4), 1-13.

Dasgupta, P., 1986, "The Theory of Technological Competition", in: J.E. Stiglitz and G.F. Mathewson (Editors), New Developments in the Analysis of Market Structure (*The MIT Press, Cambridge,* MA), 519-547.

Diawara, B., Mughal, M., 2014, "Does education matter for the adoption of information and communication technologies (ICT) in developing countries? Evidence from Senegal", Working Papers 2103, Groupe ESC Pau.

Dosi, G., 1988, *Technical Change and Economic Theory*, Pinter Publishers Ltd.

Drew, S. 2003, "Strategic uses of e-commerce by SMEs in the east of England», *European Management Journal*, 21(1), 79-88.

Ennen, E., Richter, A., 2010, « The Whole Is More Than the Sum of Its Parts Or Is It? A Review of the Empirical Literature on Complementarities in Organizations », *Journal of Management*, 36(1), 207-233.

Fabiani, S., Schivardi, F., Trento, S., 2005, "ICT adoption in Italian manufacturing: firm-level evidence", *Industrial and Corporate Change*, 1-25.

Fambeu, A. H., Bakehe, N. P., 2015, "Interaction sociale et Usages de l'internet au Cameroun", *L'Actualité Economique, Revue d'analyse économique*, 91(4).

Foong, S. Y., 1999, "Effect of end-user personal and systems attributes on computerbased information system success in Malaysian SMEs», *Journal of Small Business Management*, 37(3), 81-87.

Frambach, R.T., Schillewaert, N., 2002, "Organizational innovation adoption: A multi-level framework of determinants and opportunities for future research", *Journal of Business Research*, 55, 163-176.

Fudenberg, D., Tirole, J., 1985, "Preemption and Rent Equalization in the Adoption of New Technology",*Review of Economic Studies*, vol. 52, 383-401.

Fuller-Love, N., 2006, "Management development in small firms", *International Journal of Management Reviews*, 8(3), 175-190.

Gallego, J. M., Gutiérrez L. H., Lee, S. H., 2015, "A firm-level analysis of ICT adoption in an emerging economy: Evidence from the Colombian manufacturing industries", *Industrial and Corporate Change*, 24(1).

Galliano, D., Roux, P., 2006, « Les inégalités spatiales dans l'usage des TIC. Le cas des firmes industrielles françaises », *Revue économique*, 57(6), 1449-1475.

Galia, F., Ballot, G., Fakhfakh, F., Salter, A., 2013, « The fathful triangle: complementarities in performance between product, process and organizational innovation in France and the UK », EURAM. Istanbul, Turkey.

Gatignon, H., Robertson, T.S., 1989, "Technology diffusion: an empirical test of competitive effects", *Journal of Marketing*, 53, 35-49.

Ghobakhloo, M., Zulkifli, N. B., Aziz, F. A., 2010, "The interactive model of User information technology acceptance and satisfaction in small and medium-sized enterprises". *European Journal of Economics, Finance and Administrative Sciences*, 19(1), 7-27.

Ghobakhloo, M., Benitez-Amado, J., Arias-Aranda, D., 2011a, "Reasons for information technology adoption and sophistication within manufacturing SMEs", POMS 22nd Annual Conference: Operations management: The enabling link. Reno, USA, April 29 to May 2.

Ghobakhloo, M., Arias-Aranda, D., Benitez-Amado, J., 2011b, "Information technology implementation success within SMEs in developing countries: An interactive model", POMS 22nd Annual Conference, Reno, USA, April 29 to May 2.

Gnansounou, S.U., 2010, « Utilisation des Technologies de l'Information et de la Communication dans les Entreprises Béninoises : Niveau d'Adoption et Effets sur la Performance », Projet de Renforcement des Capacités en Conception et Analyse des Politiques de Développement, Document de Travail n°005/2010.

Greenan, N., Mairesse, J., Bensaid, T., 2001, « Information technology and research and development impacts on productivity and skills, looking for correlations on french firm level data », *NBER WP 8075*, Cambridge, MA.

Greene, W.H., Hensher, D.A, 2008, *Modeling Ordered Choices: A primer and recent developments*, Cambridge: Cambridge University Press.

Grolleau, G., 2001, « Adoption et diffusion des systèmes de management environnemental en agriculture », INRA Paris, 20-21 septembre.

Gutiérrez, L.H., 2011, "ICT and labor productivity in Colombian manufacturing industry", in Vergara, S., Rovira, S. and Balboni, M., *ICT in Latin America: A Microdata Analysis*, ECLAC - United Nations, and MPRA Paper No. 34598.

Haller, S.A., Siedschlag, J., 2011, "Determinants of ICT adoption: evidence from firm-level data», *Applied Economics,* 43(26).

Hempell, T., 2003, "Do Computers Call for Training? Firm-level Evidence on Complementarities between ICT and Human Capital Investments", ZEW Discussion Paper No. 03-20, Mannheim.

Hollenstein, H., 2004, "Determinants of the Adoption of Information and Communication Technologies: an Empirical Analysis Based on Firm-Level Data for the Swiss Business Sector", *Structural Change and Economic Dynamics*, 15(3), 315-342.

Hollenstein, H., Woerter, M., 2008, "Inter- and intra-firm diffusion of technology: The example of E-commerce. An analysis based on Swiss firm-level data", *Research Policy*, 37, 545-564.

Holt, L., Jamison, M., 2009, "Broadband and Contributions to Economic Growth: Lessons from the US Experience", *Telecommunications Policy*, 33, 575-581.

Hur, J. J., Seo, H. J., Lee, Y. 2005, "Information and communication technology diffusion and skill upgrading in Korean industries", *Economics of Innovation and New Technology* 14, 553-71.

Ireland N., Stoneman P., 1985, "Order effects, perfect foresight and inter-temporal price discrimination", *Recherches économiques de Louvain*, 51(1), 7-20.

Jeffcoate, J., Chappell, C., Feindt, S., 2002, « Best practice in SME adoption of eCommerce, Benchmarking", *An International Journal*, 9(2), 122-132.

Jorgenson, D.W., Stiroh, K., 2000, "Raising the Speed Limit: US Economic Growth in the Information Age", *Brookings Papers on Economic Activity*, 1, 125-211.

Kamien, M.I., Schwartz N.L., 1982, "Market structure and innovation", Cambridge Univ. Press.

Karshenas, M., Stoneman, P., 1993, "Rank, Stock, Order and Epidemic Effects in the Diffusion of New Process Technology", *Rand Journal of Economics*, 24(4), 503-527.

Kossai, M., Lapa de Souza, M.L., Roussel, J., 2010, « Adoption des technologies de l'information et capital humain : le cas des PME tunisiennes », *Management et Avenir*, 31, 131-159.

Kretschmer, T., 2012, "Information and Communication Technologies and Productivity Growth: A Survey of the Literature", *OECD Digital Economy Papers*, 195.

Kutlu, B., Özturan, M., 2008, "The Usage and Adoption of IT Among SMEs in Turkey: An Exploratory and Longitudinal Study", *Journal of Information Technology Management*, 19(1), 12-24.

Lal, K., 2007, "Globalization and Adoption of ICTsin Nigerian SMEs", *Science, Technology Society*, 12(2), 217-244.

Lal, K., 2004, "E-business and Export Behavior: Evidence from Indian Firms", *World Development*, 32(3), 505-517.

Lehr, B., Lichtenberg, F., 1999, "Information Technology and its Impact on Productivity: Firm Level Evidence from Government and Private Data Sources, 1977-1993", *Canadian Journal of Economics*, 32, 335-362.

Machikita, T., Tsuji, M., Ueki, Y., 2010, "How ICTs Raise Manufacturing Performance: Firm-level Evidence in Southeast Asia", Papers DP-2010-07, Economic Research Institute for ASEAN and East Asia.

Majumdar, S. K., Venkataraman, S., 1992, "New technology adoption in US telecommunications: The role of competitive pressures and firm-level inducements", *Research Policy,* 22, 521-536.

Mansfield, E., 1968, *Industrial Research and Technological Innovation*, Norton.

Mansfield, E., 1961, "Technical Change and the Rate of Imitation", *Econometrica* 29, 741-766.

Matteucci, N., O'Mahony, M., Robinson, C., Zwick, T., 2005, "Productivity, Workplace Performance and ICT: Industry and Firm-Level Evidence for Europe and the US", *Scottish Journal of Political Economy,* 52(3), 359-386.

Milgrom, P., Roberts, J., 1995, « Complementarities and fit strategy, structure and organizational change in manufacturing », *Journal of Accounting and Economics*, 19, 179-208.

Milgrom, P., Roberts, J. 1990, « The Economics of Modern Manufacturing: Technology Strategy and Organization », *The American Economic Review*, 80(3), 511-528.

Miller, D., 1986, « Configurations of strategy and structure: Towards a synthesis », *Strategic Management Journal*, 7(3), 233-249.

Mughal, M., Diawara, B., 2011, "Human Capital and the Adoption of Information and Communications Technologies: Evidence from Investment Climate Survey of Pakistan", Economics Discussion Papers, No 2011-21, Kiel Institute for the World Economy.

Mukoko, B., 2012, "Determinants of Computer and Internet Adoption and Use in Cameroon", *African Review of Economics and Finance*, 3(2), 96-703.

Ndiege, J. R. A., Herselman, M. E., Flowerday, S. V., 2014, «Absorptive capacity and ICT adoption strategies for SMEs », *The African Journal of Information Systems,* 6(4).

Nguyen, T. U. H., 2009, "Information technology adoption in SMEs: an integrated framework", *International Journal of Entrepreneurial Behaviour and Research,* 15(2), 162-186.

Nour, S., 2011, "The Use and Economic Impacts of ICT at the Macro-Micro levels in the Arab Gulf Countries", Maastricht Economic and social Research Institute on Innovation and Technology, UNU-MERIT Working Papers, 059.

OECD, 2004, *The Economic Impact of ICT, Measurement, Evidence and Implications*, OECD, Paris.

OECD, 2003, *ICT and Economic Growth – Evidence from OECD Countries, Industries and Firms*, OECD, Paris.

Oliner, S.D., Sichel, D.E., 2000, "The Resurgence of Growth in the Late 1990s: Is Information Technology the Story?", *Journal of Economic Perspectives*, 14, 3-12.

Oyelaran-Oyeyinka, B., 2004, "Learning and Local Knowledge Institutions in African Industry", In UNU-INTECH. Maastricht: DP 2004-2.

Porter M. E., 1980, *Competitive Strategy*, The Free Press, New York.

Quirmbach, H., 1986, "The Diffusion of New Technology and the Market for an Innovation", *Rand Journal of Economics,* 17, 33-47.

Raymond, L., St-Pierre, J., 2005, « Antecedents and performance outcomes of advanced manufacturing systems sophistication in SMEs", *International Journal of Operations and Production Management*, 25, 6, 514-533.

Reinganum, J.F., 1981, "On the Diffusion of new Technology: A Game Theoretic Approach", *Review of Economic Studies*, 48, 395-405.

Riemenschneider, C. L., Mykytyn, P. P., 2000, "What small business executives have learned about managing information technology", *Information and Management*, 37, 257-269.

Robertson, T. S., Gatignon H., 1986, "Competitive effects on technology diffusion", *Journal of Marketing,* 50.

Royston, P., 2004, "Multiple Imputation of Missing Values," *The Stata Journal,* 4 (3), 227-241.

Rubin, D. B., 1987, *Multiple Imputation for Nonresponse in Surveys*, J. Wiley and Sons, New York.

Rubin, D. B., 1978, « Multiple Imputations in Sample Surveys- a Phenomenological Bayesian Approach to Non-response », *The Proceedings of the Survey Research Methods Section of The American Statistical Assciation*, 20-34.

Sajaia, Z., 2008, « Maximum likelihood estimation of a bivariate ordered probit model : implementation and Monte Carlo simulations », *The Stata Journal*, The World Bank Washington, DC, 4 , 1-18.

Smith, M., 2007, « Real managerial differences between family and non-family firms », *International Journal of Entrepreneurial Behaviour and Research*, 13(5), 278-295.

Ssewanyana, J., Busler, M., 2007, "Adoption and Usage of ICT in developing Countries: Case of Ugandan Firms", *International Journal of Education and Development using ICT*, 3(3).

Steinmueller, E., 2001, « Les TIC et les possibilités pour les PED de brûler les étapes », *Revue internationale du travail*, 140(2).

Stoneman, P., Kwon, M-J., 1994, "The diffusion of multiple process technologies", *The Economic Journal*, 104, 420-431.

Tamokwe Piaptie, G. B., 2013, « Les déterminants de l'accès et des usages d'internet en Afrique Subsaharienne Analyse des données camerounaises et implications pour une politique de développement des TIC », *Réseaux*, 180(4), 95-121.

Tello, M. D., 2011, « Science and technology, ICT and profitability in the manufacturing sector in Peru », in Vergara, S., Rovira, S. and Balboni, M., *ICT in Latin America: A Microdata Analysis*, ECLAC - United Nations, and MPRA Paper No. 34598.

Thong, J. Y. L. (1999), « An integrated model of information systems adoption in small businesses », Journal of Management Information Systems, 15(4), 187-214.

Thong, J.Y.L., Yap, C.S., 1995, « CEO characteristics, organizational characteristics and information technology adoption in small businesses », *Omega*, 23(4), 429-442.

Timmer, M., Van Ark, B., 2005, "Does Information and Communication Technology Drive EU-US Productivity Growth Differentials?", *Oxford Economic Papers*, 57, 693-716.

Tseng, C.-H., Tansuhaj, P.S., Rose, J., 2004, « Are strategic assets contributions or constraints for SMEs to go internationanal? An empirical study of the US manufacturing sector », *Journal of American Academy of Business*, 5, 1/2, 246-255.

World Bank, 2016, *World Development Report 2016: Digital Dividends*, World Bank, Washington DC.

ANNEXES

Tableau 1. Structure de la population mère et de l'échantillon selon la taille

	Population mère		Echantillon	
	N	%	N	%
TPE	9858	84.36	513	50.89
PE	858	7.34	205	20.34
ME	740	6.33	197	19.54
GE	229	1.97	93	9.23
Total	**11685**	**100**	**1008**	**100**
Khi2 = 913,16	**ddl = 3**			

Source : auteur.

Tableau 2. Structure de la population mère et de l'échantillon selon le secteur d'activité

	Population mère		Echantillon	
	N	%	N	%
Extraction	25	0.21	14	1.39
Industries alimentaires	695	5.95	210	20.83
Autres industries manufacturières	10227	87.52	443	43.95
Electricité – eau et gaz	74	0.63	48	4.76
Construction	664	5.68	293	29.07
Total	**11685**	**100**	**1008**	**100**
Khi2 = 1904,42	**ddl = 4**			

Source : auteur.

Tableau 3. Proportion des entreprises selon le secteur d'activité (population mère) (%)

	Sous-secteurs industriels					
	Extraction	Industries alimentaires	Autres industries manufacturières	Electricité, eau et gaz	Construction	Total
TPE	0.05	3.57	93.55	0.21	2.62	100.00
	(5)	(352)	(9222)	(21)	(258)	(9858)
PE	0.58	14.57	59.79	1.28	23.78	100.00
	(5)	(125)	(513)	(11)	(204)	(858)
ME	0.68	20.81	50.41	3.92	24.19	100.00
	(5)	(154)	(373)	(29)	(179)	(740)
GE	4.37	27.95	51.97	5.68	10.04	100.00
	(10)	(64)	(119)	(13)	(23)	(229)
Total	**0.21**	**5.95**	**87.52**	**0.63**	**5.68**	**100.00**
	(25)	**(695)**	**(10227)**	**(74)**	**(664)**	**(11685)**

Les effectifs sont entre parenthèses.
Source : auteur.

Tableau 4. Proportion des entreprises selon le secteur d'activité (échantillon) (%)

	Sous-secteurs industriels					
	Extraction	Industries alimentaires	Autres industries manufacturières	Electricité, eau et gaz	Construction	Total
TPE	1.17	13.45	43.86	4.48	37.04	100.00
	(6)	(69)	(225)	(23)	(190)	(513)
PE	0.98	26.34	40.49	5.85	26.34	100.00
	(2)	(54)	(83)	(12)	(54)	(205)
ME	1.52	31.47	42.13	5.08	19.80	100.00
	(3)	(62)	(83)	(10)	(39)	(197)
GE	3.23	26.88	55.91	3.23	10.75	100.00
	(3)	(25)	(52)	(3)	(10)	(93)
Total	**1.39**	**20.83**	**43.95**	**4.76**	**29.07**	**100.00**
	(14)	**(210)**	**(443)**	**(48)**	**(293)**	**(1008)**

Les effectifs sont entre parenthèses.
Source : auteur.

Tableau 5. Description des variables

Variables	Définition
Variables dépendantes	
NATIC	0 si pas de TIC ; 1 si une TIC ; 2 si deux TIC ; 3 si trois TIC ; 4 si quatre TIC
NPO	0 si pas de pratique ; 1 si une pratique ; 2 si deux pratiques ; 3 si trois pratiques ; 4 si quatre pratiques
Variables de rang	
age	Age de l'entreprise : 0-4 = 1 (groupe de réf.); 5-9 =2; 10-14 = 3; 15 et plus = 4
taille	Nombre d'employés permanents : 0-9 = 1 (groupe de référence); 10-19 = 2 ; 20-99 = 3 ; 100 et plus = 4
salaire	Log du salaire moyen des employés permanents
Rd	rd = 1 si l'entreprise a investi en R&D ou a fait de la R&D expérimentale dans l'établissement et 0 sinon
groupe	1 si l'entreprise appartient à un groupe ; 0 sinon
ide	1 si l'entreprise est une filiale étrangère ; 0 sinon
si	Société individuelle = 1 ou société à responsabilité limitée unipersonnelle = 1 et 0 sinon
sa	société anonyme = 1 et 0 sinon
hhi	$hhi = \sum_{i=1}^{N}(PM)^2*10000$ Indice de concentration d'Herfindahl-Hirschman mesurant la concurrence domestique. Cet indice est déterminé par la somme des carrés des parts de marché (PM) des entreprises dans un secteur d'activité
export	1 si l'entreprise a une production destinée principalement à l'exportation ; 0 sinon
Variable de stock-ordre	
stockordre	Niveau moyen d'adoption des TIC ou niveau de pratiques organisationnelles dans le secteur de l'entreprise concernée
Variable épidémique	
epidémique	Niveau moyen d'adoption des TIC ou niveau de pratiques organisationnelles dans la région de l'entreprise concernée
Caractéristiques du dirigeant	
homme	homme=1 si le dirigeant est un homme et 0 sinon
Cameroun	Cameroun=1 si le dirigeant est camerounais et 0 sinon
France	France=1 si le dirigeant est français et 0 sinon
Eurhorsfce	Eurhorsfce=1 si le dirigeant est européen, hormis français et 0 sinon
secondaire	secondaire=1 si le niveau scolaire le plus élevé du dirigeant est le secondaire et 0 sinon
bac	bac=1 si le niveau scolaire le plus élevé du dirigeant est le Bac et 0 sinon
bacplus	bacplus=1 si le niveau scolaire le plus élevé du dirigeant est au moins Bac + 2

Source : auteur.

Tableau 6. Statistiques descriptives

Variables	Réponse	Non réponse	total	Taux de réponse (%)	Taux de non réponse (%)	Mean	Std.Dev.	Min	Max
NATIC	587	421	1008	58.23	41.77	2.40	1.32	0	4
NPO	871	137	1008	86.41	13.59	1.30	0.73	0	4
age	941	67	1008	93.35	6.65	2.18	0.84	1	3
salaire	421	587	1008	41.77	58.23	6.95	1.23	2.02	11.99
rd	528	480	1008	52.38	47.62	0.08	0.27	0	1
groupe	636	372	1008	63.10	36.9	0.14	0.35	0	1
ide	642	366	1008	63.69	36.31	0.06	0.25	0	1
export	783	225	1008	77.68	22.32	0.06	0.24	0	1
homme	799	209	1008	79.27	20.73	0.93	0.26	0	1
taille	1008	0	1008	100	0	1.87	1.03	1	4
si	1008	0	1008	100	0	0.28	0.45	0	1
sa	1008	0	1008	100	0	0.16	0.37	0	1
hhi	1008	0	1008	100	0	2003.87	1051.99	646.78	4791.51
Cameroun	1008	0	1008	100	0	0.78	0.41	0	1
France	1008	0	1008	100	0	0.04	0.20	0	1
Eurhorsfce	1008	0	1008	100	0	0.03	0.17	0	1
secondaire	1008	0	1008	100	0	0.13	0.34	0	1
bac	1008	0	1008	100	0	0.10	0.30	0	1
bacplus	1008	0	1008	100	0	0.37	0.48	0	1
epidemiquetic	1008	0	1008	100	0	2.40	0.49	0.80	2.73
stockordretic	1008	0	1008	100	0	2.43	0.42	1.63	3.43
Epidemiquepo	1008	0	1008	100	0	1.51	0.26	0.87	2.07
Stockordrepo	1008	0	1008	100	0	1.52	0.14	1.34	1.65

Source : auteur.

DETERMINANTS OF ICT ADOPTION IN DEVELOPING COUNTRY: AN ECONOMETRIC ANALYSIS ON INDUSTRIAL FIRMS IN CAMEROON

Abstract - *The objective of this study is to analyze the factors responsible for ICT adoption in developing country. For this, we estimate ordered probit bivariate model on a sample of 1008 industrial firms in Cameroon. In addition to traditional determinants cited by the technological diffusion models and expected profitability (rank, stock-order and epidemic effects), we highlight the complementarity factor organizational practices cited by the theory supermodularity one hand and secondly the characteristics of leaders (manager). Our econometric results show that ICT adoption depends mainly on organizational practices, size, human capital of leader and adoption of peers. Thus we find that there is a positive and bidirectional link between ICT adoption and level of organizational practices. This work also highlights the importance of leadership, often neglected role in the literature of ICT adoption in firms.*

Key-words - ICT ADOPTION, COMPLEMENTARY ORGANIZATIONAL PRACTICES, ORDERED BIVARIATE PROBIT, CAMEROON

LES MOTIVATIONS MICROÉCONOMIQUES DES TRANSFERTS DE FONDS AU BURKINA FASO : LA CULTURE EST-ELLE DÉTERMINANTE ?

Okayo Alphonsine COULIBALY[1]

Résumé - *Cet article analyse les déterminants des transferts de fonds des migrants burkinabè vivant en Côte d'Ivoire. Pour ce faire, nous avons effectué une enquête de terrain où les migrants interrogés ont été sélectionnés par la méthode « boule de neige ». A l'aide d'un modèle Tobit les résultats économétriques montrent que les transferts de fonds des migrants burkinabè sont guidés par des motifs subjectifs et des traits culturels où dominent le sentiment d'attachement à leur pays, l'altruisme, l'entraide, l'esprit communautaire, la solidarité et le conformisme.*

Mots-clés - MIGRANTS, TRANSFERTS DE FONDS, CULTURE AFRICAINE

Classification JEL - J61, F24, Z19

L'auteur remercie le référé anonyme et la rédaction de la revue pour les remarques pertinentes qui ont aidé à améliorer significativement l'article. Nos remerciements vont également au Professeur Zié Ballo.

[1] Université Félix Houphouet Boigny, Côte d'Ivoire ; okayocool@yahoo.fr

1. INTRODUCTION

La croissance rapide des transferts de fonds des migrants, comparativement à l'aide publique au développement (APD) et aux investissements directs étrangers, a suscité l'intérêt de bon nombre de chercheurs. Plusieurs motifs sont avancés pour expliquer le comportement de transfert : d'un côté des motifs objectifs allant du pur altruisme au pur intérêt personnel en passant par des motifs d'arrangement mutuel entre le migrant et sa famille restée dans le pays d'origine ; d'un autre côté, des motifs subjectifs comme l'attachement au pays d'origine (Funkhouser, 1995 ; Miotti et al., 2012), l'honneur du clan (Azam et Gubert, 2002), l'histoire et le contexte institutionnel de l'émigration (Miotti et al., 2012). L'honneur du clan met en avant la structuration de la société en castes. Il va sans dire que les traits culturels sont des déterminants des transferts de fonds des migrants. Cet article s'inscrit dans ce cadre en se focalisant sur la culture africaine fondamentalement basée sur l'esprit communautaire dont découlent les obligations d'entraide, le sentiment d'appartenance, les obligations de solidarité et le conformisme. De plus, il constitue le premier travail portant sur les déterminants microéconomiques effectué sur des migrants burkinabè.

Ce travail est basé sur une enquête de terrain que nous avons réalisée en 2014 auprès de 600 migrants burkinabè vivant en Côte d'Ivoire.

Le Burkina Faso est un pays enclavé de l'Afrique de l'ouest qui fait frontière au nord et à l'ouest avec le Mali, à l'est avec le Niger et au sud avec le Bénin, le Togo, le Ghana et la Côte d'Ivoire. Le Burkina Faso est caractérisé par un faible revenu, une population à 80% rurale, un indice de développement humain faible de 0,331 qui place le pays au 181e rang mondial (Gilligan, 2013) et une forte migration soit 9,7% de la population en 2010. Les transferts de fonds représentent en moyenne 7,9 % du PIB et sont en hausse sensible (BAD, 2012). Le Burkina Faso dépend sensiblement de transferts de fonds des migrants qui proviennent de la Côte d'Ivoire, premier pays d'émigration (UEMOA, 2013). Le corridor Burkina Faso-Côte d'Ivoire est le premier corridor de migration d'Afrique sub-saharienne et le troisième des pays à faible revenu (World Bank, 2011).

Pour déterminer des facteurs explicatifs des transferts des migrants burkinabè, nous privilégions le modèle Tobit car nous examinons uniquement le comportement des individus qui envoient effectivement de l'argent dans leur pays, de manière à tenir compte de la nature censurée de la variable dépendante.

La suite de l'article est présentée comme suit. D'abord nous présentons une revue de la littérature portant sur les déterminants microéconomiques des transferts de fonds, ensuite nous exposons la méthodologie et les données utilisées, enfin nous examinons les résultats empiriques obtenus.

2. REVUE DE LA LITTÉRATURE

L'importante revue de la littérature portant sur les déterminants des transferts de fonds des migrants recense plusieurs motifs qui peuvent êtres altruistes, d'intérêts personnels ou encore d'accords de bénéfices mutuels. Avant d'exposer quelques études empiriques sur les déterminants des transferts de fonds, nous présentons les traits caractéristiques de la culture africaine que nous considérons dans notre étude.

La culture est « l'ensemble des structures sociales et des manifestations artistiques, religieuses, intellectuelles qui définissent un groupe, une société par rapport à une autre » (D'Adesky, 1998). Elle permet de comprendre les habitudes, les manières de penser des membres d'une société. La culture africaine, bien que diverse sur le plan géographique, a pour socle l'esprit communautaire (Zadi, 1998) dont découlent l'entraide et un fort sentiment d'appartenance à un groupe social, le « village » (Ponson, 1990). Comme tout pays d'Afrique subsaharienne, la société burkinabè est une société communautariste (Fiske, 1990) dans laquelle la communauté a une emprise sur l'individu (Mbiti, 1990 ; Ponson, 1990). L'individu est donc connu et identifié dans, par et à travers sa communauté (Onyedinma et Kanayo, 2013). Ses obligations sont le fondement de l'esprit communautaire dans la société africaine reléguant les droits de l'individu au second rang. L'individualisme est donc un mode de vie condamné dans la société africaine. Onyedinma et Kanayo (2013) le traduisent par cette expression « suis le chemin que la majorité d'individus suit. Si tu t'en écartes, tu auras des raisons de te lamenter »[2]. La conséquence de ce mode de vie est le conformisme qui constitue une entrave à l'innovation et à l'investissement (Ponson, 1990). Cette vie communautaire implique pour l'individu l'obligation de participer à la protection et à l'épanouissement de chacun des membres de la communauté comme les travaux champêtres, la construction des logements… Celui qui faillit à ces obligations est sanctionné de bannissement, la mort sociale (Mbiti 1990 ; 1991, Ojapinwa, 2012, Onyedinma et Kanayo, 2013). Durant toute la durée de son éloignement, le migrant doit rester en contact avec sa communauté en lui évitant le déshonneur, en répondant à ses demandes, en lui offrant des cadeaux en un mot l'absence du migrant ne doit se ressentir que par son absence physique. Cela se traduit chez le migrant par des réalisations effectuées dans sa communauté d'origine comme la construction de logements modernes, l'achat de matériel agricole, la construction de routes, etc. pour améliorer le bien-être de la famille et de la communauté. Cette obligation de participer à la vie communautaire explique également les transferts d'argent que les migrants effectuent pour les événements familiaux comme la naissance d'un enfant, le mariage d'un proche, les festivités et les fêtes religieuses (Tall, 2003) ou encore les funérailles (Gubert, 2002), en d'autres termes les obligations de solidarité. L'étude de Fleischer (2007) au Cameroun illustre bien ce phénomène. Il constate que les enfants sont contraints par leurs parents de quitter le pays pour trouver un emploi et leur envoyer de l'argent. Une fois les enfants à l'étranger, les parents exercent une énorme pression sur eux pour qu'ils satisfassent leurs demandes d'argent.

Le motif altruiste comme déterminant des transferts de fonds est unanimement reconnu par la littérature (Gupta, 2005). Il est généralement lié au revenu des bénéficiaires. Les transferts de fond diminuent lorsque le revenu de la fa-

[2] Cela s'exprime aussi dans la langue mossi par l'expression : « tond (faa) yaa a yemre » qui signifie « nous sommes tous un », ou encore « tond yaa bumb a ye » qui signifie « nous sommes un et la même chose » (Fiske, 1990).

mille augmente (Stark, 1991). Il implique que le migrant envoie de l'argent à sa famille pour subvenir aux besoins de celle-ci sans rien attendre en retour (Chami et al., 2008). C'est ce qu'illustre les études de Black et al. (2003) en Côte d'Ivoire et au Ghana, Nwajiuba (2005) au Nigeria, De Haas (2006) au Maroc, Lindley (2006) en Somalie, Aguinias (2006) en Amérique du Sud, Kireyev (2006) au Tadjikistan, Ratha et Mohapatra (2007) en Indonésie, au Mexique et aux Philippines. Par ailleurs l'altruisme est perçu à travers la durée de la migration (Stark et Lucas, 1985 ; Funkhouser, 1995), dont la question est largement débattue dans la littérature. Pour certains auteurs, plus la durée de migration est longue moins le migrant transfère de fonds à cause des liens qui se distendent (Funkhouser, 1995 ; Glytsos, 2002 ; Amuedo-Dorantes et Pozo, 2006, Arun et Ulku, 2011). Pour d'autres auteurs au contraire, les migrants conservent des liens transnationaux solides pendant de longues périodes, parfois même d'une génération à l'autre (Mc Dowell et de Haan, 1997 ; Grieco, 2004 ; Sinning, 2007 ; De Haas, 2008 ; Goya et Ryabov, 2012 ; Orozco, 2012). Pour Merkle et Zimmermann (1992), Brown (1998), Konica et Filer (2005), la durée de migration n'a aucune influence sur les transferts de fonds des migrants dans leur pays d'origine.

Les transferts de fonds des migrants dans leurs pays peuvent être déterminés par les contrats d'arrangement mutuels qui existent avec leurs familles (Rapoport et Docquier, 2005). Il s'agit soit de réaliser des investissements qu'ils ne peuvent pas réaliser eux-mêmes et de garantir ses investissements jusqu'à leur retour, soit de protéger leur héritage. Les motifs d'échange dans lesquels s'inscrivent les motifs de remboursement et le partage des risques trouvent leur explication dans le contexte d'imperfection des marchés de capitaux (Sark, 1991).

L'intérêt personnel concerne les investissements réalisés par le migrant dans son pays (Lucas et Stark, 1985), son intention de retour (Funkhouser, 1995 ; Stanwix et Connell, 1995) et son intention d'hériter (De Haas, 2007). Lucas et Stark (1985) expliquent que les migrants envoient de l'argent à leur famille pour effectuer des investissements qu'ils ne sont pas en mesure d'effectuer eux-mêmes. Pour entretenir ces investissements, les migrants utilisent les membres de leur famille et leur versent en contrepartie une compensation. L'analyse de Stark (2009) confirme ce résultat : les transferts de fonds servent de salaire à la famille du migrant assurant la rentabilité des investissements réalisés par ce dernier. En outre, Stark montre que le migrant transfère de l'argent par pur intérêt personnel. Il envoie de l'argent pour éviter que d'autres membres de la famille migrent à leur tour et viennent réduire leur gain en revenu. Brown (1997) arrive à la conclusion que les migrants des Tonga et des Samoa occidentales installés à Sydney transfèrent des fonds par intérêt personnel afin d'investir dans leur région. Dans la même veine, Coulibaly (2009) trouve qu'une hausse des transferts de fonds des migrants s'aligne sur le différentiel du taux d'intérêt traduisant ainsi des motivations d'investissement et de profit. Dans leur étude sur un échantillon de 100 pays, Giuliano et Ruiz-Arranz (2006) trouvent que les transferts de fonds sont principalement motivés par des intérêts personnels et sont surtout pro-cycliques. Selon Stanwix et Connell (1995), les migrants qui envisagent leur retour transmettent plus pour protéger leurs investissements. Par exemple, les migrants pakistanais qui envisagent leur retour ou qui ont leur activités dans leur pays envoient plus de fonds que les autres migrants (Nishat et Bilgrami, 1993). Les transferts de fonds peuvent être vus comme un retour sur investissement des ménages garantissant l'héritage du migrant (De Haas, 2007). Lucas et Stark (1985) montrent que les transferts de fonds aux ménages botswanais ont augmenté pendant la période de sécheresse pour pouvoir préserver le bétail. Dans une étude au Kenya, Hoddinott (1994) souligne que la famille fait pression sur les migrants pour qu'ils augmentent les transferts de fonds en les menaçant de les déshériter des terres familiales. Schrieder et Knerr (2000) confortent le motif d'héritage au Cameroun. Ils trouvent que les transferts diminuent lorsque les migrants n'espèrent pas un héritage important. De la Brière et al. (2000) par contre observent que les migrants dominicains aux Etats-Unis envoient de l'argent à leurs parents pour investir et accroître leur futur héritage. Stark (2009) compare deux migrants issus d'une même famille avec une tradition de succession dirigée par la primogéniture et leurs motifs de transferts de fonds à leur famille. Il remarque que l'aîné est plus disposé à transmettre de l'argent parce qu'il est celui qui héritera des parents. Les montants qu'il transfère sont investis dans la ferme familiale et partant augmenteront son héritage. Bohra-Mishra (2011), dans une étude réalisée sur les migrants népalais, confirme l'hypothèse du rôle de l'héritage.

Selon la théorie néo-classique de la nouvelle économie de la migration, la migration d'un individu est une décision prise par toute la famille ou par toute la communauté pour pallier les absences ou les incertitudes dans les pays concernés : diversification des sources de revenus, réduction des risques de revenus, surmonter les barrières de crédit et de capital (Stark, 1991).

Ilahi et Jafarey (1999) font une analyse du motif de remboursement dans leur étude sur le Pakistan. Les auteurs comparent la famille du migrant à une banque qui finance la migration de certains de ses membres. Selon eux, les membres de la famille prêtent de l'argent aux migrants que ceux-ci remboursent par leurs transferts de fonds et qui est utilisé pour financer l'éducation et les futures migrations. C'est ce qu'observe Poirine (1997) aux Tonga et aux Samoa occidentales. Le modèle de l'accord de prêt est également confirmé par l'étude de l'OCDE (2006) au Botswana. Les résultats empiriques montrent que le niveau de scolarisation des migrants et celui de leurs enfants sont positivement corrélés. Les migrants envoient de l'argent à leur famille pour trois raisons : rembourser les prêts contractés pour leur voyage, prêter de l'argent pour la formation des futurs migrants et investir dans le pays pour le retour. Les transferts de fonds sont un mécanisme par lequel naissent les arrangements de partage de risques (Chami et al., 2008). Stark (1991) compare la famille à une compagnie d'assurance qui protège les membres contre les chocs. Au Mali, Gubert (2002, 2006) fait remarquer que les transferts de fonds constituent non seulement une assurance contre le risque mais aussi une prévention pour les destinataires contre d'autres risques, par exemple la mort ou l'organisation de funérailles... Au Burkina Faso et au Ghana, Lachaud (1999) et Quartey et Blankson (2004) présentent les transferts de fonds comme la solution aux situations de crise, de chocs macroéconomiques et de détresse. Selon OCDE (2006) et Chami et al., (2008), la motivation des transferts de fonds est expliquée par deux modèles :

un contrat de co-assurance et un contrat de prêts. Dans le contrat de co-assurance, pendant la migration le migrant est considéré comme l'assuré et la famille l'assureur. La famille finance alors les coûts de la migration trop élevés pour l'individu et après la migration, les rôles s'inversent. Le migrant devient l'assureur et la famille l'assuré. Le migrant envoie l'argent pour assurer la famille contre les risques et les chocs. Dans certains cas, après la migration, la famille reste l'assureur pendant une certaine période. En effet, les migrants vulnérables se servent toujours de leur famille comme assureur. Cette hypothèse est vérifiée par l'étude de Hanson (2006) et de Black et al., (2003) respectivement au Mexique, en Côte d'Ivoire et au Ghana. Hanson explique que les migrants vulnérables, en l'occurrence en situation irrégulière aux USA, transfèrent plus d'argent que les migrants en situation régulière. Black et al. constatent que les migrants issus de familles pauvres sont plus disposés à transmettre que les migrants issus de familles riches. Amuedo-Dorantes et Pozo (2006) trouvent que les migrants envoient des fonds comme paiement d'une prime d'assurance pour recevoir de l'argent de la famille dans le futur. Pour Ahouré (2008), en Côte d'Ivoire, les migrants envoient de l'argent dans leur communauté pour remédier au défaut d'assurance contre les risques (mauvaise récolte, perte d'emploi, etc.). Stark (2009) observe que les migrants envoient de l'argent à leur famille pour les assurer contre l'insuffisance de revenus et comme prime d'assurance pour les services futurs qu'elle leur rendra.

Les caractéristiques démographiques comme l'éducation et l'âge influencent également les transferts de fonds des migrants. Concernant l'éducation, certaines études comme Schiopu et Siegfried (2006) trouvent que plus les migrants sont éduqués plus ils transmettent de l'argent. Au contraire, Kuckulenz et Bush (2004) et Adam (2008) remarquent que le taux d'analphabétisme influence positivement les transferts de fonds. Au Sénégal, les émigrés moins éduqués transmettent plus que leurs concitoyens alors que le contraire est observé au Burkina Faso et en Ouganda (UNCTAD, 2012). Markova et Reilly (2007) montrent que les transferts de fonds augmentent avec l'âge alors que Goza et Ryabov (2012) constatent que les plus jeunes transmettent plus que les plus âgés, jusqu'à un certain seuil. Cependant cette influence est modeste. Les transferts de fonds des migrants peuvent être expliqués par plusieurs facteurs à la fois, ce que Lucas et Stark (1985) qualifient d'altruisme tempéré.

D'un autre point de vue, les transferts de fonds sont également motivés par des facteurs subjectifs comme le prestige de la famille du migrant auprès de la communauté (Glytsos, 2002), l'honneur de la famille (Tall, 2003) et du clan (Azam et Gubert, 2002), la primogéniture (Gundel, 2002), l'influence politique du migrant (Kane, 2001), l'attachement au pays (Funkhouser, 1995 ; Bouhga-Hagbe, 2004). Les transferts de fonds résistent mieux que les autres aides parce qu'ils reposent sur des principes de solidarité et d'entraide (CNUCED, 2011). Les normes sociales comme le rôle du voisinage (Bohra-Mishra, 2011) ou la discrimination sociale (Kato, 2012) influencent les transferts de fonds. Miotti et al. (2012) élargissent ces facteurs à l'histoire et au contexte institutionnel de l'émigration. Les auteurs montrent que les transferts de fonds des migrants sont guidés par les traits culturels comme la division de la société en clans, la primogéniture, la solidarité et l'entraide. A la suite de ces travaux, nous considérons les motifs subjectifs tels que l'attachement au pays, l'esprit communautaire, les obligations d'entraide, la solidarité, le conformisme, comme des déterminants possibles des transferts de fonds.

3. MÉTHODOLOGIE

Notre étude est basée sur les données d'une enquête réalisée en 2014 auprès des migrants burkinabè en Côte d'Ivoire. En l'absence d'une base de sondage, construire un échantillon représentatif avec des méthodes probabilistes est impossible. Parmi les méthodes non-probabilistes les plus répandues figure la méthode « boule de neige », adéquate pour l'étude des populations difficiles à joindre (Goodman, 1961). Les résultats issus de cette enquête ne concernent que les migrants burkinabè vivant en Côte d'Ivoire.

3.1. La méthode d'échantillonnage « boule de neige »

Cette méthode a été abondamment utilisée pour étudier les populations migrantes partout dans le monde (Mooney, 2003; McKenzie et Mistiaen, 2007; Markova et Reilly, 2007; Niaz et al., 2010; Aromolaran, 2013; Fatoki, 2013; Kwarteng, 2013; Hansing et Orozco, 2014… respectivement au Mexique, au Brésil, en Bulgarie, au Pakistan, au Nigeria, en Afrique du Sud, au Ghana, à Cuba...). Utilisée la première fois par Martin (1957), la méthode boule de neige est formalisée par Coleman (1959) mais popularisée par Goodman (1961). Cette méthode passe par plusieurs étapes : d'abord on sélectionne un échantillon pas nécessairement probabiliste de la population cible (première vague) et cet échantillon sert de contacts initiaux. Ensuite on demande à chaque individu de la première vague de fournir des noms d'autres individus qui constituent la deuxième vague. Il est demandé à la deuxième vague de fournir des noms d'autres individus qui ne font pas partie ni de la première vague ni de la deuxième vague. Ce processus continue jusqu'à ce qu'on atteigne le nombre d'individus visé. La méthode boule de neige est rapide, elle facilite l'accès à la population d'intérêt à moindre coût. Toutefois, elle est sujette à tous les biais inhérents aux méthodes par chaînage (Erickson, 1979). Premièrement l'échantillon de départ n'étant pas aléatoire, les biais liés à cet échantillon se transmettent à la population finale. Le deuxième biais est le « biais de volontarisme » qui est engendré par une grande coopération des participants notamment si l'échantillon de départ est constitué de volontaires. Le « biais de masquage » apparaît lorsque certains individus essaient de protéger certains de leurs amis en ne les mentionnant pas. Enfin on enregistre le « biais de surreprésentation » dû aux individus qui ont un large réseau de connaissances, par exemple chez les riches et les plus éduqués (Erickson, 1979).

Pour tendre vers un échantillon aléatoire nous avons utilisé plusieurs techniques. Pour réduire le biais lié à l'échantillon de départ, nous avons procédé à un tirage aléatoire simple dans les associations. Nous avons choisi cinq différentes zones d'enquête dans la région de Soubré qui regroupe la plus grande majorité d'immigrants selon le recensement de 1998 (Bouquet, 2003). Les cinq zones d'enquête sont Grand-Zatry (Z1), Mayo (Z2), Méagui (Z3), Petit Ouaga (Z4), Yabayo (Z5). Pour le biais de volontarisme nous avons évité les volontaires en choisissant aléatoirement les individus dans les associations. Aussi, notre population est relativement homogène concernant le niveau de vie et les plus éduqués sont très minoritaires (voir Tableau 1). Concernant le biais de masquage, les migrants considérés sont des individus pour lesquels la société n'a aucun préjugé. Le migrant n'a donc aucune raison de protéger ses amis en ne les mentionnant pas. Ce biais est donc inexistant dans notre cas d'étude. Il en est de même pour le biais de surreprésentation (Erickson, 1979 ; Heckathorn, 1997) car notre échantillon est constitué d'une population majoritairement analphabète. Conformément à ces auteurs nous avons limité le nombre d'individus recrutés à 1 et le nombre de chaînes. Pour ce faire, nous avons demandé à chaque enquêté de nous fournir les noms de trois connaissances ; lorsqu'un des trois individus mentionnés accepte de répondre aux questions, les deux autres ne sont plus interrogés. Nous avons aussi limité la longueur des chaînes à six en nous basant sur les résultats de Killworth et Bernard (1978/1979). Dans une expérience réalisée aux USA pour étudier la cognition sociale des individus à travers des comportements sous conditions spécifiques, les auteurs trouvent que chaque américain est indirectement associé à un autre à travers approximativement six intermédiaires. De plus Erickson (1979) et Heckathorn (1997) déclarent que les biais liés aux méthodes par chaînage proviennent de la longueur des chaînes. Ils proposent donc des chaînes à 6 vagues pour remédier à ces biais. Le taux de réponse de 88,67% de notre enquête de terrain indique que ces biais sont très minorés dans notre cas.

Z1 (20 graines)	20	→	20	→	20	→	20	→	20	Total = 120
Z2 (20 graines)	20	→	20	→	20	→	20	→	20	Total = 120
Z3 (20 graines)	20	→	20	→	20	→	20	→	20	Total = 120
Z4 (20 graines)	20	→	20	→	20	→	20	→	20	Total = 120
Z5 (20 graines)	20	→	20	→	20	→	20	→	20	Total = 120
										600

3.2. Le modèle retenu

Selon la théorie de la nouvelle économie de la migration, l'utilité du migrant est fonction de l'utilité de la famille : $Um = f(cm, Uf)$, avec *Um* l'utilité du migrant, *cm* la consommation du migrant et *Uf* l'utilité de la famille. En envoyant de l'argent, l'utilité du migrant correspond à celle de la famille, donc $Um = Uf$. Le comportement de transfert est donc formalisé ainsi : $Tm = f(Uf)$, avec *Tm* le comportement de transfert du migrant. Or l'utilité de la famille correspond à la satisfaction de ses besoins et à l'obligation du migrant à assumer ses responsabilités dans la société, en d'autres termes au respect de la culture.

Pour estimer les paramètres de nos variables explicatives, nous utilisons le modèle Tobit pour tenir compte de la nature censurée de la variable dépendante car nous examinons uniquement les réponses à l'enquête des personnes qui envoient effectivement de l'argent à leur famille. Le modèle de régression Tobit censuré est de la forme :

$$y^* = \beta Xi + \epsilon i \qquad \begin{array}{l} yi = 0 \; si \; y^* \leq 0 \\ yi = y^* \; si \; y > 0 \end{array}$$

où *y* représente les transferts de fonds effectués par les migrants burkinabè en Côte d'Ivoire, β est un vecteur de k coefficients fixes, *Xi* est un vecteur de k variables explicatives et εi est un vecteur de résidus indépendants normalement distribués de moyenne nulle et de variance σ^2. L'objectif de ce modèle est d'estimer les paramètres β sur la base des individus (Xi, yi) qui effectuent des transferts de fonds.

Aux variables explicatives traditionnellement retenues comme l'âge, le niveau de l'éducation, l'intention de retour, la durée de migration, l'altruisme, les intérêts personnels, l'assurance, l'épargne, nous ajoutons les traits culturels tels que la vie communautaire, les obligations d'entraide, le sentiment d'appartenance, les obligations de solidarité et le conformisme. Ces variables sont mesurées par les questions posées dans les rubriques du questionnaire données dans l'annexe 2.

La variable « *Age* » influence négativement les transferts de fonds si avec l'âge la capacité de travail du migrant et son revenu sont plus faibles.

La variable « *Education* » influence positivement les transferts de fonds. Plus le migrant est éduqué plus il tend à recevoir un revenu élevé et donc à transférer davantage de fonds.

La variable « *Retour* » implique des transferts de fonds plus élevés car elle exprime le sentiment d'attachement du migrant à son pays d'origine.

La variable « *Durée de la migration* » influence négativement les transferts de fonds car plus la durée de migration est longue plus les liens sociaux se distendent.

La variable « *Famille* », qui mesure l'altruisme, augmente les transferts de fonds car les migrants envoient de l'argent à leur famille pour satisfaire leurs besoins de première nécessité.

La variable « *Investissement* » exprime le fait que le migrant envoie de l'argent pour effectuer des investissements dans son pays.

La variable « *Assurance* » traduit le fait que les migrants envoient de l'argent pour protéger leur famille en milieu rural des risques liés aux aléas climatiques.

La variable « *Epargne* » augmente les transferts de fonds lorsque le migrant a pour but d'augmenter ses revenus dans son pays.

La variable « *Bonnes relations* » influence positivement les transferts de fonds. Elle traduit l'esprit communautaire qui fait de la culture africaine un contrat qui exige du membre de la famille qu'il assume ses obligations vis-à-vis de sa famille de peur d'être banni. Les transferts de fonds constituent donc le lien social entre le migrant et sa famille. Il envoie de l'argent dans son pays pour conserver son droit de membre, son identité dans la communauté.

Les variables « *Education et Santé* » augmentent les transferts de fonds car le migrant rembourse la dette contractée auprès de la société du fait de son absence. En fait, son absence est un manque à ses obligations d'entraide aux plus faibles (les enfants et les plus âgés).

La variable « *Conformisme* » influence positivement les transferts de fonds. Elle correspond à la réponse « je n'en sais rien je le fais parce que tout le monde le fait ». Elle traduit l'obligation de se conformer aux rites et aux traditions de la culture.

La variable « S*entiment d'appartenance* » a une influence positive sur les transferts de fonds. Le migrant envoie de l'argent pour construire des logements, des infrastructures comme des centres de santé, des écoles, des commissariats... La variable est évaluée par la question « pour participer au développement de mon pays ».

La variable « *Solidarité* » exprime le fait que le migrant est obligé de soutenir les autres pour bénéficier à son tour de cette solidarité quand il sera dans le besoin (elle est évaluée par la réponse « Parce que dans la vie il faut être solidaire pour qu'on puisse m'aider à mon tour quand j'aurai des problèmes »).

En prenant en compte ces variables explicatives, notre modèle s'écrit :

$$Tm = \beta 0 + \beta 1\, Age + \beta 2\, Educ + \beta 3\, Ret + \beta 4\, Dm + \beta 5\, Fam + \beta 6\, Inv + \beta 7\, Ass + \beta 8\, Epg + \beta 9\, Rel + \beta 10\, Sco + \beta 11\, San + \beta 12\, Conf + \beta 13\, Sentapp + \beta 14\, Sol + \mathcal{E}t$$

avec *Age* : l'âge du migrant, *Educ* : le niveau d'éducation du migrant, *Ret* : l'intention de retour, *Dm* : durée de la migration, *Fam* : subvenir aux besoins de la famille, *Inv* : investir dans son pays, *Ass* : assurer ma famille, *Epg* : épargne dans mon pays, *Rel* : garder de bonnes relations, *Sco* : dépenses d'éducation, *San* : dépenses de santé, *Conf* : conformisme, *Sentapp* : sentiment d'appartenance, *Sol* : obligations de solidarité.

4. RÉSULTATS ET INTERPRÉTATION

4.1. Les réponses à l'enquête

Le traitement des données a été réalisé avec le logiciel Statistique Package for Social Sciences (SPSS), Version 20. Comme l'indique le tableau 1, la population burkinabè en Côte d'Ivoire est majoritairement constituée d'hommes et de jeunes à faible niveau d'éducation. Ces caractéristiques correspondent à celles trouvées par Boutin (2014) dans son étude sur les migrants burkinabè en Côte d'Ivoire. Il constate 9,2% de femmes contre 90,8% d'hommes. L'âge moyen des migrants est de 31 ans contre 33 ans pour notre étude et 64% des migrants ne sont jamais allés à l'école contre 62,9% dans notre échantillon. 64,9 % des individus interrogés envisagent de retourner dans leur pays d'origine, après une durée moyenne de migration de 17 ans.

Les raisons évoquées par les migrants transférant des fonds sont consignés dans le tableau 2. La principale raison évoquée est de subvenir aux besoins de la famille (96,3%). Ensuite viennent le fait de garder de bonnes relations avec la famille (32,6%) et la scolarisation des membres de la famille (21,1%).

Les migrants qui envoient de l'argent à leur famille participent également au développement local de leur pays. Ils le font « parce que tout le monde le fait »

(36,7%), « pour être solidaires afin d'être aidés à leur tour » (33,6%), « pour participer au développement de leur pays » (26,7%), pour d'autres raisons (3,6%). Les différents domaines d'investissement sont : santé (18,1%), éducation (38,9%), logement (29,2%), PME (2,8%), eau potable (11,1%), agriculture (6,9%), élevage (4,2%) électrification (2,8%), tourisme (1,4%), assainissement (1,4%) et autres (11,1%).

Tableau 1. Caractéristiques socio-démographiques des migrants

Caractéristiques	Pourcentage (%)
Genre	
Hommes	89,8
Femmes	10,2
Age	
19-29	39,1
30-39	43,2
40-49	13,6
50 et plus	4,1
Niveau d'éducation	
Aucun	37,8
Coranique	25,1
Primaire	30,1
Secondaire	6,2
Supérieur	0,8
Nombre d'observations	532

Source : Enquête de l'auteur.

Tableau 2. Raisons évoquées par les personnes transférant des fonds dans leur pays

Caractéristiques	(%)
Subvenir aux besoins de ma famille	96,3
Aider mes amis	3,4
Investir dans mon pays	4,7
Assurer ma famille contre les risques	5,4
Garder de bonnes relations avec ma famille	32,6
Epargner dans mon pays	0,7
Scolariser les membres de ma famille	21,1
Payer les soins de santé de ma famille	9,3
Autres	2,7

Source : Enquête de l'auteur.

4.2. Les résultats du modèle

Les résultats de l'analyse économétrique sont consignés dans le tableau 3. Le test de spécification de Linktest, le test de multicolinéarité et le test de Breusch-Pagan associés à la régression sont donnés pour évaluer la robustesse du modèle.

Tableau 3. Estimation des déterminants des transferts de fonds à l'aide du modèle Tobit

Variables indépendantes	Coefficients estimés	Probabilités	Statistiques de colinéarité (VIF)	1/VIF (tolerence)
Age	-0.4532195	0.943	1.01	0,990099
Educ	1.7139564	0.218	2.19	0,456621
Ret	0.0584917	0.043**	1.27	0,787401
Dm	-1.114839	0.682	1.51	0,662251
Fam	1.021332	0.024**	1.14	0,877191
Inv	0.071543	0.291	1.83	0,546448
Ass	0.583817	0.167	1.19	0,840336
Epg	-0.776478	0.623	1.11	0,900900
Rel	0.756318	0.049**	1.95	0,512820
Sco	0.547008	0.026**	2.16	0,462962
San	1.450122	0.068*	1.35	0,740740
Conf	1.121342	0.011**	1.87	0,534759
Sentapp	1.378965	0.004***	1.38	0,724637
Sol	2.001245	0.009***	1.71	0,584795
β0	1.174896	2.292	-	
Nombre d'observations = 532 Prob > F = 0.0012 R-squared = 0.4985 Adj R-squared = 0.4347				

**** significatif à 1% ; ** significatif à 5% et * significatif à 10%.*

Test de specification: Linktest

Moyenne	Coef.	Std.err.	t	P>|t|	[95% conf. interval]	
hat	1,896315	1,451592	1,31	0,205	-1,12202	4,914651
hatsq	-1,833099	0,1337811	-0,62	0,684	-0,361523	0,1949033
Cons	-2,007568	3,395956	-0,59	0,561	-9,069845	5,054709
F(2,532)= 14,53 Prob>F = 0,0001 R-Squared= 0,5805 Adj R-Squared= 0,5405						

Test de Breusch-Pagan

Chi (1)	3,48
Prob>chi2	0,4021

D'après le test de Linktest, le modèle est correctement spécifié : la pvalue du coefficient du carré du prédicteur est de 0,684 (supérieur à 0,05), le coefficient n'est donc pas significatif.

La statistique VIF (very inflation factor) est construite à partir de régressions de chaque variable explicative par rapport aux autres variables explicatives du modèle. Les valeurs de VIF = 1/ 1-R^2 pour toutes les variables explicatives sont nettement inférieures à 5, qui est le seuil à partir duquel la présence de colinéarité devient probable. La régression ne souffre donc pas de problème de multicolinéarité.

Le test de Breusch-Pagan permet de tester l'hypothèse d'homoscédasticité du terme d'erreur d'un modèle de régression linéaire. Le test Prob>chi2 est égal à 0,4021 est supérieur à 0,05, montrant que le modèle est homoscédastique.

Les résultats montrent que 49,85% de la variance est expliquée et le modèle est globalement significatif car la p-value (Prob > F = 0,0012) est inférieure au seuil de 1 %. Ce qui permet de dire que les variables explicatives prises ensemble ont un effet global sur la variable expliquée.

D'après l'analyse économétrique, les variables indépendantes comme l'âge, l'investissement et l'épargne ne sont pas statistiquement significatives. Les signes et la significativité des variables explicatives Ret, Fam, Educ, San, Rel, Conf, Sentapp et Sol sont conformes à nos attentes.

La variable *Retour* (Ret) est positive et significative au seuil de 5%. Les migrants burkinabè envoient de l'argent parce qu'ils sont attachés à leur pays. Ce résultat confirme ceux de Elkhider et al. (2008) au Maroc et de Miotti et al. (2012) dans les pays du sud de la Méditerranée et d'Afrique Subsaharienne.

La variable *Besoins de la famille* (Fam) est positive et significative au seuil de 5%. Elle conforte donc la revue de littérature sur le motif altruiste. Les migrants envoient de l'argent pour prendre soin de leurs familles. La population burkinabè est une population largement rurale qui vit dans des conditions précaires.

Les variables *Education* (Educ) et *Santé* (San) sont toutes les deux positives et significatives respectivement au seuil de 5% et de 10%. Ces résultats impliquent que les migrants burkinabè envoient de l'argent dans leur pays pour assumer leurs responsabilités d'entraide. Elle réfute les résultats de OCDE (2006) au Botswana et de Paris et al. (2009) au Vietnam, en Thaïlande et aux Philippines selon lesquels les migrants envoient de l'argent pour rembourser les prêts contractés pour payer leur voyage. En effet, dans notre cas, 30 % seulement des migrants burkinabè ont bénéficié de l'aide de la famille, 62,5% ont payé eux-mêmes leur voyage, d'autres sont passés par un réseau de migration ou ont utilisé d'autres moyens.

La variable *Garder de bonnes relations* (Rel) est positive et significative au seuil de 5%. Elle exprime l'esprit communautaire. En envoyant l'argent dans leur pays les migrants conservent leurs droits de membre et leur identité. Ce résultat rejoint ceux de Hoddinott (1994) au Kenya, Osili (2004) au Nigéria, Fleischer (2007) au Cameroun, Zongo (2009) au Burkina Faso.

La variable *conformisme* (Conf) est positive et significative au seuil de 5%. Elle traduit la loyauté du migrant. Les migrants envoient de l'argent pour respecter les rites et les traditions.

La variable *Sentiment d'appartenance* (Sentapp) est positive et significative au seuil de 1%. Elle exprime le sentiment d'appartenance des migrants à leur communauté. En leur absence, les migrants envoient de l'argent pour participer à l'épanouissement de la communauté à travers l'embauche d'ouvriers pour les travaux champêtres ou l'achat de matériels...

La variable *Solidarité* (Sol) est positive et significative au seuil de 1%. La solidarité dans la culture africaine se manifeste aussi bien pour les évènements heureux que pour les évènements malheureux. Ce résultat rejoint ceux de Gubert (2002) au Mali, de Tall (2003) au Sénégal, de la CNUCED (2011).

Ces résultats obtenus dans le contexte burkinabè nous emmènent à questionner la notion de l'altruisme telle que définie dans la littérature. Nous mettons ici en évidence que les variables culturelles influencent significativement les transferts de fonds à destination du Burkina Faso, rejoignant l'étude d'Ojapinwa (2012) au Nigéria qui explique que l'altruisme n'est autre que le motif de remboursement implicite et informel d'une dette définie par le contrôle social, les valeurs culturelles de solidarité et de loyauté et par la menace de la perte du support de la famille au dernier stade de sa vie.

5. CONCLUSION

Cette étude a analysé les déterminants des transferts de fonds des migrants burkinabè vivant en Côte d'Ivoire. En nous appuyant sur différents travaux (Funkhouser, 1995 ; Azam et Gubert, 2002, Gundel, 2002 ; Glytsos, 2002 ; Miotti et al., 2012 ; Kato, 2012), l'objectif était de voir dans quelle mesure les traits culturels comme l'esprit communautaire, les obligations d'entraide, le conformisme, le sentiment d'appartenance, la solidarité, influencent les transferts de fonds à destination de leur pays. Les résultats indiquent que les transferts de fonds à destination du Burkina Faso sont déterminés par les traits culturels que nous avons considérés. Il serait donc intéressant de tester l'influence de ces traits culturels sur les transferts de fonds dans d'autres pays africains.

Par ailleurs, les motivations des transferts de fonds des migrants permettent aux décideurs d'orienter les politiques concernant la gestion des flux migratoires et l'impact des transferts de fonds des migrants sur l'économie. Des raisons altruistes permettent de développer des politiques pour stimuler la demande intérieure alors que des motifs d'intérêt personnel permettront plutôt de mettre en place des politiques d'entrepreneuriat.

REFERENCES

Adam Jr. R.H. (2008), « The Demographic, Economic and Financial Determinants of International Remittances in Developing Countries », *World Bank Policy Research Working Paper* 4583.

Agunias D. (2006), « Remittances Trends in Central America », Migration Information Source, Migration Policy Institute.

Ahouré A.A.E. (2008), « Migrations, transferts, gouvernance et croissance dans les pays d'Afrique sub-saharienne : une analyse à partir de données de panel », Communication pour l'Université Ouverte sur les Migrations : Migrations, Liberté de Circuler et Développement, Dakar, 2-5 juin.

Amuedo-Dorantes C., Pozo S. (2006), « Remittances as insurance: evidence from Mexican immigrants », *Journal of Population Economics*, 19, 227-254.

Aromolaran A.K. (2013), « Assessment of Benefits Associated with Rural-Urban Migration among Non-Migrants in Odeda Area, Ogun State, Nigeria », *International Journal of Pure and Applied Sciences and Technology*, 14(2), 31-38.

Arun T., Ulku H. (2011), « Determinants of Remittances: The Case of the South Asian Community in Manchester », *Journal of Development Studies,* 47(6), 894-912.

Azam J-P., Gubert F. (2002), « Those in Kayes. The impact of remittances on their recipients in Africa », Document de travail Développement Institutions &Analyses de Long terme / Unité de Recherche Croissance Inégalité Population et Rôle de l'Etat, N° 11.

BAD (2012), « Burkina Faso document de stratégie pays 2012-2016 », Département des opérations pays - Région Afrique de l'Ouest.

Black R., King R., Tiemoko R. (2003), « Migration, return and small enterprise development in Ghana: a route out of poverty », Sussex Migration Working Paper, N°9.

Bohra-Mishra P. (2011), « Motivations to Remit - Evidence from Chitwan, Nepal », Working Paper Office of Population Research-2011-04, Office of Population Research.

Bouhga-Hagbe J. (2004), « A theory of workers' remittances with an application to Morocco », International Monetary Fund, Working Paper 04/194.

Bouquet C. (2003), « Le poids des étrangers en Côte d'Ivoire », *Annales de Géographie*, 112.

Boutin D. (2014), « Remittances and Child Labour in Africa: Evidence from Burkina Faso », Institute for the Study of Labor (IZA) Discussion Papers Series No. 8007.

Brown R.P.C. (1997), « Estimating remittance functions for Pacific Island migrants», *World Development*, 25(4), 613-626.

Brown R.P.C. (1998), « Do Migrants' Remittances Decline over Time? Evidence from Tongans and Western Samoans in Australia », *The Contemporary Pacific,* 10(1), 107-151.

Chami R, Barajas A., Cosimano T., Fullenkamp C., Gapen M., Montiel P. (2008), « Macroeconomic Consequences of Remittances », International Monetary Fund, Occasional Paper No. 259.

CNUCED (2011), « Optimisation de la contribution au développement des envois de fonds », Conférence des Nations Unies sur le commerce et le développement, Genève.

Coleman J.S. (1959), « Relational analysis: The study of social organization with survey methods », *Human Organization*, 17(4), 28-36.

Coulibaly D. (2009), « Macroeconomic Determinants of Migrants' Remittances: New Evidence from a Panel VAR », Documents de travail du Centre d'Economie de la Sorbonne.

D'Adesky F. (1998), « Culture et Développement en Afrique », Extrait d'un discours donné lors d'une conférence à Dakar, Sénégal.

De Haas H. (2006), « Migration, Remittances and Regional Development in Southern Morocco », *Geoforum*, 37(4), 565-580.

De Haas H. (2007), « Remittances, Migration and social Development: A Conceptual Review of the Literature », Program on Social Policy and Development, Paper No. 34, United Nations Research Institute for Social Development, Geneva.

De Haas H. (2008), « Migration and development: A theoretical perspective », *International Migration Review*, 44(1), 227-264.

De la Briere B., Sadoulet E., De Janvry A., Lambert S. (2002), « The roles of destination, gender, and household composition in explaining remittances: an analysis for the Dominican Sierra », *Journal of Development Economics,* 68(2), 309-328.

Elkhider A., El Bouhadi A., El Kchirid M. (2008), « Les déterminants de transferts des résidents marocains à l'étranger : étude empirique de 1970 à 2006 », Commission Economique pour l'Afrique.

Erickson B.H. (1979), « Some problems of inference from chain data », *Sociological Methodology*, 10, 276-302.

Fatoki O. (2013), « An Investigation into the Financial Bootstrapping Methods Used by Immigrant Entrepreneurs in South Africa », *Journal of Economics*, 4(2), 89-96.

Fiske A.P. (1990), « Relativity within the Moose ("Mossi") Culture: Four Incomensurable Modelss for Social Relationships », *Ethos*,18 (2), 180-204.

Fleischer A. (2007), « Family, obligations, and migration: the role of kinship in Cameroon », *Demographic research,* 16(13), 413-440.

Funkhouser E. (1995), « Remittances from International Migration: A Comparison of El Salvador and Nicaragua », *The Review of Economics and Statistics*, 77(1), 137-146.

Gilligan M. (2013), « Burkina Faso », Données par pays de la Banque mondiale, Rapport 2012/2103.

Glytsos N.P. (2002), « Dynamic Effects of Migrant Remittances on Growth: An Econometric Model with an Application to Mediterranean Countries », Centre of Planning and Economic Research No. 74.

Goodman L.A. (1961), « Snowball sampling », *Annals of Mathematical Statistics,* 32(1), 148-170.

Goza F., Ryabov I. (2012), « Remittance Activity among Brazilians in the US and Canada », *International Migration,* 50(4), 157-185.

Grieco E. (2004), « Will Migrant Remittances Continue Through Time? A New Answer to an Old Question », *International Journal on Multicultural Societies*, 6(2), 243-252.

Gubert F. (2002), « Do Migrants insure those who stay behind? Evidence from the Kayes Area (Western Mali) », *Oxford Development Studies*, 30(3).

Gubert F. (2006), « Migration and development. Evidence from the Kayes area (Western Mali) », Institut de Recherche pour le Développement, Développement Institutions & Analyses de long terme.

Giuliano P., Ruiz-Arranz M. (2006), « Remittances, Financial Development, and Growth », Institute for the Study of Labor (IZA) Discussion Paper No. 2160.

Gundel J. (2002), « The migration–development nexus: Somalia case study », *International Migration*, 40(5), 255-281.

Gupta P. (2005), « Macroeconomic Determinants of Remittances: Evidence from India », International Monetary Fund Working Paper, 05/224.

Hansing K., Orozco M. (2014), « The Role and Impact of Remittances on Small Business Development during Cuba's Current Economic Reforms », Working Paper N°69.

Hanson G.H. (2006), « Illegal migration from Mexico to the United States », *Journal of Economic Literature*, 44(4).

Heckathorn D.D. (1997), « Respondent driven sampling: A new approach to the study of hidden populations », *Social Problems*, 44, 174-199.

Hoddinott J. (1994), « A Model of Migration and Remittances Applied to Western Kenya », *Oxford Economic Papers*, 46, 459-76.

Ilahi N., Jafarey S. (1999), « Guest worker Migration, Remittances and the Extended Family: Evidence from Pakistan », *Journal of Development Economics*, 58, 485-512.

Kato M. (2012), « The role of migration and remittances in a growing economy: perspectives on social classes in rural India and Bihar », Economic Research Center discussion paper, 187.

Killworth P.D., Bernard H.R. (1978/1979), « The Reversal Small-World Experience », *Social Network*, 1, 159-192.

Kireyev A. (2006), «The Macroeconomics of Remittances: The Case of Tajikistan», International Monetary Fund Working Paper 06/02.

Konica N., Filer R.K. (2005), « Albanian Emigration: Causes and Consequences », Working Paper, Prague, Center for Economic Research and Graduate Education-Economics Institute.

Kuckulenz A., Buch C.M. (2004), « Worker Remittances and Capital Flows to Developing Countries », Zentrum für Europäische Wirtschaftsforschung Discussion Papers, N° 04-31.

Kwarteng K. (2013), « The Remittance Intentions of Second-Generation Ghanaian-Americans », Capstone Collection Paper 2615.

Lachaud J-P. (1999), « Envois de fonds, inégalité et pauvreté au Burkina Faso », Document de travail N° 40, Centre d'Economie du Développement, Université Montesquieu-Bordeaux 4.

Lindley A. (2006), « Migrant Remittances in the Context of Crisis in Somali Society », Humanitarian Policy Group, Overseas Development Institute, London.

Logossah K. (2007), « Ethique sociale et trappe à sous-développement: le cas de l'Afrique sub-saharienne », Les cahiers du Centre de Recherche en Gestion et Economie du Développement, 3, 57-73.

Lucas R.E.B., Stark O. (1985), « Motivations to Remit: Evidence from Botswana », *Journal of Political Economy*, 93(4), 901-918.

Markova E., Reilly B. (2007), « Bulgarian migrant remittances and legal status: some micro-level evidence from Madrid », *South-Eastern Europe Journal of Economics*, 1, 55-69.

Mbiti J.S. (1990), *African religions and philosophy*, Heinemann 2nd Edition.

Mbiti J.S. (1991), *Introduction to African religion,* Heinemann 2nd Edition.

McDowell C., De Haan A. (1997), « Migration and Sustainable Livelihoods: A Critical Review of the Literature », Institute of Development Studies: Sussex.

McKenzie D.J., Mistiaen J. (2007), « Surveying Migrant Households: A Comparison of Census-Based, Snowball, and Intercept Point Surveys », *World Bank Policy Research Working Paper* 4419.

Merkle L., Zimmermann K.F. (1992), « Savings, Remittances and Return Migration», *Economic Letters*, 38, 77-81.

Miotti L., Mouhoud El M., Oudinet J. (2012), « Migrations et déterminants des transferts de fonds vers les pays du sud de la Méditerranée », Laboratoire d'Economie de Dauphine (LEDA) et IRISES UMR CNRS 7170.

Mohapatra S., Ratha D., Silwal A. (2010), « Outlook for Remittance Flows 2011-12: Recovery after the crisis, but risks lie ahead », Migration and Development Brief 13, Migration and Remittance Unit of the World Bank.

Mooney M. (2003), « Migrants' Social Ties in the U.S. and Investment in Mexico», *Social Forces*, 81(3), 1147-1170.

Niaz M., Mushtaq A., Nisar A., Musawar S., Intikhab A., Muhammad J. (2010), « The impact of foreign remittances on the socio-economic conditions of households (a case study of rural areas in DIR LOWER, NWFP) », *Sarhad Journal of Agriculture*, 26(1).

Nishat M., Bilgrami N. (1993), « The determinants of worker's remittances in Pakistan », *The Pakistan Development Review*, 32(4), 1234-1245.

Nwajiuba C. (2005), « International Migration and Livelihoods in Southeast Nigeria », Global Commission on International Migration, Geneva.

OCDE (2006), Les transferts de fonds internationaux des émigrés et leur rôle dans le développement - Partie III, Perspectives des migrations internationales.

Onyedinma E.E., Kanayo N.L. (2013), « Understanding Human Relations in African Traditional Religious Context in the Face of Globalization: Nigerian Perspectives », *American International Journal of Contemporary Research*, 3(2).

Ojapinwa T.V. (2012), « Determinants of Migrants' Remittances in Nigeria: An Econometrics Analysis », *International Journal of Humanities and Social Science*, Special Issue 2(14).

Osili U.O. (2004), « Migrants and Housing Investments: Theory and Evidence from Nigeria », *Economic Development and Cultural Change*, 52(4), 821-849.

Paris T.R., Joyce L., Villanueva D., Rola-Rubzen M.F., Chi T.T.N., Chaicharn W. (2009), « Labour out migration on rice farming households and gender roles: synthesis of findings in Thailand, the Philippines and Vietnam », Paper presented at the FAO-IFAD-ILO Workshop on Gaps, trends and current research in gender dimensions of agricultural and rural employment: differentiated pathways out of poverty, Rome.

Poirine B. (1997), « A Theory of Remittances as an Implicit Family Loan Arrangement », *World Development*, 25, 589-611.

Ponson B. (1990), *Individualisme ou communauté : quelques implications managériales pour l'entreprise en Afrique*, in Hénault G., M'Rabet R., *L'entrepreneuriat en Afrique francophone : culture, financement et développement*, John Libbey, Paris.

Quartey P., Blankson T. (2004), « Do Migrant Remittances Minimize the Impact of Macro-Volatility on the Poor in Ghana? », Final report submitted to the Global Development Network. http://www.gdnet.org/pdf2/gdn_library/global_research_projects/macro_low_income/Quartey.pdf.

Ratha D., Mohapatra S. (2007), « Increasing the Macroeconomic Impact of Remittances on Development », Development Prospects Group at the World Bank, note prepared for the G8 outreach Event on Remittances, Berlin.

Rapoport H., Docquier F. (2005), « The Economics of Migrants' Remittances », Institute for the Study of Labor (IZA) Discussion Papers Series No. 1531.

Schiopu I., Siegfried N. (2006), « Determinants of workers' remittances: Evidence from the European neighbouring region », European Central Bank, Working Paper Series (688).

Schrieder G., Knerr B. (2000), « Labour migration as a social security mechanism for smallholder households in Sub-Saharan Africa: The case of Cameroon », *Oxford Development Studies,* 28(2), 223-236.

Sinning M. (2007), « Determinants of savings and remittances: empirical evidence from immigrants to Germany », *Ruhr economic papers*, 23.

Stanwix C., Connell J. (1995), « To the Islands: The Remittances of Fijians in Sydney », *Asian and Pacific Migration Journal*, 4(1), 69-87.

Stark O. (1991), *The migration of labor*, Oxford: Blackwell.

Stark O. (2009), « Reasons for Remitting », *World Economics*, 10(3), 147-157.

Tall S.M. (2003), « Les migrants sénégalais et les nouvelles technologies de l'information et de la communication », Programme de l'United Nations Research Institute for Social Development Technologie, Entreprise et Société, Document N° 7.

UEMOA (2013), « Synthèse des résultats des enquêtes sur les envois de fonds des travailleurs migrants dans les pays de l'UEMOA », Banque Centrale des Etats de l'Afrique de l'Ouest (BCEAO).

UNCTAD (2012), « Harnessing Remittances and Diaspora Knowledge to Build Productive Capacities », The Least Developed Countries Report 2012.

World Bank (2011), *Migration and remittances Factbook 2011*, 2nd Edition Washington, DC: World Bank.

Zadi M.K. (1998), « la privatisation pour quel résultat ? », Culture africaine et gestion de l'entreprise moderne, Editions Centre d'Edition et de Diffusion Africaines, Abidjan, 1998.

Zongo M. (2009), « L'italian dream : côté cour. L'impact des transferts financiers des migrants bissa en Italie sur les villages de départ dans la province du Boulgou au Burkina Faso », Annales de l'Université de Ouagadougou - Série A, 008.

ANNEXE
Questionnaire concernant l'étude

Partie III : les modalités liées aux transferts d'argent

QUESTIONS ET INSTRUCTIONS	RÉPONSES ET CODES
Transférez-vous de l'argent dans votre pays ?	• Non • Oui
Si non pourquoi ?	• Parce que j'économise pour investir • Ce n'est pas à moi de m'occuper de ma famille • Parce que je n'ai assez d'argent • Autre à préciser
Si oui, pourquoi ? (Plusieurs réponses possibles)	• Subvenir aux besoins de ma famille • Aider mes amis • Investir dans mon pays • Rembourser mon voyage • Assurer ma famille contre les risques (assurance) • Garder de bonnes relations avec ma communauté • Epargner dans mon pays • Scolariser les membres de ma famille • Pour les soins de santé de ma famille • Autre à préciser
A quelle fréquence envoyez-vous cet argent ?	• Annuellement • Trimestriellement • Mensuellement • Rarement • En cas de problème • Dès que l'on vous le demande • Autre à préciser
A quel moment envoyez-vous le plus d'argent ?	• Pendant les périodes de fêtes • Pendant les périodes de crises • Pendant les périodes de soudure (période des travaux agricoles) • Pendant les funérailles • A la rentrée scolaire • Pour les manifestations de mariage ou baptême • Autre à préciser
Par quels moyens envoyez-vous l'argent dans votre pays ?	• Banques • Maisons de transfert d'argent (Western Union/Money Gram) • Amis/famille • Mains propres (moi-même) • Compagnies de transport • Autre à préciser
Pourquoi ?	• Plus sûr • Plus rapide • Moins cher • Autre à préciser

Partie V : financement du développement local

QUESTIONS ET INSTRUCTIONS	RÉPONSES ET CODES
L'argent que vous transférez sert-il au développement de votre pays ?	• Non • Oui
Si oui pourquoi ?	• Je n'en sais rien je le fais parce que tout le monde le fait • Pour participer au développement de mon pays • Parce que dans la vie il faut être solidaire pour qu'on puisse m'aider à mon tour quand j'aurai des problèmes • Autres
Si oui par quel canal avez-vous envoyé cet argent ?	• Une banque • Une ONG • Une caisse de solidarité • L'association des émigrés • Autre à préciser
Dans quels domaines avez-vous investi ? (Plusieurs réponses possibles)	• Santé • Education • Logement • PME • Eau potable • Agriculture • Elevage • Electrification • Tourisme • Assainissement • Autres à préciser
Cette partie concerne le financement des investissements productifs (agriculture, élevage, ...) réalisé par les communes de votre pays. L'idée est de faire de vous des créanciers de ces communes à des intérêts bas.	
Accepteriez-vous de prêter aux communes pour le financement de ces projets ?	• Non • Oui
Si oui, pourquoi ? (Plusieurs réponses possibles)	• Faire du profit • J'aime mon pays • Par solidarité pour mon pays • Aider mes parents restés au pays • Je suis citoyen de ce pays et qu'il a besoin de moi • Réduire la pauvreté dans le pays • Je compte retourner vivre au pays • Pour créer des emplois • Dans la vie il faut s'aider les uns les autres • Attirer la bénédiction de Dieu • Tout ce que j'ai appartient à ce pays et ce qui appartient au pays est à moi • Tous les burkinabés sont mes frères • Participer au développement du pays • Autres à préciser
Quel montant seriez-vous prêt à prêter annuellement ?	|__|__|__||__|__|__||__|__|__| F CFA
A combien voulez-vous être remboursé ?	|__|__|__||__|__|__||__|__|__| F CFA

Dans quels domaines voulez-vous investir ? (Plusieurs réponses possibles)	• Santé • Education • Logement • PME • Eau potable • Agriculture • Elevage • Electrification • Tourisme • Assainissement • Autres à préciser
Sinon, pourquoi ?	• Parce que personne ne m'a aidé • Mauvaise gestion • Instabilité politique • Parce que dans la vie, c'est chacun pour soi • Autres à préciser

MICROECONOMICS MOTIVATIONS OF REMITTANCES IN BURKINA FASO: IS CULTURE DETERMINANT?

Abstract **-** *This article analyses remittances determinants from burkinabè migrants living in Côte d'Ivoire. To do this we carried out of survey. Individuals interrogated were selected with « snowball method ». The econometrics results established with the help of Tobit model show that remittances in Burkina Faso are guided by subjective motifs and cultural traits like attachment feeling, altruism, mutual assistance, community spirit, conformism, membership feeling and solidarity.*

Key-Words **-** MIGRANTS, REMITTANCES, AFRICAN CULTURE

COMPTE RENDU

Olivier Morrisey, Ricardo A. Lopez, Kishor Sharma, *Handbook on Trade and Development*, Edward Elgar, 2015, 480 p.

Cet ouvrage collectif, qui réunit près de quarante auteurs, traite des liens entre commerce, croissance et développement, thème souvent abordé dans la littérature, particulièrement dans le cas des pays en développement. L'interrogation majeure est de savoir si l'ouverture commerciale est ou non un facteur de croissance, et à quelles conditions.

L'ouvrage est structuré autour de quatre parties. La partie 1 analyse huit thèmes dont le commerce international, les préférences commerciales, le rôle des firmes, le travail des enfants, le tout en lien avec la croissance et la pauvreté. Les trois autres parties concernent chacune une aire distincte : l'Afrique subsaharienne, l'Amérique latine et l'Asie de l'Est.

Dans l'introduction, les coordinateurs rappellent le bouleversement induit par la globalisation depuis les années 1980 où le commerce y tient une place importante via la libéralisation et la progression des échanges, la fragmentation de la production, les flux d'IDE et le poids des firmes multinationales... L'essentiel est de mesurer les effets de ces multiples bouleversements sur les perspectives des pays en développement en matière de croissance, de revenus et de pauvreté.

Les multiples facteurs qui permettent au commerce de soutenir la croissance et le développement, ont été identifiés dans la littérature : outre les ressources naturelles et les exportations de matières premières, qui peuvent être impactées par les prix mondiaux, citons le niveau d'éducation prompt à élever la qualification de la main d'œuvre, le degré de diversification des exportations et les niveaux de compétitivité prix et qualité, l'accès aux technologies, une demande domestique solvable relayant la demande mondiale, le degré de dépendance aux partenaires commerciaux, le niveau des infrastructures, le développement financier, la qualité des institutions et la bonne gouvernance...

Si la théorie standard est convaincue des effets positifs de l'ouverture commerciale et du libre-échange, les faits sont plus ambigus. Il convient de bien prendre en compte les spécificités des pays ou des régions. Ce souci explique la structure de l'ouvrage où les bienfaits (ou non) du commerce sont abordés par grande région distincte.

L'Afrique subsaharienne (ASS) est une région où les performances commerciales et la croissance ont été limitées, du moins jusqu'à la fin du siècle précédent. L'ASS est représentative des pays à faible revenu. L'Amérique latine, de son côté, comprend de nombreux grands pays à revenus intermédiaires supérieurs, traditionnellement en proie à de fortes instabilités macroéconomiques. Jusqu'à la première moitié du siècle dernier, ils prenaient part activement aux exportations avant de se replier sur des pratiques protectionnistes qui ont perduré jusqu'au début des années 1990. Enfin, l'Asie de l'Est a été la région la plus dynamique au cours de ces cinquante dernières années où de nombreux pays ont connu une forte croissance en lien avec les investissements directs étrangers et le développement de leurs exportations.

Depuis le milieu des années 1980, la plupart des pays africains ont libéré leur commerce et réduit de nombreuses barrières commerciales. Ils ont dû tenter de diversifier leurs exportations. On ne peut pas conclure que la libéralisation a été un échec total mais les problèmes de compétitivité en matière d'offre d'exportation ont été et restent bien réels. C'est la raison pour laquelle les réformes commerciales et la multiplication des accords régionaux peuvent ne pas atteindre les effets attendus en matière de croissance.

L'ouvrage a le grand mérite de couvrir trois espaces géographiques distincts avec pour certains d'entre eux des approches pays, même si les échanges commerciaux de certaines économies ne sont pas (ou peu) abordés comme l'Inde ou la Russie. Le risque dans ce type d'exercice est de proposer un ensemble de contributions hétérogène. C'est au contraire une somme originale qui offre des perspectives d'analyses importantes sur les relations entre le commerce et le développement. Il comprend à la fois des critiques et des mises à jour sur des questionnements anciens ou classiques et des contributions sur des interrogations plus récentes, comme la place du commerce transfrontalier informel, un thème non négligeable exploré dans cet ouvrage. L'ouvrage mobilise les outils théoriques, appliqués tout en s'attachant aux spécificités locales. Enfin, il cherche à comprendre les raisons pour lesquelles l'ASS a des difficultés à bénéficier des échanges commerciaux, contrairement à l'Asie de l'Est et à l'Amérique latine. Pour ces diverses raisons, sa lecture peut être recommandée aux chercheurs et aux praticiens.

Jean-Claude Vérez,
LEAD, Université de Toulon

Jean-Paul Carrière, Abdelillah Hamdouch, Corneliu Iaţu (dir.), ***Développement durable des territoires*****, Economica, Anthropos, 2016, 234 p.**

Comment penser et mettre en œuvre le développement durable à l'échelle des territoires ? Cet ouvrage, coordonné par J-P. Carrière, A. Hamdouch et C. Iaţu tente d'offrir des points d'éclairage sur la notion de « développement territorial durable » (DTD) et vise à ouvrir des pistes de réflexion.

Depuis les années 1980, les territoires, à différentes échelles, sont confrontés à de nouvelles problématiques interpellant le développement durable : tendance à la concentration géographique des potentiels de développement et métropolisation, accroissement des inégalités socioéconomiques, questions concernant la disponibilité et l'utilisation de différentes ressources, pollution et changement climatique...

Si l'on comprend intuitivement que le développement durable ne peut se penser sans sa composante territoriale, l'« hybridation », selon l'expression des auteurs, entre développement durable et développement territorial est loin d'être aboutie, tant sur le plan de la réflexion théorique que pour les praticiens. Le DTD reste un concept à définir. Il s'agit « d'intégrer les deux approches en dépassant leurs limites respectives » : insuffisante prise en compte ou sous-évaluation des dimensions environnementales et sociales par les politiques de développement territorial ; manque d'opérationnalité, d'articulation entre les différentes dimensions de la durabilité, de systèmes d'indicateurs locaux pour le développement durable.

La tâche s'annonce ardue. D'abord parce qu'il serait illusoire d'imaginer une universalité des modèles d'action, le DTD concernant toute la « gamme » des territoires, du rural des pays du Sud aux grandes métropoles des pays développés. Ensuite parce qu'il faudra souvent résoudre des conflits d'objectifs entre soutenabilité socio-environnementale et attractivité/compétitivité des territoires.

Plus concrètement, la première question abordée par l'ouvrage est celle des « échelles territoriales de la durabilité », donc du bon périmètre d'action. Sont traités le développement durable à l'échelle rurale inspiré d'expériences québécoises ; la difficulté de mise en place des politiques de DTD à l'échelle des petites villes sur la base d'enquêtes menées en Auvergne ; l'identification de profils résidentiel, productif ou créatif des villes petites et moyennes pour mieux calibrer les politiques de développement local ; la contribution des Parcs Naturels Régionaux au développement durable du Grand Paris ; une réflexion sur la décentralisation française dont le cadre politique rend difficile la mise en place d'une DTD réellement démocratique.

Le deuxième champ de réflexion porte sur les questions de gouvernance et de mise en œuvre du DTD. Sont ainsi abordés la politique de régionalisation en Roumanie face à l'amplification des disparités interrégionales de développement ; la question de la participation des acteurs locaux dans la gouvernance d'une wilaya en Algérie ; la reconstruction de la gouvernance locale en Roumanie ; la place des pratiques de DTD dans la reconfiguration de la gouvernance territoriale au Québec.

L'ouvrage consacre enfin une troisième partie à la mise en valeur du paysage et à l'essor du tourisme : l'exemple de Blois où le paysage est envisagé comme vecteur du DTD avec une gouvernance associant acteurs ruraux et urbains ; le tourisme comme moteur du DTD dans une région périphérique de la Roumanie et les types de gouvernance à instaurer ; l'« innovation durable » à l'échelle locale sur la base d'enquêtes dans des stations alpines françaises.

Au final, l'hétérogénéité des approches, générales ou appliquées, la diversité des échelles spatiales et des territoires considérés s'accommodent mal d'une lecture linéaire de l'ouvrage. Cette somme de contributions n'ambitionne pas de couvrir toutes les questions ouvertes par ce champ relativement récent et extrêmement large. Le lecteur n'y trouvera pas non plus de réelle cohérence ni de réflexion théorique sur ce qui pourrait servir de soubassement conceptuel au DTD, ni de questionnement sur ses indicateurs ou sa mesure, enjeux néanmoins soulignés par les auteurs. Cependant, chercheurs et praticiens trouveront dans cet ouvrage des cas d'étude et des illustrations concrètes qui pourront nourrir leurs réflexions.

Christophe Van Huffel,
LEAD, Université de Toulon

Hommage au Professeur Jean-Claude Perrin

C'est avec une profonde tristesse que j'ai appris le décès le 8 février 2016 de Jean-Claude Perrin. Je tiens à témoigner toute ma reconnaissance au Professeur avec qui j'ai fait mes premiers pas dans la recherche et qui a accompagné mon parcours jusqu'à la fin des années 1980 au sein du centre d'Economie Régionale à Aix-en-Provence.

Jean-Claude Perrin a été, après l'agrégation de sciences économiques, Doyen de la Faculté de Droit et des Sciences économiques de Tananarive à Madagascar, Directeur de l'IAE d'Aix-Marseille et Directeur de l'Institut d'Aménagement Régional d'Aix-Marseille qu'il a contribué à créer. Il a exercé un rôle important, avec notamment le regretté Denis Maillat, dans le lancement du GREMI et les travaux menés sur les milieux innovateurs.

Surtout, il a créé le Centre d'Economie Régionale (CER) en 1965 à l'Université d'Aix-Marseille, et l'a dirigé jusqu'à sa retraite en 1986. Le CER a été un des laboratoires majeurs dans les années 1970 et 1980 qui, avec quelques autres (à Bordeaux, à Dijon, etc.), ont animé et développé la recherche en économie spatiale en France. Le CER a été à cette époque le creuset qui a formé de nombreux chercheurs en économie régionale.

Même si ces travaux ont souvent échappé à l'économie conventionnelle, je voudrais mettre en exergue que Jean-Claude Perrin est notamment l'auteur de l'ouvrage *Le développement régional*, paru aux Presses Universitaires de France, Collection Sup, en 1974, qui a posé les premiers jalons d'analyse liant approche régionale et économie du développement. L'ouvrage tente de décrire les principaux mécanismes économiques qui jouent sur le plan territorial au cours des différentes phases de développement, en puisant largement ses illustrations dans l'histoire économique des Etats-Unis, de la Grande-Bretagne...

Jeune assistant, je me souviens, lors de la rédaction de cet ouvrage, que Jean-Claude Perrin avait souhaité bénéficier de mes remarques et des longues discussions que nous avions eues ensemble, ainsi qu'avec Paul Carrère, avec qui j'ai longtemps collaboré à l'INSEE, au sein du Centre d'Etude Statistique du Développement Régional qu'il dirigeait.

Faut-il rappeler enfin, si l'on suit le cheminement historique, que j'ai créé la revue *Région et Développement* en 1995, avec le Professeur Gilbert Benhayoun, et que c'est le Centre d'Economie Régionale qui en a assuré la gestion à l'origine.

Maurice Catin
Professeur émérite, Université de Toulon
Directeur de la revue *Région et Développement*

REVUE RÉGION ET DÉVELOPPEMENT

Site Web : www.regionetdeveloppement.org

Recommandations aux auteurs

La Revue Région et Développement publie en français ou en anglais des articles originaux, des notes et documents et des comptes rendus de lecture. Pour soumission à publication, l'auteur doit adresser à la rédaction de la revue le texte par courrier électronique ou le manuscrit dactylographié en deux exemplaires. La présentation des chapitres, des références bibliographiques et des notes de bas de page doit être conforme à celle de la revue. Les articles doivent être accompagnés d'un résumé en français et en anglais d'une dizaine de lignes, des mots-clés correspondants et de la classification du JEL. Le nom de l'auteur, l'institution à laquelle il appartient et l'adresse complète doivent figurer en page de garde.

Les articles proposés à la revue Région et Développement sont évalués par le Comité de rédaction puis soumis de manière anonyme à un ou deux referees. L'auteur reçoit un rapport d'évaluation, lui aussi anonyme, concluant à publication, révision ou refus.

Après avis favorable à la publication dans la revue, il sera demandé à l'auteur un envoi par mail du texte en Word (y compris figures, tableaux et formules mathématiques compatibles avec Word 2010).

Les propositions d'articles doivent être adressées à la rédaction de la revue :

Professeur Maurice Catin
Revue Région et Développement
LÉAD - Faculté de Sciences Économiques et de Gestion
Université de Toulon
70 Avenue Roger Decouvoux
83000 Toulon

Mail : maurice.catin@univ-tln.fr

Secrétaire général de la rédaction : Christophe Van Huffel
Tel : 04 83 36 63 02 - Mail : vanhuffel@univ-tln.fr

BULLETIN D'ABONNEMENT

Revue "Région et Développement"

• **Je désire souscrire un abonnement pour l'année 2016 (deux numéros) :**

☐ France, DOM-TOM : 37 € ☐ Étranger : 40 €

• **Règlement :**

☐ CCP ☐ Chèque bancaire ☐ Mandat international

Pour l'étranger, merci d'effectuer un virement en euros sur le ***CCP 23 625 44 N Paris*** ou bien un règlement par chèque bancaire en euros sur une banque domiciliée en France ou par carte de crédit internationale.

N° de la carte : |_|_|_|_|_|_|_|_|_|_|_|_|_|_|_|_|

Date d'expiration : |_|_|_|_|_|_|_| Banque : ....

Nom et Prénom : ....
Adresse :...
....
Code Postal : .... Ville : ....
Pays : ....

Date :

Signature :

Ce bulletin d'abonnement à la Revue "Région et Développement" et votre règlement sont à retourner à :

Éditions L'HARMATTAN - 7, rue de l'École-Polytechnique, 75005 PARIS
Tél. : 01 40 46 79 14 - fax : 01 43 29 86 20 - site web : www.librairieharmattan.com

Abonnement annuel : 2 numéros	
France, DOM-TOM :	37 €
Étranger :	40 €

L'HARMATTAN ITALIA
Via Degli Artisti 15; 10124 Torino
harmattan.italia@gmail.com

L'HARMATTAN HONGRIE
Könyvesbolt ; Kossuth L. u. 14-16
1053 Budapest

L'HARMATTAN KINSHASA
185, avenue Nyangwe
Commune de Lingwala
Kinshasa, R.D. Congo
(00243) 998697603 ou (00243) 999229662

L'HARMATTAN CONGO
67, av. E. P. Lumumba
Bât. – Congo Pharmacie (Bib. Nat.)
BP2874 Brazzaville
harmattan.congo@yahoo.fr

L'HARMATTAN GUINÉE
Almamya Rue KA 028, en face
du restaurant Le Cèdre
OKB agency BP 3470 Conakry
(00224) 657 20 85 08 / 664 28 91 96
harmattanguinee@yahoo.fr

L'HARMATTAN MALI
Rue 73, Porte 536, Niamakoro,
Cité Unicef, Bamako
Tél. 00 (223) 20205724 / +(223) 76378082
poudiougopaul@yahoo.fr
pp.harmattan@gmail.com

L'HARMATTAN CAMEROUN
BP 11486
Face à la SNI, immeuble Don Bosco
Yaoundé
(00237) 99 76 61 66
harmattancam@yahoo.fr

L'HARMATTAN CÔTE D'IVOIRE
Résidence Karl / cité des arts
Abidjan-Cocody 03 BP 1588 Abidjan 03
(00225) 05 77 87 31
etien_nda@yahoo.fr

L'HARMATTAN BURKINA
Penou Achille Some
Ouagadougou
(+226) 70 26 88 27

L'HARMATTAN SÉNÉGAL
10 VDN en face Mermoz, après le pont de Fann
BP 45034 Dakar Fann
33 825 98 58 / 33 860 9858
senharmattan@gmail.com / senlibraire@gmail.com
www.harmattansenegal.com

L'HARMATTAN BÉNIN
ISOR-BENIN
01 BP 359 COTONOU-RP
Quartier Gbèdjromèdé,
Rue Agbélenco, Lot 1247 I
Tél : 00 229 21 32 53 79
christian_dablaka123@yahoo.fr

Achevé d'imprimer par Corlet Numérique - 14110 Condé-sur-Noireau
N° d'Imprimeur : 130489 - Dépôt légal : juillet 2016 - *Imprimé en France*

www.ingramcontent.com/pod-product-compliance
Lightning Source LLC
LaVergne TN
LVHW010924061026
849535LV00007B/2225